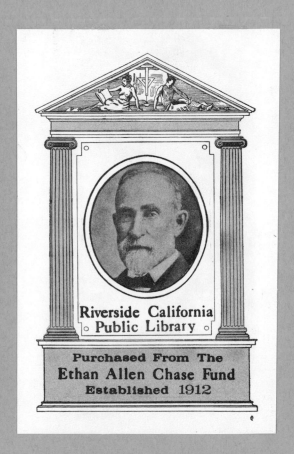

CROMER IN EGYPT

CROMER IN EGYPT

JOHN MARLOWE

PRAEGER PUBLISHERS

New York Washington

BOOKS THAT MATTER
Published in the United States of America in 1970
by Praeger Publishers, Inc., 111 Fourth Avenue,
New York, N.Y. 10003

© 1970 in London, England, by John Marlowe

Library of Congress Catalog Card Number: 71-125390

Printed in Great Britain

CONTENTS

ILLUSTRATIONS

Nos. 1, 2, 4, 5, 6, 7, 8 by courtesy of the Radio Times Hulton Picture Library, Nos. 3, 9, 10, 11, 12, 13 by courtesy of the London Electrotype Agency.

ACKNOWLEDGEMENTS

To the Keeper, Department of Manuscripts, British Museum, for access to the D'Abernon, Gladstone, Hamilton and Iddesleigh Papers deposited there, to the Trustees of the estate of the late Viscountess D'Abernon for permission to quote from the D'Abernon Papers, and to the Most Hon. the Marquess of Salisbury KG FRS for permission to quote some letters in the Iddesleigh Papers written by the 3rd Marquess of Salisbury.

To the Librarian, Christ Church, Oxford, for access to the Salisbury Papers deposited there, and to the Marquess of Salisbury for permission to quote therefrom.

To the Librarian, New College, Oxford, for access to the Milner Papers deposited in the Bodleian Library.

To St Antony's College, Oxford, for access to the Boyle and Gorst Papers deposited in the Middle East Centre there, and to Mrs K. R. Thomas for permission to quote from the Gorst Papers.

To the Librarian, School of Oriental Studies, Durham University, for access to the Wingate Papers deposited there.

To the Foreign Office Library for access to various published State Papers deposited there.

To the London Library for access to most of the published books, papers, articles included in the List of Sources.

Transcripts of Crown copyright records in the Public Record Office appear by permission of the Controller of HM Stationery Office.

To the following Publishers, Agents, and Copyright holders for permission to quote from the works listed below:

H. E. Bowman, *Middle East Window*, Longman, 1942
reprinted by permission of A. D. Peters & Company
Clara Boyle, *Boyle of Cairo,* Titus Wilson & Son Ltd, Kendal 1965
Clara Boyle, *A Servant of the Empire*, Methuen, 1938
by permission of the Executors of the Estate of the Late Mrs Boyle
Lady Gwendolen Cecil, *Life of Robert Marquis of Salisbury*,
4 vols, Hodder & Stoughton, 1921–32
by permission of the Executors of the Estate of Lady Cecil
A. E. Crouchley, *The Economic Development of Modern Egypt*, Longman,
1938
by permission of the Longman Group Ltd
Viscount d'Abernon, *Portraits and Appreciations,* Hodder & Stoughton,
1931
by permission of Hodder & Stoughton Ltd

W. S. Blunt, *Secret History of the British Occupation of Egypt*, Martin Secker, 1906

W. S. Blunt, *My Diaries*, Part II 1900–1904, Martin Secker, 1920

Reprinted from both books by permission of the Syndics of the FitzWilliam Museum, Cambridge

Lord Grey of Falloden, *Twenty Five Years*, 2 vols, Hodder & Stoughton, 1925

by permission of the Executors of the Estate of Lord Grey

M. A. Hollings, *Life of Sir C. Scott Moncrieff*, Murray, 1917

by permission of John Murray (Publishers) Ltd

H. E. Hurst, *The Nile*, Constable, 1952

by permission of Constable Publishers

Lord Lloyd, *Egypt Since Cromer*, 2 vols, Macmillan, 1933

by permission of Macmillan & Company Ltd

A. Lutfi as-Sayyid, *Egypt and Cromer*, Murray, 1968

by permission of John Murray (Publishers) Ltd

C. J. Lowe, *The Reluctant Imperialists*, 2 vols, Routledge & Kegan Paul, 1967

by permission of Routledge & Kegan Paul, and also Macmillan Co., Inc., USA

Philip Magnus, *Kitchener; Portrait of an Imperialist*, Murray, 1958

by permission of John Murray (Publishers) Ltd

Lord Newton, *Life of Lord Lansdowne*, Macmillan, 1929

by permission of Macmillan & Company Ltd

Sir J. Rennell Rodd, *Social and Diplomatic Memories*, Vol 2, Arnold, 1923

by permission of Edward Arnold (Publishers) Ltd

J. M. Robertson, (ed) *Letters upon the Affairs of Egypt*, Routledge & Kegan Paul, 1908

Robinson, Gallagher & Denny, *Africa and the Victorians*, Macmillan, 1961

by permission of Macmillan & Company Ltd

G. N. Sanderson, England, *Europe & the Upper Nile 1882–1899*, Edinburgh University Press, 1965

by permission of the Syndics of the Edinburgh University Press

Robert L. Tignor, *Modernisation and British Colonial Rule in Egypt, 1882–1914*, Princeton Studies on the Near East (Copyright © 1966) by Princeton University Press

by permission of Princeton University Press

'If the world were falling to pieces round his ears,
but Egypt was left intact,
Lord Cromer would not ask for more.'

LORD SALISBURY 1896

1
EGYPT IN 1876

THE BRITISH GOVERNMENT'S interest in Egypt stemmed from the acquisition of British India at the Treaty of Paris in 1763. But it was not seriously manifested until nearly forty years later, after Bonaparte's invasion of Egypt in 1798. One of the objects of that invasion, as laid down by the Directory in their instructions to Bonaparte, was to use the French possession of Egypt as a means of attacking the British possessions in India. This threat, in so far as it was taken seriously by the British Cabinet, was considered by them to have been exorcised by Nelson's destruction of the French fleet at Abuqir Bay and by Bonaparte's subsequent failure to capture Acre. Nelson's victory deprived the French of naval command of the Mediterranean and conferred it on the British, thus cutting off the French in Egypt from regular reinforcement from France. Bonaparte's failure before Acre disposed of the possibility that Asiatic Turkey might fall under French control. Thereafter, at least half of the British Cabinet considered that the presence of a French expeditionary force in Egypt was less of a menace than the return of that force to Europe, and the despatch of Abercromby's force to Egypt was intended to secure the alliance of Turkey against France by assisting the Sultan to recover his lost dominion. There was certainly no intention to substitute a permanent British for a French occupation of Egypt and, at the short-lived Peace of Amiens, concluded in 1802, provision was made for the evacuation of the British occupation force and the restoration of Egypt to effective Turkish sovereignty. However, the British Government were determined not to relinquish the naval command of the Mediterranean won by Nelson at Abuqir Bay, and their refusal to evacuate Malta under the terms of the Peace of Amiens was the principal reason for the resumption of hostilities against France in 1803. This refusal can be taken as the genesis of that British Mediterranean strategy which was to persist for over 100 years and which developed, as its principal aim, the preservation of the effective sovereignty and, as far as possible, the territorial integrity, of the Ottoman Empire.

By the beginning of the nineteenth century the Ottoman Empire was well advanced in its long process of decline, although its dominions were still very extensive. These comprised the whole of the Balkan Peninsula, Asia Minor, much of the Caucasus, the Fertile Crescent (what is now Syria, Lebanon, Iraq, Jordan and Israel), the Arabian Peninsula, Egypt, the whole of North Africa, and all the islands in the Eastern Mediter' ranean. Their hold on many of these regions was extremely tenuous. The predominantly Christian nationalities of the Balkan Peninsula, who enjoyed varying degrees of autonomy, were in an endemic state of near' revolt, encouraged by Russia, posing as their protector and anxious to dominate Turkey so as to win uninterrupted access from the Black Sea through the narrow Turkish Straits to the Mediterranean. Farther east, Russia was nibbling away at the Caucasus. Austria had designs on the Turkish ports of the Adriatic. Difficulty of communication had reduced Ottoman control of most of the Arabian Peninsula to a nullity. The lands of the Moghrib—Tunis, Algiers and Morocco—had for decades been virtually independent under hereditary rulers. Egypt, before Bonaparte's invasion, had been ruled by a military oligarchy known as the Mamluks under the usually nominal supervision of an Ottoman Pasha, or Gov' ernor. The French and the subsequent Anglo'Turkish occupations were followed by a period of confusion from which, in 1805, there emerged the figure of Mohamed Ali, an Albanian soldier who had come to Egypt with the Turkish invading force and who succeeded in making himself master of Egypt under the nominal suzerainty of the Ottoman Sultan, who appointed him Viceroy.

The British policy of propping up the Ottoman Empire, which was sought to be secured by the maintenance of naval supremacy in the Mediterranean, was motivated by a desire to avoid the aggrandisement of, and the probable contentions between, the European Great Powers resulting from that Empire's dissolution. In that event, Russia would probably occupy Constantinople and most of Asia Minor; Austria and Russia would dispute the control of the Balkan Peninsula; France would lay claim to Egypt, Syria, and most of North Africa. The results would be, first, the risk of a European war arising from quarrels over a division of the spoils and, secondly, the presence of two powerful and potentially hostile Powers—France and Russia—on the landward approaches to India, with the possibility of sending their armies there far more quickly than British sea'borne reinforcements could reach India via the Cape.

In practice, British Mediterranean policy during the nineteenth century successfully concentrated, until its closing years, on trying to prevent the formation of a common front between France and Russia, which might well have led to a partition of the Ottoman Empire between them. In this Great Britain could usually rely on diplomatic support from Austria, since the Habsburg Empire was, for different reasons, also interested in preventing the formation of this common front. What successive British Governments aimed at, and what they usually achieved in any crisis affecting the future of the Ottoman Empire, was the creation of a Concert of European Powers in which either France or Russia was the odd man out. This happened over the Greek War of Independence, and over Mohamed Ali's invasion of Asia Minor in 1831, when Russia was the odd man out; over Mohamed Ali's bid for independence in 1839–41, when France was the odd man out; and over the Crimean War and the Russo-Turkish war of 1877–78, when Russia was again the odd man out.

British policy over Egypt was conditioned by Mohamed Ali's expansionist policy and his ambitions for independence. Before 1820, he had, at the request and in the name of the Sultan, defeated the Wahhabi schismatics in Arabia and made himself master of much of the Arabian Peninsula. In 1820 he started colonising the Sudan. During the Greek War of Independence the Egyptian army and navy bore the brunt of the fighting on the Turkish side and the Egyptian fleet, together with the Turkish, was destroyed by the Anglo-French squadron at Navarino. Already stronger militarily than his by now nominal suzerain, Mohamed Ali invaded and occupied Syria and defeated a Turkish force in 1831 at Konia in Asia Minor. The threat thus presented to Constantinople induced the Sultan to call for Russian assistance. During a few hectic weeks of diplomatic activity it seemed as if the partition of the Ottoman Empire between Russia and Egypt was about to be consummated. The threat was averted by Anglo-French solidarity; the Russians withdrew from Constantinople and the Egyptians from Asia Minor. Mohamed Ali retained possession of Syria. After an uneasy truce lasting for seven years trouble again erupted. In 1839 an Ottoman army, against the advice of the Ambassadors of the Powers, invaded Syria. It was defeated by Ibrahim Pasha, Mohamed Ali's eldest son and principal General, at Nezib, near Aleppo. Soon afterwards, the Ottoman fleet deserted to Mohamed Ali. Once more, the Ottoman Empire seemed on the verge of dissolution.

On this occasion the principal threat to British policy was seen to be presented not by Russia but by France. Ever since Bonaparte's invasion forty years before, successive French Governments had shown a constant interest in Egypt. French officers had helped to train the Egyptian army. French experts had been made available to assist in Mohamed Ali's various modernising schemes. Attempts (frustrated by British diplomacy) had been made to associate Mohamed Ali with the French occupation of Algiers in 1830. After Mohamed Ali's invasion of Asia Minor and threat to Constantinople in 1831–32 (during which the British and

3

French Governments had made common cause in order to avoid a Russian occupation of Constantinople), French policy tended to support Mohamed Ali's claims to independence in Egypt and Syria. The British Government saw this tendency as evidence of French determination to acquire a protectorate over an enlarged Egypt. This was regarded as a threat to British naval supremacy in the Mediterranean, and as a prelude to an agreement with Russia for a partition of the Ottoman Empire, which would have upset the balance of power in Europe and jeopardised the security of increasing British interests in India and around the Indian Ocean. British diplomacy after the battle of Nezib, therefore, concentrated on isolating France in the Concert of Europe by forming a united front of the other Powers in opposition to Mohamed Ali's pretensions. Palmerston, the British Foreign Secretary, was so far successful that Mohamed Ali, with the assistance of a British naval force, and with the backing of all the European Powers except France, was ejected from Syria and was compelled to relinquish to his suzerain all his territorial acquisitions outside Egypt and the Sudan. In return he was confirmed in the hereditary rulership of Egypt and given a fairly wide measure of autonomy in the government of that Province, subject to the acknowledgement of Ottoman suzerainty, the payment of tribute, and a strict limitation of his military and naval armaments.

This was a considerable victory for what, by this time, had become traditional British policy in the Eastern Mediterranean—the preservation of the effective sovereignty and territorial integrity of the Ottoman Empire. It had been achieved as a result of British naval supremacy in the Mediterranean won by Nelson at Abuqir Bay and confirmed by the outcome of the Napoleonic wars. It was a corresponding defeat for traditional, and much longer-standing, French ambitions in the Eastern Mediterranean. Henceforward, French Mediterranean policy became concentrated on the possibilities of expansion in Africa, and their Egyptian policy was designed, not so much to ensure an exclusive French position in Egypt as to prevent the British from obtaining such a position. Since the British did not, until some time later, desire such an exclusive position, there followed a period of relative detente in Anglo-French relations over Egypt. This was cemented by the Anglo-French alliance against Russia in the Crimean war, was not seriously threatened by British opposition to the French-sponsored Suez Canal between 1855 and 1865, and lasted until the British occupation in 1882.

Bonaparte's invasion brought Egypt into the field of European diplomacy and Mohamed Ali's expansionist designs kept it there. The same factors caused Egypt to emerge from the cocoon of obscurantism in which the country had been enwrapped since the Ottoman conquest at the beginning of the sixteenth century. The Ottoman conquest, coinciding approximately with the opening of the Cape route to the Indies and the discovery of the Americas, had pushed Egypt, together with most of the rest of Islam, into a cultural, economic and military backwater. The great trade routes between Europe and the East no longer ran through Moslem lands. The Mediterranean ceased to be the hub of the civilised world and the centre of power, riches and creativity shifted westwards from the Mediterranean littoral to the shores of the Atlantic. That great impulse of geographical and scientific discovery, of cultural achievement, and of religious and political enlightenment which started with the European Renaissance and which, for the next 300 years, transported into a new order of magnitude the wealth, the knowledge, the industrial and agricultural productivity, and the military capacity of western Europe, completely by-passed Egypt. By the end of the fifteenth century Egypt, in all these things, was hardly, if at all, inferior to the West. By the end of the eighteenth century, after 300 years of isolation, Egypt, together with the rest of the Ottoman Empire, was immeasurably behindhand in nearly all the material arts of peace and war.

Mohamed Ali recognised Egypt's backwardness and sought to pursue his policy of aggrandisement by using the rich agricultural resources and the industrious population of Egypt to finance the purchase of Western equipment and Western techniques. This involved a rehabilitation of Egypt's irrigation system, which had gone to rack and ruin under Mamluk rule, and a merciless exploitation of Egypt's peasantry. Cotton became for the first time an important export crop and agricultural production generally was greatly increased. But all agricultural exports, as well as most imports, were placed under a strict State monopoly, with the result that the peasant was compelled to sell cheaply to, and to buy dearly from, the State which by this means derived virtually all the profit from his labours. These profits were principally spent by Mohamed Ali on the maintenance of his army and navy.

Mohamed Ali's defeat in 1841 put an end to his military adventures and, in consequence, to most of his military expenditure. It also put a virtual end to his sytem of State monopolies. The British Government, which was interested in free trade with Egypt, since it meant cheap imports of cotton from, and dear exports of manufactured goods to, that country, successfully insisted on the application to Egypt of a Commercial Treaty concluded with Turkey in 1838, the terms of which, in effect, prohibited State monopolies.

At the beginning of the nineteenth century, Egypt's geographical position as a staging post on the direct route between Europe and India had only been of negative interest to the British Government in that they had been concerned merely to prevent Egypt from falling under the dominance of some other Great Power. With the invention of the steam-ship, this negative interest began gradually to be reinforced by a more positive appreciation of the possibility of using the short overland route through Egypt as a means of expediting mail and passengers between England and India. This route had been used to a small extent before and during the Napoleonic wars, but it was not until the invention of the steamship that the British Government and the East India Company began to be seriously interested. By 1840, after an abortive attempt had been made to develop a regular overland mail route via the Euphrates Valley, a regular mail service between England and India via Egypt was in existence, with steamers plying between England and Alexandria, and between Suez and Bombay, and with mail and passengers being carried across Egypt between Alexandria and Suez by river and desert transport. The use of this route considerably shortened the length of the journey between England and India as compared with the Cape route and the volume of traffic carried by it steadily increased. It was not long before the British Government, and various British capitalists, began to be interested in the possibility of constructing a railway across Egypt, between Alexandria and Suez via Cairo, as a means both of increasing the speed and efficiency of transit and of exporting British capital goods at the height of what was then the Railway Age. There was another, more ambitious, and mainly French-sponsored, scheme in the air for the con-struction of a ship canal through the Isthmus of Suez linking the Mediter-ranean with the Red Sea. Neither of these schemes made any progress during the lifetime of Mohamed Ali, who died in 1849.

In spite of the frustration of his plans for expansion and independence, Mohamed Ali succeeded, up to the end of his life, in avoiding any serious European encroachment on the domestic administration of Egypt. His success was due to his being able, by his monopolies, by his use of forced labour, and by merciless taxation, to finance his military and modernising expenditure out of current revenue, and without raising foreign loans which, as his successors found out, would in effect have mortgaged Egypt to its creditors. He was also adamantly opposed to the grant to Europeans of any 'public utility' concessions—such as a railway or a canal—which might have served as an excuse for some European Power to establish a *pied à terre* in Egypt. He even took over the transit organisa-tion, which had been inaugurated as a result of the private enterprise of a few British individuals and Companies, and had it run as a department of Government.

Mohamed Ali was succeeded by his grandson, Abbas, a son of Ibrahim Pasha, Mohamed Ali's eldest son and greatest General, who predeceased his father by a few months. Abbas was uninterested in modernisation but, like his grandfather and his successors, was interested in loosening the bonds attaching Egypt to Constantinople, forged as a result of Mohamed Ali's defeat in 1840–41. By means of a momentary, entirely opportunistic, tergiversation of their traditional policy, the British Government, by interceding at Constantinople on his behalf in connection with the interpretation to be placed on the relations between Abbas and his Suzerain, induced Abbas to grant concessions to a British Company for the construction of railways between Cairo and Alexandria and Cairo and Suez. When Abbas died in 1854, construction of the Cairo-Alexandria line had almost been completed, and that of the Cairo-Suez line was about to begin.

Abbas was succeeded by his uncle, Mohamed Said, the youngest son of Mohamed Ali, who was somewhat younger than his nephew. (Among the terms of the settlement imposed on Mohamed Ali in 1841 was the traditional Ottoman order of succession to the throne of Egypt by which a deceased ruler was succeeded, not by his eldest son, but by the eldest living male in the direct line of succession.) One of the new ruler's first acts was to grant a concession for the cutting of a ship canal across the Isthmus of Suez to Ferdinand de Lesseps, a retired official of the French diplomatic service, apparently on the strength of an old acquaintanceship dating from the time, twenty years before, when Lesseps was a Consul in Egypt and Mohamed Said a young man about his father's Court.

The grant of this concession was bitterly opposed by the British Government. Palmerston, by that time Prime Minister, professed to regard it as a French plot to separate Egypt from the Ottoman Empire, to make it a French colony, and to interpose a French military presence on the road to India. His thinking was out-of-date. The Suez Canal project, although it contained elements of political, as well as financial, chicanery, was a commercial and financial speculation, and not a French Imperialist plot. But for ten years successive British Governments hampered its construction by diplomatic activity in Paris, Constantinople and Cairo. All they succeeded in doing, by the imposition of delays and by insistence on changes in various terms of the concession, was to saddle the Egyptian Government with an immense bill of costs for indemnities. The Canal was opened to traffic in 1869 and, within a few years, had revolutionised the pattern of mercantile traffic between Europe and the East. Almost from the beginning, the British were the major users of the Canal, both for naval and military communications east of Suez, and for their rapidly increasing mercantile traffic with India, East Africa, Australasia and the Far East. The importance, from the British point of view, of a guarantee of unimpeded passage through the Canal greatly enhanced the need for preserving the independence and territorial integrity of the Ottoman Empire, and of retaining effective means of bringing diplomatic pressure to bear in Constantinople. This meant the maintenance of British naval supremacy in the Mediterranean and the absence of any European alliances capable of outweighing and opposing British influence in Constantinople.

The game of diplomatic chess involved in trying to avoid the latter had been affected by changes in the Great Power structure coinciding with and immediately following the construction of the Canal. During the early 1860s Italy became a unified and independent Power. In 1866 Austria was defeated by Prussia and lost her previous primacy among the German States. In 1870 Prussia defeated France, from which victory emerged the powerful new German Empire incorporating all the Con- federated German States under Prussian leadership. The old British policy of avoiding a combination between France and Russia had become complicated by a French desire for *revanche* and the recovery of the lost Provinces of Alsace and Lorraine, by the German desire to keep France quarrelling with as many other Powers as possible, and by the emergence of Italy as a Mediterranean Power.

The grant of the Suez Canal concession was the first episode in an era of extravagant 'development' and foreign speculation in Egypt which, in the space of twenty-one years, was to burden Egypt with a foreign debt of some £90 million and reduce it to bankruptcy. In Europe, speculators were looking for opportunities to invest money, mostly borrowed, with the prospect of a large and rapid return; manufacturers for opportunities to import raw materials cheap and export finished goods dear; and entrepreneurs for opportunities to conclude lucrative contracts. With competition as keen as it was in Europe, they were looking particularly for opportunities in the less sophisticated, less 'developed' countries, where profit margins might be inflated and business risks minimised by the use of shrewd business sense and the resources of diplomatic bullying.

For some years many of these speculators, manufacturers, and entre- preneurs had been casting longing eyes towards Egypt which was, in many respects, an ideal field for the exercise of their talents and for the satisfaction of their cupidity. It was an 'undeveloped' country with increasing agricultural exports and, consequently, foreign currency to spare. It was readily accessible to Europe and communications within Egypt were comparatively easy. It had a docile and industrious population and conditions of public security were good. Under Mohamed Ali the country had acquired a taste for Westernisation and several prosperous foreign merchants were already established there. Most important of all, there were the foreign privileges deriving from the system of Ottoman Capitulations.

Originally, the Capitulations had been unilateral grants made by Ottoman Sultans to European Governments, which enabled companies of European merchants to live and to trade in Ottoman cities and ports under the jurisdiction of their Consuls, and to be generally exempt from the ordinary processes of Ottoman law—which was mostly the Islamic law—as applied to Ottoman subjects. The first of these Capitulation grants (they were grants and not treaties since there was no reciprocity) was in 1535, from Sultan Suleiman the Magnificent to the French. During the next 100 years or so similar privileges were accorded to the nationals of most European countries. Up to the end of the eighteenth century European merchants led something like collegiate lives, bound by their Company rules and under the control of their Consuls. They lived in more or less segregated compounds, owned no real property, and rarely mixed with the native inhabitants except in the way of business. The Capitulatory privileges impinged hardly at all on the rights of the Ottoman State or of the local inhabitants and indeed provided for the Consul a necessary measure of authority over the merchants, for whose behaviour he was responsible to the Ottoman Government and to the trading Company by whom he was appointed.

But, in Egypt in the nineteenth century, under Mohamed Ali the conditions under which European merchants lived entirely changed. The old monopolistic trading companies, such as the English Levant Company and the French Compagnie du Levant, under whose aegis and subject to whose discipline the European merchants had previously lived and traded, were no longer in effective existence. Merchants traded for their own account and made their own contacts with local governments and merchants. They no longer lived together in segregated ghettos. Except in the matter of criminal jurisdiction they were no longer prepared to accept the discipline, although they continued to shelter behind the authority, of their Consuls. They frequently came to own real estate and other property, to enter into partnerships with local inhabitants, to have business transactions with other foreign residents, to conclude contracts with local government administrations, and so on. Mohamed Ali, in his anxiety to encourage foreign merchants, who supplied him with short-term loans and acted as import and export agents for his monopolies, greatly extended the Capitulations privileges. By the end of his reign European residents, generally speaking, enjoyed extra-territorial rights, were exempt from the processes of Egyptian civil and criminal law, and from direct taxation; free from arrest or domiciliary search by the Egyptian authorities, and able to enter or leave Egypt at will. Criminal charges against European foreigners could only be tried in the Consular Court of the accused. Civil suits between foreigners of the same nationality were

9

also tried in the suitors' Consular Court. Civil suits between foreigners of different nationalities were tried in the defendant's Consular Court in accordance with the legal maxim *actor sequitur forum rei*. Europeans engaged in litigation with Ottoman subjects successfully refused to plead before Ottoman Courts and, during the reign of Mohamed Ali, a system of Commercial Courts, with both Egyptian and European assessors, was inaugurated to try such cases, which were becoming increasingly numerous. These Courts were not very successful, and the usual method of settling such cases, particularly in suits to which the Egyptian Government was a party, was by pressure or persuasion exercised by the European suitor's Consul.

The position was to some extent improved and regularised in 1876 when, after a long process of diplomatic haggling between the Egyptian Government and the European Powers, the 'Mixed Courts' were inaugurated. These Courts, in which there was a majority of European judges, nominated by the European Governments and appointed by the Egyptian Government, had jurisdiction over all civil suits between foreigners of different nationalities, and between Ottoman and foreign nationals, and in all civil suits in which there was deemed to be a foreign interest. They had no jurisdiction in criminal suits or in civil suits between foreigners of the same nationality, which continued to be tried in the Consular Courts. It was specifically provided that the Mixed Courts had jurisdiction over the Egyptian Government and over the Ruler personally in civil suits in which a foreign national was either plaintiff or defendant. It was provided in the Règlement setting up the Mixed Courts that they had jurisdiction over acts of administration by the Egyptian Government 'prejudicing rights acquired by foreigners' and this came to be interpreted by the Courts as meaning that any Egyptian Government legislation 'which may affect a foreigner must be accepted by the governments of the States represented in the Mixed Courts before it can be made applicable to their subjects or is in fact valid.'[1] This interpretation, generally speaking, meant that European foreigners could still not be subjected to Egyptian law without the unanimous consent of the Capitulatory Powers. In effect, therefore, the inauguration of the Mixed Courts left foreign privileges unimpaired, although their existence provided a reasonably efficacious and expeditious means of settling civil disputes between Egyptians and foreigners. It also provided a means of curbing the absolutism of the Ruler by placing him under the law in his dealings with foreigners or with foreign interests.

With foreigners in such a privileged position, foreign nationality became a prized asset, and acted as a powerful magnet attracting to Egypt foreigners from all over Europe, and particularly from the impoverished and overpopulated districts of southern Italy and Greece. This magnet only exercised a limited attraction until after the death of Abbas in 1854. Mohamed Ali was discriminating in his favours towards foreigners and quite able to protect his people from exploitation by anyone except himself and his agents. Abbas was not interested in modernisation and discouraged foreign enterprise and the influx of foreigners. But, with the accession of Mohamed Said, a new era set in. During the course of the next twenty years the number of European nationals resident in Egypt increased from about 15,000 to about 85,000. More important than the numerical increase was the fact that, during this period, European individuals and European interests, under the protection of the Capitulations and, in many cases, assisted by diplomatic intervention, acquired a stranglehold over the economic life of the country.

Mohamed Said was a fat, good-natured, French-educated, extravagant voluptuary. He fell an easy prey to the hordes of European adventurers who descended on Egypt. The usual method of these adventurers was to cajole Said into granting some unreasonable or unworkable con-cession which they had no intention of operating, and then to demand and obtain a substantial indemnity in return for relinquishing it. Other 'ploys' were the use of bribery to obtain from the Egyptian Government large orders for unnecessary items at inflated prices, and the use of diplomatic pressure to obtain exaggerated financial compensation for real or imag-inary injury or damage to person or property. As Mohamed Said had not his father's ruthlessness in tax-collecting, this kind of expenditure, added to a lavish building of palaces, stocking of harems et cetera, soon emptied the Egyptian Treasury. Said sought to rectify matters by dimin-ishing the size of his army, by neglecting the maintenance of the railways and irrigation canals, and by borrowing money against short-term Treasury bills. He also contracted two long-term foreign loans for a total of about £3¼ million from two European Banks—one French and one Anglo-German. When he died in 1863 the Egyptian Treasury owed about £9½ million in fixed term and floating debts, which represented some two years' revenue at that time.

Early in Said's reign, Bruce, the British Consul-General, presciently drew his Government's attention to the impolicy of encouraging the Egyptian Government to contract foreign loans. In 1857 he told them that the Egyptian revenue was 'quite sufficient to meet every legitimate expense and to execute such internal improvements as the interests of Egypt render desirable. But, if (Said) were permitted to borrow on the security of the revenue, no hope would remain of economy or good administration, and the country would descend to his successors with its revenue alienated to foreign speculators.'[2] But, in their anxiety to retain and reinforce their influence, and to advance the commercial and financial interests of their nationals, the British and other European Governments were soon neglecting this prudent advice and instructing their Consuls to apply diplomatic pressure in order to assist their nationals in negotiating improvident loans at exorbitant rates of interest. For example, in 1861, Beauval, the French Consul-General, told his Government: 'If the Viceroy wants a further loan, would it not be better for him to obtain it from France rather than from any other country? When one is authorised, as a result of arrangements made in the interests of our capitalists, to exercise some measure of control over the finances of the State, one is well on the way to controlling the affairs of the State.'³ And, in 1862, Colquhoun, the British Consul-General who succeeded Bruce, was instructed by his Government to give 'moral support' to Henri Oppenheim, a British subject, in the negotiation of Said's second loan, and actually threatened Said with a demand for an indemnity if he did not take up the loan for which he was said to have contracted.⁴ In connection with this loan, the services of the British Embassy at Constantinople were also employed to obtain the permission of the Ottoman Government for it, since the Egyptian Ruler was not supposed to contract foreign loans without Ottoman consent.

Ismail, the eldest surviving son of Ibrahim Pasha, who succeeded his uncle in 1863, was more active, more intelligent, and much more self-confident than Mohamed Said. He had large and ambitious ideas about achieving independence of the Sultan, about agricultural and industrial development, and about extending the Egyptian dominions in the Sudan. He was a great speculator and fancied himself as a sophisticated man of business. He was encouraged in this by a great boom in Egyptian cotton at the beginning of his reign, caused by the blockade of the Southern cotton ports by the North during the American Civil War. He was determined to modernise Egypt, to enrich his own extensive private estates, to establish an Egyptian Empire in an enlarged Sudan, and to purchase his independence of the Sultan, by means of money borrowed from foreign merchants and long-term loans contracted with foreign banking houses. He calculated that the money borrowed could be repaid and the foreign loans serviced from the proceeds of the development which all this borrowed money was intended to finance. But he was not nearly as astute as he thought. The money was borrowed at ruinous rates of interest. Most of the development projects either came to nothing or else failed to produce the expected income. He was worsted in his attempts to wrest the Canal out of the hands of Lesseps and had to pay the Company vast sums in indemnities. The American Civil War came to an end and the cotton boom collapsed. His military exploits in the

13

Sudan proved expensive and unrewarding. The progressive instalments of independence which he succeeded in extracting from the Sultan cost him large sums in bribes and increased tribute payments. The Egyptian Treasury got more and more heavily into debt. Taxation was increased and collected in advance. One particularly improvident device, known as the Muqabala loan, was to grant to landowners remission of half their land-tax in perpetuity in return for the payment of the equivalent of six years' land-tax in instalments payable over twelve years. Foreign loans had to be raised not for development but in order to pay off pressing short-term indebtedness. The terms of borrowing naturally became more onerous as Egypt's creditworthiness deteriorated under the burden of all this extravagance.

The British Government and the Governments of the other Great Powers viewed this Rake's Progress with a curious passivity. The British Government which, in 1841, had been instrumental in devising the bonds of vassalage which subordinated Mohamed Ali to the Sultan, watched without protest while Ismail loosened these bonds by a lavish application of bribes, and used his freedom to contract large and ex-tortionate loans (often from British subjects), to levy improvident and oppressive taxes, and to indulge in unproductive and extravagant expenditure. In the Autumn of 1875, Disraeli, the Prime Minister, took advantage of Ismail's financial difficulties to negotiate the purchase of Egypt's holding of Suez Canal Company Ordinary Shares for £4 million. By this time Ismail's financial plight had become so acute that he needed this ready money in order to meet the next half-yearly coupons on his foreign loans. He was determined to remain technically solvent in order to leave the door open for further borrowing. He was also determined to avoid anything in the nature of Turkish or European interference. So far as Turkey was concerned he had succeeded by bribery in winning back, by successive Firmans from the Sultan, rather more than the independence which Mohamed Ali had forfeited in 1841. He tried to combat European—which principally meant British and French—interference by playing off one country against the other. Since the French Government had shown an excessive tendency to protect the interests of its nationals in Egypt in negotiations over the Mixed Courts, and was pressing him hard over the funding of his short-term indebtedness, much of which was held by the Crédit Foncier, Ismail was not dis-pleased by the hostile French reaction provoked by the sale of the Canal Shares to the British. He improved the occasion by informing the British Government that he was 'anxious to engage the services of two gentlemen to superintend, under the Minister of Finance, the receipts and revenues of the country' and to 'advise the Government on all financial matters.'[5]

14

His presumable object was to try to obtain some assistance from the British Government over his financial difficulties, while relying on Anglo-French rivalry, exacerbated by the British purchase of the Canal Shares, to prevent this degenerating into British control and to provoke a counter-offer of French assistance. The British Government, in dealing with this request, 'determined that the preferable course to adopt in the first instance . . . will be to send out a special envoy to confer with the Khedive (a royal title conferred on Ismail by the Sultan in 1867, together with the right of succession to the throne of Egypt by primogeniture) and his Government as to the financial position and administration of Egypt.'[6] The envoy selected was the Rt Hon. Stephen Cave MP, Paymaster-General.

The sinecure office of Paymaster-General was used then, as it is some-times used now, as a convenient niche for an *homme de confiance* of the Prime Minister who can be made available for special, more or less confidential, missions in which the Prime Minister has a special interest. Not unnaturally, the Cave Mission, coming on top of the purchase of the Canal Shares, was ill-received in France where, in spite of the British Government's assurance that their action 'must not be taken to imply any desire to interfere in the internal affairs of Egypt';[7] it was regarded as one more stage in a concerted British plan to assume control of Egypt.

Cave arrived in Cairo on 17 December 1875. Ismail immediately made it clear to him that 'it was utterly out of his power to permit any official enquiry into the finances of Egypt,' as such an enquiry 'would be virtually allowing foreign intervention in the affairs of the country.'[8] He also provided Cave with information, mostly inaccurate, about proposals he was receiving for obtaining money from French sources, with the presumable object of exciting British emulation. Cave was sufficiently impressed to suggest to the British Government the possibility of a British guaranteed loan. But the British Government, whose real motives in sending Cave to Egypt are obscure, refused to have anything to do with the idea. So Ismail had perforce to turn to the French Government, which was anxious to make some arrangement for the funding of the floating debt, and agreed to receive a French financial mission, which arrived in Egypt in the middle of January 1876.

Cave returned to England at the end of February and wrote his report, which was published on 3 April.[9] It opened by stating: 'The Viceroy has attempted to carry out with a limited revenue, in the course of a few years, works which ought to have been spread over a far longer period and which would tax the resources of far richer Exchequers.' It made some reference to waste and extravagance, but commented that 'probably nothing in Egypt has even approached the profligate expenditure which characterised the commencement of the railway system in England.' It went on to describe the Egyptian system of agriculture, irrigation and land tenure and to criticise the improvidence of the Muqabala. It estimated the current annual revenue at £10,698,070 and current expenditure at £9,080,681, of which £5,036,675 was devoted to debt service. After giving details of the various loans and the arrangements for servicing them, Cave commented: 'None of these loans cost less than 12 per cent p.a., while some of them cost 13¼ per cent and the railway loan 29·9 per cent including sinking fund.' He estimated the sums paid in interest and sinking fund for loans up to the end of 1875 at £24,570,994, and added: 'For the present large amount of indebtedness there is absolutely nothing to show but the Suez Canal, the whole product of the loans and floating debt having been absorbed in the payment of interest and sinking fund, with the exception of the sums debited to the Suez Canal.' He stated that 'the immediate pressure arises from the Khedive's inability to take up the Bonds of his unfunded floating debt now falling due at short intervals and estimated at £18,243,076 at least.' He then made a detailed proposal for refunding and consolidating most of the longterm and floating debt into a loan of £72 million at 7 per cent interest and sinking fund repayable over fifty years. The balance of the longterm debt was to be serviced out of the proceeds of the Muqabala loan. He considered such a plan practicable provided that 'the Khedive should place a person who would command general confidence . . . at the head of a Control Department which would receive from the tax collector certain branches of revenue to be defined . . . and have a general supervision of the incidence and levying of taxes.' He concluded: 'Egypt is well able to bear the charge of the whole of her indebtedness at a reasonable rate of interest, but cannot go on renewing floating debts at 25 per cent and raising fresh loans at 12 per cent and 13 per cent to meet these additions to her debt which do not bring in a single piastre to her Exchequer.'

Meanwhile, the French mission pursued their negotiations. The British Government, after Cave's departure from Egypt, sent there instead Mr Rivers Wilson, Commissioner of the National Debt, ostensibly to advise Ismail about his finances, in reality to keep an eye on the French negotiations and to try and arrange, on behalf of Rothschilds, a loan which would keep Ismail out of French clutches. On 6 April, three days after the publication of the Cave Report, the Egyptian Government, on Rivers Wilson's advice, decreed a threemonth moratorium on obligations falling due during April and May pending arrangements for the consolidation and refunding of the debt. Ismail tried to get off the French hook by negotiating a loan with Rothschilds through Rivers Wilson. But Rothschilds insisted in a British guarantee which the British Government refused to give. So Ismail had to turn to the French mission, from whom he had already borrowed £5 million on the understanding that this sum would subsequently be included in a comprehensive re-funding arrangement. Details of this arrangement were agreed with the French mission and published on 7 May, having been communicated to the British Government a few days earlier. It provided (a) for the conversion of the whole long-term and floating debt, calculated at £91 million, into a Consolidated Debt, bearing interest and sinking fund at 7 per cent and repayable over sixty-five years, and for the allocation of certain State revenues for the service of the debt, which was estimated at £6,343,600 p.a.; (b) for the setting up of a Caisse de la Dette, administered by French, British, Austrian and Italian Commissioners, who would be responsible for collecting the allocated revenues from the Egyptian Treasury and for distributing them to the bondholders. A group of French capitalists was to manage the conversion operation.

The British Government, which had not been consulted over the arrangement, expressed their regret that 'HH has not been able to induce the leading houses of Europe to act for him,' and 'had not thought fit to adopt Mr Cave's recommendations for dealing with the debt.'[10] Rivers Wilson expressed his disapproval, thinking that the settlement placed too heavy a burden on the Egyptian taxpayer, and was unduly favourable to the floating debtholders. (The main purpose of the settlement, from the French point of view, was to get some security for the repayment of the floating debt, of which a large part was held by the Crédit Foncier.) He advised Northcote, the Chancellor of the Exchequer, against any official British nomination to the Commissionership of the Caisse and, soon afterwards, at the request of the British Government, returned to England.

The other three Governments nominated Commissioners and the new arrangement came theoretically into force. But it soon became clear that the British Government, and the British bondholders, objected to it. Several floating debtholders started suing the Egyptian Government in the Mixed Courts, which decided that they were not bound by any legislative acts of the Egyptian Government affecting the rights of foreigners, and proceeded to give judgements in favour of the creditors. In October the Mixed Courts decided to postpone all suits against the Egyptian Government for a month 'to give the Viceroy time to negotiate an amicable arrangement with his creditors and to learn the views of the European Governments about the powers of the Courts.'[11]

Meanwhile, Mr (afterwards Lord) Goschen, a Liberal MP and a member of the Anglo-German banking house of Fruhling & Goschen, which had negotiated several of Ismail's foreign loans, had been appointed by the British bondholders as their representative. He went to Paris in August to confer with M. Joubert, the representative of the French bond-holders, about possible modifications to the settlement arranged in May with the French mission. The two men produced a draft plan which was agreed by the French Government. In September, the Egyptian Govern-ment invited them to Cairo at the suggestion of the French Government, who made it clear to Ismail that they would insist on the original settle-ment being implemented unless it were varied as the result of an agreement with MM. Goschen and Joubert. The British Government, who had indicated their agreement with the Mixed Courts' view of their jurisdiction over the Egyptian Government, in spite of the opinion of their Law Officers,[12] instructed their Consul-General in Cairo to 'give such unofficial assistance as you can to Mr Goschen.'[13] Although, then and later, the British Government ostentatiously dissociated themselves from any responsibility for the Goschen-Joubert mission, the intention was clear. With the French Government insisting on the fulfillment of the French-sponsored May settlement, and with the British Government upholding the Mixed Courts' view of the extent of their jurisdiction, Ismail was to be subjected to converging pressures which would compel him to agree to a revised settlement satisfactory to the British and French Governments. At the same time, the avoidance of any official commitment left them free subsequently to disclaim responsibility for any settlement which MM. Goschen and Joubert might arrive at. Ismail, who had come round to his grandfather's view that England, rather than France, was the Power which had to be conciliated, was not deceived, and treated the views of Mr Goschen with a deference quite incompatible with his apparent role of being merely a private representative of the English bondholders.

The Goschen-Joubert negotiations with the Egyptian Government in Cairo were enlivened by the dismissal, disappearance, and presumed murder of Ismail Sadiq, the Egyptian Minister of Finance. The Mufattish (inspector), as Ismail Sadiq was known, exerted all his influence to obstruct the negotiations, and it soon became clear that, if any agreement were to be arrived at, Ismail Sadiq would have to be removed. The Khedive was not unwilling to make his Finance Minister the scapegoat for Egypt's financial chaos. He also realised that he had to have an agree-ment. So the Mufattish was dismissed, arrested and, almost certainly, murdered as a result of Ismail's direct order.[14]

With the Mufattish out of the way, agreement was reached on 14 November. The capital of the Consolidated Debt was reduced from £91 million to £59 million by subtracting from it all debts owing by the Khedive's Dairas, or private estates, for which other arrangements were made, and by providing for the service of the shorter-term loans from the proceeds of the Muqabala, which had been cancelled under the May settlement and which was now restored. Interest and Sinking Fund on the new Unified Debt was retained at 7 per cent and the annual service of the debt was estimated at £6,480,000. This was about the same as in the original settlement but, unlike the original settlement, included receipts from the Muqabala, which were estimated at £1½ million p.a. for the next ten years. The settlement also provided for a limitation of the Sinking Fund, if necessary, in order to provide for a minimum sum of £4,200,000 p.a. out of revenue for Egyptian administration. The revenue estimate of some £10½ million p.a., which was derived from information supplied by the Egyptian Government, was the same as that taken by Cave and the French mission, and proved in the event to be greatly exaggerated. Even on this exaggerated estimate, some ⅗ of the revenue was to be devoted to the repayment of the debt, virtually all of which was in foreign hands. This is a measure of the extent to which the country had been mortgaged in the course of the previous twenty years.

The Goschen-Joubert settlement also provided for the appointment of a British Commissioner to the Caisse de la Dette, for the allocation to the service of the debt of certain specific revenues, which were to be paid direct to the Commissioners of the Caisse, for the appointment of British and French Controllers of Revenue and Expenditure respectively, for the setting up of an Anglo-French Railways Administration with an Englishman as Chief Commissioner (some of the short-term debt was converted under the settlement into railway debentures), and for the appointment of European advisers and officials to other revenue-producing Departments of State.

The British officials concerned were nominated by Goschen, on behalf of the British bondholders, and not by the British Government who, in reply to a suggestion by Goschen that they should make the nominations, told him that they 'accepted no responsibility but had no objection' to Goschen nominating them himself.[15]

The most important of these officials was the British Commissioner on the Caisse de la Dette. For this post, Goschen, on the recommendation of Sir Louis Mallet, Under Secretary at the India Office,[16] nominated Captain Evelyn Baring, a member of the great banking family, and an officer in the Royal Artillery, who had recently returned from India after serving for four years as Private Secretary to his cousin, Lord Northbrook, the Viceroy. Baring accepted, was duly appointed, and arrived in Egypt on 2 March 1877.

2
COMMISSIONER
OF THE DEBT

CAPTAIN EVELYN BARING was thirty-six years of age when he first came to Egypt as British Commissioner of the Debt in 1877, having been born on 26 February 1841. He had been educated as a soldier, going at the age of eleven to the Ordnance School at Carshalton, a preparatory school for the Royal Military Academy, Woolwich, which he entered at fourteen. In 1858, at the age of seventeen, he received his commission in the Royal Artillery and was posted to Corfu, the principal island in what was at that time the British Protectorate of the Ionian Islands. Here, in the intervals of his not-very-arduous military duties, he devoted much of his time to the study of ancient and modern Greek, Latin and Italian, and French and English literature. By hard work, and what must have been a considerable natural aptitude, he filled the gaps of an inadequate formal education and became a competent scholar in two ancient and two or three modern languages. It was a remarkable achievement for a young subaltern in his teens, particularly as it was combined with a serious interest in his profession, and a normal young man's love of sport, particularly shooting.

In 1862, after a period of leave in England, Baring returned to Corfu on the staff of Sir Henry Storks, Lord High Commissioner of the Ionian Islands. For two years he continued his process of self-education and was introduced, in a small way, to the world of politics and diplomacy. In 1864 the Ionian Islands were ceded to Greece and Baring found himself temporarily without employment. He passed the Summer of that year on a trip to North America with his brother, and spent a month at the HQ of Grant's Northern Army during the Civil War.

In the Autumn of 1864, after his return to England, his old chief, Sir Henry Storks, was appointed Governor and C-in-C Malta, and took Baring there with him as a member of his staff. A year later, in 1865, Storks was appointed Chairman of a Commission to enquire into the circumstances surrounding the recent suppression of an insurrection in

Jamaica where the Commission spent several months preparing its Report. Baring accompanied him.

When the work of the Commission was over, towards the end of 1866, Storks received an appointment at the War Office and Baring returned to regimental duty. After his wider experiences in Corfu, Malta and Jamaica, he found this uninteresting and soon decided to become a candidate for the Staff College. This involved a course of intensive 'cramming' in French and, early in 1868, he was admitted. He passed out first at the end of 1869 and, after a short tour of regimental duty, was appointed to the Topographical and Statistical Department at the War Office, whose functions approximated to those of an Intelligence Department. One of its principal functions was the collection of information about foreign armies, and Baring entered it at a particularly interesting time, on the eve of the Franco-Prussian War and when Cardwell, the Secretary of State for War, was intent on his reforms.

Baring made his mark at the War Office. His cousin, Lord Northbrook, was Under Secretary of State; he was in sympathy with Cardwell's reforming ideas; he attracted the favourable attention of his superiors by a comparative appreciation of the Turkish and Russian armies and by a comprehensive study of the organisation and methods of the Prussian army, whose victory over the French he accurately foretold. He seemed destined for a brilliant military career. But he was already imbued with that mistrust and dislike of the military mind which he was so often to exhibit later. In the Spring of 1872 his cousin, Lord Northbrook, was appointed Viceroy of India in succession to Lord Mayo, who had just been assassinated. Northbrook, who had seen much of Baring's work while at the War Office, invited him to come to India as his Private Secretary. Baring seems to have jumped at the opportunity.

He spent a happy, influential and hard-working four years in India. Northbrook was not a very commanding personality and Baring was very much the Viceroy's right-hand-man, becoming known to the jealous little circle of Anglo-Indian high officials as the 'Vice-Viceroy.'

Baring came back to England in 1876 at the end of Northbrook's term of office. He returned to the War Office, bought a house in London, and married Ethel Errington, a Roman Catholic lady to whom he had been engaged for some years. The marriage seems to have been delayed for so long, partly for financial reasons, and partly because of the objections of the Roman Catholic hierarchy. In spite of the strict rules of that Church, the two sons of the marriage were brought up in the Protestant faith.

As has been indicated, Baring was not happy in his military career, and his term of office as Private Secretary to the Viceroy had not increased his love of soldiering. He therefore welcomed Goschen's offer, made to him in the Autumn of 1876, to go to Egypt as representative of the British holders of Egyptian bonds and to take the post of British Commissioner on the Caisse de la Dette.

His position was an equivocal one. His French, Austrian and Italian colleagues on the Caisse had all been nominated by, and had the support of, their respective Governments, while Baring had been nominated, not by the British Government, but by Goschen, representing the British bondholders. As a Liberal, he disapproved of Disraeli's Conservative Administration, which was in office at the time, and he particularly disapproved of its Near Eastern policy. This disapproval greatly increased during his term of service as Commissioner of the Debt.

Characteristically, he set diligently to work to master the chaotic intricacies of Egyptian finance. He reported copiously and regularly to Goschen. He soon found that the real condition of affairs was much worse than had been revealed to the Goschen-Joubert mission. In addition to the debt which had been consolidated under the Goschen-Joubert settlement, there were large outstanding claims against the Egyptian Government. The pay of its employees was heavily in arrears. Taxation was being collected in advance to pay the debt coupons. Large sums of revenue were disappearing on the way between the tax-collector and the Treasury. Romaine, the British Controller of Revenue, appointed under the Goschen-Joubert settlement, of whose competence Baring formed a low opinion, had no real control over, or even knowledge of, what was happening. The Khedive himself was systematically 'milking' the revenue and making no attempt to cooperate in the implementation of the settlement.

Towards the end of 1877 Baring submitted a proposal to Goschen for dealing with the unconsolidated floating debt which he estimated to amount to £11·5 million, of which £7·5 million, mostly held by French Banks, was secured by various assets, and £4·9 million, including some £0·5 million arrears of Government employees' pay, was unsecured. Baring proposed that this debt should be paid off by raising a loan of £11·5 million, guaranteed by the British and French Governments, issued at par, and paying interest at 5 per cent. This would cost the Egyptian Government £575,000 p.a. in interest, but would enable the cancellation of £11·5 million worth of Unified Stock, then standing at 45, which was held by French Banks as security for part of the floating debt. He told Goschen that if the loan were guaranteed it might be possible to induce the Khedive to reduce the military expenditure of £1 million p.a. which 'appears to me to be out of proportion to the wants and resources of the country.' He also told him that 'a sum of £700,000 p.a. goes to the Khedive and some members of his family.

This is a monstrous charge . . . I believe that the country might perfectly well be administered for about £2·7 million p.a. To this must be added £0·7 million p.a. in tribute and £0·2 million interest on Suez Canal Shares.'[1] (The interest on the Canal Shares was payable to the British Government, representing interest on the Shares bought by the British Government in 1875 on which the interest had previously been mortgaged by the Egyptian Government for twenty-five years; it was a condition of the purchase that this interest should be paid by the Egyptian to the British Government during the period of the mortgage.) In his proposal Baring envisaged a total revenue of £8·75 million, of which £3·5 million was to be spent on administration and £5·25 million on debt service. This compared with the revenue estimate of £10·5 million on which the Goschen-Joubert settlement had been based. He recommended the guarantee of a loan by the British and French Governments on the ground that 'the benefits conferred on the Khedive would be so great that they might assume for ever afterwards the paramount ascendancy of a wholesome European influence.' The 'benefits conferred on the Khedive' by a guaranteed loan would have consisted principally in protecting the Egyptian Government from the ever-present possibility—which was in fact being realised—that some of the unsecured creditors would obtain judgements in the Mixed Courts for the sums owing to them, and proceed to execution, thus putting a further squeeze on an exhausted Egyptian Treasury, and jeopardising the payment of the half-yearly Unified coupons.

The main reason for Baring's proposal was his realisation that the controls provided under the Goschen-Joubert settlement were quite inadequate to procure that minimum of good administration which was necessary to guarantee the settlement, and that a guaranteed loan could serve as a means for insisting on more effective controls. In the event the British Government refused to consider a guaranteed loan. But, by the end of 1877, Baring's emphasis on the necessity for stricter financial control was being underlined by the increasing likelihood that the Goschen-Joubert settlement could not much longer be maintained under existing conditions. Throughout 1877 Vivian, the British Consul-General, had been warning his Government about the deteriorating financial position. He told them about the expense of the troops which Egypt was sending to Turkey to fight in the war against Russia which had broken out in April 1877, but had been instructed 'carefully to avoid joining any pressure which may be attempted to be put on the Khedive with reference to the amount of assistance he shall send to the Porte.'[2] He complained that the salaries of the European officials appointed under the Goschen-Joubert settlement added to the cost without increasing the efficiency of the administration.[3] He reported that it was only with great difficulty and by the collection of taxes in advance that the debt coupons were being paid as they fell due.[4] He wrote that the European Controllers had not succeeded 'in checking to any great extent the abuses and extortion that prevail in the provinces,' and doubted if they could tell 'whether the legal taxes and only these are being honestly collected and paid over' or whether 'the country is taxed beyond its means.'[5] He warned the British Government that 'great mischief may be done both to the country and to our own reputation, as taking a leading part among the European advisers, by the perpetuation of abuses and oppression.' As early as the end of July he came to the conclusion that the Goschen-Joubert settlement was unworkable. In September the Khedive told him that the settlement would have to be revised and Vivian told the British Government that the expenses of the war and a low Nile had brought on a crisis somewhat earlier than would otherwise have been the case. Baring and the other Commissioners of the Caisse were inclined to agree with Vivian, but insisted that any modification of the terms of the settlement must be preceded by a 'thorough and searching enquiry' into the state of Egypt's finances. Baring told Vivian that such an enquiry should be conducted by a Commission composed of the two Controllers and the Commissioners of the Caisse; it should go into the question of reducing expenditure as well as of increasing revenue, suggest means of acquiring stronger control over the collection of taxes and of protecting the taxpayer from illegal and arbitrary taxation, consider the expediency of changing the dates of the coupons to coincide with the harvests, and devise a practicable method of dealing with the floating debt.[6]

The Khedive was anxious for, and conscious of the necessity of, some modification of the Goschen-Joubert settlement, but wished to avoid any comprehensive enquiry which would reveal the extent to which he and his family had enriched themselves at the country's expense, and impose an effective check on his own arbitrary methods of rule. The British Government were reluctant to interfere. The French Government inclined to the view that the settlement was maintainable if sufficient pressure were applied, since they believed the Khedive had accumulated assets which he should be compelled to disgorge.

Baring took a leading part in trying to secure an enquiry of the kind which he, and Vivian, considered necessary. He suggested the draft of a letter to be sent by Goschen and Joubert to the Khedive, urging the necessity for a comprehensive enquiry, and told Goschen: 'It is essential to get Joubert out of the idea that the Viceroy, with a little more firmness, might be held to his engagements as they exist, I daresay there is some truth in this, but it is not the whole truth.'[7] He drew Goschen's attention to the danger lest money in the hands of the Caisse should be sequestrated as a result of Mixed Court judgements in favour of floating creditors.[8] He urged his proposal for a guaranteed loan as a means of putting pressure on Ismail to agree to a comprehensive enquiry. He warned Goschen against Romaine, the British Controller, and Money, the British Administrator of the Daira (Khedivial estates), who were apparently in favour of a straight reduction of interest on the Unified Debt. He described Romaine as 'a dangerous lunatic who should be locked up' and told Goschen that 'if by a stroke of the pen we reduced the rate to 2 per cent to-morrow, we should assuredly have the Viceroy crying out in a year that he can only pay 1 per cent.' He referred to the 'Keller judgement' in the Mixed Courts, by which a European employee of the Egyptian Government had obtained judgement for arrears of salary, and warned Goschen that 'we shall assuredly have the Khedive running up arrears of pay and then with the sanction of the law saying, "I must now alter my arrangements with bondholders in order to pay my clerks." '[9]

As a representative of the bondholders, Baring was sensitive to Vivian's criticisms, expressed to the British Government, about the responsibility of the bondholders for the oppression of the Egyptian taxpayer. On 19 December he told Goschen: 'I don't see the good of not recognising what everybody knows; that some sacrifices by the creditors are on the cards.' Later, in February, when criticising a report by Romaine stressing the impossibility of collecting sufficient taxes to pay the forthcoming coupon, he told Goschen: 'If Romaine had set to work to ameliorate the fellah's lot in a reasonable way he would have had my cordial support. As long as I consider the demands of the creditors just, I will support them, but a time may come when I think that the demands put forward . . . are unjust, and then I certainly should not support them.'[10]

Meanwhile Vivian, with Baring's encouragement, was trying to get a reluctant British Government to insist on a comprehensive enquiry. For three months, during December 1877 and January and February 1878, the struggle went on. Ismail tried to limit the scope of the proposed enquiry. The British Government refused to go further than to authorise Vivian to tell the Khedive that 'he would act wisely in consenting to a full and complete enquiry.'[11] The French Government were not anxious for any enquiry at all. Ismail continued to twist and turn. In order to try to appease the British Government and sow dissension between Britain and France he offered to appoint a British Inspector-General of Finances with undefined powers. Towards the end of January he tried to appoint a Commission of Enquiry of his own, with Gordon, at that time Governor-General of the Sudan, President, and Lesseps Vice-President, and without the Commissioners of the Caisse, in the expectation that they would recommend a reduction of interest without any very close enquiry into the finances. A Mr Walker from London, said to be representative of some of the English bondholders, arrived in Cairo to negotiate with the Egyptian Government over the heads of the Caisse.

Baring and his colleagues on the Caisse put such pressure on the Khedive as they could. At the beginning of February Baring told Goschen that the Caisse had decided to summon the Minister of Finance before the Mixed Courts to make him render a detailed account of the revenues earmarked for the service of the debt, of which he alleged that there was a short-fall compared with the estimates. 'You will see from all this that we have thrown away the scabbards of our swords and are at open war . . . I believe that the moment for compromise has passed. Vivian says that the Khedive is now deaf to any persuasion . . . He is determined to fight . . . We must fight with such means as we have at our disposal.'[12] He advocated a campaign against the Khedive in the British Press and told Goschen that 'if, frightened by public opinion, the Khedive really shows any signs of yielding, I think we should redouble our blows. I hope the English papers will not abstain from further attacks.'[13]

Baring realised that these means were inadequate and that support from the British Government would be necessary. On 15 February he told Goschen: 'The answer rests with HMG. I take it for granted that they will continue to act in harmony with the French; the active or even passive hostility of the French will cause any arrangement made without their concurrence to collapse. The two Governments must make up their minds whether to adopt a persuasive or a dictatorial policy. I hope they will make up their minds as to what they want and insist on getting it.' He went on to indicate that the two Governments should insist on an enquiry 'into the whole financial and administrative machinery of the country without any limitation whatever' as being 'the only course which will be productive of any real and permanent good.' He added: 'The French think that such an enquiry would lead to the downfall of the Khedive. Perhaps they are right. If it did it would be a good thing for all concerned.'[14] He was later to learn that Ismail's deposition created problems even more intractable than those created by his rule.

Gordon arrived in Egypt from the Sudan at the beginning of March, intent on accepting the Khedive's invitation to preside over a Commission of Enquiry with a membership and terms of reference amenable to the Khedive's ideas. Baring told Goschen that the Khedive would give Gordon a free choice of colleagues provided that the Commissioners of the Caisse were excluded and that his own attitude towards him would be not to seek him out and advise him but to 'give him the best advice I can if asked.' In the same letter he warned Goschen that 'sooner or later

26

the English Government will be drawn out of its policy of non-intervention in Egyptian affairs . . . they will be obliged to step in at last whether they like it or not.'[15]

Although Baring did not know it, the British Government were about to step in. For some weeks they had been having discussions with the French Government about the Egyptian situation. They had apparently been advised in favour of a comprehensive enquiry by Rivers Wilson, the Commissioner of the National Debt, who had been in Egypt for a short time in 1876 and who was the Government's principal adviser on Egyptian finances. During the winter of 1877/78 Wilson saw a good deal of Nubar, an ex-Minister who had fallen into disgrace with Ismail the year before and who was in exile. Nubar, who had no very kindly feelings towards Ismail, impressed upon Wilson the necessity for a thorough enquiry into expenditure as well as revenue. He also appears to have given Wilson a good deal of information about the methods by which Ismail's estates had been acquired, i.e. mostly out of the revenues of the State. So Wilson's advice was added to that of Vivian. What appears finally to have brought the British Government to act was an intimation by the French and German Governments that they proposed to make official protests to the Khedive about the non-execution of various Mixed Courts' judgements in favour of their nationals against the Egyptian Government and the Royal Estates. On 26 February Vivian was instructed by cable to associate himself with these protests.[16] The effect of these protests would probably be to induce the Egyptian Government to divert money from the Caisse in order to satisfy the judgement creditors. On 2 March the Mixed Courts gave judgement in favour of the Caisse in their action against the Minister of Finance. On 8 March Lord Derby, the Foreign Secretary, after consulting Northcote, the Chancellor of the Exchequer, and Goschen, instructed Vivian by cable to 'act in conjunction with your French colleague to support the claims of the bondholders that they should be adequately represented on the Commission of Enquiry and to say that HMG think that the enquiry should be full and comprehensive, that Captain Baring should be a Commissioner, and that if a second British Commissioner were required they would nominate Mr Rivers Wilson.' Similar instructions were sent to M. des Michels, the French Consul-General, by the French Government.

This joint action effectively torpedoed Ismail's attempts to set up a Commission under Gordon's Presidency. He threw Gordon over and, on 27 March, after a little further haggling, promulgated a Decree setting up a Commission of Enquiry on the lines stipulated, with Lesseps as President, Rivers Wilson as first Vice-President, Riaz Pasha, an Egyptian statesman, as second Vice-President, and the four Commissioners of the Caisse as the remaining members. It was understood that Lesseps would do no detailed work on the Commission and that Wilson would be *de facto* President. The Decree provided that the Commission's investigations 'porteront sur tous les éléments de la situation financière, en tenant compte des droits légitimes du gouvernement . . . Les Ministres et fonctionnaires devront fournir directement à la Commission tous les renseignments qui leur seront demandés.'

Baring met Gordon for the first time during the latter's short and somewhat ignominious stay in Cairo. Gordon had accepted Ismail's invitation to preside over a Commission from which the members of the Caisse would be excluded. He took the view that the Commissioners of the Caisse were being unduly hard on Ismail, and had already worked out a plan for postponing the forthcoming May coupon and reducing the rate of interest on the Unified Debt to 4 per cent. Vivian and the other Consuls-General warned him that he was encouraging Ismail to risk his throne, but Gordon treated their advice with disdain. He saw Baring, and took an immediate dislike to him, which was reciprocated. Baring told Goschen that he had seen Gordon for five minutes. 'I begged him not to get it into his head that we were blind to the interests of the fellah, and I pointed out to him the importance of the recent judgement . . . He is about as much fit for the work in hand as I am to be Pope.'[17] After seeing the Consuls-General and Baring, Gordon saw Lesseps, who made it clear to him that he was not prepared to go against the wishes of the British and French Governments. By this time Ismail had been informed of the identic instructions addressed by these Governments to their Representatives and was preparing to retreat. He made himself inaccessible to Gordon, who soon returned to the Sudan, and appears to have been advised by Lesseps to give way. He succeeded in insisting on having an Egyptian on the Commission. In this he was supported by Baring, who suggested Riaz' nomination. He was opposed both by des Michels, the French Consul-General, and by de Blignières, his French colleague on the Caisse, but he told Goschen that the Khedive must be given a fair chance and that he was not going to join the French in creating a state of affairs which was intended to lead to his deposition.[18]

At last Baring had got what he wanted. As he told Goschen: 'After five months of incessant labour the enquiry is settled. We have got absolutely all for which we have been contending—an enquiry into the whole financial situation without limit, the admission of the whole Caisse, the admission of an Englishman as Vice-President.'[19] He paid tribute to Vivian's persistence and also to the attitude of 'old Lesseps', without whose help, he told Goschen, it could not have been arranged. The only fly in the ointment was the nomination of Rivers Wilson as Vice-President.

He disliked Wilson personally, was a little suspicious of his integrity,[20] and considered him too much of a 'Treasury' man in his financial approach. He told Goschen that, for his part, 'the moment I become a member of the Commission I shall consider I have wider interests than those of the bondholders and shall act accordingly.' He added, 'It is not improbable that differences may arise between us and the French,' and indicated to Goschen his hope, if not his expectation, that he would be able to rely on Wilson's help and cooperation.[21]

Hardly had the matter of the Commission been settled than another serious crisis arose. It had been arranged some months previously that the half-yearly Unified Debt coupon, due on 1 April, should be split into two, one half being paid in anticipation in November 1877 and the other half in arrear on 1 May. The November half had been duly paid and the other half, amounting to about £1 million, was about to fall due. On 15 April Vivian told Lord Salisbury, who had just taken over the Foreign Office from Lord Derby, that the payment of the May coupon, on which the French were insisting, 'would absorb every available resource of the Government and leave nothing to pay the tribute which we are instructed officially to demand,[22] or arrears of pay to Government clerks who are in great distress. I contemplate that the payment of the coupon will certainly produce disastrous effects.'[23] Salisbury replied stating, (a) that the French Government had told him that there was every reason to believe that the Khedive could pay the May coupon if he chose; (b) that the institution of the Commission of Enquiry 'ought not to be made a pretext for postponing the payment of the Khedive's debts in so far as he is in a position to do so'; (c) that M. Waddington, the French Foreign Minister, had expressed a desire that the British should act with the French in this matter, and that Vivian was therefore to join with his French colleague in insisting on payment of the May coupon in full; and (d) that 'HMG consider that the payment of the tribute and the interest on the English Shares of the Canal Company are obligations of a more binding character than any other and that they have a special interest in their practical fulfilment.'[24] Baring, in a letter to Goschen on 19 April, expressed his astonishment at Vivian's instructions. 'What has made the Government depart from the general principle of leaving the bondholders to themselves? This is going further than I can go in representing the bondholders and further than, as an Englishman, I like to see an English Government go. Vivian tells me confidentially that the French Ambassador has won over Lord Salisbury to his point of view. I am a warm advocate of acting in harmony with the French but I am by no means an advocate of following their lead. Vivian finds himself in a difficult position as his instructions run diametrically contrary to all his previous instructions and language. If there is a row in Parliament I hope you will see that Lord Salisbury don't make a scapegoat of him. I have had some experience of the noble Marquis' ways.'[25] On 22 April Baring told Goschen: 'After investigation the Caisse decided that they can make no official protest,' and expressed the opinion that the French Government had forced HMG's hand. 'It is not for me to criticise the conduct of the latter. But I cannot help thinking that it would have been . . . more worthy of two great Governments to have refrained from any special pressure for the payment of the coupon and merely to have told the Khedive that he ought, if he can, to meet it as well as his other engagements . . . It is only after grave hesitation that I have come to the conclusion that I should do nothing. By protesting I should do no possible good and might materially increase the difficulties of HMG.'[26] On 29 April, in a third letter to Goschen, Baring set out his considered views on the matter, which were apparently shared by his colleagues on the Caisse: 'The English and French Governments have told the Khedive that he can and ought to pay the coupon. In my opinion they have in doing so assumed a very grave responsibility and one which neither my colleagues nor myself are prepared to take . . . It is very doubtful whether it is in the real interests of the bondholders that the coupon should be paid in its entirety. To do so will almost certainly drive the Government back on the pernicious system of taking the taxes in advance, which we have but recently got rid of after much trouble. It will largely compromise the payment of the November coupon. It will allow interest on judgements and arrears of salaries to accumulate and thus render the operation of the Sinking Fund abortive. Lastly it will certainly lead to excessive rigour and oppression in the collection of taxes . . . We do not express any opinion as to whether the Egyptian Government can or cannot or ought or ought not to pay the coupon. The whole administration of the country has been in the hands of the Khedive. We have not the means of expressing an opinion. We throw the whole responsibility of coming to a decision and the consequences of that decision on the Egyptian Government. Whatever may be the opinion of the bondholders we are not prepared to go further than this . . . It appears to me that both the British and French Governments have gone a good deal further than we are prepared to go. They have said that the Khedive can and ought to pay the coupon. We say that we are quite unable to form any opinion.'[27]

Over twenty-five years later, Baring wrote: 'The Berlin Congress was then about to sit to regulate the situation arising from the recent Russo-Turkish war,' that 'Egyptian interests had to give way to broader diplomatic considerations' and that 'it was necessary to conciliate the French.'[28] Lord Salisbury, in a contemporary note to the Chancellor of the Exchequer[29] gave this explanation of his instructions to Vivian: 'If we declined to assist the French to any extent in pressing the claims of the bondholders, we should alienate France, cause her to work against us privately, and injure our position seriously without much helping either the Canal Shares or the tribute.' This confirms Baring's view that British insistence on the payment of the coupon was due to a desire to conciliate the French, although it is not certain whether this was due to Egyptian or to wider considerations.

In consequence of the combined insistence of the British and French Governments, Baring tells us[30] that 'steps were taken to collect the money necessary to pay the coupon. Two of the most iron-fisted Pashas who could be found were sent into the Provinces. They were accompanied by a staff of moneylenders who were prepared to buy in advance the crops of the cultivators . . . The money was however obtained. The last instalment was paid to the Commissioners of the Debt a few hours before the coupon fell due. The great diversity of currency, and the fact that many of the coins were strung together to be used as ornaments, bore testimony to the pressure which had been used in the collection of the taxes.'

For the next few months, Baring was busy with his work on the Commission of Enquiry. As he had warned Goschen, he regarded himself as having wider interests than those of the bondholders, and his experience over the May coupon had confirmed him in his opinion that the interests of the bondholders could not be pursued without reference to the interests of the Egyptian taxpayer. During the course of the Enquiry he elaborated a theory that the interests of the taxpayers and the bondholders were, up to a point, identical, in that they were both interested in curbing the extravagance and the arbitrary rule of the Khedive. As Baring, together with his fellow Commissioners, spent the hot Summer months in trying to find their way through the murky labyrinth of official Egyptian finances, he became more and more convinced that Ismail was at the root of the trouble, and that it would be possible for the Egyptian Government to pay its debts without oppressive taxation if only some effective check were placed on the arbitrary power of the Khedive, and the principle and practice of Ministerial responsibility enforced. Specifically, what was needed was the acceptance by the Khedive of a Civil List, and the introduction of an effective system of ministerial government which, with European assistance, would reform and regularise the imposition and collection of taxes and keep the hands of the Khedive and his minions out of the till.

It had been arranged that the Commission of Enquiry should adjourn in August and resume its sittings in October, and that it should produce a preliminary Report before its adjournment in order, if possible, to create

31

conditions which would enable a loan to be raised to deal with the judge-ment debts and the unsecured floating debt generally. The necessity for this loan, and Baring's views about the Khedive, which were shared by his fellow-Commissioners, dictated the content of the preliminary Report, which was presented to the Khedive by Rivers Wilson, the acting President of the Commission, on 18 August.

In the first part of the Report[31] the Commissioners made a scathing denunciation of the existing administration of Egypt. They found that the system of tax-collection was arbitrary and that many of the taxes were unjustified and inequitable. They found that forced labour and military conscription were heavy burdens and that the Khedive's estates were cultivated almost entirely by forced labour. They recommended that the *corvée* (forced labour) should be restricted to 'works of unquestionable public necessity', that the taxation system should be regularised, and the native Courts of Justice reformed. They found that the system of European Controllers had failed to exercise an effective check against abuses and recommended (a) that no tax should be collected except on the authority of a Decree officially published, and (b) that the exercise of the legislative power should be so reformed as to justify the eventual application of financial laws to all residents of Egypt irrespective of nationality. They recommended that a Reserve Fund should be set up to provide for extraordinary expenses and for remissions of taxation in years of low Nile, that no taxes should be collected in advance, that the land-tax should be reviewed after the completion of a Cadastral Survey, and that the Customs tariff should be revised.

In the second part of the Report the Commissioners estimated the amount of outstanding debts for which provision had to be made at just under £5 million, but reported that 'the confused accounts and irregular system of taxation' made it impossible to estimate the real revenue. They stated that 'the absolute power and control hitherto exercised by the Khedive' made him personally responsible for the existing condition of the finances, and expressed the view that 'he cannot be released from this responsibility until time has been allowed for the introduction of a new system of administration, the central principle of which must be the limitation of the Khedive's absolute power which has resulted in the present position.' They concluded that 'before any further burdens can be imposed on the taxpayer, or any further sacrifice demanded of the creditors, the private property of the Khedive and his family are liable for the satisfaction of the debt,' and demanded the surrender of all the Khedive's property in land and houses in return for a Civil List.

Lord Salisbury was not altogether happy about this attack on the Khedive and at the prominent part in it being played by Wilson and

Baring. He feared that the French would 'double-cross' them and, by a sudden *volte face*, make themselves champions of the Khedive and so secure for themselves a predominant position in Egypt. On 25 August he wrote to Northcote, the Chancellor of the Exchequer: 'If they so treat the Khedive that he either falls or becomes recalcitrant it will be no sort of consolation that he deserves such treatment. The danger of his throwing himself into the hands of the French is not speculation . . . The French are more disloyal to an alliance than any other nation with whom we have to deal. If the screw is to be turned on the Khedive we must take care that the French have their full share in turning it.'[32] Apart from the danger of a French *volte face*, Salisbury also seems to have foreseen the difficulties which would arise, and which later did arise, as a result of the Khedive's deposition. He had minuted on one of Vivian's despatches[33] that he thought the Commission's proceedings were 'wholly wanting in commonsense. If they want to dethrone the Khedive, their policy might lead to the desired result. But they do not want to dethrone him. What then is the use of driving him to desperation? It will not increase our hold on him. These ill-gotten gains are an invaluable screw. But, once dethroned, the screw is gone.' Salisbury's view was that enough pressure should be put on the Khedive to make him subservient to British policy, but not enough to break him, and that the British Commissioners on the Enquiry should 'avoid extreme measures and exigencies which might bring about the dethronement of the Viceroy.'[34]

During the Commission's investigations, Ismail had concentrated his resistance on the question of his estates. He made no bones about the acceptance of responsible ministerial government, believing, correctly, that he would be able to reduce it to a nullity. At the beginning of May, a week or two after Wilson's arrival in Egypt, he offered him the appoint-ment of Minister of Finance in a responsible Ministry[35] and, a few weeks later, apparently at Wilson's suggestion, he sent an emissary to Europe to sound Nubar about becoming President of the Council of Ministers.[36] Nubar expressed his willingness and left for Egypt at the end of July, after having arranged with the British Government that Wilson should be appointed Minister of Finance and that a Frenchman should be appointed to some other Ministry.[37]

Ismail accepted the Commission's Report on 25 August and expressed the intention of inviting Nubar to form a Government with Wilson as Minister of Finance and a Frenchman as Minister of Public Works. Vivian told Salisbury with some disingenuousness that this had been achieved 'without any pressure on my part' and Salisbury expressed his satisfaction.[38] On 28 August Nubar was invited to form a Ministry in a Rescript by the Khedive in which he stated that he wished in future 'to govern by and through my Council of Ministers.' There followed some coming-and-going about the European Ministers. The French Government mistrusted Nubar and suspected that he was too intimate with Wilson and the British Government. The Italian Government demanded representation in the Council of Ministers. The British and French Governments combined to oppose the Italian demand and eventually agreed to the appointment of Wilson as Minister of Finance and de Blignières, Baring's French colleague on the Caisse, as Minister of Public Works. It was also agreed that the positions of British and French Controllers should be abolished as a result of the appointment of European Ministers, with the proviso that the Control should be reinstated in the event of either of the European Ministers being dismissed without the consent of their respective Governments.

And so matters were arranged. But the new Ministry, with its two European members, did not become fully operative until the end of November. Wilson spent the interval in arranging with Rothschilds for a loan of a nominal £8·5 million at 7 per cent interest, to be issued at 73, which was to provide the Egyptian Government with just under £6 million in cash, sufficient to pay the outstanding amount of unsecured floating debt as estimated by the Commission of Enquiry. This loan, which the British and French Governments refused to guarantee, was secured on the Khedivial estates (subsequently known as the State Domains) which were surrendered in accordance with the recom-mendations of the Commission of Enquiry. These were estimated to produce an annual income of some £400,000, and were to be admini-stered, in accordance with the terms of the loan, by one British and one French Commissioner. (In the event, as we shall see, there was a delay of over a year before the money was advanced by Rothschilds.)

After the completion and acceptance by the Khedive of the Com-missioners' preliminary Report, Baring went on leave at the end of August and returned to Egypt towards the end of the year. On paper, most of what he had striven for had been accomplished, although he regretted that the British Government had refused to guarantee the loan either by themselves or in conjunction with the French Government. He considered that such a guarantee would have given the guarantors some control over the future course of events, besides enabling more favourable terms to have been obtained from Rothschilds.

The Commission of Enquiry resumed its work after the Summer recess. Having, to all appearance, established the pre-conditions necessary for sound financial administration, it remained to make detailed proposals for a revision of the Goschen-Joubert settlement. With Wilson and de Blignières in the Ministry, most of the work devolved on Baring, who had little else to do, since the supervisory powers previously exercised by the Caisse were now the responsibility of Wilson as Minister of Finance. Politically, he remained in the background, watching with an increasingly critical eye the not very auspicious course of events under the new Ministry.

During the earlier investigations of the Commission, Baring, Wilson and Vivian had been closely in accord with each other about the necessity of getting the Khedive to accept responsible ministerial government and the relinquishment of his estates. This united British front had helped to secure Ismail's acceptance of the Commission's recommendations, in the same way as the united front between Vivian and Baring earlier in the year had assisted in inducing Ismail to accept the effective powers demanded for the Commission. But, after the setting-up of the new Ministry, Vivian and Wilson were soon at loggerheads. This, together with financial difficulties due to delays in receiving the loan money from the Rothschilds, and the unpopularity caused by the economies which the new Ministry imposed, made it easy for Ismail to discredit the experiment of responsible government to which he had, with apparent willingness, agreed.

The point at issue between Vivian and Wilson was that Vivian considered the new system of government could only survive so long as Ismail was prepared to support it with the prestige of his authority. If he chose to intrigue against it, it was doomed. It was therefore necessary for Ministers to go out of their way to try to conciliate Ismail by consulting him and inviting his cooperation in the business of administration. Wilson, although conscious of the need for the Khedive's support—while in Paris negotiating with the Rothschilds he told Salisbury that 'if we only have fair play I have no doubt as to the result, but if the Viceroy is against us the difficulties will be enormous'[39]—was at one with Nubar in his determination to exclude Ismail from any share in the administration. Baring, although sceptical of Ismail's good faith, believed, with Vivian, that Ismail's cooperation should be sought by the new Ministry.[40]

Wilson afterwards recorded his opinion that the new Ministry could have 'met and overcome' all their difficulties 'had we been able to present a united front with our diplomatic representatives and, above all, had the money for the recent loan been at our disposal.'[41] As it was, a crisis was not long in coming. In February 1879 some of the 2,500 Army officers thrown out of employment as a result of a cut in army strength from 15,000 to 7,000 decreed by the new Ministry made a demonstration against the Ministry in Cairo and manhandled Nubar and Wilson. They only dispersed on a direct order from Ismail, who had probably instigated the demonstration. Having effectively shown that he was still the real master of the situation, Ismail told the British and French Consuls-General that Nubar's resignation was necessary on grounds of public security and that he would himself preside in future over the Council of Ministers. Nubar thereupon resigned. Vivian advised Wilson to remain at his post and the French Government instructed de Blignières to do the same.

This incident brought the controversy between Wilson and Vivian to a head and each complained to the British Government of the conduct of the other. Salisbury instructed Vivian to give 'the most cordial support to the policy of Rivers Wilson' and told him that 'all the influence of HMG must be at his disposal.'[42] The British and French Governments also sent identic Notes to their representatives stressing that they were determined to act in concert 'in all that concerns Egypt' and instructing them to inform Ismail that 'they cannot lend themselves to any modification in principle of policies and financial arrangements recently sanctioned by the Khedive.' In spite of Wilson's protests, they did not insist on Nubar's reinstatement. But, after a flurry of telegrams between London, Paris and Cairo, they did insist that Ismail's son, Taufiq, should, instead of Ismail himself, be President of the Council of Ministers, and that the two European Ministers should have a power of veto over any measure proposed by the Ministry. Salisbury also recalled Vivian and replaced him as British Consul-General by Mr Frank Lascelles.

And so matters were patched up on the surface. But, as Baring commented later, 'a man like Ismail was not to be bound by ropes of diplomatic sand.'[43]

By the beginning of April the Commission's final Report, prepared mostly by Baring, was ready. Wilson, in his capacity as acting President of the Commission, accompanied by de Blignières, showed it in draft form to Ismail, as a matter of courtesy, before it was published. The Report was based on the assumption that Egypt was bankrupt and had been so since 1876. It proposed a composition with Egypt's creditors consisting principally of a reduction to 5 per cent of the interest on the Unified debt, the payment of unsecured creditors at a rate of about 11s in the £ and the virtual cancellation of the Muqabala. On the taxation side the Report recommended the abolition of a number of the vexatious and inequitable taxes which had been imposed over the past ten years, but recommended an increase in the land-tax paid on what were known as Ushuri lands.

Ushuri lands, comprising about one-quarter of the cultivated lands of Egypt, had originally been uncultivated land granted to magnates by Mohamed Ali at a favourable rate of land-tax in order to encourage its being brought into cultivation. In course of time they had simply become

Sir Evelyn Baring *c* 1890

Khedive Taufiq

Khedive Abbas Hilmi at his accession, 1892

lands held on favourable taxation terms by wealthy and privileged people. (According to an unpublished book written by a future Financial Adviser to the Egyptian Government—Sir Edgar Vincent, afterwards Lord d'Abernon—there were in 1887 3,554,000 feddans of Kharaj— ordinary—agricultural land paying an average land tax of PT128 per feddan per annum and 1,476,000 feddans of Ushuri land paying an average land tax of PT50 per feddan per annum. [See BM Add. MS 48960–61.] A feddan is about an acre. One piastre [PT] was worth about 2½d.) Any proposal to increase the Ushuri land tax, however equitable, was therefore certain to arouse great opposition from large landowners. The same consideration applied to the proposal to abolish the Muqabala, since a great many large landowners had subscribed to this improvident loan, which provided for the halving of their land tax in perpetuity in return for the payment of a sum equivalent to six years' tax. These two proposals by the Commission therefore represented political dynamite which Ismail was quite prepared to use. He had, some weeks previously, convoked the Chamber of Notables, a representative body of provincial magnates set up in 1866, to which proposed increases in taxation were supposed to be submitted but whose deliberations had never before been taken seriously by Ismail. In a land where there are no official secrets the recommendations of the Commission had probably been known to most of the members of the Chamber, then assembling in Cairo, long before they were presented to the Khedive. Ismail could, therefore, rely on their assistance in the *coup* which he had prepared.

Ismail, according to Wilson, 'received our remarks with outward courtesy'[44] when he and de Blignières presented him with the draft Report but, immediately afterwards, sent each of them a curt letter dismissing them from office. On the same day he wrote to Sherif Pasha, an Egyptian elder statesman, inviting him to form a Ministry. The year before, Sherif Pasha had resigned from the Government in protest against being summoned by the Commission of Enquiry to give evidence before them.

The next day, 9 April, Ismail summoned a meeting of the Consular Corps and, in the presence of a number of members of the Chamber of Notables, told them that 'the nation' demanded the formation of a purely Egyptian Ministry responsible to the Chamber of Notables. In consequence Taufiq Pasha, 'yielding to the will of the nation,' had resigned and been replaced by Sherif Pasha who would form a Ministry in accordance with the Rescript of 28 August 1878 in which the principle of ministerial responsibility was laid down. Ismail added that 'the nation' protested against the declaration of bankruptcy contained in the Commission's Report and that an alternative financial project which had been 'submitted to him signed by all classes of the population' and which was in accordance with the Decree of 18 November 1876 incorporating the Goschen-Joubert settlement, would be promulgated.

This counter-project, published as a Decree on 22 April, which estimated the revenue at a figure nearly £1 million higher than the Commission of Enquiry's estimate, provided for the payment in full of all Egypt's debts (subject to the 'temporary' reduction of Unified interest to 5 per cent) and for the maintenance of the Muqabala, without any increased taxation. It was clearly impossible to execute; apart from anything else, Ismail's *coup* made it unlikely that the balance of the Rothschild loan, which was needed for paying off the floating debt, would be forthcoming. But there was, in truth, no intention in Ismail's mind that it should be executed. It was simply a device adopted in an attempt to free himself from the shackles which Great Britain and France sought to fasten on him.

At first, it seemed that the Khedive had 'got away with it.' Wilson and de Blignières left the country, the former to be solaced with a KCMG. Sherif Pasha, in view of the stipulation that the Control over Egyptian finances should be revived *ipso facto* in the event of either of the European Ministers being dismissed without the consent of their respective Governments, invited M. Bellaigues de Bughas (who had succeeded de Blignières as French Debt Commissioner) and Baring to assume the offices of Controller of Revenue and Expenditure respectively under the terms of the Decree of 18 November 1876. Both declined on the ground that they could not associate themselves with a financial plan which they regarded as impracticable or with a change of system which they regarded as being in contradiction to the engagements recently undertaken by the Khedive towards the British and French Governments. Baring, considering that 'any hope of placing Egyptian financial affairs on a sound footing' had been 'dashed to the ground'[45] resigned his position as Debt Commissioner and left Egypt on 24 May. Mr Auckland Colvin, an Indian Civil Servant, who had been appointed by Rivers Wilson, during his term as Minister, to conduct a Cadastral Survey, was appointed British Debt Commissioner in his place.

Baring had served in Egypt as Debt Commissioner for just over two years. Working largely behind the scenes, he had been influential, persistent, and ultimately successful in obtaining the sort of enquiry he considered necessary. Once the Commission had been set up, and again working largely behind the scenes, his influence had very largely determined the course of the enquiry. By the time the European Ministry was formed in the Autumn of 1878 he had become so mistrustful of Ismail that he must have doubted whether the experiment of responsible ministerial government would work. He may well have been relieved that Wilson, and not he, had been selected to serve as Minister of Finance. With a fairly well-developed instinct for not becoming involved in a situation out of which little credit was likely to be gained, he had kept well in the background during the turbulent course of the European Ministry, and took no open part in the controversy between Vivian and Wilson, both of whom became to some extent discredited in the eyes of the British Government as the result of this controversy. In spite of a later reputation for brusqueness, he seems to have got on well enough with those with whom he had to work. He worked closely and amicably with Vivian over getting the Commission of Enquiry set up and seems to have dispelled some early suspicions expressed by Vivian that he was over-zealous in the cause of the bondholders. Although he disliked Wilson, he worked closely with him during the work of the Commission, and does not seem to have lost the goodwill either of Wilson or of Vivian during the quarrel between the two. He got on well with, without being dominated by, de Blignières, his explosive French colleague on the Caisse, and, generally, played his part successfully in the difficult game of remaining on good terms with, without becoming subordinated to, the French high officials—the Consul-General, the Debt Commissioner, and the Controller—with whom he had to work. He seems to have won the confidence of Riaz Pasha, his Egyptian colleague on the Commission of Enquiry, and Minister of the Interior in Nubar's, and then in Taufiq's, Ministry.

When he slipped unobtrusively from Egypt towards the end of May, his work there seemed to be in ruins. The financial settlement drawn up by him in the final Report of the Commission of Enquiry had been thrown into the wastepaper basket. Ismail's *coup* had destroyed all those pre-conditions for sound financial administration for which he had striven during his two years of office. To all appearance, Egypt was back in the same position as at the end of 1876. But, during the intervening two-and-a-half years, Egypt's inability to honour the terms of the Goschen-Joubert settlement, and Ismail's refusal to cooperate with his European creditors, had both clearly been demonstrated. It also seemed to have been demonstrated that, when it came to the point, neither the British nor the French Government were prepared effectively to impose their will on the Khedive.

3
CONTROLLER—
GENERAL

THE BRITISH GOVERNMENT'S reaction to Ismail's *coup* was limited both by military weakness and by the assumed necessity of keeping in step with, and avoiding being 'double-crossed' by, France. In February, just after Nubar's dismissal, Lord Beaconsfield, the Prime Minister, writing to the Queen, had told her: 'On Egyptian affairs, England and France will act together. If it were not for the South African affair (*i.e.* the Zulu War) we should prepare for the military occupation of Egypt. Let us hope that it may not be necessary or may be postponed.'[1] The French, who disapproved of Nubar, were not sorry to see him go. There-after, they probably wanted to give Ismail enough rope to enable him to hang himself, and then intervene in order to secure his deposition. This, in the event, was what happened. In the meantime both Governments reacted to Ismail's *coup* by finger-wagging despatches deploring his 'grave and apparently intentional breach of international courtesy to friendly Powers,' and stressing that 'the two Cabinets reserve to themselves an entire liberty of appreciation and action.'[2]

Salisbury, in a letter to Northcote, the Chancellor of the Exchequer, on 11 May,[3] summarised his attitude. 'The Egyptian complaint is a complicated disease which will require patient treatment. We desire and must aim at several things not wholly consistent. We wish to keep clear of entanglements—that is to avoid relations with the Khedive which put it in his power to insult us if we give him some temptation to do so. If this were all, the simple course would be to interfere as little with his internal affairs as we do with those of Italy. But we have a past which cannot wholly be sloughed off. We have not only recently lent him Rivers Wilson . . . we helped to set up the Commission of Enquiry and we received communication of his Reform Decree and of the Rothschild loan. Moreover we have a pecuniary interest in the payment of the tribute and the Suez Canal interest, and our capitalists have an interest in Alex-andria harbour which we can scarcely afford to disregard. But above all these entanglements is the apprehension that if we stand aside France will become as dominant there as she is in Tunis . . . We cannot cut the tow, rope . . . We must avoid recommending any person officially again or lending a public servant . . . But we must . . . keep abreast of France in any hold she has over the administration of the country . . . If we can make France fall back from practical interference we shall get back to the position before Rivers Wilson appeared on the scene and spoilt all. The position is an anxious one because it is ambiguous and hard to explain publicly. But the Khedive is going straight to ruin and we cannot afford to be out of the way when the crash comes.'

The crash was not long in coming. Baring later expressed the opinion that Ismail's *coup* would probably have been successful if the financial plan which he had pledged himself to carry out had been based on any solid foundation. If he had been able to pay his debts no excuse would have existed for further interference from abroad. Unfortunately for Ismail his financial plan was impossible to execute.[4]

The prime movers in Ismail's undoing appear to have been the Rothschilds, who were intimately interested in Egypt's finances in that they had recently contracted for a loan of £8·5 million on the security of Ismail's estates. They were in close touch with Wilson who, not unnaturally, was very sore about the way in which he had been treated. Whether or not moved by Wilson, the Rothschilds, 'having pulled strings both in Downing Street and on the Quai d'Orsay in vain,'[5] approached Bismarck and secured the intervention of the German Government.

On 15 May the German Ambassador in London informed the Foreign Office that the German Consul-General in Cairo had been instructed to protest against the Decree of 22 April which, 'in the opinion of the German Government was at variance with the judicial reforms.'[6] This raised, in a very acute form, the question as to whether the Mixed Courts had the power to challenge 'acts of administration which prejudice rights acquired by foreigners,' or whether such acts, not specifically directed against, but only incidentally affecting, foreigners, were sovereign acts unchallengeable in the Courts. It was clear that the German Govern- ment's action would encourage foreign floating debtholders to press for the execution of their claims if judgement had already been given, or to seek judgements if they had not been given. It was also clear that some foreign Governments might be prepared forcibly to intervene in favour of those of their nationals obtaining such judgements. On 30 May the British and French Governments sent identic Notes to their Repre- sentatives instructing them to associate themselves with the German protest.[7]

On 13 June Salisbury told Northcote: 'I have no doubt that we must come to a deposition.'[8] He added that he was apprehensive lest any resistance by Ismail 'should give to the French the opportunity of interfering alone by force' and expressed regret that available British forces were locked up in Zululand. From about the middle of June the British and French Governments started negotiations in Constantinople with a view to Ismail's deposition. The Sultan was not unwilling to use the opportunity to re-establish his authority over Egypt, which had been reduced to a nullity as a result of the successive Firmans which Ismail had obtained by bribery from his predecessor. He wanted to confer the Khedivate on Ismail's uncle Halim, which would have the effect of revoking the right of succession by primogeniture which Ismail had obtained. But the British and French Governments had no desire for the resumption of effective Turkish control over Egypt and, after much complicated bargaining, during the course of which Ismail sought in vain both for political support in Constantinople and popular support in Cairo, Firmans were issued by the Sultan on 26 June deposing Ismail and appointing his eldest son Taufiq Khedive in his stead. On 30 June Ismail left Egypt in the royal yacht *Mahroussa* for his exile in Italy. An eventful reign and a colourful epoch had come to an end. One recent comment on Ismail's financial methods describes him as 'anticipating Keynesian economic policies in a century wedded to the doctrines of Micawber.'[9] Contemporary European commentators were generally less charitable.

It remained for the British and French Governments to recreate some effective control over Egyptian finances and administration. The two Governments were at one in their desire to control Egypt between them and vigilant to ensure that neither stole a march on the other. Their relationships over Egypt were succinctly summarised by Salisbury in a letter to Northcote: 'When you have a neighbour and faithful ally who is bent on meddling in a country in which you are deeply interested you . . . may renounce or monopolise or share. Renouncing would have been to place the French across our road to India. Monopolising would have been very near the risk of war. So we resolved to share.'[10] The French attitude was probably the same. Within this general framework, British and French interests were not identical. The French, much more than the British, were interested in the bondholders. It was not quite true, as Salisbury told Northcote, that 'we have had no thought of the bondholders.' But the British Government were really interested, in Salisbury's words, in avoiding 'anarchy and the hazards in which it would involve the stability and above all the neutrality' of Egypt.[11]

The two Governments decided that British and French Controllers should be appointed to supervise the Egyptian finances and administration generally, but Salisbury did not want to get too closely involved.

'Control should take the form of inspection . . . Actual authority we cannot exercise. With European Ministers the disbanded officers proved that two pairs of arms are no use against 2,000. The only control we have is moral influence which in practice is a combination of nonsense, objurgation and worry. In this we are still supreme and have many modes of applying it—diplomatic Notes, Consular interviews, newspapers, Blue Books. We must devote ourselves to the perfecting of this weapon. We must have complete knowledge of what is going on.'[12] He insisted with Waddington, the French Foreign Minister, that the Controllers should have no executive powers, but reluctantly agreed to Waddington's insist-ence that they should be under the orders, and irremoveable except with the consent, of their respective Governments. But he complained to Lyons, the British Ambassador in Paris, that this was 'a considerable advance in the direction of *ingérence* over anything we did in the case of Rivers Wilson or Romaine.'

Having agreed over the powers of the Controllers, the next thing was to nominate them. The French nominated de Blignières, previously French Commissioner of the Debt and, later, Minister of Public Works. The nomination was accepted reluctantly by Taufiq, the new Khedive, who told Lascelles that the European Ministers had left a bad impression in Egypt.[13] Salisbury invited Baring to serve as British Controller.

When Baring left Egypt in May he had the intention of adopting a political career. He resigned from the Army with the rank of Major and a gratuity of £2,000,[14] and planned to stand as Liberal candidate for East Norfolk at the General Election due in 1880.[15] He was out of sympathy with the Egyptian policy of the Conservative Administration. But he rejoiced at Ismail's deposition and had some hope that, with proper guidance, Egypt's finances might be rehabilitated and its admini-stration reformed. Therefore, 'after some hesitation,' as he tells us, he accepted Salisbury's invitation, with the proviso that 'as soon as the immediate financial difficulties are solved I shall request that someone else be named,' and on the understanding that his position would be limited to 'the inspection of all matters relating to the financial affairs of Egypt and advice on them.' He was to receive a salary of £4,000 p.a.[16]

Baring's nomination was accepted by Taufiq with expressions of pleasure and of relief that Rivers Wilson had not been chosen.[17]

After the nomination of the two Controllers, there was a good deal of coming-and-going between the British and French Governments about the settlement of the financial situation, which was still 'in the air' after Ismail's rejection of the Commission of Enquiry's recommendations. Baring told Salisbury in September that he thought the Controllers should not proceed to Egypt until something had been settled about the

Debt. 'We can only report what we have already reported, viz, that the country is bankrupt, that legislation is absolutely necessary, and that unfortunately the legislative power resides in the different Powers which took part in the constitution of the international tribunals.[18] Hence these Powers must agree on some legislative machinery . . . We can do nothing in Egypt until the legislative *modus operandi* is settled.'[19]

Baring's point was this. If the recommendations of the Commission of Enquiry were adopted, they would have to be promulgated in a Decree issued by the Egyptian Government. But such a Decree, affecting as it would 'the acquired rights of foreigners' in Egypt, would be subject to challenge in the Mixed Courts by any foreign national affected by the Decree. Therefore, if the Decree were to be operative, it was necessary to obtain the advance consent of all the foreign Governments concerned to the terms of the Decree. It was also necessary, as Baring pointed out to Salisbury, that the British and French Governments should arrive at a complete understanding over the matter.

Salisbury, who was on holiday at Dieppe at the time, and in close touch with Paris, was in general agreement with Baring's views, and, on 19 September, addressed a despatch to Edward Malet, who was about to proceed to Cairo as Consul-General in succession to Lascelles, setting out the heads of agreement arrived at with the French Government over the proposed financial settlement. This agreement contained six points: (1) That an International Commission of Liquidation should be set up with power to deal with the Unified Debt as well as with the other liabilities of the Egyptian Government; (2) That, before any money was appropriated towards the payment of creditors, a sufficient sum should be set aside to provide for Egyptian Government administrative expenses; (3) That the 'native government' should receive the 'earnest support' of the British and French Governments; (4) That the two Governments would make the Khedive clearly understand that they 'would not tolerate the establishment in Egypt of any political influence on the part of any European Power in competition to that of England and France, and that they were prepared to take action to any extent that might be found necessary to give effect to their views in this respect'; (5) That Major Baring and M. de Blignières should meet in Paris and draw up a draft Decree for the institution of a Commission of Liquidation and draft identical instructions to be addressed to themselves as to their powers and duties; (6) That the arrangements to be made for the continuance of the Mixed Courts at the end of the five-year probationary period fixed when these Courts were set up required careful consideration. (The Courts were set up in 1876 and the five-year probationary period was therefore due to end the following year.)[20]

Baring went to Paris to discuss matters with Waddington, the French Foreign Minister, and with de Blignières, his ex-colleague on the Caisse and Commission of Enquiry, and his future colleague on the Control. He and de Blignières had no difficulty in drafting a document setting out their functions as agreed in principle between the two Governments. Two months later, on 15 November, after various minor details had been settled, and after Egyptian objections to the appointment of de Blignières had been overcome, an Egyptian Government Decree was promulgated appointing Baring and de Blignières as Controllers-General of Revenue and Expenditure respectively. The Decree provided that both Controllers had the right to be present (but not to vote) at meetings of the Council of Ministers, that they should be responsible for the preparation of annual Budgets to be submitted to the Council of Ministers for approval, and that they could not be relieved of their functions without the consent of their respective Governments.[21] Baring also agreed with Waddington that an adequate sum out of the Egyptian Budget must be assured to the Egyptian Government for administration before the creditors got anything and 'that the present powers of the Mixed Courts as regards the State are excessive.'[22]

In connection with the powers of the Mixed Courts, Baring suggested to Salisbury the possibility of setting up an International Commission on Egyptian Legislation with the object of defining and curtailing the powers of the Mixed Courts. But Salisbury was dubious: 'When so many Powers have to be consulted, the resources of obstruction are endless. It is like the *liberum veto* of the Polish Diet without the resource of cutting off the dissentient's head.' He added that it would be quite difficult enough to obtain international agreement to a Commission of Liquidation.[23]

Baring and the French agreed that the Controllers should not go to Egypt until the composition and terms of reference of the Liquidation Commission had been settled. This involved another four weeks of negotiation. There seem to have been two principal difficulties. First, the British Government wanted Rivers Wilson as Chairman of the Commission. The Khedive objected on personal grounds, and Baring was not enthusiastic. But, the French having imposed de Blignières on an unwilling Khedive, it seemed to Salisbury that he 'must insist on Wilson . . . to avoid giving the impression that our support is either less warm or less powerful than that of France.'[24] Secondly, Baring foresaw the possibility that it might be desirable for the Commission to recommend that the interest on the Unified Debt be reduced to 4 per cent. He did not therefore want the terms of reference of the Commission restricted by the recommendations of the previous Commission of Enquiry. The

French, on the other hand, were anxious to block any question of a further reduction in Unified interest. Eventually a compromise was reached by which the Liquidation Commission was to 'take account as far as possible' of the recommendations of the Commission of Enquiry.

Baring and de Blignières left for Egypt via Vienna on 20 October, leaving the British and French Governments to 'sell' to the other Capitulatory Powers the agreements at which they had arrived over the terms of reference of the Commission of Liquidation. In conversations which the two Controllers had with the Austro-Hungarian Government in Vienna on their way out, it became apparent that this would not be an easy matter,[25] and it was in fact several months before it was possible for the appointment of a Commission of Liquidation to be announced by the Egyptian Government.

Before he left England Baring had a final discussion with Salisbury and told him that, although appointed by the British Government, he regarded himself as having responsibilities towards the Egyptian Government which might conflict with the interests of HMG, and that he would regard his responsibilities towards the Egyptian Government as paramount. Salisbury, in a letter written after Baring's departure, told him: 'You are quite right to take, in some sort, an independent line in regard to HMG. Your position is not very easy to define, but you have duties to the Egyptian Sovereign and people which we have not and you cannot be guided entirely by the political interests of England as we shall be.'[26]

Baring and de Blignières arrived in Egypt at the end of October. Taufiq had been Khedive for just four months. At the beginning of his reign he had retained Sherif Pasha as President of his Council of Ministers. At the instance of the British and French Governments Sherif told the British and French Agents that the Khedive agreed to the setting-up of a Commission of Liquidation and to the 'appointment of Controllers-General nominated by France and England whose powers should be limited to investigation and verification and who should not exercise any administrative or executive functions.'[27] In the middle of August Sherif resigned office as a result of the Khedive having refused to approve a project for a Constitution which he had submitted to him. Taufiq told Lascelles that he regarded 'liberal institutions and popular rule as being entirely unsuited to the country and that the Constitution submitted to him was nothing more than a "décor de théatre." He hoped that in time the country would be fit for parliamentary government and proposed to retain the Chamber of Notables which he hoped would eventually become a really responsible body.'[28] Lascelles and Salisbury appear to have approved of the Khedive's attitude. After Sherif's resignation, Taufiq recalled Riaz Pasha, who had been a member of the Commission of Enquiry and Minister of the Interior in the two European Ministries, from the exile to which he had departed at the time of Ismail's *coup* in April, and invited him to form a Government. He accepted the invitation and became President of a new Council of Ministers, retaining for himself the portfolio of the Interior.

Riaz was an autocratic Turk of the old school, but a good administrator and an honest and brave man, who had stood up to Ismail at the time of the Commission of Enquiry. He, Baring, and de Blignières were old colleagues and had confidence in one another. For the next few months they, in effect, ruled Egypt as an autocratic triumvirate in much the same way as, but more successfully than, Nubar and Wilson and de Blignières had tried to rule Egypt a year before. But this second triumvirate had two great advantages over the first. There was no Ismail to intrigue against them. And Riaz, unlike Nubar, was a Moslem and a strong and ruthless man. Later, the gusts of public opinion and popular action released as a result of the collapse of the personal authority wielded by Ismail were to prove even more destructive of the experiment of European control without the sanction of European armed force than Ismail's intrigues had been. But these gusts took some time to develop and, for the time being, the habit of subservience survived to clothe the Dual Control in a little brief authority.

In spite of a great difference in temperament between them—de Blignières was excitable and voluble, Baring cool and measured—the two Controllers got on well together. The definition of their respective functions—Baring had been named as Controller of Revenue and de Blignières as Controller of Expenditure—caused no difficulty between them. As Baring put it later:[29] 'The solution which we adopted was a simple one. We never attempted to solve the question at all. We were in constant communication with each other, and we worked in common. Any precise definition of our respective functions would have been difficult, and was quite unnecessary.' They established a workable *modus vivendi* with Riaz who, in Baring's words, 'saw the necessity for European assistance, but, at the same time, in whatever form it was given, it was distasteful to him.' They resolved to 'pull the strings behind the scenes, but appear on the stage as little as possible.'[30] Baring, as he had already indicated to Salisbury, regarded it as his duty to stand 'as a buffer between the Egyptian Government and their creditors'[31] and the policy adopted by him and de Blignières was to 'associate ourselves as much as possible with the Egyptian Government and to defend them against any excessive demands and encroachments on their rights.' Later, this policy was to lead to a sometimes bitter struggle between the Controllers and the Liquidation Commission. For the moment, the Controllers had to try

47

to rescue the Egyptian Government from the day-to-day financial difficulties created by a chronic shortage of ready money. Because of this shortage, they had, before they arrived in Egypt, advised the Egyptian Government to postpone payment of the tribute then due, and to short-pay by 2 per cent the Unified coupon due on 1 November 1879 in order to enable Government employees to be paid and to avoid the necessity for collecting taxes in advance. They authorised the publication of a letter giving this advice, thus transferring the responsibility from the Egyptian Government to themselves and, by implication, to the British and French Governments.

One of the reasons for the shortage of ready money was that only £1 million of the Rothschild loan negotiated by Wilson on the security of the Khedivial estates had so far been paid over to the Egyptian Government, although Rothschilds were demanding, and receiving, interest payments on the whole loan, amounting to a nominal £8¼ million. In February 1879, while Wilson was Finance Minister, Rothschilds had suspended further payments until the matter of outstanding suits against the Khedivial estates had been cleared up. After much negotiation this was arranged and, on 15 November, with the agreement of the Capitulatory Powers, a Decree was promulgated barring all suits against the Khedivial estates after their transfer from the Khedive to the State Domains administration. Rothschilds, nevertheless, continued to refuse payment of the balance of the loan on the ground that the Greek Government had not yet given their consent to the Decree. One of Baring's first acts after his arrival in Egypt was to write extremely energetic letters of protest both to Salisbury and to Baron de Rothschild against what, as he clearly indicated to both his correspondents, he regarded as sharp practice. He was most dissatisfied with the lack of support which he received from Salisbury over this matter. In a letter to Goschen written in the middle of March 1880 he expressed his indignation: 'I am perfectly prepared to aid the Government in carrying out a policy which I believe to be in the best interests of Egypt and of England, but if HMG come forward and say that all interests, native and European, are to give way before those of the Rothschilds, if they are thus to declare that a powerful special interest of this sort is to outweigh all considerations of policy, justice and law, then all I can say is that I will be no party to carrying out a policy which I believe to be immoral and contrary to the true interests of England. I should regret that someone else may be appointed to take my place and I shall shake the dust of Egypt from my feet with a consciousness of failure.'[32] The fact that the balance of the loan was handed over to the Egyptian Government about a fortnight later may have had some connection with the implied threat contained at the end of this letter. The incident sharpened Baring's mistrust of Rivers Wilson who, in his dealings with Egypt, seems to have regarded himself, and was certainly regarded by Baring, as an unofficial agent of Rothschilds.

Baring, with the approval of the British Government, considered that the rate of interest on the Unified Debt should be reduced from 6 per cent to 4 per cent. He seems to have converted de Blignières to his point of view. But any such proposal was bound to be resisted by the bond-holders, by most of the European Governments and, in consequence, by the Commission of Liquidation when it was finally set up. So the Controllers, who had already advised the Egyptian Government to pay only 4 per cent on the November coupon, prepared a proposal to the Egyptian Government, recommending that the rate of interest on the Unified Debt be reduced to 4 per cent. This proposal was published in January 1880 with the surprising and encouraging result that the price of Unified rose from 51 to 56.[33]

Having thus presented the Liquidation Commission with what was virtually a *fait accompli*, the Controllers proceeded to frame an Egyptian Budget for 1880. On the revenue side they cut the Commission of Enquiry's estimate which had been framed by Baring himself, from £9,067,000 by £½ million to £8,562,000. On the expenditure side they earmarked £4,323,000 for administrative expenses and tribute, leaving £4,239,000 available for the Debt. Here again, they endeavoured to limit the field of manoeuvre available to the Liquidation Commission. These figures, which compared with the revenue estimate of £10½ million accepted by MM. Goschen and Joubert, and with an annual sum of £6½ million for the service of the Debt provided in the Goschen-Joubert settlement, gave point to the Controllers' opinion, expressed in the published note recommending the reduction of interest on Unified, that 'the main defect of all former attempts to regulate the Egyptian financial situation has been that they have been too optimistic.'[34]

Within the framework of these Budget estimates, the Controllers pro-ceeded to carry out most of the taxation recommendations of the Com-mission of Enquiry. On 6 January the Muqabala was abolished. On 17 January the poll tax was abolished. On 18 January the land-tax on Ushuri lands was increased. 'Twenty-four petty taxes of a vexatious nature were abolished by a stroke of the pen.' The salt-tax was reformed and the collection of land-tax regularised. On 23 January Baring wrote a somewhat euphoric letter to Salisbury: 'Certain measures which were absolutely necessary have been carried out. (1) The abolition of the Muqabala. Not a voice has been raised against this. I always knew it would be popular with the mass of the people but distasteful to the upper classes. Almost simultaneously with this promulgation we swept away a number of petty and vexatious taxes which have rendered the Government so popular as to enable them to face the opposition from a few malcontents.'

He went on to tell Salisbury that he now considered the Liquidation Commission undesirable. 'Things are going very well now, and by the creation of a new and very powerful body . . . you run a risk of undoing the good that has been done . . . I am afraid of the Commission turning out to be a veritable Old Man of the Sea which, once created, we shall not be able to get rid of . . . I cannot yet positively say that we shall be able to pay the whole floating debt in full, but I think we can and, if so, the necessity for a Commission falls to the ground. It is true that we cut deep into bondholders' rights, but the rise in stock after it was known that the rate of interest was to be reduced, enables us to liquidate on favourable terms the creditors who hold Unified stock as a pledge. On these grounds I deplore the appointment of a Commission . . . Opinion here on the subject is unanimous.'[35] Salisbury told Baring in reply that a Commission was necessary to prevent any settlement promulgated by the Egyptian Government without international agreement being chal-lenged in the Mixed Courts.[36]

The Controllers had to accept this. But, in fact, a Mixed Courts judgement in February, which was later upheld in the Court of Appeal, appeared to vindicate the Controllers' view about the validity of Egyptian Government financial legislation and to invalidate not only the assumption on which the necessity for a Liquidation Commission was based but also the legal justification for the protests against the Decree of 22 April 1879 which led to Ismail's deposition. As a result of the Decree abolishing the Muqabala, a foreign plaintiff sued the Egyptian Government in the Mixed Courts for specific performance of the Law of the Muqabala, demanding that the balance of the twelve-year annuities be accepted and remission of half his land-tax thereafter confirmed according to the pro-visions of that law. He lost his case in the Court of First Instance, whose judgement was later upheld in the Court of Appeal which found that 'the Tribunals have jurisdiction between foreigners and the Egyptian Government when either the Capitulations or international Treaties have given to foreigners acquired rights. But they have no jurisdiction in the case of Decrees made by the Egyptian Government alone and not by agreement with the Powers, even though these Decrees may affect the general interests of foreigners. Such Decrees have no real international character and are simple expressions of the will of Egypt which is sovereign in its internal affairs.'[37]

Curiously, Baring does not seem to have realised the importance and significance of this judgement, and accepted Salisbury's argument about the necessity for the Commission. But he told Salisbury that the Controllers should not be members of the Commission and that they should 'stand between the Commission and the Government and see that the latter get fair play.' He continued his letter with an attack on Rivers Wilson, who had been named as President of the Commission, but whose nomination had not yet been published. 'Wilson ... is exceedingly unpopular and has no authority with any class. The danger consists in his excessive admiration for Nubar, who is triumphant at the idea of a Commission, and especially one presided over by Wilson, and lets it be known that he foresees the downfall of the Ministry and the Control ... Nubar will try and get Wilson to quarrel with me and push him on to extend the powers and demands of the Commission. I have no confidence in Wilson's judgement.' He went on to ask Salisbury to warn Wilson that any idea of another European Ministry was 'out.' 'My own opinion is strongly adverse to the exercise of any direct executive authority by Europeans except in purely departmental places like the Post Office.'[38]

Baring eventually had to give way about Wilson as well, after having again warned Salisbury about the danger of Nubar intriguing with Wilson against the Government and the Control and using the Commission as a means of discrediting them. By the end of March agreement had been reached with the principal Capitulatory Powers and, on the last day of the month, a Declaration was signed and a draft Decree setting up the Commission approved by representatives of the six Powers in Cairo.[39]

The Commission, which started its sittings in Cairo at the beginning of May, consisted of Wilson as President, the four Commissioners of the Caisse, the German Consul-General, the Secretary-General of the Egyptian Ministry of Justice,[40] and a French Secretary. Russia had been invited to nominate a member but had refused. It was provided in the Decree of appointment that decisions should be taken by a majority of votes.

The British and French Consuls-General had instructions from their respective Governments to give 'earnest support' to the 'native government.' In view of this, and of the attitude of the Controllers, who saw themselves as protectors of the Egyptian Government against the Commission, relations between the Commissioners on the one hand and the Consuls-General and the Controllers on the other were sometimes a little strained. The two principal bones of contention were the estimate of current revenue, on which the settlement was to be based, and the disposition of future surplus revenue. The Controllers pressed for a much lower estimate of current revenue than had been taken by Goschen and Joubert and a figure was finally agreed at £E8,361,622. (One £E, or Egyptian Pound, was equal to about £1 : 0 : 6.) Of this, £E4,897,888 was reserved for administration, leaving £E3,463,734 for the service of the Debt. This was even more favourable to Egypt than the Controllers' Budget estimate for 1880 and involved the reduction to 4 per cent on the interest on Unified as recommended, and as virtually enforced, by the Controllers. The abolition of the Muqabala was confirmed and arrangements made for the payment of some compensation to those who had contributed to it. The other clash with the Commissioners was over surpluses which, for the time being, was an academic question. The Controllers wanted any revenue surpluses, after provision had been made for the service of the Debt, to be unreservedly at the disposal of the Egyptian Government. The Commissioners considered that Egyptian Government expenditure should be pegged, and that any future surpluses should be devoted to extinction of the Debt. By the terms of the settlement it was provided that any surplus on the revenues earmarked for the service of the Debt should be devoted to the extinction of the Debt and that any surplus on the 'free' revenue should also be devoted to the extinction of the Debt to the extent of making up, together with any surplus on the 'earmarked' revenue, a sum equal to $\frac{1}{2}$ per cent of the capital of the Unified Debt. After providing for this, any additional surplus on the 'free' revenue was to be at the disposal of the Egyptian Government. Any deficit on the 'earmarked' revenue had to be made good from the 'free' revenue, whether or not there was a surplus on this.

The findings of the Commission were embodied in the Law of Liquidation promulgated on 17 July 1880.[41]

In June 1880, about a month before the Law of Liquidation was promulgated, Baring was appointed Finance Member of the Viceroy of India's Council. He was succeeded as British Controller-General by Mr Auckland Colvin, the British Commissioner of the Caisse, who had succeeded Baring in that capacity a year before. There had been a General Election in England in March and, as a result of a Liberal victory at the polls, a Liberal Government with Gladstone as Prime Minister had replaced Lord Beaconsfield's Conservative Administration. As one of the results of this change Lord Lytton had resigned as Viceroy of India and Lord Ripon had been appointed in his place. This involved some changes in the Viceregal Council. Baring, at that time, was still a staunch Liberal in his political allegiance. Before his appointment as Controller he had intended standing as a Liberal candidate at the General Election. He particularly disapproved of the Conservative Government's Near Eastern policy, and attributed what he regarded as Salisbury's feeble Egyptian policy to the subordination of England to France in Egyptian affairs imposed by the necessity of securing the approval of the French Government to the Cyprus Convention at the Berlin Congress in 1878.

The Third Marquess of Salisbury, 1885

The Fifth Earl of Rosebery

Sir Herbert Kitchener as Sirdar of the Egyptian Army

In a letter to Goschen in January 1880 he wrote: 'I have a heavy charge against the present Government . . . I am an advocate of the French alliance . . . but I think that the Government have increased their difficulties by their Cyprus action . . . I know for a fact with what eagerness they sold themselves to France as regards Egypt to square France at Berlin and in that way they tied their hands unnecessarily.'[42]

The financial policy adopted by the Control during Baring's term of office was to lighten and regularise taxation as much as possible in order to enable the country to recover from the merciless and arbitrary taxation which had afflicted it during the previous ten years. Baring believed that moderate and equitable taxation, combined with the industry of the Egyptian peasant and the fertility of the Egyptian soil, would increase the country's productivity and so gradually increase the revenue without increasing the incidence of taxation. For this reason he was particularly insistent in trying to secure that future revenue surpluses should be available to the Egyptian Government in their entirety instead of being devoted, in whole or in part, to the extinction of the Debt, so as to make possible either further decreases in taxation or public works of unquestionable utility. He secured something, but not all, of what he wanted from the Commission, who would undoubtedly have imposed much heavier burdens on Egypt in the interest of the bondholders, both in respect of interest and of sinking fund provisions, had it not been for the resistance of the Controllers, both before and during the sittings of the Commission.

The Control's policy necessarily involved a stringent economy in expenditure. In the 1880 Budget the Army estimates were cut from £E1 million to £E430,000, the lower figure being considered by the Controllers as 'sufficient for defensive purposes.' Public Works were cut down to £E430,000, but provision for education was raised from a derisory £E13,000 to £E60,000. The process of rehabilitating the countryside was assisted by a good Nile—not too high and not too low—in the Autumn of 1879, and Malet quoted travellers' reports that 'the fellah has never looked so well nor appeared so contented.' Malet, the British Consul-General, may have been biased in favour of the Control, but the same could not have been said of W. S. Blunt, the Egyptian nationalist sympathiser and propagandist, who, travelling in Egypt in the Autumn of 1880, wrote: 'I find a great change for the better here since five years ago . . . The country people now look fat and prosperous, and the few I have talked to, people who in former years complained bitterly of their condition, now praise the Khedive and his administration. They seem for once to have gone the right way to work.'[43]

One of the Control's transactions is of some historical interest. The Crédit Foncier held, as security for a loan of £5 million, some £2 million (nominal) worth of Unified stock and the whole of the Preference Shares of the Suez Canal Company, owned by the Egyptian Government and entitling the owners to 15 per cent of the Company's net profits. These Preference Shares had been allocated to the Egyptian Government as consideration for the grant of the Suez Canal Concessions and, since the Egyptian Government's Ordinary shareholding had been sold to the British Government in 1875, represented their only remaining financial interest in the Canal Company. In February 1880 the amount owed to the Crédit Foncier and secured by these assets amounted to £4,212,600. The Controllers arranged for the liquidation of this debt by making over the whole of the security to the Crédit Foncier. This must have seemed a good bargain for the Egyptian Government at the time, since the market price of Unified was only about 56 and since 15 per cent of the Canal Company's net profits did not, at that time, amount to very much. But, in the long run, the bargain was as good a one for the Crédit Foncier (and as bad a one for the Egyptian Government) as the purchase of the Egyptian Government's Ordinary shareholding was for the British Treasury.

The essential weakness of the Control, which was to become apparent over the next two years, was that it possessed no sanction, either of force, or of traditional authority, or of popular approval, to reinforce its rule. Instead of force, the British and French Governments relied, in Salisbury's words, on 'moral influence . . . a combination of nonsense, objurgation and worry.' This was to prove insufficient. The traditional authority of the Khedivate had been shattered by Ismail's deposition. It was almost impossibly difficult for a Government, controlled to a large extent by foreigners, and wedded to a policy of administrative economy, to win very much popular approval. Such popularity as was gained by taxation reliefs and the regular payment of Government salaries, was more than counterbalanced by the offence given to particular interests by the reduction in Army establishments, the cancellation of the Muqabala, and the increase in the Ushuri land-tax, and by the offence given to nascent but growing popular feeling by the increasing number of Europeans recruited into Government service, by the absence of any representative institutions, and by the oppressiveness and inefficiency of the whole cumbersome administrative machine. This offence was only very slightly mitigated, and that only in so far as the collecting of taxes and the payment of Government salaries were concerned, by the exertions of the Controllers and the European heads of the various revenue-producing Departments.

By the time Baring left Egypt in the middle of 1880 none of these forces of protest and discontent had made their way to the surface. The Army demonstration of February 1879, and the demands of the 'nation' as expressed by the Notables in April 1879, could plausibly be put down to Ismail's machinations. The new Khedive had brushed aside the idea of representative institutions as a '*décor de théatre.*' The peasants were reported to be happy and contented. The presence of Riaz Pasha at the Ministry of the Interior, presiding over the antique and time-honoured instruments of oppression and repression at his disposal, seemed a sufficient guarantee for the preservation of internal order. If the British and French Governments could continue acting in unison, if the intrigues of the Sultan, of Nubar, and of Sherif could be checkmated, if reasonably able and reasonably tactful people could be retained in the British and French Agencies and in the Controllers' offices, if the judges of the Mixed Courts and the Commissioners of the Caisse could be induced to moderate their sense of their own importance, it must have seemed to Baring, when he visited Egypt on his way to India in December 1880, that the work of reform which he and de Blignières had set in train would go steadily forward. From what he recorded afterwards,[44] it appears that he did have some apprehension about possible trouble with the Army, but that on the whole he believed that 'all that was required was time to complete the superstructure of which the foundations had been so laboriously laid.'

4

THE BRITISH
OCCUPATION

IT IS NECESSARY briefly to outline the course of events in Egypt during the three years between Baring's resignation of the Controllership in June 1880 and his return as British Agent in September 1883.

As has been indicated, there were a number of discontents simmering below the surface in Egypt during 1880. Some of these were of long standing; others had been created or exacerbated by the policies of the Dual Control. The manifestation of all of them was facilitated both by the collapse of the traditional Khedivial authority which had resulted from Ismail's deposition and by Ismail's exploitation of these discontents during the last few months of his reign.

There were several sources of discontent:

(a) Under Mohamed Ali the Egyptian Army had been officered by 'Circassians'—a generic term comprising Kurdish, Albanian, Georgian and other non-Egyptian citizens of the Ottoman Empire. Said and Ismail had encouraged the promotion of native-born Egyptians, and rivalries and jealousies had grown up between Egyptian and Circassian officers, each considering that the other was being unduly favoured. By the end of Ismail's reign, the Circassians, although outnumbered by the Egyptians, still held most of the senior posts and were still, as a whole, more professionally competent than the Egyptians. Consequently, the cuts in the Army establishment insisted on by the European Ministry and, later, by the Dual Control, fell with particular force on the Egyptian officers, many of whom were forcibly retired on half-pay, and for most of whom there was little prospect of alternative employment. The consequent discontent of the Egyptian officers and ex-officers was, to some extent, a reflection of the more general and increasingly articulate Egyptian resentment against the ruling-class, the Turkish-Albanian-Kurdish-Georgian 'establishment' which had tyrannised over Egypt for centuries and which was now being held responsible, not without reason, for having betrayed the Egyptian people to European moneylenders.

(b) The catastrophic impact of the West on the Moslem world during the previous quarter-century had led to increasing financial indebtedness to the West and a consequent assumption by the West of financial and, to some extent political, control. Moslem reactions to this had ranged from the relatively intellectual movement of Islamic Modernism to an atavistic undercurrent of xenophobia. Islamic Modernism, the leader of which was Jamal ad-Din el-Afghani, who had spent several years in Egypt before being expelled by Ismail, regarded despotism as a perversion of the original democratic and elective principles of Islam and objected both to Western domination and to indigenous tyranny. Jamal ad-Din's disciples in Egypt, who included some of the Ulema of el-Azhar, were opposed to the Dual Control, as they had been opposed to Ismail, both because of the autocratic methods employed and because of the Western influence behind it.

(c) In this respect the Islamic Modernists were in sympathy with the fashionable doctrine of constitutionalism, which had seeped into the Ottoman Empire from Western Europe, which had led to the grant of a Constitution (later abrogated) in Turkey in 1876, to which Ismail had paid lip-service in 1879, and with which Sherif Pasha, one of Egypt's three leading statesmen (the other two being Riaz and Nubar), was known to be sympathetic. The constitutionalists, like the Islamic Modernists, objected to the despotism of Riaz and the Dual Control, as they had objected to the despotism of Ismail, and deplored the Khedive's rejection of Sherif's constitutional proposals in 1879, which rejection, they rightly suspected, had been encouraged by European influence.

(d) The xenophobic feelings of the less sophisticated Moslems were encouraged by the increasing number of European officials under the Dual Control, by the abuse of Capitulatory privileges on the part of many of the rapidly increasing European population, by the fact that a great many landowners, particularly some of the smaller ones, had become indebted to European moneylenders, and by the pressure of taxation, most of the proceeds of which were devoted to the servicing of a foreign debt which had been contracted on extortionate and near-fraudulent terms and from which the Egyptian people had derived no benefits whatever.

(e) Certain acts of the Dual Control, particularly the abolition of the Muqabala and the increase in the Ushuri land-tax, alienated many of the richer landowners who would not normally have been in sympathy with the other dissident forces.

(f) The influx of foreign officials, not all of whom were very competent, and who were paid more highly than their Egyptian colleagues, alienated the majority of the Egyptian Government officials who felt that their chances of promotion were blocked and their prospects of a career jeopardised.[1]

The local Press which, mainly by reason of the immunity afforded by the Capitulations, was a relatively free one, and had attracted to Egypt liberal journalists from other parts of the Ottoman Empire, publicised and disseminated these diverse aspirations, ambitions, rancours and discontents which coalesced into a more or less coherent Egyptian nationalist movement that in 1882 rose in rebellion against the established Government.

The first overt sign of rebellion was in February 1881 when three regiments commanded by dissident Egyptian officers mutinied in a successful attempt to compel the Khedive to replace the Circassian Minister of War by a nominee of their own. This success was followed in September 1881 by another mutiny, as a result of which Riaz Pasha's Government was ousted and replaced by one approved by the mutineers and headed by Sherif Pasha, who advised the Khedive to convoke the Chamber of Notables, which met towards the end of December.

By this time a fairly large measure of common purpose had been achieved between the various dissident groups. The mutinous Colonels —from whom Ahmed Arabi had emerged as leader, apparently by reason of his eloquence—had acted, or been used, as 'front runners,' because they were in a better position than anybody else to take action against the Government, and had gradually broadened their professional and sectional grievances to embrace the more general reformist demands of the constitutionalists and the Islamic Modernists. As a result of their mutinies they had not only secured satisfaction for their own grievances but had also served the turn of the reformers in that they had discredited the Khedive, evicted a despotic Government, and secured the convocation of the Chamber of Notables, which was seen by the reformers as the nucleus of a constitutional parliament.

The Chamber of Notables, which Ismail had set up in 1866, was elected, for the most part, by the Omdehs, or headmen, of villages. It was representative of the large and medium-sized landowners and was a fairly conservative body. But its members had suffered from, and objected to, government despotism, and they particularly objected to the abolition of the Muqabala at the instance of the Dual Control. (Their support for Ismail in 1879 was largely the result of the Commission of Enquiry's recommendation for the abolition of the Muqabala.) Also, as indigenous Egyptians, they were in sympathy with the Egyptian Army officers in their objections to the Circassians in the army and elsewhere. Sherif Pasha, the new Prime Minister, attempted to take the edge off the prevailing discontent by conferring limited constitutional powers on the

Chamber of Notables, following the suggestions he made to Taufiq in September 1879. In this way he hoped to be able to restore the authority of the Government, to turn the Khedivate into something like a constitutional monarchy, to moderate the demands of the army, and to preserve some sort of *modus vivendi* with the Dual Control. He failed in his attempt for a number of reasons. First, he himself was lacking in energy and in the imperious personality necessary for the task. Secondly, the mutinous Colonels, driven both by ambition and by the fear of reprisals, and concerned lest any compromise with the Government might expose them to Taufiq's vengeance, gradually shed their enthusiasm for a constitution and determined upon the installation of a military dictatorship. Thirdly, the British and French Governments, acting under the influence of Gambetta, who had come into office in France in November, and encouraged by the advice of their Controllers (and, to a lesser extent, of their ConsulsGeneral) in Egypt, adopted a hard line in response to the notveryextreme demands put forward by the Chamber of Notables for an extention of their powers.

What happened was this. When the Chamber met at the end of December, Sherif presented for their approval a draft Organic Law defining their powers. The Chamber replied with their own version of an Organic Law, of which the principal point of difference was that the Chamber demanded the right of voting what was known as the 'unaffected' part of the Egyptian Budget—that is to say, that part of the Budget which had not been earmarked, in accordance with the Law of Liquidation, for the servicing of the Debt. This demand was rejected by Sherif on the insistence of the British and French Governments who, on the advice of their Controllers and ConsulsGeneral, took the view that, in the light of the current atmosphere in Egypt, and, particularly, of the army's clamour for increased establishments and pay, the Chamber's demand would inevitably lead to deficits on the 'unaffected' part of the Budget. This in turn would lead to an increase in the floating debt and, eventually, to a collapse of the financial settlement imposed by the Law of Liquidation. It would also have led immediately to the virtual abdication of the Controllers from their effective control over Egyptian finances and reduced them to the status of supernumerary Commissioners of the Debt.

There was some substance in this view, but a compromise might have been negotiable, which would have driven a wedge between the Chamber and the Army, produced a viable system of constitutional government in Egypt, and safeguarded legitimate European interests in Egypt at the certain expense of some relaxation of the AngloFrench Control and at the probable expense of some eventual further 'sacrifices' by the bond holders. This would not have been unpalatable to the Liberal Government in England. But, in France, Gambetta was determined to maintain the extent of Anglo-French influence unimpaired and was quite prepared to intervene by force if necessary. In an attempt to overawe the forces of opposition in Egypt, he prevailed upon a somewhat unwilling Lord Granville, the British Foreign Secretary, to send a Joint Note, which was published, to their respective Representatives in Egypt, stressing the determination of the two Governments, 'in the light of recent circum-stances and especially the meeting of the Chamber of Notables,' 'to afford the Khedive and his Government support against the difficulties of various kinds which might interfere with the course of public affairs in Egypt,' and 'to guard by their united efforts against all causes of com-plication, internal or external, which might menace the order of things established in Egypt.'² This 'Joint Note' was despatched and published on 6 January 1882. As Baring commented later, 'foreign intervention became an almost inevitable necessity from the moment it was issued,'³ although Granville 'failed to appreciate the effect which the Note would produce.'⁴ For the process of disaffection in Egypt had passed far beyond the point at which it could have been checked and reversed by finger-wagging from the British and French Governments. The immediate effects of the Note were to demonstrate the extent of the Khedive's sub-ordination to and reliance on foreign influence, to discredit Sherif Pasha, who was trying to play the Chamber off against the Army, and to drive the Chamber into the arms of the mutinous Colonels. The Note also annoyed the Sultan, Taufiq's Suzerain, who had not been consulted, and whose armed intervention, if armed intervention became necessary, was regarded by the British Government as a preferable alternative to intervention by themselves and the French.

Gambetta, who had inspired the Joint Note, was, unlike Granville, quite aware of its possible effects. He was not prepared to consider Turkish intervention and was quite prepared for, if not anxious to provoke, an Anglo-French military occupation. But, by the end of January, Gambetta was out of office. His successor as Prime Minister and Foreign Minister, de Freycinet, was no more willing than Granville to contemplate the logical consequences of the Joint Note and just as unwilling as Gambetta to encourage any intervention by the Sultan.

Meanwhile, in Egypt, events moved steadily towards a military dictatorship. The Sherif Government resigned at the beginning of February and was replaced by a Government, virtually nominated by the Army, in which Arabi was Minister of War. The new Government, having secured the promulgation of the Organic Law as demanded by the Chamber of Notables, concentrated on increasing Army establishments and officers' pay, and on paying off old scores. The Dual Control no longer had any effective existence.

In May things came to a crisis between the Khedive and the army-dominated Government. A number of Circassian officers, including the ex-Minister of War who had been dismissed on the demand of the mutineers in February 1881, were tried by Court Martial on an almost certainly trumped-up charge of conspiracy against Arabi. They were convicted and sentenced to dismissal from the Army and perpetual banishment 'to the furthest limits of the Sudan.' The Khedive, with the encouragement both of the Sultan and of the British and French Agents, and believing the convicted officers to be innocent, used his prerogative to reduce the sentences to simple banishment from Egypt. The Council of Ministers then broke off all relations with the Khedive, and committed the illegality of summoning the Chamber of Notables (whose previous session had finished at the end of March) with the object of inducing them to vote for the Khedive's deposition. This represented the first formal break between the Khedive and his Ministers, and imposed on the British and French Governments some action in order to preserve the Khedive's throne, unless they were prepared openly to repudiate the policy laid down in the Joint Note.

Neither Government was anxious for armed intervention. The British Government was prepared for armed intervention by Turkey as the least of a number of evils. But the French Government was opposed to this. After hearing from Cairo of the threatened deposition of the Khedive, the two Governments agreed on the despatch of British and French naval squadrons to Alexandria. At the same time they instructed their Representatives in Cairo to advise the Khedive to take advantage of the arrival of the squadrons to 'dismiss the present Ministry and to form a new Cabinet under Sherif Pasha or any other person inspiring the same confidence.'[5]

Meanwhile Mahmud Sami, the Prime Minister, and the Army Colonels were having trouble with the Chamber of Notables, the majority of whom objected to their illegal convocation and were by no means disposed to depose the Khedive in order to facilitate the establishment of a dictatorship of army officers who were already proving themselves to be venal, predatory, incompetent and vindictive. Malet and Siencowicz, the British and French Agents, used this divergence between the Notables and the Army to try to negotiate a settlement in line with the instructions received from their Governments which would have provided for a change of Government and for the temporary removal of Arabi from Egypt. These attempts did not succeed. The Government resigned in protest against the Khedive's acceptance of foreign advice in preference to their own. Having failed to procure his deposition by means of the Chamber of Notables, Arabi and his supporters were now deter/ mined to bring about his submission by a direct appeal to public opinion. The result, obtained with the aid of a certain amount of coercion and terrorism, was that a powerful deputation of Notables and Ulema and leading citizens of Cairo waited on the Khedive on 29 May and prayed him to restore Arabi as Minister of War. The Khedive yielded. Whether he yielded to the popular will or, as Malet told Granville, to the threat of a massacre, must remain uncertain. From the point of view, not only of the Army, but of a great many intelligent and respectable Egyptian civilians, Arabi was fighting against a corrupt and tottering despotism which sought to maintain itself with foreign aid, and which had set its face against any sort of reform. These civilian 'constitutionalists' were not wholly in agreement with the Army, and they probably regarded Arabi as the arrogant and illiterate braggart that he was. But military rule, with all its disadvantages, was probably seen by them as a lesser evil than the alternative, as they saw it, of a return to an Ismailian despotism buttressed by European ironclads.

Arabi was duly reinstated as Minister of War. As there were no other Ministers he was, in effect, Prime Minister, as well as virtually C/in/C of the Army. There was no longer any serious possibility of offsetting his influence, except by force.

On 13 June the Khedive and his Court moved from Cairo to Alex/ andria. Most of the Consuls/General followed him. On 17 June, at the request of the German and Austrian Consuls/General, he appointed a 'neutral' Government under the Presidency of a nonentity, Ragheb Pasha. But Arabi remained Minister of War and master of the situation.

Over the weeks of negotiation in which the British Government had been engaged with the Porte, with France, and with the other Powers, over Egypt, they had become aware of four things. First, that the other Powers were suspicious of any Anglo/French action taken over Egypt without consultation with them. Secondly, that all the Powers except France wanted armed intervention, if it proved necessary, to be under/ taken by Turkey. Thirdly, that the French Government were becoming less and less enamoured of the prospect of Anglo/French, or indeed of any, armed intervention. Fourthly, that the Sultan was playing a double game, running with the Khedivial hare and hunting with the Arabist hounds, and generally unprepared to act as the obedient instrument, either of the British and French Governments, or of the Powers generally, in restoring the authority of the Khedive. He wanted to see who was going to win in Egypt, and then to back the winner. To this end, at the beginning of June, on the Khedive's invitation he sent to Egypt Darwish

Pasha, a distinguished soldier, with the ostensible and unrealistic object of restoring order there. There was no expectation that this mission would do more than give some time for manoeuvre, but this was welcome to all parties.

The British Government still hoped to avoid any armed intervention, either unilaterally or collectively, and welcomed a suggestion from Freycinet that the two Governments should propose to the Porte and the Powers the immediate assembly of an International Conference at Constantinople. A joint proposal was therefore made to the Porte and the Powers that such a Conference should be held, with a representative of the Turkish Government, and the Ambassadors of Great Britain, France, Germany, Austria-Hungary, Italy and Russia participating, with a view to agreeing on steps (a) to maintain 'the rights in Egypt of the Sultan and the Khedive'; (b) to procure 'the observance of international engagements and the arrangements existing under them, whether with England and France alone, or with those two nations and the other Powers'; (c) to provide for 'the preservation of the liberties secured by the Firmans of the Sultan'; and (d) to secure 'the prudent development of Egyptian institutions.'[6] The other Powers agreed, but the Porte entered upon a characteristic course of procrastination. Eventually the Conference met in Constantinople on 23 June without the participation of the Porte.

Meanwhile, the urgency of the situation had been sharpened by the outbreak of anti-European and anti-Christian violence in Alexandria on 11 June, during which an unknown number, but probably about 300, Christians, and a smaller number of Moslems, were killed. The incident was inevitably linked, in the minds of European observers, and of European Governments, with the anti-foreign and anti-Christian propaganda and incitement which had lately been rife in Egypt, and a bad impression was created by the tardiness of the local authorities in restoring order.

This incident had a decisive effect on a wavering British Cabinet. Nobody in the Cabinet was really interested in the bondholders. With the exception of Hartington, the Secretary of State for India, none of the members of the Cabinet had much enthusiasm for the Dual Control, which had been set up by their Conservative predecessors, or for Taufiq, and many members of the Cabinet had some sympathy with the Khedive's opponents. But in the minds of all of them was one overriding consideration—the necessity to preserve freedom of passage through the Suez Canal, which meant the avoidance of anarchy in Egypt and the avoidance of any situation which might lead to the predominance in Egypt of any other Great Power. The objective was traditional in British policy, although the situation was new, and the Cabinet at first tried to meet it in the traditional way by invoking Turkish suzerainty over Egypt. But the problem was complicated by several factors. There was some reason to believe that, not only the Turks, but the French as well, were contemplating doing a deal with Arabi. The combination of Ottoman trimming and procrastination on the one hand, and the French reluctance to admit Turkish intervention on the other, more or less put the possibility of such intervention out of court. It was fairly clear that any intervention by England alone, or by France and England, would provoke the combined hostility of Turkey and the other Powers. There were differences of opinion in the Cabinet over the extent to which Arabi and his supporters could be regarded as a potential menace to freedom of passage through the Canal. Up to the time of the Alexandria massacre only Hartington, and probably Northbrook and Childers, who were responsible for India, the Admiralty and the War Office respectively, had made up their minds about the necessity for some sort of armed intervention. After the Alexandria massacre, Chamberlain, President of the Board of Trade, Dilke, Under Secretary of State for Foreign Affairs, and even Gladstone himself, became convinced that Arabi was, in Chamberlain's words, 'a military adventurer, that there was no national party in the true sense, (and) that his uncontrolled supremacy would very shortly bring about bankruptcy and anarchy.'[7] This coalescence between the Whig Imperialists and the Radicals meant that there was an almost certain majority in the Cabinet for military action of some sort. On 20 June Hartington told Granville that he would resign unless some arrangements were made for sending a military expedition to Egypt and suggested the immediate preparation of a British force in an attempt to stimulate the French or the Turks to action.[8] As a result of Hartington's insistence two battalions of reinforcements were sent to Cyprus and conversations opened with the French about the best method of protecting the Suez Canal should this become necessary. The French were unenthusiastic and informed the British Government that the Canal Company were confident that there was no threat to the Canal and that the only danger which might arise would be in the event of foreign intervention to protect it.

This was the position when the Constantinople Conference opened on 23 June. The proceedings opened with the signature by all the delegates of a self-denying Protocol, proposed by the French Government, by which all the participants bound themselves not to use the situation in Egypt to seek for themselves any exclusive position or advantages.

After the Conference had been sitting for just over a week, without achieving any decisive results, the Admiralty received a disquieting signal from Sir Beauchamp Seymour, the Admiral commanding the British squadron in Alexandria harbour. Some weeks before, Seymour had complained that shore batteries were being mounted to command the anchorage of the British squadron. Work on the batteries had been discontinued at the request of the Sultan, to whom the British Government had appealed. But, on 3 July, Seymour reported that work on the batteries had been resumed and asked permission to bombard them if it were not stopped. There followed a series of agitated discussions between various members of the Cabinet. The French Government made it clear that they would not associate themselves with a bombardment. All the members of the Cabinet seem to have appreciated that a bombardment would probably have to be followed by a military expedition to, and a temporary military occupation of, Egypt. Nobody seems to have enquired about the extent to which the British squadron was really endangered by the Egyptian batteries. Nobody, except Bright, who resigned from the Cabinet in protest against the bombardment, seems to have suggested that the object in view—the safety of the Suez Canal—was more likely to be jeopardised than secured by the bombardment of Alexandria.[9] Nobody seems to have considered the serious implications, from the point of view of the safety of European lives and property, of a naval bombardment which was not immediately followed by a military landing in force. Eventually, on 9 July, Seymour was authorised to issue an ultimatum to the Egyptian authorities stating that the forts would be bombarded unless the batteries were removed within twenty-four hours. At the same time the War Office was authorised to prepare an expeditionary force to be sent to Egypt.

The French squadron at Alexandria under Admiral Conrad sailed for Port Said. On the morning of 11 July Seymour, who had apparently exceeded his instructions by demanding the surrender of the batteries and their removal under British supervision,[10] ordered his squadron to open fire on the forts. The fire was returned and a brisk cannonade exchanged all day. Some British ships were damaged. Next morning the Egyptian batteries were silent and it soon became apparent that the Egyptian Army had abandoned the town, setting fire to it in the course of their retreat. On 13 July Seymour landed a small force of Marines to try to preserve order. (Looting Beduin had already entered the town.) They were assisted, at Seymour's request, by detachments from some foreign warships in the harbour. On 17 July some 3,000 British troops arrived from Cyprus and established themselves in and around Alexandria. Meanwhile, the Egyptian Army started digging in at Kafr ed-Dawar, some eight miles south-east of Alexandria, in the narrow isthmus between Lake Edku and Lake Mariut. This isthmus, through which the Alexandria-Cairo railway and the Mahmudieh Canal (connecting Alexandria with the Nile) passed, commanded the only direct land route between Alexandria and the Nile Valley. From Kafr ed-Dawar Arabi issued a Proclamation stating that 'irreconcilable war existed between the Egyptians and the English' and threatening the 'severest punishment by martial law to all Egyptians who cooperated with them.' This Proclamation was principally directed towards the Khedive and the remainder of the Government, who had remained in Alexandria and put themselves under the protection of the British squadron. The Khedive, who had now become the mouthpiece of the British, ordered Arabi to return to Alexandria and, on his refusal to do so, formally dismissed him from office, and issued a Decree declaring him to be a rebel and a Proclamation forbidding all Egyptians to assist him. Darwish, The Turkish Commissioner, who was also in Alexandria, with his mission effectively at an end, returned unobtrusively to Constantinople.

Some members of the Cabinet, and particularly Granville, seem to have imagined that the bombardment of Alexandria might by itself lead to the collapse of Arabi and the restoration of the Khedive's authority.[11] They were soon undeceived. As we have seen, they ordered a small force of British troops from Cyprus to occupy Alexandria with a view to keeping order there and preventing its reoccupation by the Egyptian Army. But they were still, most of them, desperately anxious to avoid a unilateral British occupation. Most of them appreciated the nature of the trap into which this would lead them. It would earn them the hostility of the French and the Turks who, unlike the British, still had their options open between the Khedive and Arabi, and who might thus have the power of making things very difficult indeed. It would expose them to the blackmail of the other Powers, whose support they would need in combating French and Turkish hostility. It would make them responsible for the foreign debt, to which was likely to be added large claims in respect of the destruction of foreign property in Alexandria. However, it was impossible to do nothing. The bombardment had closed the door on any possibility of an accommodation with Arabi. The alternative prospects were, on the one hand, a chaos of fanaticism, looting and xenophobia and, on the other hand, a military dictatorship which was irretrievably hostile to England and which might well do a deal with Turkey and the Powers behind the British Government's back. In either event the security of passage through the Canal, the principal, and only vital, British interest in Egypt would be jeopardised. And so British diplomatic efforts—in Constantinople, in Paris and in London—were concentrated on attempts to secure some sort of concerted action against Arabi by the Powers. What they tried, and failed, to achieve over the next few weeks was: (1) Immediate steps for the protection of the Suez

Canal by Anglo-French naval forces, if possible with, if necessary without, the consent of Turkey and the other Great Powers; (2) an eventual Turkish military expedition which would restore the *status quo ante* Arabi and then evacuate. The attempt to secure French cooperation over the Canal failed because the Freycinet Government was defeated in the French Chamber on 29 July when it asked for the necessary credit for the purpose. The attempt to arrange for a Turkish military expedition failed, partly because of a natural Turkish reluctance to be used by the British Government as a fire brigade, and partly because the Sultan wished to retain the option of coming to an agreement with Arabi, whose cause was probably supported by the majority of Moslems in the Ottoman Empire.

While these negotiations were going on, a section of the British Cabinet, led by Hartington, continued to insist on the necessity for contingent arrangements to occupy Egypt in the event, in Gladstone's words, of 'the exhaustion of every effort to procure collective or joint action.'[12] On 20 July the Cabinet decided to send an expeditionary force, which the War Office had been preparing in England for some weeks, to Cyprus and Malta, where it would be ready 'for operations in any part of Egypt.'[13] On 24 July the Government asked for and obtained from the House of Commons a credit of £2,300,000 for the expedition. Gladstone himself, asking for the money, explained to the House that such an expedition was necessary for the protection of the Suez Canal which was menaced by 'disturbed and anarchical conditions in Egypt.' For this reason, Gladstone explained, England must 'substitute the rule of law for that of military violence in Egypt, in partnership with other Powers if possible, but alone if necessary.'[14] Dilke, the Foreign Office spokesman in the Commons, explained that England had a double interest in the Canal: (1) Commercial in that 82 per cent of the traffic through the Canal was British; and (2) Political in that the Canal was the 'principal highway to India, Ceylon, the Straits, and British Burmah, where 250,000,000 people live under our rule, and also to China, where we have vast interests . . . It is also one of the roads to our Colonial Empire in Australia and New Zealand.'[15]

The Commons voted the money by 275 votes to 19. This was perhaps a surprising result in view of the Liberal majority and large Radical element in the House. The Conservatives, the Liberal Imperialists, the bondholders, and shipping and Eastern trading interests, might have been expected to agree, as they did. The support of the Radicals was secured by an argument developed, and possibly even believed in, by Gladstone in which he represented the proposed British intervention as being a means of giving to the Egyptian people 'hope . . . for free institutions . . . and . . . for the attainment of those blessings of civilised life which they see have been achieved in so many countries in Europe.'[16] The British invasion of Egypt was thus based on a precarious alliance of consent between a number of normally opposed forces which the Cabinet had momentarily been able to bring together under the stress of the necessities created by the bombardment of Alexandria, which had made military intervention inevitable, and which limited both the time and the area of manoeuvre available to the British Government in their efforts for a concerted arrangement with the Powers.

The British expedition, under the command of Sir Garnet Wolseley, proceeded direct to Egypt and started disembarking at Alexandria from 11 August onwards. From there, leaving the Cyprus force which had been landed in July to defend Alexandria and to divert Arabi's attention from his Suez Canal flank, the main force sailed to Port Said, entered the Canal in face of protests from the Canal Company against a violation of its alleged neutral status and disembarked at Ismailia, half-way through. The intention was to advance into the Delta by way of the Wadi Tumulat and the Sweet Water Canal, and so to capture Cairo. Just as Kafr ed-Dawar was the key to the Delta on the west, so the village of Tel el-Kebir, between desert and Delta on the Sweet Water Canal, was the key on the east. It was at this point that Wolseley's force met and defeated the Egyptian army on 13 September. Cairo was occupied the following day without further resistance. The 'Grand National Council,' which Arabi had set up in Cairo, hastened to make its submission. Within a week the rebellion had collapsed. Arabi and the principal rebel leaders surrendered to the British. The rank and file of the Egyptian troops dispersed to their homes and the Egyptian Army, as it then existed, was formally disbanded. The Khedive who, a few weeks before, at British instigation, had formed a Government with Sherif Pasha as Prime Minister and Riaz Pasha as Minister of the Interior, returned to Cairo. It only remained to clear up the mess.

The British Government continued their efforts to secure concerted action in Egypt right up to the eve of Tel el-Kebir, and an Anglo-Turkish Convention, regulating the conditions of Ottoman intervention, was about to be signed when the news of the British victory arrived in Constantinople. But the Sultan had hesitated too long before deciding to commit himself against Arabi. By the time he had made up his mind, it was too late. The British Government no longer required his assistance and, courteously but firmly, broke off negotiations. France was already *hors de concours* after Freycinet's defeat in the Chamber at the end of July. A half-hearted invitation to Italy to participate in the occupation was turned down by the Italian Government.

Once the British Cabinet had, as most of its members saw it, been manoeuvred by the course of events into a unilateral occupation of Egypt, they naturally tended to think of the opportunities rather than of the perils of the situation in which they found themselves. They were all agreed on the necessity for an early withdrawal. But, before withdrawing, certain steps had to be taken with a view to securing those vital British interests which had made the occupation necessary. The consensus of their ideas, discussed and canvassed in a number of Cabinet memoranda during September and October, were set out in the instructions sent by Granville to Lord Dufferin, the British Ambassador in Constantinople, whom the Cabinet sent to Egypt in November 1882 to 'advise the Government of the Khedive in the arrangements for re-establishing HH's authority and providing for the well-being of all classes of the population.'

Dufferin was told that 'HMG, while desiring that the British occupation should last for as short a time as possible, feel bound not to withdraw from the task imposed on them until the administration of affairs has been reconstructed on a basis which will afford satisfactory guarantees for the maintenance of peace, order and prosperity, for the stability of the Khedive's authority, for the judicious development of self-government, and for the fulfilment of obligations towards the Powers ... All measures bearing on the reconstruction of government should be submitted to Y.E. before they are adopted or made public, and you should as far as possible be consulted at every stage of their preparation.' The instructions went on to outline the main questions with which it was considered that Dufferin should deal. These included: (1) The reorganisation of the army and police; (2) The substitution of 'some better system' for the Dual Control; (3) An improvement of those services 'now managed in great part by Europeans' and a 'gradual reduction of foreign elements and an increased employment of Egyptians in all branches of the administration'; (4) 'An improved system of justice for natives'; (5) Equal taxation for foreigners and Egyptians; (6) 'The establishment of institutions favourable to the prudent development of liberty, either by the re-assembly of the Chamber of Notables or otherwise'; (7) The prevention of the slave trade; (8) 'Security of transit across Egypt between Europe and the East, and especially freedom of passage through the Suez Canal.'[17]

These instructions reflect the very wide spectrum of views represented in the Cabinet on the subject of Egypt. It was generally agreed that the main reason for British intervention had been to protect 'freedom of passage through the Suez Canal.' It was also widely agreed that this necessitated the effective restoration of law and order, involving the reorganisation of the army and police, and also the 'fulfilment of obligations towards the Powers' in order to avoid giving 'the Powers' a colourable excuse for interfering in Egypt themselves. But the Radicals, who believed, or wished to believe, in the British rôle as liberators of Egypt, also wanted to see the occupation justified by an 'improved system of justice for natives,' by the 'establishment of institutions favourable to the prudent development of liberty,' and by the removal of some of those foreign privileges and abuses which they equated with the Dual Control (set up by their Conservative predecessors), and which they considered, not without reason, to have been partly responsible for all the trouble. In this the Radicals were at one with Whig Imperialists, like Hartington, who were incensed by the vacillating behaviour of successive French Governments over the previous year, and who were determined not to accept the concept of equal Anglo-French rights in Egypt. There was, therefore, a firm Cabinet majority in favour of the abolition of the Dual Control. This was accomplished in January 1883, after bitter negotiation with the French Government, who, at the conclusion of the negotiation, expressed their intention of 'resuming their liberty of action in Egyptian affairs.' This marked the formal end of close Anglo-French cooperation over Egypt based on a mutual acknowledgement of equal rights, and no outside interference, initiated at the Berlin Congress in 1878. The two Controllers were replaced by a single British Financial Adviser who, on paper, inherited much the same powers as the Controllers. The first Financial Adviser was Sir Auckland Colvin, who had been the British Controller, and wielded a much more dominating influence than Malet, the British Consul-General, had done in determining the course of British policy in Egypt between the mutiny of September 1881 and the bombardment of Alexandria in July 1882.

The abolition of the Dual Control formalised and set the stage for that bitter history of Anglo-French rivalry over Egypt which lasted for the next twenty-one years and which, more than anything else, determined the course of British policy in Egypt.

The other instructions given to Dufferin were more immediately important in that their attempted implementation produced a series of contradictions which, for a time, paralysed and discredited British policy in Egypt and, by a process of infection, threatened to do the same for the whole of British foreign policy. It is of the essence of Baring's achievement in Egypt, after he returned there in 1883, that he succeeded in rescuing British policy from this state.

It might just have been possible to secure vital British interests in Egypt—freedom of passage through the Suez Canal—by a rapid restoration of the authority of the Khedive under effective Ottoman suzerainity, by some debt settlement which would probably have involved an internationally guaranteed loan and some increased international interference in Egyptian finances, and by some sort of guarantee of Egyptian 'neutralisation' obtained from the Powers in return for a speedy military evacuation. But this would have meant allowing the Khedive and his Ministers to govern in their own way, with some European technical assistance, if necessary, with the assistance of Turkish arms, and without any question of an 'improved system of justice for natives' or 'the establish, ment of institutions favourable to the prudent development of liberty.' It would also have meant abandoning any hopes for 'the well-being of all classes of the population.' The pressure of discontent created by such a solution would certainly have necessitated the 're-organisation of the army and police.' It is not unlikely that this pressure would, before long, have started the same cycle of events all over again, leading to a second insurrection and a second foreign intervention. But it might have worked.

On the other hand, the schemes of reform—improved justice, repre, sentative institutions, and the other matters adumbrated in Dufferin's instructions, were irreconcilable with a speedy restoration of Khedivial authority and, to the extent that they were seriously pursued, involved both a prolongation and extension of effective British authority. One of the lessons of the Dual Control had been that effective European authority could not be sustained without the backing of armed force; the authority of the Dual Control had been whittled away because it had not had this backing. But a prolongation and extension of the British occupation was regarded, not only by the Liberal Government, but also by the Con, servative Opposition, as being out of the question, both for domestic and for international reasons.

Dufferin, in his final Report written in February 1883,[18] shewed himself as being aware of, without being able to resolve, the inherent contradiction in his instructions; 'Had I been commissioned to place affairs on the footing of an Indian State, the outlook would have been different. The masterful hand of a Resident would have quickly bent everything to his will and, in the space of five years, would have greatly added to the national well-being of the country. But the Egyptians would have justly considered these advantages dearly bought at the price of their political independence. Moreover, HMG and public opinion in England have pronounced against such a solution. But it is absolutely necessary to prevent the fabric we have raised from crumbling to the ground as soon as our hand is withdrawn.'

The first problem which Dufferin had to deal with after his arrival in Egypt illustrated the contradictory aims inherent in the official British attitude. Arabi and the principal military leaders had surrendered to the British Army, which handed them over to the Egyptian Government.

They had been in armed rebellion against the Khedive and had had the certain intention of deposing him. By Oriental, and by some Western, standards they deserved the death penalty and might well have expected to suffer it. Left to themselves, the Egyptian Government would certainly have executed them. But, in England, there was some spontaneous, and much organised, sympathy for the rebels. The British Army was inclined to regard them as prisoners of war. But the official attitude was that the British had come to Egypt in the name, and at the request, of the Khedive to put down a rebellion and restore the Khedive's authority. An important element in the restoration of that authority, in the eyes of Egyptian public opinion and in the eyes of the Egyptian Ministers, was condign punish-ment for the rebels. Although not regarded as such at the time, the fate of Arabi and his associates was an important test case to determine whether the British Government really intended to restore the Khedivial authority in fact as well as in name, or whether they intended to exercise their own authority behind the Khedivial façade. What they did was, in effect, to opt for the latter without immediately pursuing their choice to its logical conclusion in the other matters at issue with which they had to deal.

Unless it had been determined to leave the prisoners to their fate, undoubtedly the best solution would have been for the British authorities to have exiled Arabi and his associates while they were still in British hands, and not to have handed them over to the Egyptian Government. But, having recognised the Khedive's authority to the extent of handing them over, they proceeded to undermine that authority by dictating to the Egyptian Government the nature of the punishment to be meted out. After some negotiation, it was arranged that Arabi and his principal associates should plead guilty before an Egyptian Court to treason and rebellion, that they should be sentenced to death, and that the Khedive should immediately use his prerogative to commute the sentences to perpetual exile and confiscation of property. The British Government provided a place of exile in Ceylon and transported them there. Riaz Pasha, the Minister of the Interior, and the 'strong man' in the Govern-ment, who was stigmatized by Dufferin as 'narrow, obstinate, arbitrary and an enemy of liberal institutions,'[19] resigned his office in protest against the leniency shown.

Apart from the leaders of the rebellion, many hundreds of others had been arrested on charges of arson, murder and for other crimes in con-nection with the Alexandria massacre and fire, and the massacres of Europeans which had taken place in various provincial towns during Arabi's period of ascendancy. Most of these were tried over the next few months before Egyptian Military Courts. British military observers were appointed to attend the trials and appear to have satisfied themselves that no serious injustice was done to those who were convicted and sentenced either to execution or to long terms of imprisonment. British influence was also used to expedite the release of many of those awaiting trial against whom no serious charge could be preferred.[20]

Dufferin's principal business during his assignment in Egypt, which lasted from November 1882 to April 1883, was to inaugurate the various reforms adumbrated by Granville in the instructions given to him.

(1) The reorganisation of the army and police. This was the most immediately urgent task, since both had become completely disorganised as a result of the rebellion. After Tel el-Kebir a garrison of 12,000 British troops was retained in Egypt; by March 1883 this had been reduced to 9,500 and the intention was to reduce it progressively to nil as soon as Egyptian forces could be raised and trained to undertake internal security duties and frontier defence. General Sir Evelyn Wood, VC, a distinguished British officer, was appointed Sirdar, or Commander-in-Chief, of the new Egyptian Army, and a number of British officers were seconded to serve under him in the superior commands and on the staff. The size of the new army was provisionally fixed at 6,000. A Gendarmerie, which was intended as a para-military force for Beduin control and for policing the villages, was established under the command of General Valentine Baker, a British ex-officer previously employed by the Sultan, who was assisted by a few other British ex-officers. A police force, with a strength of about 2,000, for the purpose of policing the main towns, and commanded by Europeans, was also raised.

(2) The substitution of 'some better system' for the Dual Control has already been described above.

(3) 'An improvement in the services managed in great part by Europeans' and 'an increased employment of Egyptians in all branches of the administration.' Dufferin severely criticised the cost and effectiveness of the Cadastral Survey then being undertaken by Europeans and arranged for the whole Survey to be reorganised under British control. On the general question of the increased employment of Egyptians, Dufferin pointed out that there were about 20,000 Government employees in Egypt, which was 'greatly in excess' of needs. Of these, just over 1,000 were Europeans who, however, absorbed about 20 per cent of the total salary bill. Dufferin agreed that the total number of Europeans should be reduced, but told Granville: 'I cannot conceive anything more fatal to the prosperity and good administration of the country than a hasty and ill-considered extrusion of any large proportion of Europeans in deference to the clamour which has been raised against them.'[21]

(4) 'An improved system of justice for natives.' A Commission for

the Reform of Native Tribunals, which had started sitting in 1880, was revived, and Nubar Pasha added to it to strengthen its councils and expedite its proceedings. Criminal and Civil Codes were drawn up on the model of the Code Napoleon. A system of Courts of First Instance and Appeal was elaborated. A number of foreign judges were engaged. An Anglo-Indian lawyer, Sir Benson Maxwell, was appointed Procureur-Général. The new Courts were inaugurated by Decree on 14 June 1883.[22]

(5) Equal taxation for foreigners and Egyptians. Dufferin concentrated on an attempt to get foreign residents to pay a house tax, imposed on Egyptians by a Decree promulgated under the Dual Control in January 1881, amounting to 1/12th of the annual '*valeur locataire.*' Since this was held to have been legalised by the Ottoman law of 1867 providing for the payment of local taxation by foreigners in the Ottoman Empire on property owned by them, and was not, therefore, new taxation affecting foreigners, which came under the jurisdiction of the Mixed Courts, there appeared to be no legal impediment to this. But, as a result of pre-dominantly French objections, this tax was not finally applied to foreigners until March 1884. In spite of Dufferin's confident assertion that 'it is scarcely to be supposed that any Power in Europe would . . . refuse their assent to the removal of this and other cognate grievances,' it proved impossible, either then or later, to obtain the necessary unanimous consent to the application of any other direct taxes to foreigners.

(6) 'The establishment of institutions favourable to the prudent development of liberty.' Dufferin soon decided against the reconstitution of the Chamber of Notables on the ground that it would provide an opportunity for intrigue both by the Porte and by foreign Representatives in Egypt, and that it might well stop Egyptian Ministers from governing by reason of their inability to manage it.[23] The system eventually worked out and promulgated by a Decree dated 1 May 1883[24] consisted of:

Councils of from four to eight members for each Province elected by representatives from the villages. Their powers were purely advisory, and they met as and when convoked by the Mudirs (Governors) of Provinces.

A Legislative Council consisting of twenty-six members, of which twelve were nominated by the Khedive and sixteen elected by the Provincial Councils. Its functions were confined to examining, debating, and making recommendations to the Government about all proposed legislation. It had no power of initiating legislation, and its views on laws submitted to it were not binding on the Government.

A General Assembly consisting of eighty members—eight Ministers, the twenty-six members of the Legislative Council, and forty-six delegates from the Provinces. Its principal function was to approve new taxes, which could not be levied without the consent of the General Assembly.

Probably the most important of the reforms initiated by Dufferin, although it attracted little notice at the time, was the engagement in Egyptian Government service of Colonel Scott Moncrieff, a British irrigation engineer from India, as Inspector-General of Irrigation in the Ministry of Public Works, with the assignment of reorganising and rehabilitating the Egyptian irrigation system, which had fallen into great decay. Scott Moncrieff later engaged a small staff of British irrigation engineers from India. An efficient irrigation system was basic to Egypt's economic prosperity and financial solvency, and the appointment of Scott Moncrieff was the first step towards the material rehabilitation of Egypt achieved under Baring's long proconsulship.

Dufferin also arranged for the engagement by the Egyptian Government of Mr Clifford Lloyd, an Anglo-Irish magistrate, who was later appointed Under Secretary in the Ministry of the Interior, with the rather vague assignment of 'superintending internal reforms.' This, as we shall see, was to cause a good deal of trouble later.

All the difficulties which the British Government had to grapple with in Egypt were overshadowed by the financial question. In the instructions to Dufferin, and in a later Circular to the Powers,[25] the British Government had made it clear that existing international agreements, such as the financial settlement imposed by the Law of Liquidation, international privileges, such as the Capitulations and the regime of the Mixed Courts, and international interests, such as the right of navigation through the Suez Canal, would be respected and only amended as the result of prior consultation and agreement with the interested Powers.

Of these international agreements, the most immediately important and relevant was the financial settlement imposed by the Law of Liquidation. Apart from England, whose interest was mainly strategic, the direct interest of the Powers in Egypt was almost entirely financial. The successive international encroachments on Egypt—the installation of the Mixed Courts in 1875, the Goschen-Joubert settlement in 1876, the European Ministry in 1878, the deposition of Ismail and the establishment of the Dual Control in 1879—had all been motivated by a European desire for the better security of their Egyptian loans and investments. The Anglo-French Joint Note, which had ended any hope of accommodation with the national movement, had been provoked by the assumed danger to the Law of Liquidation presented by the Chamber's demand to vote the 'unaffected' part of the Budget. From the point of view of the Powers, therefore, and particularly that of France, the main object of, and only justification for, the British occupation was to safeguard the operation of the Law of Liquidation. This, in their eyes, also involved the maintenance, and perhaps even the intensification, of the various international checks and controls—the Mixed Courts, the Caisse de la Dette, the international Boards administering the railways, the Daira, the State Domains and all the other arrangements with which Egypt was encumbered. Even within these limits, such freedom of action as remained to the British Government in Egypt was dependent on the observance of the conditions laid down in the Law of Liquidation. If it became impossible to service the foreign debt as provided for in that Law, it was certain that the Powers would demand further interference in Egypt's internal affairs. By their occupation, the British Government had, willy-nilly, made themselves the guarantors of Egypt's foreign indebtedness. It was, as Baring was to remark later, simply a question of who was to do the paying—the British or the Egyptian taxpayer. And on this point all parties in the House of Commons were quite unanimous—the British taxpayer was not going to pay a penny. Income tax had been increased by three-halfpence in the £ to pay for Wolseley's expedition, and this was to be the maximum extent of the British financial contribution to the Egyptian imbroglio, in spite of the fact that the real reason for the British occupation had been the protection of British strategic interests.

All might have been comparatively well if Egyptian finances had been buoyant enough to bear the weight of the settlement embodied in the Law of Liquidation. But various factors had contributed to a considerable deterioration since 1880. The Arabi regime had been inefficient and extravagant. Tax collecting had been neglected and large sums had been spent on the army. The floating debt had consequently increased. The burning and looting of Alexandria had given rise to large claims for compensation, mainly from European property-owners. These claims were adjudicated by an International Commission set up in January 1883,[26] whose awards amounted to just over £4 million. The internationally managed Daira and Domains administrations showed an annual deficit which had to be made good. There was a cholera epidemic in the Spring of 1883 which interfered with agricultural productivity and retarded tax collection. This was followed by a low Nile in the Autumn. The British Government insisted that the costs of the army of occupation must be paid by the Egyptian Treasury. Payment of the interest on the British holding of Suez Canal Shares was exacted by the British Treasury. The Ottoman tribute had to be paid. Rebellion had broken out in the Sudan, which necessitated the raising—from the debris of the old Egyptian army—and the equipping of an emergency force to try to deal with it.

These increasing expenditures and commitments created an intractable situation. The conditions of the Law of Liquidation on the one hand prevented any deficits in the administrative revenue being made up from surpluses on that part of the revenue 'affected' to the service of the debt, and on the other hand provided that deficits in the 'affected' revenue must be regarded as a first charge on the administrative revenue. No foreign loan of more than £1 million could be raised without the consent of the Powers who were parties to the Law of Liquidation. Additional taxes on foreigners could not be imposed without the unanimous consent of the Capitulatory Powers. The run-down state of the agricultural economy, the heavy agricultural indebtedness, the unpopularity and the precarious authority of the Egyptian Government, all militated against the desir-ability, or even the possibility, of increased land-taxes (the principal source of Egyptian revenue). The rehabilitation of the irrigation system embarked on by Scott Moncrieff and his assistants could not immediately be expected to produce dividends in the form of increased productivity. All that the British occupiers, exercising their authority through the Financial Adviser, could do was to try to encourage a strict economy, a cutting-down of establishments, and a meticulous collection of taxes. Such a programme was not likely to enhance the popularity either of the British occupiers or of the Egyptian Government, particularly in view of the extravagant promises made by the Arabi regime which had, *inter alia,* promised to repudiate all public and private debts owing to foreigners. Also, Governmental economy, and particularly a restric-tion of expenditure for irrigation, although immediately necessary, only made matters worse in the long run by eroding the agricultural economy on which the possibility of future financial improvement depended.

The British Government were inhibited from thinking in terms of 'the long run' by their frequently expressed, and sincerely meant, determination to evacuate Egypt as quickly as possible. Having agreed to the various 'instant' reforms initiated by Dufferin—the new Courts of Justice, the various Councils and Assemblies, the abolition of the Dual Control, the British-officered security forces, the appointment of a British Financial Adviser and the engagement of British experts in the Ministries of Public Works and the Interior—they shewed an increasing reluctance to extend their interference in any way which might involve a continuing commit-ment to maintain a military presence in Egypt. This particularly applied to the rebellion in the Sudan. In spite of a recommendation made by a British officer sent there to report on the situation, the British Government refused to give the Egyptian Government any advice at all, on the ground that any mandatory advice given on the subject might involve subsequent British military operations in the Sudan. They even passively acquiesced in the employment by the Egyptian Government of half-pay British officers in command of a 'scratch' Egyptian force raised in a desperate and ill-advised attempt to reconquer the whole of the Sudan. This passivity was to have important and unfortunate consequences later.

The British Government's reluctance to involve themselves too deeply in Egypt was not entirely due to considerations of financial parsimony, any more than the determination of the other Powers to insist on the letter of Egypt's financial obligations was due entirely to financial greed. At this time, Bismarck, the German Chancellor, was the principal arbiter in European diplomacy. His foreign policy was dictated by a determination to prevent France from building up a series of alliances which might enable her to embark on a war of *revanche* for the recovery of Alsace-Lorraine. To this end he had cultivated the Dreikaiserbund—a general understanding between the three Empires of Germany, Austria-Hungary and Russia which involved, *inter alia,* mutual consultation over matters concerning the Ottoman Empire—and had just buttressed this by a Triple Alliance between Germany, Austria-Hungary and Italy. He was also prepared to welcome any opportunity of embroiling France with England, since this would enable him either to appease France by supporting her diplomatically against England, or to threaten France by supporting England against her. In the same way he was able to put pressure on England, in matters of European policy and in pursuit of Germany's nascent colonial ambitions, by threats of diplomatic hostility and promises of diplomatic support. He therefore welcomed the potential Anglo-French discord inherent in the British occupation of Egypt, did his best to encourage that occupation, and, when it had been accomplished, exploited it to the top of his bent.

To Bismarck, the British occupation was an opportunity for diplomatic manoeuvre. To France it was a serious political defeat. Bismarck did not want the British occupation to end since this would have deprived him of the opportunity for *chantage.* The French, for a variety of reasons in which outraged national pride was uppermost, did want it to end, and concentrated their efforts on trying to bring about a system of international control which they recognised as the only immediately practicable alternative. Neither was primarily interested in the payment of the debt. Both used the question of the debt for the attainment of their ends.

The part played by Turkey and the other Powers was secondary. The Turks wanted the British out of Egypt and realised that they could only achieve this with the assistance of the other Powers. Austria-Hungary followed the German lead. Italy's designs on the remains of the Egyptian Empire in the Horn of Africa inclined her towards an accommodation with England, in so far as this could be arranged without antagonising Bismarck. Russia who, throughout the 1880s, was drawing steadily closer to France, in reaction against the Triple Alliance, saw in the Egyptian situation an opportunity of giving diplomatic support to France at no cost or risk to herself. Bismarck therefore held the key to the trap in which the British had become entangled in Egypt. He had the option either of effectively supporting England by carrying with him Austria-Hungary and Italy against France and Russia, or of effectively opposing England by joining France and Russia, taking Austria-Hungary with him, and leaving England with the dubious, conditional, and ineffective support of Italy. The Turkish attitude would, in effect, be decided by Bismarck. For, in view of Bismarck's ascendancy, and the rapprochement between France and Russia, British influence in Constantinople was no longer sufficient to swing the Porte in the required direction.

Egypt had become a kind of prison for British diplomacy. The British Government wanted to replace the British occupation by an arrangement for the 'neutralisation' of Egypt designed to safeguard those strategic interests which they regarded as vital and which had been the real reason for the occupation. But such an arrangement was only negotiable from a position of comparative strength. As a precondition of effective 'neutralisation,' Egypt must be made stable, solvent and secure. It had apparently been hoped that stability, solvency and security could be achieved by a process of 'instant' reforms—a quick spring-cleaning—followed by a rapid military evacuation, leaving behind a rehabilitated native government, buttressed by a few British officials, inspired by an enthusiasm for reform, capable of paying its debts, and ruling over a contented and subservient population. Under such conditions an effective guarantee of 'neutralisation' could have been obtained in return for evacuation. By the Autumn of 1883 it was obvious that all this was a pipe-dream. Except on paper, there had been no reform at all, apart from the abolition of the kurbash as an official instrument of punishment and some slight improvement in the appalling conditions prevailing in Egyptian prisons. It seemed probable that the Sudanese rebels would be threatening the frontiers of Egypt before long. Riaz Pasha, almost the only capable indigenous administrator in Egypt, had resigned from the Government in dudgeon. The personal authority of the Khedive was almost non-existent. It was doubtful whether any coherent authority could have long survived the removal of British troops from Egypt. Financially, the country was well on the way to another bankruptcy. There was an unsecured floating debt of about £6 million, consisting of the accumulated deficits of the last three years, plus approximately £4 million of indemnities awarded by the International Commission for damage sustained to property in Alexandria. There was the prospect of having to incur further heavy expenditure in dealing with the Sudanese rebellion. Taxation receipts were in arrears, partly as a result of the inability of large landowners to make tenants pay their rents.[27] The shortage of cash in the Egyptian Treasury was so acute that in August 1883 the Government had to borrow £50,000 from Awqaf (religious) funds to pay official salaries.

It was in these depressing circumstances that Sir Evelyn Baring, KCSI (Knight Commander of the Star of India), arrived in Cairo on 11 September 1883 to take over from Sir Edward Malet the position of British Agent and Consul-General in Egypt. Baring had served for nearly three years in India as Financial Member of the Viceroy's Council and, on the eve of his departure, had been knighted for his services in that capacity. He was forty-two years old, with a quarter of a century of varied military, financial, administrative and diplomatic experience behind him. He had filled with distinction a number of posts of progressively increasing importance and responsibility, and, as a result of his previous service in Egypt as Commissioner of the Debt and Controller-General, he was already experienced in Egyptian affairs.

5

THE HOUSE
OF BONDAGE

BARING PROCEEDED TO Egypt directly from India. He received no general instructions from the British Government, except an injunction from Granville to 'act on the basis of the instructions to Lord Dufferin and on his Report.' It was made clear to him, both by Granville and by his cousin and old chief, Lord Northbrook, who was First Lord of the Admiralty in the Gladstone Administration, that the Cabinet attached great importance to an immediate reduction in the strength of the British garrison and to the total withdrawal of that garrison within a period to be measured in months rather than years. Granville also told him that he thought the French had 'pretty well made up their minds to our preponderating position in Egypt,' but were very sensitive about it for traditional and financial reasons.[1]

When Baring arrived in Cairo, some of Dufferin's reforms were already under way, at all events on paper. The new Native Tribunals had been set up and a number of European judges engaged. Elections for the Provincial Councils had been held. The use of the kurbash—rhinoceros-hide whip—as an instrument for extracting confessions, inducing the payment of taxes, and compelling forced labourers to work, had, Baring reported, been abolished in theory and all but abolished in practice. There had been some improvement in prison conditions. A start had been made on the rehabilitation of the irrigation system under the auspices of Colonel Scott Moncrieff. Sir Benson Maxwell was Procureur-Général of the new Native Tribunals. Clifford Lloyd had, on Dufferin's insistence and much against the will of Sherif Pasha the Prime Minister, been given a temporary assignment for introducing various reforms into the Ministry of the Interior. He arrived in Egypt a week or two after Baring. Sir Auckland Colvin, the Financial Adviser, had left to replace Baring as Finance Member on the Viceregal Council. After consultation with Baring, Edgar Vincent,[2] a young man of twenty-seven, had been appointed to succeed him, on the understanding that most of the responsibility for Egyptian finances would devolve on Baring himself. Vincent also arrived in Egypt a week or two after Baring. Sir Evelyn Wood and a number of seconded British officers had made a start with the formation of the new Egyptian Army. Valentine Baker was raising an Egyptian Gendarmerie. The police in the main town were being reorganised under British auspices.

The members of the Cabinet attached great importance both to reforms and to early evacuation. They were actuated by motives both of principle and of prudence. On the point of principle, Liberal acquiescence in the invasion of Egypt had been secured on the understanding that its object was to relieve the Egyptian people from oppression, bring them the benefit of Western institutions, and enable them to work out their own future destiny under the protection of these institutions. In this light, the British invading force was seen not as an army of occupation but as a liberating force, to be withdrawn as soon as the work of emancipation had been completed. And the process of reform was regarded as being largely self-generating once the appropriate constitutional instruments had been introduced. This was in accordance with the Liberal philosophy of the age, which regarded liberal institutions as a necessary precondition, and a sure guarantee, of social amelioration. On the prudential side, there was a general desire to avoid financial commitments and international complications by a speedy evacuation, after the introduction of reforms designed to create those conditions of stability, solvency and security which would preserve Egypt from armed European interference and enable the country to be effectively neutralised in accordance with traditional British policy.

Baring soon came to the conclusion that the policy which he had been charged to implement was based on an inherent contradiction. Writing to Granville on 9 October, after he had been in Egypt for about a month,[3] he warned him that the withdrawal of the garrison depended on the restoration of an effective native government in Egypt. He explained that 'recent events' had greatly weakened the authority of the native government, and that the effect of the reforms introduced by Dufferin tended to weaken this authority still further in that 'the essence of the most important of these reforms is to afford protection to the people against the arbitrary rule of the government.' He went on to make it clear that a policy of rapid withdrawal was only possible at the expense of watering down many of the reforms and of allowing the Egyptian Government to rule the country in its own arbitrary way. This statement of the incompatibility of the Cabinet's two principal objectives in Egypt was most unpalatable to its members, who insisted on a considerable bowdlerisation of Baring's official despatch on the subject before releasing it for publication.[4] Baring did, however, agree to an immediate reduction of the British garrison from 6,700 to 3,000 and to the withdrawal of British troops from Cairo.

Apart from the incompatibility between effective reforms and speedy evacuation, Baring's principal worry, during his first few weeks in Cairo, was the financial situation. Most of the reforms militated against the first of the three desiderata—stability—which the British had set themselves to restore in Egypt. The labyrinth of international commitments in which Egypt was involved militated against the second—solvency. The Capitulations made it impossible to tax foreigners without the unanimous agreement of some sixteen foreign Governments. The Mixed Courts made it possible for any foreign individual or interest to challenge any Egyptian Government Decree affecting their 'acquired rights,' which consisted of all the privileges and immunities which had grown up under the Capitulations, the provisions of the Law of Liquidation, and the cumbersome and expensive international Boards which had been set up to administer the Caisse de la Dette, the railways, the Daira, the State Domains, the Customs and the Quarantine service. They included the award of just over £4 million made by an International Commission (considered by Baring to have been grossly over-generous) to various interests and individuals, mostly foreign, as compensation for losses incurred in the riots and fire at Alexandria. All these international restrictions and stipulations were not only a source of great expense to the Egyptian Treasury, which had to pay the salaries and expenses of all the numerous officials involved. More importantly, they deprived the Egyptian Government of freedom of action in financial matters, in that they hampered the search for new and equitable sources of taxation, made the service of the foreign debt a prior charge on all Egyptian revenue, restricted the Government's borrowing powers, and made it necessary to devote the bulk of any revenue surpluses to a sinking fund for the repayment of the debt instead of to remissions of taxation or beneficial public works.

On 28 October Baring, in the course of a long letter to Granville, told him that the greatest obstacle in the way of any move forward was 'the necessity for consulting every Power in Europe before any important decision can be taken,' and that 'we ought not to leave the Egyptian Government in such a position that they may plead as an excuse for future misgovernment that their hands are so tied as to make it impossible for them to execute reforms. On the other hand we must not stay too long.' He went on: 'If we are to wait until all essential reforms have been carried out by the process of international consultation we shall wait a long time and be in danger of drifting into annexation. If we cut the knot by withdrawing, without having done our work and leaving Egypt to stew in its own juice, there will be a risk that something will occur as soon as our backs are turned which will raise up the whole Egyptian question again. I do not see any way out of this dilemma . . . (We have) in Egypt a top-heavy and exotic superstructure and an enormous external debt, Western law courts, complete liberty of contract, and all the paraphernalia of European civilisation with some of its corrupt and not many of its best features. I do not suppose that Europe will stand aside and let the superstructure crumble to pieces. We are making very fair progress with all matters within the competence of the Egyptian Government, but as regards international subjects we are at an absolute standstill . . . Would it not be possible to issue a Circular to the Powers . . . saying that we did not propose to consult them any more on each detail, but that when we had put matters straight we should ask them to accept the settlement *en bloc* and then we should at once withdraw our troops?' He concluded with unaccustomed euphoria: 'Give me 2,000 men and power to settle matters between the British and Egyptian Governments, and I will guarantee that in twelve months there will not be a British soldier in Egypt . . . But if we adhere to our present procedure I really despair of doing much within any reasonable period of time.'[5] Replying on 9 November, Granville told him that 'the remedy you suggest is too drastic!'[6]

Baring accepted this, albeit with reluctance, and devoted his efforts to persuading the British Government to negotiate with the Powers for an amendment of the Law of Liquidation and for the raising of a loan to enable the Egyptian Government to pay off the Alexandria indemnities and other pressing obligations. In his dealings with the British Government on these financial matters, Baring had to correspond with Childers, the Chancellor of the Exchequer, and with Rivers Wilson, who was Childers' principal adviser on Egyptian affairs. He did not get on well with either of them but, warned by Northbrook not to antagonise Rivers Wilson, he seems to have tried his best. He had already, on 4 November, told Rivers Wilson that it would not be possible to avoid a loan and that the Law of Liquidation would have to be amended.[7] In order to avoid the possibility of additional restrictions and, perhaps, some sort of International Commission of Enquiry into Egyptian finances, he was anxious to avoid asking the Powers for a reduction in the rates of interest fixed in the Law of Liquidation, and recommended instead that the British Government should relieve the Egyptian Treasury of some of the occupation costs and agree to a reduction in the rate of interest on their holding of Suez Canal Shares. As he put it to Childers:[8] 'The real question is, who is to pay—the British taxpayer or the bondholders?' Baring thought that the British taxpayer should do so in view of British strategic interests in Egypt, and in order to avoid further international interference in Egypt's finances. But Childers was unsympathetic and the members of the Cabinet were quite definite that the House of Commons would not look at any proposal for bearing part of the costs of the occupation. A long and somewhat acrimonious correspondence followed, in which Baring frequently complained of the parsimonious attitude of the Treasury, objected to various Treasury proposals for economies and tax increases in Egypt which he regarded as impracticable, and protested against the unwarrantedly optimistic view which Childers was taking about Egyptian finances. Eventually, in April 1884, an International Conference on Egyptian finances was arranged to take place in London at the end of June, and Baring was invited to England to take part in preliminary discussions and in the Conference itself.

Meanwhile, the whole position of affairs in Egypt had been changed by the imminent collapse of the third of the three desiderata—security—which the British intervention in Egypt had been designed to secure.

For about two-and-a-half years rebellion had been raging in the Sudan. The Sudan, meaning in Arabic 'the country of the black people,' was a vast undefined area comprising the African hinterland of Egypt, extending along the valley of the Upper Nile from the second cataract in the north to the Great Lakes in the south, and from the Red Sea coast in the east to the deserts of Darfur in the west.* It had been invaded by Mohamed Ali in 1820 and Egypt had maintained a tenuous hold on it ever since. The country, to about as far south as Latitude 10 N was inhabited by Arabic-speaking Moslems; the rest by savage pagan tribes. Its economic life was largely based on slave-holding, slave-raiding and slave-trading. The Moslem northerners were the slavers and the pagan southerners the victims. Egyptian rule was oppressive in the north and non-existent in the south. The northerners had particularly resented the efforts made by Egypt, under pressure from the Great Powers and from England in particular, to suppress the slave trade. These efforts, which had been pursued with undiscriminating vigour by 'Chinese' Gordon, whom Ismail had appointed as Governor-General of the Sudan from 1877 to 1879, had caused much discontent, particularly among the slave-trading tribes of Baqqara Arabs who inhabited the central Sudan. This discontent, combined with the more generalised discontent caused by Egyptian oppression, ensured widespread support for the rebellion proclaimed at Aba Island, on the White Nile about 200 miles south of Khartum, in May 1881 by Mohamed Ahmed, who announced himself

* See map pp 204—5

as the Mahdi, and proclaimed that 'whosoever doubts my mission does not believe in God or in his Prophets, and whosoever is at enmity with me is an unbeliever and whosoever fights against me will be forsaken and unconsoled in both worlds.'

In the strict theological sense Mahdism has no place at all in the orthodox beliefs of Sunni Islam. It derives from the messianic doctrines of the heretic Shiis, who believe that divine attributes have descended from the Prophet Mohammed by a sort of apostolic succession through a line of Imams, and that either the twelfth of this line (according to the majority of Shiis) or the seventh (according to some Shii sects) has been taken up into Heaven and become the 'hidden Imam' who will one day become manifest on earth as the Mahdi, meaning 'one who guides people aright.' This Shii belief has been popularly adopted in many unsophisticated Sunni Moslem communities and, from time to time in such communities, some local holy man has proclaimed himself the Mahdi, usually as a preliminary to leading a rising against authority. This was the case with Mohammed Ahmed, who had for long enjoyed a local reputation as a holy man. His rising soon became menacing as a result of the oppressiveness, unpopularity, and weakness of Egyptian rule. He raised his standard in Kordofan, west of the White Nile and about 250 miles south-west of Khartum, in the midst of the territory of the warlike Baqqara. He recruited an army by appeals to religious fanaticism and maintained it in a state of fighting fitness by the application of a strict code of religious discipline.

Egyptian ability to deal with the rebellion was limited by financial stringency, by domestic chaos and, finally, by the British occupation and the disbandment of the Egyptian army. By the time of the occupation in September 1882, the Mahdi had defeated two Egyptian forces which had been sent against him, and his army was besieging el-Obeid, the capital of Kordofan, and Sennar, on the Blue Nile, and was in effective occupation of most of the Moslem areas of the country south of Khartum. The Egyptian Government, reconstituted under the British occupation, were determined to crush the rebellion. The British Government, anxious to limit their responsibilities in Egypt, neither vetoed nor assisted this determination. A 'scratch' force of about 10,000 men, raised from the debris of the old Egyptian army, was sent to Khartum under the command of General Hicks, a retired officer of the Indian Army, who, together with a few European ex-officers, was engaged by the Egyptian Government. Hicks' instructions were to seek out and destroy the Mahdi's army in Kordofan and so put an end to the rebellion. He and his army left Khartum on this mission a few days before Baring's arrival in Cairo. A few weeks before he left the rebellion had spread to the Red

Sea coast where Osman Digna, one of the Mahdi's lieutenants, had raised the standard of revolt, was besieging two inland Egyptian garrisons in the area, and was threatening the port of Suakin.

During his first few weeks in Cairo, Baring, preoccupied with pressing financial and other difficulties, seems to have attached comparatively little importance to events in the Sudan, apart from attempts which he made, on Granville's instructions and against French opposition, to obtain for a British syndicate a concession for the construction of a railway between Suakin and Berber. But, on 29 October, he warned Granville that 'the Sudan business will give us a great deal of trouble,' and that although he assumed 'we shall under no circumstances send British troops to the Sudan,' he would have to 'keep in touch with Sudan affairs.'[9] In the same letter, he echoed Sherif Pasha's confidence that Hicks would be able to 'dispose of' the Mahdi and thought that an Englishman should be included in a Commission which Sherif proposed sending to the Sudan to make recommendations for the future administration of that region.

On 22 November news reached Cairo that Hicks' force had been defeated and annihilated in Kordofan. Reports from Khartum indicated that that town was in danger of falling to the Mahdi. In the eastern Sudan two attempts to relieve Tokar and Sinkat, where Egyptian garrisons were being besieged by Osman Digna, had been defeated. Suakin was said to be seriously threatened, and the road between Suakin and Berber, in the Nile Valley, the normal route for the reinforcement of Khartum, was held in force by the rebels. The Egyptian Government were arranging for a force of Gendarmerie, under the command of Valentine Baker, to go to Suakin to defend that port, to relieve Tokar and Sinkat, and to re-open the Suakin-Berber road.

Baring, with the support of the Egyptian Government, recommended an indefinite postponement of the withdrawal of the British garrison from Cairo, to which the Cabinet agreed. He also, on the advice of Generals Stephenson (commanding British forces in Egypt) and Wood (C-in-C of the Egyptian Army), and in the light of Egypt's financial and military situation, pressed upon both the British and Egyptian Governments the necessity for evacuating the whole of the Sudan, with the exception of Suakin, down to Wadi Halfa, and pointed out to Granville that the British would, willy-nilly, have to assume responsibility for the defence of 'Egypt proper' and Suakin.

The Egyptian Government indicated their unwillingness to evacuate the Sudan in accordance with this advice, taking the view that the Sudan was an integral part of Egypt and that its possession was essential to Egypt's security and well-being. But it was clear to Baring, first that

Egypt had neither the financial nor the material forces to defeat the rebellion, and secondly that the British Government were not prepared to supply the deficiency. Even if, *per impossibile*, the British Government were to supply troops, Egypt would have to pay for them, and this Egypt was unable to do. The possibility of asking the Sultan for assistance was canvassed, but the Cabinet considered the prospect unwelcome in so far as it was not illusory. They had no wish again to be pushed into armed intervention as a result of the Sultan's dilatoriness and double-dealing.

On 13 December, Granville, after some hesitation, recommended the Egyptian Government to 'take an early decision to abandon all territory south of Wadi Halfa,' and intimated that the British Government would be 'prepared to assist in maintaining order in Egypt proper and in defending it as well as the ports of the Red Sea.' In view of the Egyptian Government's continued reluctance to accept this recommendation, Baring, on 22 December, cabled Granville asking for authority to inform the Khedive that the British Government insisted on their recommendation for the abandonment of the Sudan being adopted and that 'if the present Ministry will not carry it out he must find others to do so.' In the same telegram he told Granville that, in order to carry out the policy of abandon-ment, 'it would be necessary to send an English officer of high authority to Khartum with full powers to withdraw all the garrisons from the Sudan and to make the best arrangements possible for the future govern-ment of the country.' He also suggested that the Cabinet, before coming to a decision, should consult Mr Cross, the Under Secretary at the India Office, who had been staying in Egypt for the past few weeks, who was arriving in England on Christmas Eve, and with whom Baring had discussed the matter at length.[10]

On the following day Baring, who was obviously not very happy about the prospects of abandonment, and who, in a letter to Granville written on 10 December, had inclined to the view that handing over the Sudan problem to Turkey would be 'the least of three evils,' told Granville: 'I think that the policy of abandonment is on the whole the best, but I am not sure that the extreme difficulty of carrying it out is appreciated at home.'[11]

Baring's telegram of 22 December was circulated to members of the Cabinet, who had plenty of time over the Christmas holiday for con-sidering its implications. It was discussed at a Cabinet meeting held on 3 January, as a result of which two telegrams were sent to Baring on the following day, accepting his recommendations. The first of these telegrams reiterated the British Government's refusal to employ British or Indian troops in the Sudan, but raised no objection either to the use of Turkish troops at Suakin, 'provided that this would not increase the expenditure falling on the Egyptian Treasury or cause the Egyptian Government to delay coming to a decision as to the movements of their troops from the interior of the Sudan,' or to the handing over of the eastern Sudan to Turkey. It stated that the British Government 'do not believe it to be possible for Egypt to defend Khartum,' and urged that 'all military operations excepting those for the rescue of the outlying garrisons' should cease. It promised British assistance for the protection and the defence of 'Egypt proper' north of Wadi Halfa or Aswan. The second telegram laid down the principle that 'in important matters affecting the administration and safety of Egypt the advice of HMG should be followed as long as the provisional occupation lasts. Ministers and Governors must carry out this advice or forfeit their offices.'[12]

Baring had got what he asked for, so far as the immediate crisis was concerned. But the Cabinet's agreement to insist on evacuation had been taken against the advice of Wolseley, the Adjutant-General and their principal military adviser, who considered it militarily impracticable and who advocated British military assistance in order to enable the Egyptians to hold on to the Sudan as far south as Khartum. As a result of Wolseley's advice, Hartington, the Secretary of State for War, and probably some other members of the Cabinet, were doubtful about the evacuation policy. But all, or nearly all, were still wedded to the idea of a speedy withdrawal from Egypt, and realised that this would be delayed by any assumption of responsibility in the Sudan.

No reference was made in the telegrams to Baring's request for 'a British officer of high authority . . . to withdraw all the garrisons . . . and make the best arrangements possible for the future government of the country.' Baring tells us[13] that he was already having second thoughts about this and was no longer in favour of sending any Englishman to Khartum.

The prospect of having to assume the direct administration of Egypt in the event of the Khedive being unable to find anyone to form an Egyptian Ministry must have been a daunting one for the Cabinet, but Cross had told Granville that there was very little risk of this.[14] It therefore must have seemed likely that acceptance of Baring's recommendation was the best way of limiting their responsibilities in Egypt, and of leaving the way open for a speedy withdrawal, although Baring had warned Granville that the evacuation policy, and the consequent necessity for defending Egypt for an indefinite period against a possible Mahdist invasion, would 'involve a considerable increase in the British garrison and delay the prospect of evacuation.'[15]

On 7 January Sherif Pasha and his Government resigned after being informed by Baring of the Cabinet's decision. Nubar Pasha, summoned by the Khedive, agreed without much ado to form a Government, telling Baring that he 'entirely concurred with the wisdom of abandoning the Sudan, retaining possession of Suakin.' He also agreed with Baring that the best person to conduct the evacuation would be, not an English-man, but the new Egyptian Minister of War, Abdul Qadir Pasha, who had previously been a very efficient Governor-General of the Sudan. Abdul Qadir Pasha at first accepted the assignment but, a few days later, changed his mind, on the ostensible ground that announcement of the policy of evacuation, on which Baring was insisting, would convert a difficult task into an impossible one. It seems likely that he chose this ground as a pretext for declining a mission which he came to realise could not successfully be carried out with the means at his disposal. At all events, he seems to have convinced Baring, who may not have fully realised it before, of the very great physical difficulties involved. On 14 January, after discussions with Abdul Qadir, and before Abdul Qadir changed his mind about going to Khartum, he wrote a private letter to Granville, explaining the long distances to be traversed, the scarcity of provisions, the difficulties of navigating the Nile at low water, and the certain expense of the whole operation.[16]

On 16 January, when Abdul Qadir had changed his mind, Baring, after consultation with Nubar, reverted to his request of 22 December, and telegraphed Granville that 'the Egyptian Government would feel obliged if HMG would send at once a qualified British officer to go to Khartum with full powers, military and civil, to conduct the retreat.'[17] It was as the result of this request that General Gordon was sent on his ill-fated mission to Khartum.

As a young man Gordon had gained a great reputation as a guerrilla leader in China. He had had previous experience of the Sudan, having served the Egyptian Government there as Governor of Equatoria Province from 1874 to 1876 and as Governor-General of the Sudan from 1877 to 1879. He had a great reputation, similar to that later enjoyed by T. E. Lawrence, as an eccentric, 'anti-Establishment' figure of genius. On two occasions, at the beginning of December and early in January, just after Nubar had taken office, Granville had proposed to Baring that Gordon should be employed in some undefined capacity in the Sudan. On both occasions Baring, with the concurrence first of Sherif and then of Nubar, had rejected his services. It was only when these services were offered for the third time that he accepted. He tells us that he did so 'against my own judgement and inclination, because I thought that, as everybody differed from me, I must be wrong,' and because he thought that 'I might be unconsciously prejudiced against General Gordon from the fact that his habits of thought and modes of action in dealing with public affairs differed widely from mine. I made a mistake which I shall never cease to regret.'[18]

The Cabinet's choice of Gordon was dictated partly by the pressure of public opinion and partly by the advice of Wolseley, but mainly perhaps because they were deceived by the optimistic views about the Sudanese rebellion expressed and publicised by Gordon himself, who professed to believe that the business could be settled without much bloodshed, difficulty or expense, provided that the whole problem were handed over to him. The Cabinet's almost desperate desire to limit their responsibilities in the Sudan caused them to accept Gordon at his own valuation, and to become the unconscious dupes of the Gordon charisma.

Baring's *ex post facto* explanation is not altogether convincing. When Gordon's services were offered to him by Granville for the third time in a telegram dated 15 January they were offered, not in reply to Baring's request, which was only sent the next day, for an officer to conduct the retreat, but as the result of a proposal by Wolseley that Gordon should go to Suakin to report on the situation in the Sudan. When Granville's telegram arrived in Cairo on 16 January, just after the request for 'a qualified British officer' had been sent off, Baring, for some reason, instead of accepting or rejecting the 'reporting' proposal, replied accepting Gordon as 'the best man to carry out the policy of withdrawal from the Sudan,' provided that he accepted that policy.[19] The truth seems to be that there was no one else available to carry out that policy. Abdul Qadir had declined. There was no other qualified Egyptian. If Baring had refused Gordon it is unlikely that the British Government would have offered anyone else. The implementation of the evacuation policy, on which Baring had successfully insisted, depended on his using Gordon for the purpose, whether he liked it or not.

It is not proposed to follow here in detail the well-known and melancholy story of Gordon's mission to Khartum, or to consider whether or not Gordon disobeyed the instructions which he had been given.[20] Baring afterwards expressed the opinion that Gordon 'threw his instructions to the winds.'[21] There is no evidence from contemporary telegrams or letters that he thought this at the time, although he was frequently exasperated by the discursiveness of, and the inconsistencies in, Gordon's telegrams from Khartum.

Soon after Gordon left Cairo for Khartum at the end of January it became apparent, both to Gordon and to Baring, that some sort of political settlement of the Sudan was a necessary prior condition of the evacuation of Egyptian garrisons and civilians. This involved either an agreement with the Mahdi or the establishment of some effective, if temporary, form of government in opposition to the Mahdi. Since everybody, or almost everybody, including Baring and Gordon, was agreed that the former was impracticable, Baring endeavoured to persuade the Cabinet to accept a proposal urged by Gordon that Zubair Pasha, a great Sudanese magnate and famous slave-dealer, then living in exile in Cairo, should be sent to Khartum with the authority of the British Government, and a subsidy from the Egyptian Government, to succeed Gordon as Governor-General and try and rally sufficient local support to enable him to set up an effective government which would contain the Mahdi in Kordofan and so enable the Egyptians to be evacuated from the rest of the country. In addition, Zubair might be able to establish a semi-independent State in the northern and eastern Sudan which would serve as a 'buffer' between 'Egypt proper' and the territory controlled by the Mahdi. Gordon made this proposal immediately after his arrival in Khartum towards the end of February. It was a considerable derogation from the euphoric prospects which he had publicised just over a month earlier, but it is difficult to reconcile it with Baring's later charge that Gordon 'tried to force the hand of the Government and oblige them to send an expedition to the Sudan.'[22] At the time, Baring supported Gordon's proposal and urged its acceptance on the Cabinet. Gladstone, the Prime Minister, was disposed to accept, but the rest of the Cabinet, frightened by a virtual unanimity of Parliamentary and public opinion, which was up in arms against the proposal on account of Zubair's unsavoury slave-dealing past, would have none of it.

By mid-March, when the Zubair proposal was finally rejected, Gordon was shut up in Khartum. Baker's Gendarmerie had been ignominiously defeated outside Suakin. The tribes along the Nile between Khartum and Berber had joined the rebellion. Telegraphic communication between Cairo and Khartum was cut. A small British expedition sent to Suakin, against the advice of both Baring and Gordon, on Wolseley's mistaken calculation that a token manifestation of force would be sufficient to re-open the Suakin-Berber road, was about to be withdrawn after a couple of inconclusive victories near Suakin, and after the Cabinet, on Wolseley's advice, had refused to agree to its advancing into the interior.

Towards the end of March, Baring pointed out to Granville that a British expeditionary force would now be necessary to extricate Gordon from Khartum. After the Cabinet had rejected his proposal, backed by Generals Stephenson and Wood, that the British force still at Suakin should, in the light of Gordon's precarious position, advance forthwith across the desert to Berber in spite of the risks involved, he proposed that Gordon should be told to try and maintain himself in Khartum until the early Autumn, when climatic conditions and the season of high Nile would enable an expeditionary force to be sent to his relief. But the Cabinet, a majority of whom appear to have been converted to the view, later adopted by Baring, that Gordon was trying to 'force the hand of the Government,' categorically refused to commit themselves to an Autumn expedition.

Hartington, backed by Wolseley, and some other members of the Cabinet, was already becoming convinced of the eventual necessity for a relief expedition. Over the next few months, to the accompaniment of Parliamentary, Press and public agitation, which was stimulated by occasional messages coming through from Gordon expressing his indignation with the Government, a battle was waged in the Cabinet between a growing minority demanding an expedition and a decreasing majority determined not to send one. Eventually, just before Parliament rose for the Summer recess, at the end of July, the minority became a majority and Gladstone reluctantly gave way. The Commons were asked for, and granted, a credit for the preparation of a relief expedition. This was placed under the command of Wolseley who, in opposition to most military opinion, insisted on an expedition via the Nile instead of Suakin-Berber. Thereafter, the matter passed out of the hands of the politicians and into those of the soldiers. The expedition was hampered by a late start, which meant that it missed most of the season of high Nile. It was delayed by Wolseley's insistence on having specially made boats, manned by Canadian boatmen, instead of using indigenous resources. It was hindered by inefficient supply arrangements. In consequence, it was too late. Khartum was taken by storm and Gordon killed on 26 January 1885.

The Cabinet, after initially expressing their determination to recapture Khartum, smash the Mahdi and avenge Gordon, decided in April 1885 to recall the relief expedition and revert to the original policy, recommended by Baring, of withdrawing the Egyptian frontier to Wadi Halfa and maintaining an Egyptian foothold in Suakin and the Red Sea ports. Their decision seems largely to have been influenced by Baring, who developed the case for withdrawal in a long and lucid letter to Granville, which was circulated to the Cabinet.[23] He told him that there was no object in the expedition going on to Khartum and 'smashing the Mahdi' unless it was proposed to establish a settled government in the Sudan. He warned him that, even in the event of withdrawal from the Sudan, the British occupation of Egypt would have to be a long one because of the necessity of defending whatever frontiers were selected from possible incursions by the victorious rebels. But, 'if we are to become responsible for the government of the Sudan, we may at once for all practical purposes abandon any hope of getting away from Egypt at all.'

He went on to point out that an indefinite occupation would almost certainly involve the necessity for a fundamental change in the 'present system of government in Egypt. It is a highly delicate mechanism and its efficient working depends very greatly on the judgement and ability of a few individuals. Its continuance can however be justified if we are able to keep before our eyes the possibility of evacuation, even at a somewhat distant date. If that possibility becomes so remote as to be of no practical account, I really see no object in continuing the present system. It would be better to arrange, if possible with the other Powers, that we should take over the government of the country, guarantee the debt et cetera.' He concluded that they should not attempt to establish a settled government in the Sudan and should in consequence withdraw Wolseley's expeditionary force from that country. He was, however, in favour of extending the Egyptian frontier some few hundred miles up the Nile to include the province of Dongola, which could be administered by a local ruler under Egyptian suzerainty. He realised that this meant a defeat for Egypt and might still necessitate what he was trying to avoid— a quasi-permanent occupation as a result of Egypt's inability to defend itself unaided against the Mahdist regime in the Sudan. But 'I should prefer the permanent occupation by British troops of Egypt without the Sudan to the occupation of Egypt with the Sudan.' He thought that the best solution would be to try to get the Sultan to assume responsibility for the Sudan. He told Granville that this would probably involve the payment of a subsidy to Turkey, and that the British Government would have to pay it, since Egypt could not afford to do so. 'But that would be cheaper than conquering the Sudan with British troops.'

The Cabinet, once the wave of popular indignation over Gordon's death had subsided, and under the cover of a war scare over Russian movements towards the North-West frontier of India, accepted Baring's advice, although they insisted on a withdrawal to Wadi Halfa instead of retaining Dongola.

The British Government's conduct of the Sudan episode had been unsuccessful and discreditable from start to finish. In spite of advice from Colonel Stewart, whom they had sent to the Sudan at the end of 1882 to report on the situation there (and who later accompanied Gordon to Khartum), they had refused to veto the disastrous Hicks expedition and to insist on an Egyptian withdrawal at a time when such an operation was still practicable. When eventually, on Baring's recommendation, they insisted on withdrawal, they did not, in spite of Wolseley's advice, sufficiently consider the military difficulties, and uncritically accepted Gordon's ill-considered assurances that he could arrange everything. When it became clear, as it did very quickly, that he would be unable to do so, they neither recalled Gordon, nor assisted him with troops, nor accepted his (and Baring's) recommendation to send Zubair to Khartum to try to accomplish what he was unable to do himself. Instead, refusing to recognise the fact of Gordon's failure, and inventing the grotesque fiction that Gordon was trying to blackmail them into reconquering the Sudan, they procrastinated until, almost compelled by public opinion, they belatedly sent a relief expedition which arrived too late either to rescue Gordon or to accomplish what he had failed to do.

Baring, as the British Government's Agent, shared much of the public odium for all this. He was blamed by the Jingoes for having advocated withdrawal in the first place. He was compelled by the Cabinet to accept Gordon and then criticised by them for supporting Gordon's recommendations. He was vilified by Gordon and his friends for obstructing Gordon and for influencing the Cabinet against him. In fact, the measure of his responsibility was confined to his successful insistence on withdrawal from the Sudan, which was made within a month of the news of the Hicks disaster being received in Cairo, and to his request for a British officer to conduct the withdrawal. Apart from that, he did his best to promote the success of Gordon's mission as long as there was any possibility of its being successful, and to get the Cabinet to accept the implications of its failure as soon as it became clear that it had failed.

Over the matter of withdrawal, he had no choice. Militarily and financially, the Egyptian Government were unable, unaided, to put down the rebellion. The British Government had refused categorically to assist them to do so, either with arms or with money. The Sultan would probably have been unwilling and unable to do so and the Cabinet, in any case, refused to invite him to do so on any terms which he might conceivably have accepted. (This was the solution which Baring, on the whole, was inclined to favour most.) It was probably a mistake to have asked for a British officer to conduct the withdrawal. Baring regretted his first request, made on 22 December, and did not renew it until 15 January, after Abdul Qadir had refused to go. When he renewed it, it seems that he did so at Nubar's request, and not on his own initiative. Since Nubar had accepted office on the understanding that he would implement the very unpopular British insistence on the abandonment of the Sudan, and since there was no one else in Egypt of comparable stature to Abdul Qadir who might have been able to accomplish it, it would have been difficult to refuse a request of this kind. British insistence on withdrawal imposed some sort of responsibility for assisting in it, and the loan of a British officer to conduct it at the expense of the Egyptian Government was the smallest possible coin with which to acknowledge that responsibility.

Nubar, whose acceptance of office was, in effect, conditional on the problems of finance and the Sudan being handled by the British, might well have resigned if Baring had refused his request. It was desirable to avoid this as it would have presented the British Government with the immediate necessity of assuming the direct government of Egypt. In that sense, the despatch of a British officer on a forlorn hope was a necessary sacrifice to the maintenance of a precarious *status quo*. Baring's reasons for accepting Gordon, whom he did not want, have already been discussed. But here again, he really had no choice. By that time, Gordon's self-promoting activities, and the clamour of popular opinion, had eliminated anyone else from serious consideration. If Baring had had the choice, he would probably have chosen Colonel Stewart, whom Dufferin had sent on a reporting mission to the Sudan at the end of 1882 and who subsequently accompanied Gordon as Military Secretary. Writing to Granville on 7 January, the day of Sherif's resignation, he told him that he might ask for Stewart 'for temporary Sudan work.'[24]

One important effect of the Sudan business was to secure a general acceptance of the fact that the British occupation would have to be measured in terms of years rather than months. There was already a growing body of opinion in England, represented strongly in the Press, in favour of annexation. As early as October 1883 Baring had complained to Granville that 'the English Press are almost 100 per cent pro-bondholders and anti-withdrawal.'[25] And, in April 1884, Granville told Baring: 'There is an immense and powerful combination to force us into a more exclusive administration of Egypt—the bondholders, businessmen, the English and foreign Press, the Tories and the Jingoes.'[26] The annexationists were variously motivated. Business and financial interests thought that existing investments could best be secured, and future investments best promoted, by annexation. Many imperialists and progressives—and the two terms were not at that time mutually exclusive—thought that the interests of the Egyptian masses would be best served by sweeping away the discredited apparatus of Khedives and Pashas and by the introduction of effective reforms under direct British administration. The Jingoes simply wanted to paint more of the map red. The Cabinet, conscious of the international, financial and military embarrassments involved in the occupation, were still anxious to withdraw but, apart from being affected by the climate of public opinion, were impressed by Baring's frequent expositions of the difficulties in the way of doing so. Baring, writing to Granville on 3 January 1884, and warning him of the probability of Sherif's resignation over the Sudan question, mentioned a period of five years: 'I do not think there is the smallest chance of our getting away in a shorter time'—and suggested that some announcement be made to this effect.[27] The Cabinet did not agree to this, but they seem tacitly to have accepted Baring's view.

The British Government's other preoccupations in Egypt—reforms and finance—continued concurrently with the Sudan imbroglio and were in many ways intensified by it. Nubar's assumption of office led to some difficulties over the reforms. In the circumstances, his position was a strong one vis-à-vis the British. His resignation would have presented them with the problem, which they were anxious to avoid, of administering Egypt directly. He was prepared to cooperate in maintaining the *status quo*, and to give the British a free hand over finances and the Sudan. He was, as Baring remarked, 'penetrated with the idea that Nubar's bread is buttered on the English side, and not on the French, Turkish, or any other.'[28] His principal disadvantage was that, as an Armenian and a Christian, he was very much disliked by the old Turkish ruling class who, Baring told Granville[29] 'hate Nubar worse than they do us, which is saying a great deal.' But, for the time being, Nubar was all-but-essential to the British, and he was astute enough to realise it and to drive a hard bargain. The essence of the bargain was that, in return for giving the British a free hand over finance, defence and international relations, he should himself be given a free hand in Egyptian domestic affairs. This immediately brought up the question of the reforms.

The resultant difficulties were accentuated by the fact that Baring and Nubar did not get on very well together. Their previous relationships had not been very cordial. As Commissioner of the Caisse in 1878 Baring had disapproved of the close alliance between Nubar and Rivers Wilson. Later, as Controller-General, he had suspected Nubar of intriguing against Riaz and the Dual Control. He was irritated by Nubar's temperamental nature and his frequent '*crises des nerfs*.' He underestimated Nubar's remarkable intellectual and political capacity, and had an exaggerated mistrust of him. He told Granville: 'He is no administrator, he has no courage, and I don't believe what he says.'[30]

The difficulties became concentrated on reforms in the Ministries of the Interior and Justice. Clifford Lloyd, who had come to Egypt in September 1883 to supervise reforms in the Ministry of the Interior, had been made Under Secretary at the Ministry on the formation of the Nubar administration. Sir Benson Maxwell had been appointed Procureur-Général of the new Native Courts. The reforms which these two officials had the task of inaugurating, implementing and supervising were all, or almost all, designed, in Baring's words, 'to afford protection to the people against the arbitrary rule of the Government,' and, as such, had the tendency still further to weaken the authority of the Government. But they had been warmly advocated by Dufferin and endorsed by the Cabinet, and British officials had been imposed on the Egyptian Government to ensure that they were carried out.

Specifically, the object of the new Native Courts was to substitute, over a fairly wide area, the judicial authority of the Courts for the executive authority of the provincial Governors. Baring thought that 'it was not possible to reform things in such a desperate hurry' and that 'we shall certainly have to make some changes.'[31] He regretted that he had arrived in Egypt too late to prevent the new Code from being promulgated in its existing form. The reforms at the Interior, which Clifford Lloyd was trying to implement, consisted of police, sanitary and prison reorganisa, tion, and the establishment of municipalities in the principal towns. All might have been negotiable if the two British reformers concerned had been less inflexible. As it was, they quarrelled with each other over the respective attributes of the police and the Courts, and with their respective Ministers and with Nubar over the extent of their own powers. Baring, who described Lloyd as 'a bull in an administrative china shop,' and who complained of Maxwell's 'irascibility and unjudicial fervour,' tried to keep the peace. But he eventually came to the conclusion that Lloyd, at all events, would have to go. Just before he left for England in mid-April 1884 he wrote: 'I cannot carry him on my back much longer ... Lloyd is convinced that we must assume the direct government of Egypt sooner or later. He may be right, but that is not the policy of HMG ... We must get rid of Lloyd without allowing Nubar to sing paeans of victory.' He added that 'Maxwell is only one degree less impracticable than Lloyd, and again, it is not so much his opinions as his methods of enforcing them.'[32]

The problem of getting rid of them both was facilitated by their own obstreperous and tactless behaviour. Lloyd made the mistake of addressing direct to Granville a complaint against Nubar and, by implication, against Baring. Baring, who had just arrived in England, was not pleased. At a Cabinet meeting held early in May it was decided, on Baring's advice, that Lloyd would have to go in order to avoid the risk of Nubar's resigning. And so Lloyd went. Two months later Maxwell resigned. Baring, on his return to Egypt in September, told Granville: 'There is much less friction between British officials and the native Government, due largely to the removal of Lloyd and Maxwell.'[33] For the next three years reforms at the Ministries of Interior and Justice were shelved and Nubar allowed to do much as he liked in these Departments of State. There were other, more urgent, matters to attend to.

There was no trouble with Nubar over the other reforms. Baring successfully insisted that the new Egyptian Army being raised under the command of Sir Evelyn Wood should not be used for operations in the Sudan until it had been properly trained. The irrigation reforms instituted by Colonel Scott Moncrieff, who had been made Under Secretary in the

Ministry of Public Works in the Nubar administration, and who had recruited a team of some half-dozen British irrigation engineers from India, were welcomed by Nubar, who got on well with Moncrieff and was interested in his plans.[34]

Thus, by the early Autumn of 1884, a *modus vivendi* had been arrived at between Baring and Nubar over the domestic administration of Egypt. Baring told Granville in June 1885 that 'since Clifford Lloyd left I have hardly ever intervened in matters of internal administration.'[35] But no progress had been made with the financial problem, or with the various international questions bound up with it.

As has been related, Baring, in April 1884, in the middle of all the alarms and excursions over Gordon in Khartum on the one hand and Clifford Lloyd in Cairo on the other, was summoned to London to take part in an International Conference on Egyptian finances. He was not anxious for a Conference but, since the Cabinet had refused either to guarantee a loan or to give Egypt sufficient financial assistance to enable her to continue paying the annuities laid down in the Law of Liquidation, it had become necessary to seek the assistance of the Powers both in raising a loan and in obtaining some amendment to the Law of Liquidation. On 19 April Granville, on the basis of information and recommendations supplied by Baring, addressed a Circular to the Porte and the five Great Powers setting out the current financial situation of Egypt and proposing: (a) an amendment to the Law of Liquidation giving the Egyptian Government freedom to deal with any surpluses arising either from the 'affected' or 'non-affected' parts of the revenue; and (b) an internationally guaranteed loan of £8 million in order to pay the Alexandria indemnities, and the floating debt, representing the accumulated deficits of the last three years, and to enable a credit of £1 million to be opened for irrigation works for the purpose of improving the productive capacity of the country. This Circular was followed by a series of informal conversations between the British and French Governments which dealt both with the financial problem and with the wider political aspects of the British occupation. On the financial side the French indicated that they would only agree to the British proposals provided that the powers of the Caisse were extended to include some supervision over the 'non-affected' parts of the Budget. On the political side the French undertook that, in the event of a British withdrawal from Egypt, they would not themselves attempt to occupy the country without prior discussion with the British Government, and proposed that an engagement to this effect should be included in an agreement between the two Governments, in which the British Government should agree to evacuate Egypt within a fixed period, 'which would not be prolonged

without a fresh consultation of the Powers.' In reply the British Government stated that they were willing that the withdrawal of British troops
should take place at the beginning of 1888, 'provided that the Powers are
then of opinion that such withdrawal can take place without risk to
peace and order.'

Baring, who was in England, kept a watchful and jealous eye on these
conversations. He secured the rejection of the French demand for an
increase in the powers of the Caisse and vigorously protested against the
proposed commitment to withdraw from Egypt in 1888. He told Granville
on 30 May: 'If I understand rightly, HMG is about to take an engagement
to evacuate Egypt at the beginning of 1888 unless, when the time arrives,
the Powers consider it desirable that the occupation should be prolonged.
I think this arrangement is open to great objection.' He pointed out that
he had already told the Cabinet that 'five years was the lowest period
which could be named with any degree of safety' and that 'under the new
arrangement' they would be forced to leave in 1888, whether they wanted
to or not, if the Powers insisted. He warned Granville that 'in Egypt the
effect will be to destroy confidence in the prospect of maintaining a stable
government.'[36] Whether or not as the result of Baring's protest, the
British Government's expression of willingness to withdraw in 1888 was
never formalised into an agreement.

The financial Conference met on 28 June and broke up on 3 August
without reaching any agreement. Lord Granville presided, and Childers,
the Chancellor of the Exchequer, and Baring were among the British
delegates. Among the French delegates was de Blignières, Baring's old
colleague on the Caisse, the Commission of Enquiry, and the Dual
Control. There was a certain unreality about the deliberations of the
Conference. Ostensibly it was concerned with the financial minutiae of
Egypt's revenue and expenditure. Actually it was engaged in an intricate
political manoeuvre in which the British delegation was trying to reduce,
and the French delegation trying to increase, the existing extent of international control over Egypt's finances. In this manoeuvre the French
delegation was supported by the delegates of Germany, Austria-Hungary
and Russia. The Italian delegation remained on the sidelines.[37] The
British Government's state of isolation and estrangement from the Powers
in the matter of Egypt was thus grimly exposed.

After the Conference had broken up, the Cabinet asked Lord
Northbrook, First Lord of the Admiralty, to go to Egypt as a 'Special
Commissioner' to 'report and advise HMG as to what counsel they should
offer the Egyptian Government in the present state of affairs,' with special
reference to 'the present exigencies of Egyptian finance.'[38] It seems likely
that this appointment was no more than a device, dear to most Govern-

The ceremonial opening of the Aswan Dam, 10 December 1902

General view of the Aswan Dam

Lord Cromer arriving at the Abdin Palace to present the Order of the Bath to
the Khedive, 29 December 1892

Queen's Birthday Parade at Cairo—British troops saluting the flag, 4 May 1899

ments, and particularly to Mr Gladstone's Government, for shelving a decision on a difficult and contentious matter in the hope that it will eventually, in some sort, solve itself. As Baring later remarked: 'There was really little about which to report' since 'the main facts with which the Government had to deal were patent to all the world.'[39] But the appointment was in some respects welcome to Baring. He was related to, and intimate with, Northbrook. He had served as his Private Secretary in India and had a great deal of influence over him. After the breakdown of the London Conference he undoubtedly hoped to be able to use Northbrook to impose upon the Cabinet his own solution of the Egyptian problem, which he had adumbrated to Granville a year before, but which Granville had rejected as being 'too drastic.'

The two men, accompanied by Wolseley, who was going out to command the Gordon relief expedition, left England for Egypt together at the beginning of September, arriving in Cairo on 9 September.

The financial situation was becoming desperate. There was no money to pay the Alexandria indemnities. The Sudan rebellion was adding to the Government's expenses. No agreement had been reached about the taxation of foreigners. The English Treasury insisted on exacting its pound of flesh over the occupation expenses and the Suez Canal interest. Pending an arrangement for a loan it had been necessary to borrow £1 million from Rothschilds. One major difficulty was caused by the stipulation embodied in the Law of Liquidation by which any surpluses on the 'affected' revenue had to be paid into the Caisse and devoted to a reduction of the funded debt. The regular deficits on the Daira and Domains revenues allocated to the service of the loans raised on the security of these estates had to be made up from the 'non-affected' revenue at the disposal of the Egyptian Treasury. This created an absurd situation in which the Egyptian Treasury had to increase its floating debt in order to decrease its funded debt. In an attempt to remedy this, Northbrook, urged by Baring, and Vincent, the Financial Adviser, advised the Egyptian Government only to pay to the Caisse enough of the 'affected' revenue to meet the service of the funded debt and to pay the rest into the Treasury. The foreseeable result was that the Caisse sued the Egyptian Government in the Mixed Courts and, on 15 December, obtained judge-ment for payment to them of the moneys so diverted.

Meanwhile, towards the end of November, Northbrook had com-pleted his investigations and returned to England. His financial recom-mendations were very similar to those which Baring had pressed on Granville a year previously and which Granville had rejected as being 'too drastic.' It seems fairly certain that they were inspired almost entirely by Baring. 'The hand was the hand of Esau but the voice was the voice of Jacob.' He accepted two principal points about Egyptian finance which Baring had been trying in vain to impress on Childers: (1) that all previous estimates about Egyptian finances had been too optimistic both as regards maximum maintainable revenue and minimum necessary expenditure; and (2) that a greater measure of autonomy in the management of revenue and expenditure was a *sine qua non* of the rehabilitation of Egyptian finances. He estimated the maintainable revenue at £E8,910,000 p.a. and minimum expenditure at £E4,708,000, excluding the cost of occupation troops, which he recommended should be fixed at a maximum of £E160,000 p.a. based on an occupation strength of 4,000. With the service of the debt, at existing rates of interest, costing £E3,915,000 p.a., this left a nominal surplus of £E160,000 p.a. which, as he pointed out, was 'obviously insufficient' for the servicing of the new loan which was necessary.

He recommended (a) that the British Government should guarantee a loan of £8·7 million, secured on the Domains and Daira estates, to pay off the Alexandria indemnities and accumulated deficits and enable a sum of £1 million to be spent on irrigation projects over the next five years; (b) that the existing Daira and Domains loans should be added to the funded debt and any deficits met out of 'affected' revenue; (c) that all surpluses, whether on 'affected' or 'non-affected' revenue, should be at the disposal of the Egyptian Government, which would be responsible for meeting any deficits. Northbrook concluded that 'Egypt, when any danger of attack from without has ceased to exist, when her fiscal system has been improved and her resources developed, will be able to meet the cost of her administration and the service of her debt, provided that she is set free from the trammels which now hamper the action of the Government, increase the cost of the administration and diminish the resources of the country.' He acknowledged that the effect of his proposals would 'undoubtedly be to substitute the financial control of England for the international control which was proposed at the Conference.'

In a general report Northbrook recommended an immediate reduction of the army of occupation to a strength of 4,000, but expressed the 'decided opinion that it would not be safe or wise to fix any definite time' for its entire withdrawal. He assumed that 'a prompt settlement' of the finances would be effected 'through the instrumentality of HMG so that the difficulties in which the country is now placed may cease and the salutary influence of HMG be sustained.'[40]

Baring had high hopes, and indeed good reason to believe, that Northbrook's recommendations, which were to all intents and purposes his own, would be implemented. Northbrook was a senior member of the Cabinet who had been delegated by his colleagues, and his recommendations might be expected to carry weight. He wrote to Granville on 10 November urging a prompt consideration of Northbrook's financial Report and warned him that 'unless a solution is found which will deal promptly with the financial situation there will be local discontent and disappointment, (but) . . . if only the financial trouble is solved our main Egyptian troubles will be at an end.'[41] On the assumption that North-brook's financial recommendations would be accepted, he was not too worried about the Caisse's lawsuit, nor at demands being made by the Russian and German Governments for the representation of their countries on the Caisse, and the consequent prospect of 'six gentlemen all doing nothing at high salaries and with plenty of leisure for intrigue.'

But Northbrook's proposals ran into difficulties with the Cabinet, who were frightened of the reactions of the Powers, frightened of reactions in the Commons to the proposal for a guaranteed loan, and frightened of the implications of a prolongation of the occupation. Baring himself had told Childers eight months previously that he could not recommend a British-guaranteed loan because 'it would involve England virtually ruling Egypt for the next fifty years.'[42] Eventually, mainly as a result of the insistence of Childers, who was supported by Gladstone, North-brook's proposals were rejected, and the Treasury devoted themselves to negotiating an agreed settlement with the Powers with the object of arranging for an internationally guaranteed loan and some immediate relief from the provisions of the Law of Liquidation. Granville told Baring that he would 'have been glad if Northbrook's proposal had been carried,' but explained that 'the House of Commons members (of the Cabinet) were almost unanimous that it could not be put through the House.'[43]

This was the same reason which Granville had given Baring for the rejection of his recommendation about Zubair, and Baring was getting rather tired of it. Brought up in the Anglo-Indian tradition of benevolent autocracy, he was impatient of the restraints imposed by what he once described as the 'fitfulness and impulsiveness' of parliamentary democracy. But there was more to it than that. He suspected, probably correctly, that Granville was using the Commons to excuse the indecision and pusillanimity of the Cabinet themselves. He told him that the Khedive and Nubar were 'very discouraged at the reception given by HMG' to Northbrook's recommendations, and added that he too was 'getting discouraged at the way the whole business has been treated. It is uphill work to be obliged always to *faire bonne mine à mauvais jeu*. Northbrook's mission was an excellent idea and really gave us a good opportunity if we had only acted promptly and decisively, but it seems to me that we have thrown our opportunity away.'[44]

In this mood of discouragement Baring resumed his acrimonious correspondence with the Treasury, broken off the previous April, about the bases of a settlement with the Powers. As a result of negotiations in Paris, execution of the Caisse's judgement was postponed in anticipation of such a settlement. Eventually Baring gave a reluctant assent to a draft Convention which was ratified by the Powers and, on 18 March 1885, embodied in the London Convention.[45] The terms of this Convention provided: (1) for the raising of an internationally guaranteed loan of £9,424,000 at 3 per cent to produce a net sum of £9 million for the payment of the Alexandria indemnities, for the covering of accumulated deficits for the years 1882–85, and for the provision of £1 million for irrigation works. In order to service this loan an annual sum of £315,000 was added to the sums already payable to the Caisse for the service of the funded debt; (2) for various amendments to the Law of Liquidation; (a) that any Egyptian Government expenditure authorised by the Caisse over and above the proceeds of the 'non-affected' revenue could be financed out of any surpluses on the 'affected' revenue after paying the service of the funded debt; (b) that any surpluses after meeting the debt service plus 'authorised' additional expenditure should be divided equally between the Egyptian Government and the Caisse; (c) that the interest on the funded debt for the years 1885 and 1886 should be reduced by $\frac{1}{20}$ on condition that, if the full rates of interest could not be resumed in 1887, an International Commission should be set up to conduct a general enquiry into Egyptian finances; (d) for the abolition of the sinking fund provisions of the Law of Liquidation; (e) for the addition of German and Russian representatives to the membership of the Caisse.

The effect of the Convention was to provide Egypt with some immediate and necessary relief from the tight financial strait-jacket of the Law of Liquidation at the expense of a considerable increase in the powers of the Caisse and the prospective threat of an international Commission of Enquiry. Writing two years later to Goschen, who was Chancellor of the Exchequer in Salisbury's Conservative Government, Baring told him that his difficulties over finance had been 'greatly increased by the unwise provisions made in the Convention under which a rigid limit was fixed to expenditure.' He told him that he had protested as strongly as he could 'against this cumbersome method of ensuring economy which puts us at the mercy of the French. But the Treasury would not listen to me.'[46]

At the time, he put the best face he could on it. He told Granville: 'I cannot say that I like the financial arrangement, but we must try to make the best of it. I hope the Treasury will not be too exacting.'[47] He stressed the necessity for 'doing everything possible to resume payment of interest in two years' in order to avoid an International Commission. 'Nubar believes that it is impossible. I am not so despondent, although I much fear we shall be swamped by Sudan expenses.' He added that Nubar was very discouraged and that 'he must be prevented from resigning as there is no one to take his place. Great kindness and a good deal of flattery are what he requires.'[48]

In the event, over the next two years, Vincent, the Financial Adviser, spurred on by Baring, successfully employed all his considerable financial ingenuity to enable the payment of the full rate of interest on the funded debt to be resumed in 1887, thus avoiding the threatened enquiry. In this successful struggle, the £1 million obtained out of the London Convention for irrigation, which had been Baring's own idea, and for which he had resolutely pressed, was an essential factor because of the contribution which it made to increased productivity. Another essential factor was the withdrawal from the Sudan, which took place a few weeks after the signature of the Convention.

The hostile attitude of the Powers, and particularly of France, made it probable that the increased powers and membership of the Caisse, conferred by the London Convention, would be exploited to the maximum possible extent for the embarrassment of the Egyptian Government. The other international servitudes with which Egypt was bound were already being exploited to the same end. The cumbersome international Boards administering the railways, the Daira and the Domains had been left untouched by the London Convention. The regular deficits of the Daira and Domains still had to be made good by the Egyptian Government out of the 'non-affected' revenue. A fixed proportion of railway receipts still had to be paid into the Caisse as part of the 'affected' revenue irrespective of the capital and maintenance requirements of the railways. An International Judicial Commission, convened in Cairo the previous year, had failed to agree over any modification in the powers of the Mixed Courts. The foreign privileges acquired under the Capitulations were still being insisted on as jealously as ever.

One particular instance of this in the Spring of 1885 gave Baring a great deal of trouble and once more brought Nubar to the brink of resignation. *Bosphore Egyptien* was a French-owned, French-language newspaper published and circulating in Egypt. Ever since the British occupation it had violently denounced the Egyptian Government and the British occupiers. In February 1885, the Egyptian Government, on Baring's advice and under the authority of a Press Law promulgated in 1881, issued a Decree suppressing the paper on the ground of its being prejudicial to public order. On the advice of Barrère, the French Consul-General, who maintained that the Law of 1881 had no application to foreigners, the Editor of *Bosphore* ignored the Decree of suppression and continued to publish. The Egyptian Government took no action until April 1885 when *Bosphore* published, in French and Arabic, a proclamation by the Mahdi calling on the people of Egypt to rise in rebellion. The Egyptian Government thereupon, after consultation with Baring, and after advising Barrère of what they were about to do, in order to give him an opportunity of being present, raided the building in which *Bosphore* was printed and shut down the printing press. There followed a storm of protest from Barrère, from the French colony in Egypt, and from the French Government in Paris. The French position was that, under the usages which had grown up under the Capitulations, a domiciliary search of the premises of a foreign national could only be carried out with the concurrence of that national's Consul, which concurrence had not been given and had, in fact, been expressly withheld. There were long exchanges between the British and French Governments which resulted in Nubar having to apologise to Barrère for a technical breach of the Capitulations, in the Editor of *Bosphore* promising to behave in future, and in the French Government undertaking not to oppose the promulgation of a new Press Law applicable to foreigners. In the event, *Bosphore* ceased publication for a time, but then reappeared with its tone more or less unchanged, and nothing was done about a new Press Law. Faces were more or less saved all round and Granville told Baring that 'we are well out of it.'[49] But neither Baring nor Nubar were happy and the incident accentuated the pessimism which Baring was feeling at the time. In a bitter outburst against the French he told Granville that 'the French colony in Egypt contains some of the most unscrupulous blackguards it has ever been my fortune to come across.' He complained that Barrère, the French Consul-General, had 'performed no single act of any kind which proves a wish to put matters on a more friendly footing.'[50] He was still sore about the rejection of Northbrook's financial proposals. He was annoyed about the Cabinet's insistence on withdrawing from Dongola and complained: 'Why does the Government always go to extremes? At one moment we are to go on to Khartum and reconquer the whole country, and then, almost before we can turn round, we are told to scuttle out of the whole country as fast as we can.'[51]

Baring had no illusions about the unpopularity of the occupation. 'I do not think it is so much the presence of the army of occupation as the employment of Europeans rather than natives in administrative capacities.'[52] He complained of British officials wanting to resign because they could not always get their own way.[53] He realised that the Khedive and Nubar were unpopular with all classes.[54] But 'the more I see of the working of the present system the more clear does it become to me that it depends entirely on the personalities of three individuals—the Khedive, the Prime Minister and the British Agent. Of these the last is in some respects the least important, as plenty of men could be found to do my work. But there is no one to replace Nubar. He is getting on, he is rich, he is disappointed at the turn things have taken. I do not think he would cling to office. He is between the devil and the deep blue sea. The Khedive and all the Pashas detest him but think him indispensable.' He went on to compare Nubar's position in Egypt with that which Disraeli had occupied in the Tory Party. Both were regarded as detestable but indispensable. He thought that 'it would take very little to upset the whole thing.'[55]

It was in this mood that Baring received, in the middle of June, news of the fall of Mr Gladstone's Government. Granville told him: 'I now understand the feelings of a stage coach horse unharnessed at the end of a hilly stage.'[56] Baring, as one of Granville's passengers, may have shared his feelings of relief. He still professed himself a Liberal,[57] but twenty months of service under a Liberal Government had given him an abiding dislike of Gladstonian Liberalism, which he was apt to translate into a dislike of parliamentary democracy. In his correspondence with Granville over Zubair he had told him: 'I venture to think that any attempt to settle Egyptian questions by the light of English popular opinion is sure to be productive of harm, and in this as in other cases it would be prefer-able to follow the advice of responsible authorities on the spot.'[58] He was continually irritated by Granville's pleas about the necessity for consulting Parliamentary or public opinion. He probably realised, but certainly despised, the necessity in which the Liberal Government found themselves of having to try to reconcile contradictory strands of opinion within their own Party. He detested what he regarded as Mr Gladstone's evasiveness, his refusal to face unwelcome facts, his obstinacy, and his insincerity, and he regarded his Government as having been infected with all these defects. He was contemptuous of what he regarded as that Government's mishandling of foreign affairs which, as he saw it, resulted in almost unanimous international opposition to the British occupation.

This attitude was, to a large extent, a natural reaction from the frustrations attendant on his first two difficult years in Egypt. Later on, he learnt to accept, to work within, and to get most of what he wanted in spite of, the limitations imposed by parliamentary democracy in England, by international servitudes in Egypt, and by Great Power rivalries in Europe. He may even, over the years, and without realising it, have learnt something from Nubar, who had twenty years' experience of international politics.

During his first two years in Egypt Baring laboured under difficulties over and above those imposed by the political situation and by working under political masters with whom he felt less and less in sympathy. The Agency was inadequately staffed. For his first few months he did not even have a shorthand writer. Until the arrival of Mr Egerton in March 1884 he had no trained diplomat to assist him. He received frequent rebukes from London for the cost of his telegraph bills. His office and residential accommodation were inadequate. He told Granville in February that, when he put up Lord and Lady Ripon in the British Agency, he had to send his children to an hotel, that he had to turn out of his office whenever they gave a party, and that one of his Chancery staff had to be accommodated in his drawing-room. In these circum-stances he was very much overworked and without the feeling of very much positive achievement to sustain him. There are frequent signs of acerbity in his official and demi-official correspondence. His judgement of individuals was often unwarrantably harsh. Scott Moncrieff, the irrigation engineer, and one of the two or three most important British officials in Egypt, writing at the end of December 1883, described him as 'a rough, rude sort of fellow, but a strong, able man,[59] and suggested that he would 'be a far greater success if he had just a little *suaviter in modo*.'[60] He received the nickname of 'Over-Baring.'

His career in Egypt was still in the balance. In England the Jingoes regarded him as having been partly responsible for the Gordon débâcle, the Radicals were inclined to regard him as an incipient annexationist, and the Conservatives, who were about to come into office, looked at him askance as a professed Liberal. The British officials in Egypt were irritated with him for curbing their reforming zeal and considered that he was insufficiently sympathetic to them in their numerous differ-ences of opinion with the Egyptian authorities. The British business community in Egypt thought he was insufficiently devoted to their interests and unenthusiastic about safeguarding their privileges. His *alliance de convenance* with Nubar was an uneasy one, neither appreciating the other's considerable qualities. If things went wrong—if Nubar should resign, if there were another *Bosphore* incident, or some Press agitation inspired by someone on whose corns he had trodden, if he let himself go in his correspondence with Salisbury as he had sometimes with Granville—it was quite possible that he might be replaced. All his political connections were with the Liberal Party which had just gone out of office. And, unlike his predecessor, Malet, he was no career diplomat who could be kicked upstairs into the dignity of a Legation at Brussels or the Hague.

6

THE DRUMMOND
WOLFF NEGOTIATIONS

THE EUROPEAN SITUATION, as seen by Salisbury on his assumption of office as Prime Minister and Foreign Secretary in June 1885, is described thus by Lady Gwendolen Cecil in her biography of her father:

'Turkey had been finally lost as a dependent ally . . . and the extinction of our paramountcy at Constantinople had deprived England of all solid basis for further interference. France had been alienated by the Egyptian adventure, while . . . the quarrel which Liberal statesmen had fastened upon Austria in their anxiety to dissociate themselves from the anti-Russian policy had as its result the conversion of Russia's latent into active hostility. This adapted itself to the fundamental aim of Bismarck's policy. The Austro-German alliance of 1879 and the adhesion of Italy to the Triple Alliance three years later had been a counsel of despair and he had reverted to the Dreikaiserbund policy with British interests as the sacrificial offering. He had recommended the Sultan to close the Dardanelles in the event of a war between England and Russia . . . The Russians had substituted India for Constantinople as the inspiration of their dreams and Central Asia for the Balkans. Jules Ferry had proposed to Bismarck that a truce should be called at British expense; Bismarck, irritated by colonial differences with England, had agreed and offered diplomatic support for France against England in Egypt.'[1]

So Salisbury was anxious to mend diplomatic fences with Germany, and to get out of Egypt, which he regarded as an 'incubus' which exposed England to German blackmail. Therefore, although 'the more ardent spirits of his Party would have welcomed annexation,' and although Bismarck, who was anxious to embroil England with France, continued to advise it, Salisbury was opposed to annexation and wanted to get out of Egypt as soon as possible. But he was convinced that England 'should not leave Egypt until we had restored to her a solvent and matured administration and a settled frontier and, in leaving her, we must ensure as against other Powers those Imperial interests involved in her geographical position . . . The assertion of this claim and the provision of conditions under which it could be maintained were thus the immediate requirements of his policy . . . The restoration of the Sudan must wait.'²

To this end, Salisbury, a very few weeks after assuming office, sent Sir Henry Drummond Wolff, a Conservative MP and an associate of Lord Randolph Churchill and his Fourth Party, to Constantinople as 'Envoy Extraordinary and Minister Plenipotentiary' to negotiate with the Porte over Egypt. In his official instructions Drummond Wolff was told: 'The general object of your mission will be to secure for this country the amount of influence which is necessary for its own imperial interests and, subject to that condition, to provide for a strong and efficient Egyptian Government as free as possible from interference . . . There is a growing impression that the influence of England has been injured and the cause of true progress in Egypt arrested by the precipitancy with which an Oriental population has been compelled to accept reforms conceived in the spirit of Western institutions.' He was told that it was necessary to maintain 'a strict observance of the various international agreements binding on the Khedive,' and not to 'give the Khedive the slightest reason for apprehending that HMG are wavering in their deter-mination to support him.'³

In a private letter to Drummond Wolff dated 13 August Salisbury was rather more specific. 'The end to which I would work is evacuation, but with certain private reservations, e.g. a Treaty right to reoccupy Alexandria when we pleased and predominant control of the Egyptian railways. These terms may be hard to obtain but I would not cut myself off from them until the state of Europe has cleared up. If we come back strong from the Elections, and if we can persuade Germany to go with us . . . I do not see my way to bind myself to a fixed date for evacuation. I am quite content that the Turks should be there as long as we are. Nor would I pledge myself to obtain the formal consent of the Powers to anything we do. I quite agree in objecting either to annexation or to international control.'⁴ In a private letter to Sir Augustus Paget, British Ambassador at Vienna, written at about the same time, Salisbury told him: 'We are anxious to get Turkish soldiers to Egypt for convenience and for a political reason . . . We cannot fix a date for leaving Egypt. If we did so, or talked of leaving soon, we should make ourselves power-less for all purposes of internal government and reform. But we wish to give a token that we harbour no intention at variance with the Treaty of Paris. Turkish troops will regularise our position. They will not really interfere with our power. Whether we shall be able to get over Turkish apathy and French jealousy remains to be seen, but we want what assistance Austria can give.'⁵

Baring was on holiday in Austria when Drummond Wolff went to Constantinople in August. He wrote to Salisbury from Austria in the middle of September, telling him: 'It would be a great point if Wolff can really negotiate a satisfactory arrangement with the Porte and, even if he fails, it was no doubt quite right to try. It is impossible to feel sanguine that he will succeed . . . nor am I sanguine as to winning the battle against internationalism in Egypt, although it is not yet lost . . . The movement in this direction began after the break-up of the Confer-ence *without* a distinct declaration of policy by HMG, and was greatly accelerated by the break-down of the Northbrook mission. I doubt whether so good an opportunity of settling the whole question will occur again. The conclusion of the financial Convention, much as I disagree with many of its details, gave us a breathing space . . . (We must) take advantage of any events which may occur in European politics in 1886 to settle the Egyptian question.'[6] It is apparent from this letter that Baring had only a limited enthusiasm for the Drummond Wolff mission.

In October 1885, after two months' negotiation, Drummond Wolff signed a preliminary Convention in Constantinople, which was ratified by the Sultan in November. By the terms of this Convention, British and Turkish High Commissioners were to be sent to Egypt to discuss with the Khedive 'arrangements for the reorganisation of the Egyptian Army and for any necessary changes in the civil administration.' The Convention also provided that the Turkish High Commissioner should discuss with the Khedive arrangements for the re-establishment of order in the Sudan, with the proviso that nothing in this respect should be decided without the consent of the British High Commissioner, the Sudan being regarded as 'an integral part of the general settlement of the affairs of Egypt.' Finally, it was provided in the Convention that, as soon as the two High Commissioners had satisfied themselves of the security of the Egyptian frontiers and the stability of the Egyptian Government, their respective Governments would proceed to negotiate a second Convention providing for the evacuation of Egypt by British troops.[7]

Most of this preliminary Convention was window-dressing. The real point at issue was the evacuation of British troops. The British Govern-ment were still anxious to evacuate, provided that they could leave a reasonably stable situation behind them, and provided that they had a recognised right of re-entry in the event of that stability being subsequently threatened. The Porte wished for a reassertion of the Sultan's suzerainty over Egypt which recent events had whittled down almost to nothing. Nobody really believed that the presence of a Turkish High Com-missioner could make any contribution either to a reorganisation of the

Egyptian Army, or to a settlement of the Sudan, or to an improvement in the civil administration.

As a result of this preliminary Convention, Drummond Wolff was appointed British High Commissioner, and Ghazi Mukhtar Pasha, a distinguished Turkish soldier, as Turkish High Commissioner. Thus, for the second time, Baring was virtually superseded as senior British Representative in Egypt. His supersession by Northbrook had not been disagreeable to him. His supersession by Drummond Wolff was so, since he did not particularly like the man, and since the policy he was instructed to pursue was not altogether agreeable to him. However, he told Salisbury, on 26 January 1886, that he was getting on well with Wolff.[8]

Mukhtar Pasha, taking the view that the best way to deprive the British of any excuse for retaining their forces in Egypt would be to make the Egyptian Army capable of defending the Egyptian frontiers and guaranteeing internal security, concentrated his efforts on plans to this end. In February 1886 he submitted a Report to the Khedive and to Drummond Wolff in which he recommended that the strength of the Egyptian Army should be increased to 18,000 combatants 'composed exclusively of Egyptians and commanded either by Egyptian officers or by foreigners who, by reason of long service in the Egyptian Army, can be regarded as Egyptians.' He recommended that the major part of this army be used to recapture and hold the province of Dongola in order to safeguard Egypt from the Mahdists. He suggested that it would be possible to finance the enlarged army out of the existing Army Budget of £E130,000 p.a., plus the £E200,000 p.a. approximately which Egypt was paying for the British occupation force, and which would be saved as the result of a British evacuation.[9]

At the beginning of February, before Mukhtar's Report had been received in London, there was a change of Government as the result of a General Election. The short-lived Conservative Administration was replaced by a Liberal one, with Gladstone as Prime Minister and Rosebery as Foreign Secretary. The new Government had a majority of only one in the House of Commons and only lasted for six months, being defeated in the Commons as the result of the defection of the Irish Nationalists. After another General Election in July 1886, it was replaced by a Conservative Administration in which Salisbury was Prime Minister and Sir Stafford Northcote, raised to the Peerage as Lord Iddesleigh, Foreign Secretary. The new Administration was twenty short of a majority in the Commons and relied for its mandate on the votes of the Liberal Unionists, who had split off from the main Liberal Party on the issue of Irish Home Rule.

The short-lived Liberal Administration instructed Drummond Wolff to reject Mukhtar's recommendations and to continue negotiating. These negotiations dragged on without result until November, when the new Conservative Administration recalled Drummond Wolff to London for consultations.

During Rosebery's short first term of office as Foreign Secretary, and later, during a visit by Rosebery to Egypt in the Winter of 1886–87, Baring seems to have laid the foundations of a close alliance with him over Egyptian policy and to have convinced him, probably in advance of Salisbury, of what he had by this time come to regard as the impracticability of evacuating Egypt. In two letters written to Rosebery immediately after he came into office he set forth his views about the international and local aspects of the Egyptian problem. In the first of these letters he stressed the importance of keeping on good terms with Germany. 'Berlin and not Cairo is the real centre of gravity of Egyptian affairs. If we drift again into the same position in which we were a year ago—in which every Power except Italy was unfriendly—no effort to put matters right locally will avail.'[10] In the second letter he told him: 'When I first came to Egypt two years ago I believed that the policy of evacuation was possible and I hoped to assist in carrying it out . . . I am (now) reluctantly led to the conclusion that it is quite useless to endeavour to carry out that policy.'[11]

Baring's relations with Iddesleigh during his short term as Foreign Secretary (he was replaced, dying a few weeks later, by Salisbury, who became Foreign Secretary as well as Prime Minister in January 1887) seem to have been less happy. As soon as he had come into office, Iddesleigh warned him that 'our position in Egypt must be regularised and preparations seriously made for our ultimate withdrawal.'[12] Writing to Iddesleigh at the end of October, Baring advised against setting any fixed date for evacuation or, if a date had to be fixed, a period of ten years 'without commitment.' He warned him that the only possible independent indigenous Government would be a 'fanatical Moslem one.' 'In the Department of Justice there is not a single English Judge . . . nor is there a single Englishman in the central administration. The result is a most complete fiasco.' But, if the British Government insisted on evacuation, 'our best plan . . . is to interfere as little as possible with the administration of the Interior, properly so called, and to fix our attention mainly on one or two subjects—notably irrigation, in respect of which there is some chance that, in the event of a withdrawal, a native administration would be willing to carry on through the agency of Englishmen.'[13]

During Iddesleigh's term at the Foreign Office, arrangements were made for Baring's temporary return to India in his old position as Finance Member, on the understanding that his position in Egypt would be kept open for him. This may have been due to his obvious disagreement with the Government's policy over evacuation. Baring was not keen on the idea, but was prepared to accept it.[14] However, the arrangement was cancelled when Salisbury took over at the Foreign Office in January 1887.[15]

One of Salisbury's first acts on assuming control was to send Drummond Wolff back to Constantinople with new instructions. By that time he had become convinced of the necessity of fixing some date for a con-ditional evacuation. In his official instructions to Drummond Wolff he told him:

'The Sultan is pressing HMG to name a date for the evacuation of Egypt, and in that demand he is encouraged by one, perhaps two, of the European Powers. HMG have every desire to give him satisfaction upon this point, but they cannot fix even a distant date for evacuation until they are able to make provision for securing beyond that date the internal and external peace of Egypt. The object which the Powers in Europe have had in view, and which it is not less the desire of HMG to attain, may be generally expressed by the phrase "the neutralisation of Egypt," but it must be neutralisation with an exception designed to maintain the security and permanence of the whole arrangement. HMG must retain the right to guard and uphold the condition of things which will have been brought about by the military action and large sacrifices of this country. So long as the Government of Egypt maintains its position, and no disorders arise to interfere with the administration of justice or the action of the executive power, it is highly desirable that no soldier belonging to any foreign nation should remain on the soil of Egypt except when it may be necessary to make use of the land passage from one sea to another. HMG would willingly agree that such a stipulation should, whenever the evacuation has taken place, apply to English as much as to any other troops; but it would be necessary to restrict this provision, as far as England is concerned, to periods of tranquillity. England, if she spontaneously and willingly evacuates the country, must retain a treaty right of intervention if at any time either internal peace or external security should be seriously threatened.'[16]

In a private letter to Drummond Wolff, Salisbury told him that British public opinion was not prepared for evacuation, still less for abandonment, and would not be reconciled to it until or unless France became strong enough to enforce her views. 'But we must keep it in our power to satisfy France on account of Bismarck's attitude' which he described as 'chantage,' in that Bismarck was talking of the necessity of some return for the sacrifices Germany was making in refusing offers of conciliation from France on the basis of a joint diplomatic attack on the British position in Egypt. 'I heartily wish we had not gone into Egypt.

Had we not done so, we could snap our fingers at all the world. But the national or acquisitional feeling has been roused; it has tasted the fleshpots and will not let them go.'[17] At about the same time Salisbury told the Queen: 'It has become evident that a permanent occupation will not only be against our pledges and very costly, but it means permanent disagreement with France and Turkey. But we are pledged not to leave Egypt to danger of internal anarchy or foreign invasion. Sir Henry Drummond Wolff will propose that England undertake to leave Egypt in five years if there is no apprehension of internal or external disturbance, but retain the power of re-entry at any time, if there is danger of invasion or anarchy or of Egypt not fulfilling her international engagements.' He added that he thought it possible that Turkey would consent to such an arrangement, but that France would not.[18]

Explaining the position to Baring, Salisbury told him: 'The most important question is what security we are to have against any disturbance, internal or external, when our troops have left. It needs no proof that renewed anarchy, if not stopped by us, will not be stopped by Turkish or French troops. I want to obtain a treaty right of re-occupation . . . which would enable us to watch Egypt from Cyprus and Malta without offending the Moslem population by flaunting the infidel flag among them.'[19] Baring, who had already expressed cautious doubts about the wisdom of any negotiations at all, warning Salisbury that 'no arrangement is better than a bad arrangement,'[20] replied to this explanation expressing relief that Drummond Wolff was insisting on a treaty right of re-entry: 'I have for some time thought that such a right is an essential condition of withdrawal. But I hope that no date will be fixed at which we shall be bound unconditionally to withdraw. If we fix a date at all I think it should be under such elastic conditions as will virtually constitute us judges in our own cause.'[21]

Baring, reconciling himself with reluctance to Salisbury's evident determination to try to negotiate a conditional withdrawal, concentrated on trying to secure what he regarded as acceptable conditions. In connection with Salisbury's idea about the 'neutralisation' of Egypt, he stressed the necessity for creating a strong and viable Egyptian Government, and told Salisbury that the Caisse should be deprived of the power of bringing suits against the Egyptian Government, that criminal jurisdiction over foreigners exercised by the Consular Courts should be transferred to the Mixed Courts, and that 'some machinery should be devised for making Egyptian laws applicable to foreign residents.'[22] He begged Salisbury 'on no account to agree to fixing unconditionally a date for our departure. I think we should have a door open in case we should not think it wise to go. I am not . . . prepared to say . . . that at the end of five years we shall be able to go.'²³ He protested against the continued interference of Mukhtar Pasha, the Turkish High Commissioner, who was still in Egypt and was, in fact, to remain there indefinitely. He told Salisbury that Mukhtar was trying to persuade Nubar to remodel the Egyptian Courts on the lines of the Shari'a (Moslem religious) Courts— he might as well try to restore the Heptarchy'—and get Egypt to revert to the status of a Turkish Vilayet.²⁴

Later, realising that it would be necessary to fix some date for a with-drawal in order to get an agreement at all, Baring told Salisbury: 'If we must name a date, I think that five years' limit for Alexandria and three years for Cairo, with the proviso that we are not to go if prevented by internal or external danger, is the least which it would be prudent to accept . . . It is obviously undesirable that, having once withdrawn, we should be obliged after no long interval to fall back on the right of re-entry.'²⁵

On 6 May Salisbury told Baring that he had authorised Drummond Wolff to agree to evacuation in three years instead of five, with con-ditional right of re-entry, and with the stipulation that British officers should command the Egyptian Army for another two years. He explained that 'the change is strongly recommended by all our allies at Con-stantinople' and made it clear that the Porte would not have agreed to any longer period. 'If we only had Egyptian interests to consider' the interval would not be enough. It would be much better to remain for fifteen years, 'but the political position caused by our occupation of Egypt is one of great difficulty. It places us a good deal at the mercy of the German Powers, who have only to guarantee France from interference on their part in order to cause us a formidable amount of trouble, and we are being perpetually reminded of this liability . . . We are bound hand and foot by the pledges of retirement which our predecessors have given and which we have impliedly confirmed . . . There is no material compensation to England for the diplomatic disadvantages to which our present position exposes us.'²⁶

In reply to this somewhat apologetic letter, Baring, assuming that an agreement on these lines was now inevitable, told Salisbury: 'There will be some opposition in Egypt to withdrawal.' He added that there was some alarm in European circles, 'well represented by Moberly Bell, *The Times* correspondent.' 'The first thing that a European does in the East when he is frightened is to say that his native servants are insolent.' He went on to express his own doubts: 'It is an open question whether the Khedive will be able to keep on his legs by himself. I doubt his being able to do so unless the Egyptian Government is given much greater freedom of action.' He went on to say that he thought it would be

(*a*) The Flogging: a culprit at the triangles

(*b*) An Execution: a murderer turned off

The Earl of Cromer in 1907

necessary, before evacuation: (a) to get rid of Mukhtar; (b) to see that British officers were kept in the army and police and that the army were not allowed to get too strong, thus risking a repetition of the Arabi mutiny; (c) to get a new and more stringent Press Law promulgated and enforced; (d) to get the London Convention revised so as to enable the Egyptian Government to have uncontrolled access to revenue surpluses; and (e) to limit the powers of the Caisse and international privileges generally.[27]

The course of Drummond Wolff's negotiations was closely followed and considerably affected by the Ambassadors of the other Powers in Constantinople. Generally, the Ambassadors of France and Russia encouraged the Porte in insisting on a speedy and more or less un-conditional evacuation. The Ambassadors of Germany, Austria and Italy gave cautious support to Drummond Wolff in his insistence on some more flexible arrangement. Eventually, on 22 May 1887, a Con-vention was signed. Its terms stipulated that British troops should evacuate Egypt within three years provided that, in the meantime, there was no 'appearance of danger in the interior or from without' and that if, at any time subsequent to the evacuation, 'order and security in the interior were disturbed, or if the Khedivate of Egypt refused to execute its duties towards the Sovereign Court, or its international obligations,' both British and Ottoman troops would have the right to occupy the country. It was also provided that if 'by reason of hindrances,' the Sultan did not avail himself of the right of occupation, the British Government could take military action on their own account, the Sultan sending 'a Com-missioner to remain during the period of the sojourn of British troops with their Commander.'

The Convention also stipulated that it should be ratified by both parties within one month of signature and that the five European Powers who were signatories of the Treaty of Berlin—Germany, Austria, France, Russia and Italy—should be invited to adhere to it. This adherence was regarded by Salisbury as an essential condition of the working of the Convention and Drummond Wolff made this clear in a letter attached to the Convention, which read: 'If at the expiration of the three years stipulated in the Convention for the withdrawal of British troops from Egypt, one of the Great Mediterranean Powers shall not have accepted it, HMG would consider this refusal as the appearance of a danger from without, and the means of executing the aforesaid Convention shall be again discussed and settled between the Imperial Ottoman Government and HMG.' In other words, British agreement to evacuate depended, *inter alia,* on the agreement of the Powers to the terms of the Convention as a whole.[28]

Baring, on hearing of the signature of the Convention at the beginning of June, sent a letter of congratulation to Drummond Wolff: 'If it be considered that we have to go in a few years, I think that the terms you have made are the best possible. I recognise also that the general diplomatic arguments in favour of going must be allowed to prevail over local arguments in favour of staying. We must now try and set on its legs a machine that will work after we go.'[29]

The Convention as a whole amounted to a declaration of joint Anglo-Turkish suzerainty over Egypt, to a *de jure* recognition by the then sovereign Power of a special and exclusive British relationship towards Egypt, claimed by the British Government as a result of their intervention in 1882. This was in direct contradiction to the French position. Having reluctantly abandoned their original insistence on the special Anglo-French position in Egypt represented by the Dual Control, successive French Governments adopted the position that Egypt had, in effect, reverted to the *status quo ante* the Dual Control, *i.e.* that no Power could claim any exclusive or special privileges there, and that its future as an integral part of the Ottoman Empire was the joint and equal concern of all the six Great Powers of Europe. In support of this position France could generally rely upon Russia. At the time of the Drummond Wolff Convention, the other three Powers—Germany, Austria and Italy— were not inclined to hostility towards England because, in terms of European politics, they wished to draw England towards the Triple Alliance of these countries, and because, in terms of African politics, Germany and Italy could trade support for the British position in Egypt against British concessions towards their colonial ambitions.

The common factor in the situation was that all the Powers recognised the Sultan's *de jure* suzerainty over Egypt. From the French and Russian point of view it was therefore seen as essential to prevent the Sultan from ratifying the Convention and thereby giving *de jure* recognition to the special British position in Egypt provided for in the Convention. France, as was not unusual under the Third Republic, was in the throes of a ministerial crisis at the time of the signature of the Convention. But, by the end of May, both the French and the Russian Ambassadors at Constantinople had made it clear to the Porte that their Governments objected to the terms of Article V of the Convention by which British evacuation at the end of three years was conditional on their being no 'appearance of danger either in the interior or from without' and which conferred on the British Government the right to re-enter Egypt, either alone or in conjunction with Turkish troops, in the event of any subsequent appearance of such dangers. Since the existence or otherwise of such dangers was left to be determined by the judgement of the British

Government, it must have appeared to the Governments of France and Russia, and indeed to everybody else, that the British Government reserved for themselves the right to occupy Egypt for as long as they saw fit, and to re-occupy it whenever they wished to do so.

Montebello, the French Ambassador, had a private audience with the Sultan in which he warned him of French hostility in the event of the Convention being ratified. Nelidoff, the Russian Ambassador, made similar representations. On 9 June Kiamil Pasha, the Grand Vizier, informed Drummond Wolff that the Sultan had been much disturbed. The French and Russian Ambassadors had told him that if the Convention were ratified, their Governments would regard themselves as having the right to occupy other Provinces of the Ottoman Empire, such as Armenia and Syria, and insist on conditions for evacuation and re-entry similar to those provided for in Egypt in the Drummond Wolff Convention. He asked Drummond Wolff whether the British Government would agree to amend the offending Article to provide that British re-entry should only take place at the request of the Sultan. This proposal was rejected by Salisbury who, however, conceded that the non-adherence of any of the Great Powers to the Convention would not be made the excuse for a permanent occupation of Egypt, and declared that England would evacuate Egypt as soon as practicable whether the Convention were ratified or not. This was tantamount to saying that the Convention was meaningless in that it left the British Government with full liberty of action. This was precisely what France and Russia were complaining of. Their objection to the Convention was that its ratification by the Sultan would give legal justification to the exercise of that liberty of action.

There were other pressures operating on the Sultan against ratification. Mukhtar Pasha, from Cairo, protested against the Convention. The Ulema of Constantinople murmured against the alienation of Moslem territory to the infidel. The Sultan, harassed by these pressures, asked for an extension of the four weeks' delay provided for exchange of ratifications, which expired at the end of June, by which time the Convention had been ratified on the British side. Fifteen days' delay was granted but, by 15 July, the Sultan had still not made up his mind. At midnight on 15/16 July Drummond Wolff, in accordance with his instructions, left Constantinople, the Convention still unratified.

Salisbury telegraphed to Sir William White, British Ambassador at Constantinople, making it clear that he had no intention of re-opening negotiations with Turkey and stating: 'Great Britain will remain in Egypt until HMG have become convinced that the Egyptian Government is strong enough to protect itself from internal and external dangers.'[30]

On 23 June, when it seemed probable that the Convention would not be ratified by the Sultan, Salisbury had told the Queen: 'If we fail to obtain satisfaction, we should remain in Egypt in a better rather than a worse position than before.'[31] And to Lyons, the British Ambassador in Paris, after the negotiations had finally broken down: 'We cannot leave the Khedive to take his chance of foreign attack or native riot, and the French refuse to let us exercise the necessary powers of defence unless we do it by continuing our military occupation. There is nothing for it but to sit still and drift awhile and refuse to evacuate until conditions change ... Our relations with the French are not pleasant ... Can you wonder that there is to my eyes a silver lining even to the great black clouds of a Franco-German war?'[32]

Baring was in Europe on Summer leave when the negotiations finally broke down, and there is no contemporary record of his reaction to the news. But, in view of his lack of enthusiasm for the negotiations as displayed in previous correspondence with Salisbury, he was probably pleased that the question of withdrawal seemed to have been indefinitely postponed.

Public opinion in England expressed fairly general satisfaction at the failure of the negotiations. Newspapers of all shades of opinion criticised France and Russia, blamed the Sultan for having been influenced by their threats, and stressed that the outcome of the negotiations had given England a free hand over future policy in Egypt.

Nevertheless, Salisbury had lost a diplomatic battle. In a direct confrontation at Constantinople, the Sultan had come down on the side of France and Russia, and against England, in spite of support for England from Germany, Austria and Italy. The immediate effect of this diplomatic defeat was to deprive the British Government of any legal justification for the British position in Egypt. This, in itself, was not important. The validity and security of the British position in Egypt depended, not on any legal justification, but (a) on the extent to which the Egyptians themselves could be reconciled to the British presence, and (b) on those fluctuating international considerations which determined the strength and efficacy of Great Power hostility towards the British position in Egypt.

The long-term effect of this diplomatic defeat only became apparent retrospectively, although Salisbury seems to have had some inkling of it in a letter he wrote to Sir William White shortly after Drummond Wolff had left Constantinople. Pointing out that in the event of a war between Germany and France, Bismarck would probably bribe Russia to remain neutral with the offer of Constantinople, he went on: 'It would be a terrible blow to lose Constantinople. But have we not lost it already? ...

Have we really any arm with which we can meet Nelidoff's threats to Erzerum? And would it be worth our while to save the Sultan to prevent Germany from having a free hand with France?'[33] For the past seventy- five years British policy in the Near East, which had been concerned, partly with keeping the Russians out of Constantinople and the Mediter- ranean, and partly with preserving the security of British communications with India, had been fairly consistent in trying to maintain the territorial integrity of the Ottoman Empire, which included maintaining the theory and, to some extent, the reality of Ottoman suzerainty over Egypt. Even after the completion of the Suez Canal had so greatly increased Egypt's importance as a factor in communications with India, British policy still concentrated on influence at Constantinople as a means of exerting leverage over Egypt. Disraeli's intervention at the Congress of Berlin in 1878 provided for the extension of British influence in Asia Minor by the appointment of roving military Consuls, but he was content to subordinate British policy in Egypt to that of France. The acquisition of Cyprus was seen as an adjunct to the British presence in Asia Minor and not as a possible means of exercising British influence in Egypt.

When Gladstone's Liberal Government came into office in 1880, the Prime Minister's personal attitude towards the Bulgarian atrocities, and his expressed views about the Turks generally, were factors in weakening the Constantinople link, which was further strained by the acrimonious negotiations about intervention in Egypt before, during and after the Constantinople Conference in the Summer of 1882. What still remained of the link was strained to breaking-point as a result of the Drummond Wolff negotiations, when it became apparent that the Franco-Russian combination at Constantinople was sufficient to prevent England from using the Porte as a lever for moving events in Egypt, even when the British Government enjoyed the uncertain and vacillating support of the other three Great Powers.

And so, as an alternative to losing control over events in the Near East altogether, British policy began to look towards consolidating the British position in Cairo as a means of influencing events from there rather than from Constantinople. At the same time, British influence in Cairo began to be regarded by the Powers with much the same suspicion as Russian influence at Constantinople had been regarded by the Powers for the past seventy-five years. Just as England and France, sometimes joined by Austria, had been accustomed to make common cause at Constantinople against Russian influence, so France and Russia, some- times joined by Germany, now became accustomed to make common cause against England at Cairo. This continued until 1904, when the growing menace of German ambitions brought about a new European alignment which, for the time being, put an end to French and Russian hostility towards England in Egypt and the Near East.

But, in the Autumn of 1887, this forthcoming change in the centre of gravity of British policy in the Near East had not yet become apparent, and the failure of the Drummond Wolff negotiations was seen by Salisbury simply as another stumbling-block on the diplomatic Via Dolorosa on which the British Government had been condemned to walk as a result of their occupation of Egypt. Even Baring, much as he disliked the Drummond Wolff negotiations, and much as he probably rejoiced at their breakdown, cannot yet have seen more than the faint penumbra of the shape of things to come.

Immediately, Baring was relieved of the interference of Drummond Wolff in the affairs of Egypt, which had been a source of irritation to him for nearly two years. But he had to suffer the continued presence in Egypt of Mukhtar Pasha, whom the Porte insisted on retaining there as a quasi-permanent High Commissioner. He had no definite duties and he became a source of much embarrassment both to the Egyptian Govern-ment and to Baring.

Baring's share in the Drummond Wolff negotiations had been a passive one. While they were in progress he had been heavily engaged in what he regarded as his most urgent task—the rehabilitation of Egyptian finances in order to avoid the threat of an International Commission which, in accordance with the terms of the London Convention, was due to be convened in the event of Egypt proving unable to resume paying the full rate of interest on the foreign debt after a period of two years. The success which had been achieved in this by the middle of 1887 was the principal reason why Salisbury was able to regard the breakdown of the Drummond Wolff negotiations as philosophically as he did.

In terms of present day national finances, the sums involved were extremely small. But so was the area of manoeuvre available to the financial reformers. On the assumption of strict economy and a proper control of incomings and outgoings, the main difficulties of the situation, as described by Vincent, the Financial Adviser,[34] were (a) the over-optimistic revenue estimates on which the debt settlement was based; (b) the insufficient allowance which had been made for fluctuations of revenue due to the incidence of low Niles, cattle diseases and similar events; (c) the lack of any sufficient provision in the London Convention for extraordinary or capital expenditure; (d) the progressive fall which had taken place in the world prices of Egypt's agricultural exports since 1883; and (e) the very limited room for possible economies in Egypt's attenuated administrative Budget. Illustrating this last point, Vincent has this to say: 'Out of a total of £9 million, over £5 million consists of fixed charges for tribute and debt, plus £0·5 million for pensions which must be paid unless the Government are prepared to infringe acquired rights of the most delicate character, plus £0·3 million for the Civil List, a sum fixed by international agreement. Less than £3·5 million is left from which to effect economies. About £0·5 million of this is absorbed by the expenses of the railways,[35] and another £0·5 million by Public Works expenditure... The difference between strict economy and a lax financial administration is about £200,000 p.a.'

On the expenditure side, the only substantial scope for economy lay in the charges which Egypt had to pay to the British Government (a) for the maintenance of the occupation troops, and (b) for the interest payable on the British Government's Suez Canal Company shareholding. The Suez Canal interest amounted to about £175,000 p.a. The occupation expenses varied with the strength of the occupation forces. Under an agreement arrived at with—or rather imposed upon—the Egyptian Government in December 1882 it had been provided that the Egyptian Government should pay a sum of £4 per month per man for the maintenance of the British occupation forces, plus, in effect, whatever additional charges the War Office might raise against them in respect of ancillary charges. The size of the occupation force and the nature of the ancillary charges were determined entirely by the War Office and Treasury and the Egyptian Government had simply to foot the bill. For almost the whole of his time in Egypt Baring waged an unceasing war both with the Treasury and the War Office about these charges. The burden of his case was that, since the occupation force was there for the benefit of England at least as much as for the benefit of Egypt, the English taxpayer should pay part of the cost, and that the Egyptian share should be limited to a certain maximum, which Baring put at £100,000 p.a., irrespective of the size of the occupation force. These two matters—the occupation charges and the Suez Canal interest—had a particular urgency during the years 1885–87 when the incidence of these charges seemed likely to make all the difference between relative financial freedom and an International Commission.

On the revenue side, there could be no question of obtaining any relief from the onerous terms of the London Convention, at all events until the threat of an International Commission had been removed by a resumption of full interest payments. The patient had to be cured before medicines could be administered. An increase in landtax, from which over half the total revenue was derived, was deemed to be politically impracticable, in that it would have made an unpopular and rickety machine even more insecure, and would in any case have been economically harsh in view of the progressive fall in agricultural prices.[36] Vincent did what he could to increase Customs revenue by the conclusion of a series of Customs agreements (in which he met with the usual international obstructions), by attempts to check smuggling (in which he was hampered by the Capitulations), and by an increase in the duty on imported tobacco combined with a prohibition of local cultivation. But he concluded that the only way to obtain a sure and permanent increase in revenue was 'to increase the cultivated area, for, failing such a rise in prices as would restore the value of the produce grown in the present cultivated area to its former level, an increase in the quantity of agricultural produce is the only means by which Egypt can attain a position of financial prosperity which can satisfy foreign obligations.' It was to achieve this that Scott Moncrieff and his small band of irrigation engineers were devoting their efforts, assisted by the £1 million for irrigation purposes which had been allotted from the international loan raised under the provisions of the London Convention.

The battle for financial solvency and against international control during the years 1885–87 was therefore waged on these two fronts— on the expenditure front with the principal object of limiting the demands of the British Treasury, and on the revenue front with the principal object of increasing Egypt's agricultural productivity. At one point, as will be seen, in the matter of the abolition of the *corvée*, the two battle-fronts merged.

In the matter of the occupation expenses, Baring was almost wholly unsuccessful. Not only did the Treasury refuse any concessions; the War Office also attempted to dictate the strength and consequently the expenditure not only of the British Army of occupation but also of the Egyptian Army. On one occasion Baring complained to Salisbury that the British Treasury 'look on me as if I were some Representative of a hostile Power' and that the War Office, acting through Drummond Wolff and Stephenson, General Officer Commanding British Troops in Egypt, had ordered important additions to the Egyptian Army without consulting the Egyptian Government. 'The whole financial control of the Egyptian Army was virtually taken over by the English authorities ... A much larger force has been maintained than I thought necessary or than most of the Egyptians thought necessary . . . I had the greatest difficulty in getting Stephenson to come down to 10,000 men which, as I then thought, was in the interests of the English and not of the Egyptian taxpayer . . .' He went on to urge Salisbury to reduce Egypt's contribution to occupation expenses to a maximum of £100,000 p.a. irrespective of the size of the occupation force, and told him: 'I feel quite as secure here as far as internal tranquillity is concerned with 5,000 men as I should with 25,000. So long as they remain at all, with of course the certainty in case of real emergency of being reinforced, there will be no disturbance. The police will be able to preserve internal tranquillity. As regards external defence there is not a single British soldier on the frontier and only 150 British troops at Aswan and no other British troops south of Cairo. The whole cost of defending the frontier devolves on the Egyptian Government; the Red Sea ports are being defended by Egyptian troops.' In the same letter he recommended the reduction of the Egyptian Army from 10,000 to 6,500 in spite of Stephenson's objections, and estimated that £100,000 p.a. could be saved on the army and police.[37]

In correspondence with his old associate, Goschen, who became Chancellor of the Exchequer in January 1887, Baring was forthright about the frustrations under which he was suffering. 'The result of four years of Egyptian experience has sunk two points deeply into my mind: (1) In the present phase of our parliamentary institutions it is almost hopeless to conduct to a successful issue our task in Egypt; (2) The English administrative machine is singularly ill-adapted to the task. There is no cohesion. I hear sometimes the voice of the Foreign Office, sometimes the Treasury, sometimes the War Office, speaking in words by no means clear. We had better retire from the scene as soon as we can do so with dignity.'[38] And, two days later, he was complaining to Goschen that 'the very distinct pledges given to the Egyptian Government, especially in regard to Sudan military expenses, have been lost sight of . . . I hope you will see your way to a larger reduction of army of occupation expenses for 1887 . . . So far as I can understand we are expected to reduce the military expenditure but not to reduce the army . . . The process of making bricks without straw has been tried before on the banks of the Nile, but it was not very successful.'[39] And, on 28 March 1887, he told Goschen that '£200,000 is an excessive charge for the small British garrison now in the country' (it amounted to about 3,500 men), and that 'the principle that the occupation of Egypt is not to cost the British taxpayer a farthing is a new and impolitic one.'[40]

Later, in the Summer of 1887, when Vincent was in London negotiating with the Treasury, and when it appeared probable that the Drummond Wolff Convention was about to be signed, Baring once again requested more financial freedom for the Egyptian Government. 'Let us establish the best financial administration of which the circumstances permit, sweep away the absurd and complicated arrangements about the application of surpluses . . . and pay the whole surplus to the

Egyptian Government, and let them, acting with competent financial advice, do what they like with the money. If I were Egyptian Finance Minister I would not pay off a farthing of debt but, directly I had got a real solid surplus, I would borrow more money for canals and roads.' He pointed out the urgency of establishing a sound financial administration 'in view of our early departure' and told Goschen that it was impossible to institute various necessary reforms because they would lead either to increased expenditure or loss of revenue and that 'the counter-measures by which loss of revenue would be made good are almost always unpopular and difficult of execution. In questions of this kind the Egyptian Government will always tend to the political, *i.e.* non-financial, view. When we leave the country this tendency will receive a fresh impulse. The Government will be weak and nervously afraid of doing anything unpopular. I know that the Treasury officials at home will scorn these arguments, but I cannot afford to do so. My first duty now is to keep the Egyptian Humpty Dumpty on top of the wall, and I have to steer as well as I can between the two extremes—fiscal and political.'[41]

Baring's views met with no sympathy from Salisbury, who told him, in February 1887, that Goschen objected to 'the sort of vague reliance on the English Budget which has very naturally prevailed of late among Egyptian financiers,' and that his 'existing claims' were 'untenable in their substance and more objectionable in that they are destined to be the parents of a long and healthy chain of new claims in future.' He added that Goschen had 'cut into your Budget, with a sharp knife.'[42] A little later, referring to a 'fulminating telegram, received from Baring, he told him: 'The Treasury have all along been in favour of refusing any payment whatever from this side and taking the chance of an International Commission . . . You should not forget the extreme difficulty of persuading the H of C to incur any expenditure over Egypt. The pressure of taxation here is very heavy, and motions in the direction of economy will unite many who normally vote apart.'[43] In April 1887, when it seemed that the Drummond Wolff negotiations were succeeding, Salisbury relaxed his attitude a little. After warning Baring that 'we have to fit the Egyptian Budget within the narrow margins that international jealousy has allowed, and to do that without burdening the British taxpayer,' he indicated that it might be possible to stretch certain points in connection with the Suez Canal interest, the occupation costs, and the expenses being incurred for the defence of Suakin. 'For English reasons Suakin must be kept by Egypt, *e.g.* the suppression of the slave-trade, but, so far as the reasons are English and not Egyptian, the Egyptians ought not to pay for them.'[44] But, in the event, no assistance was given, and Egypt climbed out of her financial troubles without any assistance from the British taxpayer.

The fact that she did so was, apart from the financial expedients and controls devised by Vincent, mainly due to irrigation improvements brought about by Scott Moncrieff and his handful of Anglo-Indian irrigation engineers, which resulted not only in a steady increase in Egypt's agricultural productivity but, more importantly in the long run, in a more willing acceptance of British influence by the mass of the rural population.

In order to understand the problems faced by Moncrieff and his assistants, it is necessary briefly to describe the Egyptian irrigation system as it was at that time. Egypt is a country virtually without rainfall, depending entirely for water on the Nile which, from the southern frontier of Egypt to Cairo, runs through a valley twenty to thirty miles wide, bounded by upland desert, and fanning out between Cairo and the sea into the Delta. The area of the Delta makes up about half the total cultivated area. The Nile flood, caused by rainfall in its upper reaches— in the Sudan, Abyssinia and central Africa—lasts from July to October each year. The flood water brings down silt which is deposited on the fields, and acts as a fertiliser. In Upper Egypt—the Nile Valley upstream from Cairo—the land was mostly irrigated by the 'basin' system. 'In this system the land is divided into basins of from 1,000 to 40,000 acres by the construction of a longitudinal bank as near the river as it can safely be placed, and of cross-banks between this bank and the edge of the desert. When the Nile rises, water is let into these compartments through short canals with regulating sluices, flooding the land to a depth of . . . from one to two metres. The water is held there for from forty to sixty days and, after the river has fallen sufficiently, is drained back again. During this time it drops its silt and this process, repeated for thousands of years, has formed basins of which the surface is so perfectly graded by the deposition of silt, that it drains completely, leaving no pools behind.'[45] Lands too high to be reached by the flood water could be reached by means of canals branching off from the Nile at a point well above the area to be watered and leading downwards at a slope slightly less than the slope of the Nile itself, so that, when it reached the area to be cultivated, the water level in the canal would have reached the level of the land above the river. Such canals, if dug deep enough, could also be used for irrigation during the season of low Nile, provided that means were devised for lifting water from the canal on to the fields. In the Delta, which had been formed by thousands of years of silt deposit, the level of soil has risen too high for basin irrigation, and the normal system of irrigation was by means of such canals.

Irrigation during the time of flood only provides for one crop a year, which is sown in the newly deposited silt after the flood has subsided, and harvested in the following Spring. The land then lies fallow and dries out in the sun until the onset of the next flood. Perennial irrigation— the watering of fields for crops all the year round—started in the 1820s as a means of cultivating the valuable cotton and, later, sugar crops which grow, and have to be irrigated, during the early Summer, the season of low Nile. In order to provide for this Summer irrigation, it was necessary either (a) to sink deep wells or dig deep canals and raise water from them by some form of lifting machine, or (b) to raise the level of the water behind barrages and to transport the raised water to the summer crops through canals.

The basin system of irrigation needed relatively little maintenance. The perennial system, on which the cotton crop, and consequently the financial prosperity of Egypt, largely depended, required constant main-tenance and continual supervision. For some years before the British occupation it had not received them. Colonel Ross, one of Moncrieff's assistants, reported: 'Up to 1882, Egyptian irrigation was going down-hill. Every year, some false step was taken in spite of the engineer. Every year . . . drains were abandoned or became useless, and canals became less of artificial and more of natural channels wholly influenced by the natural rise and fall of the Nile.'[46]

Moncrieff arrived in Egypt from India, on Dufferin's recommendation, in the Summer of 1883. Before the end of the year he was joined by another four irrigation engineers from India—Ross, Brown, Willcocks and Foster, whom he appointed Irrigation Inspectors in the Provinces. His first task was concerned with the provision of Summer water for the cotton growing areas in the Delta, on the product of which Egypt's agricultural prosperity, and consequently her taxable capacity, largely depended. Nearly forty years before, Mohamed Ali had started the con-struction of a barrage at the apex of the Delta, some ten miles north of Cairo, in order to dam the river at the Summer season of low Nile, and so to raise its level and lead the water into canals to irrigate the Delta cotton crop, as an alternative to the expensive business of raising water to the fields with pumps. The barrage had been completed in 1861 but, owing to defects in construction, had not proved strong enough to dam the river. When Moncrieff arrived in Egypt, it had not been in operation for years and was regarded as a picturesque ruin. The Egyptian Govern-ment, on the advice of Rousseau Pasha, a French irrigation engineer in the Egyptian service, was on the point of signing a contract for a quarter-of-a-million pounds for the provision of steam pumps. Moncrieff, flying in the face of all local opinion, insisted that the barrage could be made to work and advised against the steam pumps. In his own words:[47] 'We resolved to see what the cracked dam was worth. About £26,000 was spent on strengthening it. As a result, in 1884, it was possible to raise the Summer water level by 7 ft 2 ins and lead it into the only one of the three canals which had been finished.' Consequently, the Delta cotton crop, which had never before exceeded 130,000 tons, amounted to 160,000 tons in 1887. As each ton was worth £35, this amounted to about £1 million worth of increased production. 'Not a bad return for the £26,000 we had spent,' as Moncrieff commented. This initial achievement was of assistance to Baring in obtaining the £1 million for irrigation out of the loan provided for in the London Convention. With the aid of this money, repairs to the barrage were completed by 1890 at a cost of some £460,000, leading to an annual increase in the order of £2½ million in the value of the Delta cotton crop.

The rehabilitation of the barrage was the most spectacular aspect of the work of Moncrieff and his assistants. But the main part of this work was the rehabilitation of the Egyptian irrigation system as a whole, and the organisation of a proper distribution of water. 'During the flood the river is highly charged with silt and every effort should have been made to keep up the current in the canals so as to carry the silt on to the fields . . . The canals were however so badly aligned that the silt came to be deposited in the first few miles of the channel, where it was useless for fertilising and had to be removed. The canals were often 20 ft deep with very steep side-slopes. Sometimes a depth of 6 ft had to be taken out of the canals during low Nile, all to be deposited again during the flood . . . When I went to Egypt in 1883, I found 85,000 men employed for 160 days a year, dragged for many miles from their villages, supplying their own tools, unpaid, unfed, unlodged . . . To carry out the system the kurbash was freely used.'[48] This system of forced labour was known to the Egyptians as 'auna' and to Europeans as the *corvée*. Its enforcement by means of the kurbash, or rhinoceros-hide whip, having been officially forbidden, on Dufferin's insistence, in 1883, Moncrieff was faced with the necessity of finding paid labour to do what had previously been done by the *corvée*. This brought him up against an intractable financial difficulty. He and his assistants were able substantially to diminish the size of the problem. By improvements to the canals and sluices, and 'by a little manoeuvring of the water during the flood,' it was found possible considerably to reduce the amount of silt which had to be removed from the canals, with a corresponding reduction in the amount of labour required. 'It was evident that the cost of keeping in order the great system of banks and channels was a proper burden on the land, but there was no use proposing anything so revolutionary as the raising of the land-tax.

Some other contrivance had to be found. Our first move was to get sanction for the *corvée* redeeming themselves by a payment of 6s per head per season. £116,535 was paid in this way in 1885. Our next step was to employ dredging machines with the money.'[49] But, after all this, Moncrieff estimated that a sum of £400,000 p.a. would be required to pay labour to get the necessary work done. The provision of part of this money was the occasion for a spectacular diplomatic crisis.

The terms of the London Convention provided for a reduction of £E450,000 p.a. in land-tax, the proceeds of which were relevant both to the 'affected' and 'non-affected' revenues. This had been recommended by Lord Northbrook and his recommendation was eventually accepted by the Powers signatory to the London Convention. Later, the Egyptian Government, on Moncrieff's advice, decided that, instead of devoting the entire sum to a reduction of land-tax, it would be preferable to devote £E250,000 p.a. of it to the substitution of paid for *corvée* labour. Accord-ing to the provisions of the London Convention, there was a technical objection to this. The annual 'authorised' expenditure by the Egyptian Government had been fixed by the Convention at £E5,237,000. Any expenditure additional to this which needed to be financed out of the surpluses in the 'affected' revenue had to be authorised by the Com-missioners of the Caisse, which meant in effect the Governments of the Powers. The £E250,000 to be spent on paid labour involved such an addition to the 'authorised' expenditure. In July 1886, after consultation with the Caisse, a draft Decree was submitted to the six Powers concerned providing for the addition of £E250,000 p.a. to the 'authorised' ex-penditure. There followed six months of what Baring afterwards described as 'international burrowing.'[50] The British Government pressed the necessity for acceptance on the Powers. The Italian Government was agreeable. The German and Austrian Governments were willing to agree if the Russian Government agreed. The Russian Government was willing to agree if no other Power objected. All therefore depended on the attitude of the French Government, who delayed their decision.

At last, after eight months' delay, and with the object of shaming the French into acceptance, on 3 February 1887, the Egyptian Government issued a public notice calling out the *corvée*. The French Government thereupon, on 8 February, signified their acceptance of the proposed Decree, but made this conditional on the insertion of a clause which would have the effect of placing all Public Works expenditure under the control of the Caisse. The Egyptians, supported by Baring, decided that this condition was unacceptable; the British Government agreed with them and told Baring that they would be prepared to consider financial assistance to enable the £E250,000 to be raised without the necessity for application to the Powers.[51] After some further negotiations it was agreed that the British Government would, in case of need, waive the payment of interest on the Suez Canal Shares (amounting to about £175,000 p.a.) for a sufficient period to enable Egypt to find the necessary money from its 'authorised' revenue, which included provision for paying this interest. This enabled the Egyptian Government to retract their notice for calling out the *corvée* and to proceed with their plans for converting a large part of the *corvée* to paid labour. (In fact, on Moncrieff's advice, they had been doing this for the past year, and the negotiations with the Powers repre-sented an attempt to regularise a *fait accompli*; this may have been one of the reasons for the French intransigence.) In the event, the French Government, at the end of March, instructed their Commissioner of the Caisse to withdraw his opposition to the proposed Decree,[52] and it thus became unnecessary for the British Government to forego their Canal interest payments.

The balance—£E150,000 p.a.—of the total of £E400,000 p.a. required was obtained five years later, again in face of French resistance, and at the price of concessions to the French in the matter of local taxation. But, by that time, the matter had become less urgent in that an improve-ment in the finances had made it possible to expand the Public Works Budget out of 'non-affected' revenue.

The first three months of 1887 were a period of high diplomatic tension as a result of the *corvée* dispute. Salisbury, at first, was not sym-pathetic. On 21 January he told Baring that, if it were not possible to get the agreement of the Powers, 'the only alternative will be that the poor wretches will be called out again, for we must not be guilty of any irregularity. It is too expensive.'[53] It no doubt seemed to him, at the time, an additional reason for trying to get out of Egypt altogether. But Baring was insistent. He told Salisbury on 7 February that the only chance of getting the French to yield was 'to show no softness and let them see that at a pinch we can get on without them. My only regret is that we did not call out the *corvée* somewhat earlier.'[54] When the crisis had been resolved as a result of the British Government's action in waiving the Canal interest he told Salisbury that it was 'the only really popular measure that we have adopted since we have been in Egypt' and urged that the British Government should publicise what they had done.[55]

In fact, as Baring did not fail to point out to Goschen, the assistance given 'did not really amount to much,'[56] particularly as, in the event, the British Government did not have to forego any interest at all. Salisbury, in a somewhat apologetic letter to Baring, explained why he could not do more and why he could not publicise what had been done: 'We have a hard game to play and a very full board. Abroad we seem to be shut up to the alternatives of two wars, either of which is liable to modify the face of Europe. At home we have an H of C paralysed by the Irish Party and governed at present by the junction of two Parties not yet united.[57] Under the circumstances our hands are a good deal tied. For instance, over the *corvée*. The right way of helping you would be by a Bill, but we cannot pass a Bill. We are obliged to adopt the circuitous method of remitting the Suez interest. If that attracts undue attention it may draw us into endless discussions which will put off the Irish measures while Ireland is getting worse and worse . . . The glory of having suppressed the *corvée* in spite of the French will exude into publicity by some opening.'[58]

During the course of the crisis Baring had a certain amount of trouble with Moncrieff who, at the beginning of February, sent a letter of resignation in the hope that it would 'stir Baring up to see what a black-guard business it is.'[59] Baring, who did not consider that he needed stirring up, was annoyed. He told Barrington, Salisbury's Private Secretary, that Moncrieff, 'instead of being helpful at a critical moment, went into hysterics. I regard it as a natural consequence of belonging to the anti-slavery, anti-opium etc., lot, who are all more or less lunatics.'[60] Advising Salisbury of the incident, Baring told him: 'The English officials here are doing admirable work. They are in a very difficult position and great allowances should be made for them. But they are occasionally very troublesome, especially the Anglo-Indians, who cannot understand that Egypt is not India . . . They sometimes get very angry when they can't get their own way.'[61] In the event, Moncrieff withdrew his resignation as the result of a 'kind and sensible letter from Baring urging me not to resign.' But he went on to comment to his correspondent: 'Baring, though just and honest, is as unsympathetic as a stone.'[62]

One way and another—with the help of Moncrieff's irrigation works, Baring's insistence on reductions in the army and police and resistance to expensive proposals for various reforms put forward by British officials, together with Vincent's financial controls and expedients—the payment of full interest on the foreign debt was resumed and the spectre of an International Commission exorcised. Writing to Goschen towards the end of 1887, Baring described the financial situation as 'promising,' due partly to a rise in the prices of sugar and cotton.[63] But he went on to tell him: 'I cannot say that events are tending rapidly towards the creation of any really autonomous Government and therefore to any diminution of our responsibility. On the contrary, new European interests are growing up and European methods of government are obtaining a firmer root. I look in vain for any real development of governing power or administrative ability among the ruling classes such as would enable them to deal adequately with the new order of things. The Nubars and the Riaz only shine by comparison. When Lord Salisbury says to me that it is illusory to suppose that the Egyptians can walk alone, I fully agree.'

Now that the immediate threat of an International Commission and the impending prospect of having to prepare for evacuation were behind him, Baring was beginning to look ahead towards a more settled future for Egypt. His hands were more firmly on the reins than they had been in 1885. The financial situation was under control. The Mahdists in the Sudan were quiescent. The English Departments, particularly the Treasury and the War Office, as well as the House of Commons, were being just as tiresome as ever, but, in spite of his earlier mistrust of Salisbury, he found his Administration infinitely more to his taste than Gladstone's had been. There were advantages in having as his chief a Foreign Secretary who was also Prime Minister. British relations with Germany had improved under Salisbury's sophisticated handling, and this, combined with the improvement in the financial situation, diminished the French capacity for mischief. The *corvée* incident had been a diplomatic victory in which he had successfully pushed a reluctant British Government into standing up to the French. There were various little clouds on the horizon, including the behaviour of Nubar, who had been intriguing against Baring and Vincent while on a visit to London in the Summer of 1887. But, now that local and international circumstances were becoming easier, Nubar was no longer as essential as he had been. In October Baring took the precaution of discreetly ascertaining that Riaz Pasha would be prepared to take office as Prime Minister if called upon to do so. 'But,' he told Salisbury, 'I do not propose to get rid of Nubar at present, mainly because everybody expects me to do so because of his attacks on me in London.'[64]

Baring had learnt to accommodate himself to the international and other limitations under which he had to work, and had realised that the incidence of these limitations would tend to diminish as the financial situation improved. He probably realised that the breakdown of the Drummond Wolff negotiations, while postponing evacuation to the Greek Kalends, had also postponed the prospect of any international agreement about financial autonomy and foreign privileges until such time as a favourable turn in the international situation might enable the British Government successfully to negotiate these matters.

He was under no illusions, either then or later, about the popularity of the British in Egypt, or about the real extent to which British-inspired reforms had benefited the people of Egypt. He realised that the overriding necessity for economy had inhibited the development of even the most rudimentary social services and that the political necessity for not interfering in the Ministries of Justice and the Interior had allowed abuses, for which the British were sometimes held responsible, to proliferate unchecked throughout these Departments. He recognised, accepted as inevitable, and treated as unimportant, the hostility of the Turco-Egyptian ruling class. He acknowledged that what he called 'the Arabi movement' was not dead but dormant. 'The Arabi movement,' he told Salisbury,[65] had taught the Egyptian people 'that they had grievances and . . . that they were of some political importance. They have not forgotten this. The Legislative Council and the General Assembly can make themselves heard. The only danger is that they may be stirred up by the French Press and intrigue and exert an influence in the army and police. Without that they can do no real harm. The great safeguard is the continued employment of British officers.'

He thought there was no chance whatever, in the foreseeable future, of the emergence of any genuinely Egyptian ruling class to replace what he regarded as the moribund Turco-Egyptians. He referred to the representatives of Egyptian nationalism among the Ulema and in the Legislative Council and General Assembly as 'corrupt and ignorant bigots,' and considered that, 'if any disturbance arises, it is more likely to come from them than from any others.' As for their being able to rule the country: 'Take away the Suez Canal, the railways, the telegraph to Europe, the European colonies and trade, the Capitulations, the external debt and the Mixed Courts, make Blunt[66] British Consul-General, and a government such as he would have might perhaps work. It would be more superstitious, rapacious, ignorant and corrupt than that of the Turkish aristocracy, about which, in spite of its many faults, some slight trace of governing capacity lingers, but it would not be altogether unsuitable for the population which, under these circumstances, would remain to be governed.'[67] He thought that the beneficent effect of the English irrigation officials, not only in improving irrigation methods, but also in ensuring a more equitable distribution of water, was having a favourable effect in the countryside, but was still a little concerned about the possibility of an outbreak of Moslem fanaticism, which he was inclined to equate with Egyptian nationalism, or what he called 'the Arabi movement.' But he was confident that, with a small garrison of British troops, and with a guarantee of reinforcement in case of serious disturbances, the rickety machine, which he had so often criticised, but which he had now learnt to drive, would continue to work without seizing up, provided that it were not disturbed by further talk of imminent evacuation.

So ended the Jubilee year 1887. In the Jubilee honours Moncrieff and Vincent, on Baring's recommendation, received KCMGs for their work in Egypt. Baring himself received the Grand Cross of the same Order.

7

THE VELVET GLOVE

THE MOVEMENT OF European politics during the five years 1888 to 1892 tended on the one hand to diminish the diplomatic disadvantages, from the British point of view, of remaining in Egypt, and, on the other hand, to reinforce the strategic desirability of doing so. Diplomatically, European alliances were becoming polarised into the Triple Alliance of Germany, Austria and Italy on one side, and the incipient Dual Alliance of France and Russia on the other. The British Government could usually rely on the conditional benevolence of the Triple Alliance in respect of Egypt. Strategically, the growing *rapprochement* between France and Russia, as manifested at Constantinople, tended still further to undermine the traditional basis of British Near East policy, which was to exert pressure at Constantinople as a means of safeguarding British communications with India. The possibility of effectively exerting this pressure depended, in the last resort, on being able to send a naval force through the Dardanelles to Constantinople. But this seemed increasingly impracticable as a result of the hostile Franco-Russian combination at Constantinople.

In 1888 the position, as seen by Salisbury, was that 'a Franco-Russian combination was the emergency against which preparations had to be made. The Channel could not be left defenceless and the Mediterranean fleet was too weak to deal with the French ships now at Toulon, apart from any detachment for operations in the Straits or Black Sea. France had been grudging no expenditure and Russia was laying down three new battleships.'[1] In the Autumn of 1888, a Cabinet Committee concluded that British naval strength must be based on the hypothesis of a hostile Franco-Russian combination.[2] An expensive and ambitious ten-year naval building programme was embarked on in order to correct the deficiency. The 'pressure at Constantinople' policy was not abandoned. But its precariousness had been demonstrated, and the need for some sort of reinsurance adumbrated.

A permanent British presence in Egypt was only tardily seen by Salisbury as a possible answer. In 1887, while the Drummond Wolff negotiations were still proceeding, he became conscious of the weakness of the British fleet and entered into a secret, limited, tripartite naval agree-ment with Austria and Italy to guarantee Turkey against Russia. He did this at the instance of Bismarck who, simultaneously, was negotiating his secret Reinsurance Treaty with Russia. This, in effect, gave Russia a free hand over Constantinople in the event of Germany being engaged in war with France. But Salisbury, although he did not know of the Reinsurance Treaty, was not deceived by what he described as Bismarck's 'pretty games.' He told White, the British Ambassador at Con-stantinople: 'If he (Bismarck) can get up a nice little fight between Russia and the three Powers (England, Austria and Italy), he will have leisure to make France a harmless neighbour for some time.'[3] Consequently, he did not commit himself very deeply in the tripartite agreement, and became increasingly sceptical about the possibility of bringing pressure to bear in Constantinople. He told White that he thought the British Government would probably have to abandon 'the ideal we have pursued since Lord Stratford's days of a leading influence at Constantinople . . . We have little to promise or give.'[4] He continued his endeavours to mitigate French hostility and tried 'to keep friends with France if we can without our paying too dear,' since 'the threat of making us uneasy in Egypt through France is the only weapon Bismarck has against us and we are free of him if we can blunt it.'[5] To this end he refused to be stampeded by the failure of the Drummond Wolff negotiations and pursued a conciliatory policy towards France. This was not very successful and, in the early part of 1888, England and France were within measur-able distance of war. In February, Salisbury told Baring that the French 'already look upon a war with England as the cheapest of three alter-natives' and complained that 'they are so unreasonable and have so much incurable hatred of England.'[6]

This hostility did not prevent the negotiation of a Convention providing for the neutrality of the Suez Canal, about which the British Government had been engaged in intermittent and acrimonious negotiations with the French Government since 1885. Agreement was eventually arrived at in October 1887 in the form of a draft Convention which was submitted to Turkey and the principal maritime Powers. The Convention in its final form was signed in Constantinople by the Representatives of the Powers on 29 October 1888 and ratifications exchanged in December 1888.[7] The Convention, which has been much quoted since, and which still forms the basis of the international status of the Canal, created little stir at the time and was not regarded as being of much importance, partly because it was provided that it should only come into force on the British evacuation of Egypt which, it was still generally assumed, would probably take place within the next few years. Briefly, the Convention provided that the Suez Canal 'shall always be open in time of peace and in time of war to every vessel of commerce or of war without distinction of flag,' that 'the Representatives in Egypt of the signatory Powers shall be charged to watch over the execution of the Convention,' that 'no rights of war, no act of hostility, nor any act having for its object the obstruction of the free navigation of the Canal shall be permitted in the Canal or in its ports of access or within a radius of three nautical miles of these ports,' and that 'other Powers shall not interfere with the measures which HM the Sultan or HH the Khedive in the name of H.I.M. (the Sultan) ... may find it necessary to take for the securing by their own forces of the defence of Egypt and the maintenance of public order.'

Baring was not enthusiastic about this Convention and told Salisbury that he regarded it as 'a sop to France,' which indeed it was. 'I would have liked to have got some Egyptian concession from them as the price of it.'[8]

Meanwhile, during the Summer of 1888, the war scare with France died down. In August, Salisbury told the Queen: 'France is and always must remain England's greatest danger. But that danger is dormant as long as the present strained relations exist between France and her two eastern neighbours (i.e. Germany and Italy). If ever France should be on friendly terms with them, the Army and Navy Estimates would rise very rapidly.'[9]

These, then, were the keys to British Near East policy: (1) To keep France and Germany apart without precipitating war between them; (2) To offset French hostility in Egypt and Franco-Russian hostility at Constantinople by a limited and secret support of the Triple Alliance, but not to join it, and to keep open the possibility of an understanding with France; (3) To try and restore the possibility of bringing pressure to bear at Constantinople by an increase in naval strength and by a secret understanding with Austria and Italy; (4) To remain in Egypt until such time as it could be evacuated as part of an arrangement which would restore effective British influence at Constantinople.

Salisbury's increasing scepticism about the possibility of doing this led gradually and almost imperceptibly towards a policy of regarding a permanent British presence in Egypt as a necessary alternative. It was not until 1896, when British inability to influence Turkey in the matter of the Armenian massacres had been humiliatingly demonstrated, that the policy of bringing pressure to bear in Constantinople was finally abandoned and the prospect of a permanent British presence in Egypt tacitly accepted as the basis of British Near East policy. But, in the meantime, largely as a result of Baring's influence and importunity, the British position in Egypt was progressively buttressed and fortified.

In his communications with Salisbury between 1887 and 1892 Baring patiently and presciently developed the case for remaining in Egypt. In a letter to Goschen—whom he knew far better than he did Salisbury—in April 1888, he set out, well in advance of Salisbury's thinking on the subject, what he regarded, and what was eventually accepted, as the logical conclusion of declining British influence at Constantinople: 'I believe that the . . . centre of gravity of our real Eastern interests in Europe has, for the last twenty-five years, been shifted from Constantinople to Cairo, that we shall never be able to get any real friendship from the Turk, and that his friendship is worth little even if we succeeded in acquiring it. It is a pity that we ever came to Egypt, but we have some real solid interests here and it would be a mistake to sacrifice them in pursuit of the phantom of Turkish good will.'[10]

But more immediately important, from the point of view of its effect on Salisbury's mind, was the thesis, which Baring started developing soon after, of the necessity for safeguarding the British position in Egypt by preventing any other Great Power from occupying any part of the upper Nile valley. His first communication on the subject was in a letter to Goschen in December 1888. After telling him that, for financial and military reasons, there could be no question of an immediate reconquest of the Sudan by Egypt, he went on: 'It would be most menacing to Egypt that a European Power should hold the headwaters of the Nile . . . We must stand on the defensive and come to terms with the tribes if we can.'[11] A year later, when the Italians, who were installed at Massawa, were threatening to occupy Kassala, on the edge of the Nile valley, he told Salisbury: 'The establishment of a civilised Power in the Nile valley would be a calamity for Egypt . . . The savage tribes who now rule in the Sudan do not possess the resources nor the engineering skill to do any real harm . . . The case would be very different were a civilised Power established in the Nile valley . . . They could so reduce the water supply as to ruin the country . . . Whatever Power holds the Upper Nile valley must by the mere force of its geographical situation, dominate Egypt.'[12]

The fear of having the supply of Nile water cut off was an ancient and traditional one in Egypt. There were various legends about blackmail having been levied on Egypt by medieval kings of Abyssinia in the form of threats to dam the Blue Nile. Traditional Egyptian hostility towards Abyssinia may indeed have been nourished by these legends, which had some basis of reality. In 1450 King Alphonso of Aragon had sent messengers to the King of Abyssinia asking him to block the Nile in order to support a projected Aragonese campaign in the Holy Land. About fifty years later, Albuquerque, trying to develop the trade route round the Cape in face of Moslem opposition, had thought in the same terms and had asked King Manuel of Portugal to send stonemasons from Madeira to assist the King of Abyssinia to dam the Blue Nile. He reported that 'Prester John' (the generic European name for Kings of Abyssinia) was 'very desirous of accomplishing it but he had no means of carrying it out; and if this had been done the land of Cairo might be entirely destroyed.' Two centuries later, in 1704, the then King of Abyssinia sent a letter to the Pasha of Egypt reminding him that 'to punish you God has put into our power His fountain, His outlet, His increase, and we can dispose of it to do you harm.' In more recent times, in 1851, C. T. Beke, an African explorer, sent Palmerston a 'Memoir on the Possibility of Diverting the Waters of the Nile so as to Prevent the Irrigation of Egypt.' In July 1884, Sir Samuel Baker, the explorer and unofficial pundit on the Sudan, in an article in the *Nineteenth Century* developing the case for the reconquest of the Sudan, stressed the danger of having the Nile water cut off unless Egypt were in control of the upper Nile, and quoted Isaiah XIX v. 6 and other Biblical texts in support of his view. He returned to the point in three letters to *The Times* on 9, 17, and 25 October in 1888. 'Should a civilised or even semi-civilised country be in possession of Khartum, the waters of the Rahad, Dinder, Blue Nile and Atbara could be diverted from their courses and dispersed throughout the desert to the utter ruin and complete destruction of Egypt proper.'[13]

Baker's letters to *The Times* in October 1888 were occasioned by the incidence of an abnormally low Nile in that year. It is probable that these letters, reinforced by a memorandum written by Riaz Pasha, then Prime Minister, in December 1888, were the immediate causes of Baring's warning to Goschen and of his subsequent development of this theme to Salisbury. Riaz, in his memorandum,[14] which stressed the necessity for Egypt retaining possession of Suakin, wrote: 'No one will deny . . . that the Nile is the life of Egypt. Now the Nile means the Sudan and the bonds and connections which unite Egypt to the Sudan are as inseparable as those which unite the soul to the body . . . No European Power would occupy Suakin without wishing to extend its power into the interior with a view to reaching richer districts. But if it attained its object and took possession of the banks of the Nile it would be all over with Egypt. Egypt could never consent to such an attack on its existence.'

From a later pronouncement by Scott Moncrieff it appears that he also was of the opinion that it was technically possible for a Power in possession of the Upper Nile to deny its waters to Egypt. In a lecture to the Royal Institute of Great Britain seven years later he said: 'A civilised nation on the Upper Nile would surely build sluices across the outlet of Victoria Nyanza and control that sea as Manchester controls Thirlmere. This would probably be an easy operation. Once done, the Nile supply would be in their hands, and if poor little Egypt had the bad luck to be at war with the people on the upper waters, they might flood them or cut off their water supply at their pleasure.'[15] Moncrieff may well have expressed this opinion to Baring in 1888 and it would have carried more weight with him than the opinions of either Riaz Pasha or Sir Samuel Baker. Unlike them, Moncrieff was an irrigation engineer. And, unlike them, Moncrieff was thinking in terms of the White, rather than the Blue, Nile. This was to be of some importance later.

With the increased importance of Summer water in the season of low Nile due to the rehabilitation of the Delta barrage and the subsequent plans for a reservoir at Aswan, the possibility of hostile control of the White Nile, which was the principal source of Egypt's precious Summer water, became more important than the possibility of damming the flood waters of the Blue Nile, which was, in any case, technically chimerical. But it would not have been technically impossible to interfere with the White Nile.

It is uncertain how far Baring himself really believed in the fears which he expressed to Salisbury. But, in their effect on Salisbury, they proved to be a very good argument. Lady Gwendolen Cecil states[16] that, from this time, 'the necessity of safeguarding the Nile Valley from the intrusion of other Powers becomes a separate and dominating factor in his policy . . . His resolve to eliminate all auxiliary occasions of differ, ence with France affected his action consciously in every quarter of the globe . . . The main action of the diplomatic drama was already shifting to the African scramble.'

Salisbury, although not abandoning the idea of a possible rehabilitation of the British position at Constantinople, began to acquiesce in, and even to encourage, Baring's policy of consolidating the British position in Egypt and preparing for an eventual reconquest of the Sudan. His public statements on the subject became more and more uncompromising. In February 1888 he was telling Baring: 'I should dread any very glaring exhibition of our sovereignty in Egypt now.'[17] But, in November 1889, in a speech at the Guildhall, he told his audience that 'that organisation of fanaticism and slave-hunting which has already caused so much misery through vast portions of what belonged to Egypt' (*i.e.* the Dervishes in the Sudan) made it necessary for the British to remain in Egypt 'whether assisted or obstructed by other Powers.'[18]

For prudential reasons Salisbury had given the Dervish danger in the Sudan, rather than the danger from European Powers, as the reason for not evacuating. But, by that time, there was no longer any real fear of a

Dervish invasion of Egypt. As Baring had just told him, 'the Dervishes have now been well beaten both in Suakin and the Nile valley. It is not probable that they will advance for some while, if at all.'[19] He had also told him, a little earlier, that the argument against evacuation based on the Dervish danger was 'an excellent working argument,' 'but it does not in reality constitute the real reason why evacuation is well-nigh impossible.' Baring went on to make it clear that the arguments he had advanced about the Nile water and the shift in the centre of gravity of British Near East policy from Constantinople to Cairo were not, in his view, the real reasons either. 'The main argument is based on the incapacity of the ruling classes in this country. I am more and more struck with this the longer I remain here. I have not yet come across a single man of the Pasha class who appears really to understand the elements of the local political problem. The ruling classes here are almost exclusively foreigners, *i.e.* Turks, with an admixture of Armenians, Syrians, Algerians etc. The Arabi movement, although in a degree anti-European, was principally anti-Turk. All this class are detested by the people and they are more disliked now than they have ever been before. I cannot say that our good government has made us popular but . . . it has made the Pashas more unpopular than before . . . The Khedive has no hold on the country. Riaz[20] is deplorably wanting in judgement and, if left to himself, would produce a revolution in six months. The argument that, if we had a right to come back, we should probably never have to exercise that right is based on a fallacy. The interests involved in bringing us back would be stronger than those involved in getting us to stay away. The more I look at it, the more does the evacuation policy appear to be impossible under any conditions.'[21]

This was a repetition of what he had been telling various Ministers over the last three years. But it now had increased weight both as a result of the wider considerations which he was simultaneously urging, and, paradoxically, as a result of the extent of success he had achieved in creating conditions of stability, solvency and security in Egypt. Whereas the achievement of these conditions had originally been regarded as justifying evacuation, it was now coming to be regarded, both by Baring and Salisbury, as a reason for staying. There was the risk, emphasised by Baring, that evacuation would put everything back to its original condition. There was also the fact that what had been achieved, on the one hand made the occupation easier to defend in the face of foreign opinion and, on the other hand, created a climate of opinion in England in favour of a quasi-permanent occupation.

Baring, encouraged by a growing sense of achievement and by the increasing confidence shown in him by Salisbury, was by this time deeply interested in Egypt and had come to regard its administration as his life's work. He was much more interested in the local than in the international aspects of the British presence there. Salisbury was mainly interested in the international aspect, and only slowly divested himself of his original view that Egypt was an 'incubus.' But he gradually came round to Baring's view, not only of the international aspects which Baring had succeeded in implanting in his mind, but also of the local aspects to which Baring so frequently drew his attention, and of which British public opinion was becoming increasingly conscious.

But Salisbury remained adamant against any move in the direction of annexation, and he made it clear to Baring that there was no question of any 'show-down' with France over the various hindrances which the French continued to put in the way of the British administration. In February 1891 he told him that he must 'make love to the French' if he wanted to get any local concessions out of them, as 'we have no means of exerting pressure on them.'[22] But, in his annual Guildhall speech on 9 November of that year, he went a long way towards a public declaration of Baring's point of view: 'England underwent great sacrifices . . . in order to rescue Egypt from evils that had overtaken her . . . If England acted alone it was not her fault . . . We cannot allow all that to be swept away as if it were last year's almanac and to suffer the country, which at so much cost has been rescued, to fall back into the condition of anarchy, confusion and danger which it occupied a few years ago.' He went on to say that the Government had no wish to divorce Egypt from Ottoman suzerainty. But, 'before England leaves Egypt she must be strong enough to repel external attack and put down internal disturbance.' He commented that the desired goal would be reached more quickly if the English in Egypt were not obstructed by others and asserted that all Parties in England were in agreement with the Egyptian policy which he was setting forth. 'I entreat those who criticise us abroad not to believe that this matter is one which will be disposed of by Party vicissitudes. The English people are proud of the splendid success of our administrators and soldiers and, whatever Party may be in power, will never withdraw their hand from the steady and vigorous prosecution of the humane undertaking with which it is their pride and honour to be connected.'[23]

The immediate occasion for this speech was 'a sudden revival of interest in Egypt among English Liberals.'[24] In September, Morley had made a public speech criticising the occupation, and Gladstone had spoken of the 'burdensome and embarrassing' occupation, 'escape from which it is to be feared that the Tory Government would hand over to its successors to deal with.' A General Election was due the following year and it was generally expected that the Liberal Party, of which Gladstone was still the leader, would be returned to office. For this reason, announcements of this kind by probable future Ministers had a good deal of significance and were regarded abroad as something like a pledge of early evacuation. Baring grumbled that the speeches had attracted a good deal of attention in Egypt and asked Salisbury to 'take some public occasion to say that HMG's policy regarding Egypt was unchanged,' because 'the talk about evacuation is doing a great deal of harm.'[25] A few days earlier, referring to the same speeches, he had told Salisbury that 'the talkative elements—the French and the Pashas and suchlike—will be in favour of evacuation . . . (But) the mass of the population, the better class of commercial men and the very small class of *bona fide* reformers, will be against evacuation but will not make their voices heard. Generally, the "classes" support Gladstone's recent utterances and the "masses" are against them.' He went on: 'Such words as "popularity" and "unpopularity" should be entirely erased from the vocabularies of those who talk seriously of Eastern affairs. In this country enlightened self-interest takes the place of patriotism and suchlike sentiments. People will assume that the Pashas are opposed to the English, and if the English are in no position to protect them, it would be well to be on the winning side and to cut their connections with English sympathisers. I should have thought that it would have been wise for Ministers who hope to get into office to avoid pledging themselves definitely to any positive line of action . . . But that is not my affair.'[26]

The Liberal speeches and Baring's protests had made Salisbury go further in his Guildhall speech than he really wished. He still wanted to keep his options open and not to bar the door to a possible understanding with France and Turkey, leading to a conditional evacuation. He told Baring that his Guildhall speech was 'a necessity under the circumstances, but it has acted as an irritant. I heartily wish the G.O.M. had spared me the necessity of making it.'[27] He was quite determined not to be driven out of Egypt as a result of the British position there being made untenable, either by a threat to the Nile water or by internal disturbances. But he was still prepared to go if he could drive a favourable bargain in terms of European politics.

This was the general framework of events in home and foreign affairs within which the administration of Egypt was carried on between 1888 and 1892.

It has already been mentioned that relations between Baring and Nubar were deteriorating (p. 133) and how Nubar, on a visit to London in the Summer of 1887, had tried to stir up trouble against Baring and Vincent. The stabilisation of the Sudan position, where the Dervishes were quiescent after having been defeated at the end of 1885 at the battle of Ginnis, just south of Wadi Halfa, the failure of the Drummond Wolff negotiations, and the removal of the threat of an International Commission on Egypt's finances, all meant that Baring was able to take a longer and calmer view of the local situation. He decided that Nubar was no longer indispensable and that the time had come to clear up some of the abuses which had resulted from the virtual British withdrawal from the Ministries of Interior and Justice since 1884. The opportunity arose with the death of Valentine Baker in November 1887. After the débâcle in the Sudan the Gendarmerie had been disbanded and Baker had been placed in command of the Police with a number of European officers under him. Not all of these were very efficient and this, combined with the friction between the Police and Parquet (the judicial organisation, independent of the Police and responsible to the Ministry of Justice, which, under the French system prevailing in Egypt, directed the interrogation of accused and the preparation of criminal prosecutions), and the inefficiency of the National Courts inaugurated by Dufferin, had resulted in an alarming increase in crime and a deterioration of public security generally. In an attempt to offset this, Nubar had set up summary Courts, known as 'Commissions of Brigandage,' under the direct jurisdiction of the Provincial Governors, which by-passed the National Courts in most criminal proceedings and dispensed a rough-and-ready justice on the old Turkish model. How rough and ready this justice was, was not yet apparent to Baring.

On Baker's death Nubar wanted to replace him by an Egyptian and gradually to eliminate the European element in the provincial police. Baring thought that this would impair public security still further and refused to agree. But he told Salisbury that he hoped to settle the question 'without raising any big question of principle.'[28] His idea was to bring the police under the control of the army and to appoint a British officer in the Egyptian Army as Inspector-General of Police. He complained that his difficulties in dealing with Nubar had been increased by the fact that he had come back from England 'with the fixed idea that he had and I had not the confidence of HMG.'[29] He was also extremely irritated by the permission given by the Foreign Office for Tigrane Pasha, Nubar's son-in-law and a rising Egyptian politician, to go to London early in 1888 as an emissary from Nubar with, as it turned out, the principal object of complaining to the British Government about Baring. He told Salisbury by telegraph: 'I have done all in my power to avoid a conflict with Nubar as it may cause Parliamentary trouble, but I doubt if I can ward it off much longer. On purely local grounds the sooner it comes the better . . . Would you mind telling me privately how far I may count on your support . . . I should be perfectly prepared to go if you thought a change desirable.' He added that Nubar's attitude towards him and the British Government had changed since his visit to London and that the Khedive, 'who has shown great weakness and want of judge-ment,' supported Nubar.[30] He was clearly very discouraged. A few days later, in a letter to Salisbury, he explained his personal position and his telegraphed offer of resignation, which he apparently already regretted. 'I have no personal wish to go. I do not want to leave the diplomatic service. The work is to me more congenial and more useful than the only other employment on which I could fall back—that of being one amongst 650 people condemned to hear the mighty lucubrations of Biggar, Labouchere, etc. The more difficult the task the less I feel inclined to go. But I do not want to embarrass HMG. The Egyptian business is the most important enterprise on which we have embarked for many years . . . We are not by a long way out of our difficulties. A great deal depends on the personal qualifications of the English Representative whose task is one of the utmost difficulty. Therefore, if you think a change advisable, do not let personal difficulties stand in the way. I did not until I had your decision express myself about Tigrane's mission. I merely told the Khedive that I thought it irregular . . . Personally I like him; he is honest and intelligent. If we had a small Ministerial storm it might be managed to be purely local . . . I shall do everything possible to continue working the present system . . . The upset of the Sherif Ministry asserted our authority; it made the Khedive and his Ministers understand that they must do what they were told. On the strength of the fright this occasioned I got on fairly well for four years . . . But Nubar's visit to London produced a complete change due to the talk of irresponsible outsiders before whom he posed as the earnest Egyptian patriot writhing in the grip of a truculent Consul-General. He came away with the impression that our intention to evacuate was much more decided than it really was. Hence he wanted to prepare for remaining in office after we left—a pure delusion, for he would not stay a week . . . His general attitude is very unfriendly . . . The whole system of government is so ill-defined and anomalous that it can only be worked successfully if loyalty and good will is shown on both sides. The Khedive is pretty straight, but weak and lately in Nubar's pocket . . . A moment comes with these people when we have to be very downright . . . The way to prevent an explosion is to show that we are the masters.'[31]

Salisbury, in reply to Baring's telegram of 15 February, tried to calm him down. He told him that no encouragement had been intentionally given to Nubar on his visit to London. 'But we are badly trained for dealing with Armenians. I suspect that he gets encouraged by Con-stantinople. But I believe that it is merely the echo of our military with-drawal. When you advance on a dog he runs away; when you walk away, he does not wait until you are far off, but begins barking at once. Even so with Nubar.' But he went on to warn Baring to 'try and postpone any break with him to a more convenient season. We are at the moment on the sharp ridge which separates the slope between peace and war . . . Therefore it is of no common importance to avoid any unnecessary cause of conflict. If you were to have a row in Egypt, the excited opinion of the French might turn that way . . . I should dread any very glaring exhibition of our sovereignty in Egypt at this moment. Of course, when the time comes, we shall support you heartily and thoroughly. I believe you are right, but even if I thought you wrong I should think it impossible to retreat before Nubar in face of the whole East. But keep the peace for the moment because I do not wish our administration in Egypt to be the cause to which a European war will be attributed by future historians.'[32]

Baring responded to this appeal. With the assistance of an official telegram from Salisbury expressing his support for Baring, the dispute over the Police was settled. Baring told Salisbury that 'the Khedive got frightened and threw Nubar over.'[33] Nubar told everybody that he had with difficulty persuaded the Khedive to accept Baring's views. 'I think he beats most other Armenians and the Armenians beat the world,' was Baring's comment.[34] So faces were saved all round. 'For the moment,' Baring reported, 'we are a happy family, but the whole machine is so fragile that it needs a very little to put it out of gear.'[35] The arrangement was that the European officers should remain in the Police and that an Englishman should succeed Baker as Inspector-General.

In fact, nothing very much had been solved. The roots of the trouble —the disputes between the European police officers and the Provincial Governors, the disputes between the Police and the Parquet, the inefficiency of the National Courts, and the abuses of the Commissions of Brigandage—remained untouched. These Baring left to be dealt with later. One step at a time. The great thing was that Nubar had been deflated, British authority upheld, and his own advice accepted; and this without any international crisis, troop reinforcements, or overt inter-vention by the British Government.

Nubar did not long survive his defeat. He had encouraged the Khedive to stand up to Baring, and then had let him down. The only thing which would have kept him in office was an intimation from Baring to the Khedive that the British Government wished him to stay. This intimation was not forthcoming, and Nubar received his congé in June. 'I stood aside,' Baring told Salisbury; 'I did not give him any personal support, (but) I took no special steps whatever to bring it about. It is as well that he is out of office.'[36] A few days later he told Salisbury, somewhat disingenuously, that he thought the Khedive had acted wisely in not consulting him over Nubar's dismissal as 'he knew well enough that he was not doing anything to which I should object.'[37]

The successful issue of this trial of strength restored Baring's confidence, which had been badly shaken at the beginning of the year. He had got the Khedive in hand again, he had got rid of Nubar, and he thought he knew how to manage Riaz, with whom he had worked in the past. He had got what he wanted without leaning very heavily on the British Government, and without provoking much criticism, either in France where Nubar was disliked, or at home.

Baring had never been really comfortable with Nubar, who was too intelligent, too much a master of intrigue, too conversant with the strings which could be pulled in the European capitals and in Constantinople. It was indeed unlikely that Riaz, any more than Nubar, would be prepared to act as Baring's puppet. But he was less intelligent than Nubar and, as such, a less formidable opponent, should it come to opposition. And, now that he had manoeuvred Sherif and Nubar successively out of office as soon as they had outlived their usefulness to the British, Baring no doubt felt that he could do the same with Riaz when the time came. But, for the moment, Riaz' stern hand, and his authority in the country, were needed to deal with the alarming state of public security. The time was not yet ripe for the puppet show.

So Baring left for his annual cure at Carlsbad, and his subsequent shooting and fishing holiday in Caithness, in a reasonably contented frame of mind.

Vincent who, as Financial Adviser, was working close to Baring at this time, afterwards wrote down his impressions of him: 'He was permeated with the heroic spirit of antiquity; its frankly avowed thirst for fame; its neglect of the insignificant; its belief in strength and power; its admiration for achievement; its contempt for weakness, whether in individuals or nations. Essentially Roman in his conception of things, his attitude in a crisis was certainly inspired by what he believed appropriate to a Pro-Consul. To this classical basis was added another source of strength. He was steeped in the severe financial tradition of Peel and Gladstone. He placed a sound financial system before every other consideration. If expenditure were demanded . . . it was only granted . . . if the money could be secured without disturbing the equilibrium of the Budget . . . Very accessible to his principal subordinates, he was always ready to listen and advise . . . For so strong-willed and self-reliant a man he referred home with surprising frequency . . . These communications he wrote out himself . . . making few corrections and sending the message as originally drafted . . . In interviews with Egyptian Ministers and officials he was civil but peremptory . . . He adhered to what he could do best—clear, straightforward, slightly paternal statement, with no flowers of speech. None of the prolixity which besets Anglo-Indian officials; no administrative jargon or periphrasis, still less a descent into the journalistic or picturesque. Rather the strength and brevity of the military commander. With a less genial appearance the plainness of his speech might have caused offence, but a faint suggestion of Pickwick made the perceptive realise that behind the curt phrase and abrupt manner lay a certain broad benevolence—a sense of what was due from the strong to the weak, a kindly superiority based upon benign self-reliance.'[38]

Soon after Baring returned to Cairo in October he was disturbed by an intimation from Salisbury that the French and Turks were likely once more to raise the question of evacuation, and by Salisbury's remark that 'it would have been better if they had accepted the Drummond Wolff Convention.'[39] In reply he expressed the hope that the question would not be raised 'in any serious form,' as no satisfactory solution was possible. 'Things on the whole are going well. It would be a great pity that everyone should be disturbed by raising the burning question of evacuation. The Drummond Wolf negotiations had one great advantage in that they gave us a case for refusing to negotiate again for the time being.'[40]

In the event nothing happened immediately to raise the question of evacuation and the year ended quietly, apart from a row with the War Office about the control of operations in the Sudan, where the Dervishes had just been defeated outside Suakin, and a quarrel between Riaz and Vincent 'which gave my Egyptian coach a serious tilt and at one time threatened to upset it.' 'But,' he commented placidly, 'Riaz and Vincent have got over their honeymoon and are settling down to the quarrels of married life. In this case Riaz was obstinate and rash, but Vincent attached more importance to the thing than it deserved. I would have supported Vincent more, but I did not want a change of Ministry. The whole thing is now settled.'[41]

The 'show-down' with Riaz did not take place until the Spring of 1891. It came over the same question as had caused Nubar's fall—law and order. But, on this occasion, it was Baring who took the initiative.

Baring got on better with Riaz than he had with Nubar. He was more in sympathy with the authoritarian, rough and rude, straight-talking Turk, than he had been with the devious, rusé Armenian. In April 1889 he told Salisbury that all was going smoothly, that Riaz was 'full of good intentions and the most honest man here. A stern disciplinarian. Does not intrigue. Inspires confidence with Moslems. Not liked, but feared and respected. An immense improvement over Nubar . . . His defects are that he is stupid, obstinate, violent and vain . . . He has not the most elementary idea of government by law. I was horrified to find that the "Commissions of Brigandage" had been freely extorting evidence by torture etc. I shut my eyes to a good deal, but there is a limit. He will one day commit an enormity which will be exaggerated by the Press and make it very difficult to keep him in office . . . If Riaz were turned out it would produce considerable difficulties. We should have to choose between (a) direct rule of the Khedive with a savage and retrograde Turk as Prime Minister, and (b) Mustafa Fahmy, a weak man whose nom/ination would mean increased British interference in reality and appear/ance. The French would not like it.'[42]

The first alternative would be no improvement; Baring was not yet ready for the second. But the Commissions of Brigandage, whose mal/practices had been exposed in a report to the Ministry of Justice by M. Legrelle, the Belgian Procureur/Général of the National Courts, had to be abolished. Their abolition led to a further deterioration in public security and gave a new urgency to the reform of the National Courts. It was some time before Baring took any action. But, in June 1890, just before he went to Europe for his annual vacation, he arranged with the Government of India for the loan of a judge—Mr John Scott. 'I want to get him permanently appointed as Judicial Adviser. Unless this is done it is useless to expect reforms in the Law Courts. The appointment would be resented by Riaz. Therefore I shall have to ask Lord Salisbury's support before I begin my fight. It will not come till the Autumn.'[43] At the same time he told Salisbury that Riaz was 'showing himself to be dogmatic, narrow/minded, obstinate and rebellious to a degree which makes him almost impossible to deal with . . . The Khedive no longer loves Riaz and I think that his fall is inevitable before long.'[44] The ground was being prepared.

Baring returned to Egypt in October after having been to Naples where he conducted some abortive negotiations with the Italian Govern/ment over 'spheres of influence' in East Africa.[45] On his return he warned Salisbury that he would have differences with the Khedive and with Riaz over Scott's appointment as Judicial Adviser 'which might upset the Ministry. If you give me authority to go on I shall choose my own time.'[46] Salisbury seems to have been a little dubious, but Baring went ahead. At the end of the year he was able to tell Salisbury: 'I have never known Riaz in such a good humour.' He had agreed without much difficulty to Scott's appointment. 'The Khedive was much more reluctant, (but) he can always be squeezed without creating any upset, whereas Riaz might resign . . . I think that a good deal of Riaz' good humour is due to the stand we have made with the Italians over Kassala.'[47]

But there was trouble ahead. Scott had just prepared a Report con/taining a comprehensive scheme of reforms for the National Courts, which he had submitted to the Minister of Justice and to the Prime Minister. Baring warned Salisbury that Scott's recommendations 'must be insisted on. We have tried twice and failed. It would not be wise to have a third failure.'[48] He also warned Salisbury that Riaz was becoming impossible. 'Palmer[49] and Scott, the most conciliatory of men, say they can't get on with him . . . I now think he had better go . . . But I want to choose an occasion which will not give an opportunity to the French to make themselves unpleasant.'[50] A few days later, he asked Salisbury for a statement from the British Government, which he could show to Riaz, indicating their insistence on acceptance of Scott's recommendations. He thought that Riaz would 'accept any scheme of judicial reform insisted on by HMG and not resign.'[51] But Salisbury was still dubious. On 23 January he had written to Baring: 'My fear is lest we shall bring our dominance so forcibly before the ordinary French elector that he will force his Government to be troublesome. Your position as *maire de palais* will be too plainly revealed if Riaz follows Nubar at a distance of two years.'[52] And, a month later, he told him that the French were grumbling about Scott's recommendations, saying that interference with the National Tribunals was equivalent to annexation.[53]

In the end Baring got what he wanted. Riaz, after having moved the Minister of Justice to reject, and the Khedive to object to, Scott's recommendations, eventually gave way. And, as had happened over Nubar, the Khedive, annoyed at having been pushed into an exposed position and then abandoned by his Prime Minister, dismissed Riaz after having assured himself that Baring would raise no objection.

Scott's reform proposals were not in fact very drastic. They included an increase in the number of European judges, the establishment of a Committee of Surveillance to watch over the proceedings of the Courts of First Instance, manned principally by European lawyers, the establish- ment of Assize Courts, and some revision of the Criminal Code. What was really at stake, as it had been in the earlier Ministerial crises of 1884 and 1889, was the question of effective British control. On each occasion Baring had won the battle, on the first occasion as a result of the decisive intervention of the British Government, on the second and third occasions largely as a result of his own manoeuvring, and in spite of doubts expressed by Salisbury. The first two occasions had not been of his seeking; on the third occasion it was he who had deliberately brought the matter to a crisis, in his own way and at his own time, when he felt himself ready to adopt the second of the two alternatives mentioned to Salisbury in April 1889.

Riaz' successor as Prime Minister, more or less nominated by Baring, was Mustafa Pasha Fahmy, on whom Baring had had his eye for some time. He was a veteran in Egyptian public life. At one time he had been an ADC to Ismail and was reputed to have had some share in the murder of Ismail Pasha Sadiq, the Mufattish, in 1876.[54] He had been a member of most Egyptian Cabinets since Ismail's time. In 1885 Baring had described him as follows: 'Mustafa Pasha Fahmy has rather played the part of the Vicar of Bray in Egyptian politics. He was a firm friend of Ismail, then coquetted with Arabi and is now devoted to the present Khedive. But I do not know that that is much against him. They all did the same and indeed could scarcely do otherwise. He is poor which, for an Egyptian who has held high office, connotes honesty. He has always been very friendly to everything British and his influence with the Khedive is considerable, although he does not have much influence in the country, and his advice has always been exerted in the right direction. He was the only Egyptian who had the sense to realise from the first that, without foreign help, the defeat of Hicks was the death-blow to Egyptian power in the Sudan. He is a civilised Turk and not in the least fanatical.'[55] This was the man who, except for an interval of two years, from 1893 to 1895, was to be Prime Minister for the rest of Baring's time in Egypt. In retrospect, his coming to office marks the end of any substantial measure of Egyptian autonomy, and the beginning of a process of increasingly overt British superintendance of all departments of the Administration. This was not accidental, or the result of ineluctable circumstances. It was something for which Baring had been deliberately working, and for which he no doubt considered that the time was ripe.

Financially and economically, great progress had been made. In October 1889 Baring had told Salisbury that 'there will be equilibrium this year and a considerable surplus next year which will give a little elbow-room for expenditure and will for the first time enable some popular measures to be taken in the direction of reducing taxes.'[56] Early in 1889 Vincent had prepared a scheme for the Conversion of the Preference and Daira Debts in the expectation that the resultant saving in interest would provide the sum needed to complete the abolition of the corvée. But, under the terms of the Law of Liquidation, the Conversion operation required the consent of the Powers, and this inevitably involved bargaining with the French Government, which, in effect, made it clear that their agreement was dependent on the fixing of a date by the British to evacuate Egypt. M. Spuller, the French Foreign Minister, pointed out with some relevance that, if the affairs of Egypt were sufficiently prosperous to justify a Conversion operation, there was no further justification for the British remaining there; if, on the other hand, conditions still justified a British occupation, these same conditions would render Conversion unjustifiable. As a result of this check the Egyptian

Government, in December 1889, on Baring's advice, submitted to the General Assembly, which had been especially convened for the purpose, a proposal for an increase in land-tax sufficient to finance the abolition of the *corvée* without the necessity for Conversion. The Assembly approved the proposal unanimously. This, however, was a piece of window-dressing and the increased tax was never levied or indeed intended to be levied. The object was to prepare the ground for a further approach to the Powers about Conversion. This approach was facilitated by the fall of the French Government in March 1890. The new French Govern-ment, of which M. Ribot was Prime Minister and Foreign Minister, was slightly more accommodating than its predecessor, and agreed to the proposed Conversion provided that the economies deriving from it were put at the disposal of the Caisse. The other Powers had no objections to offer and, in June 1890, the Conversion operation took place. The Conversion loan was for a sum of £29,400,000 at 3½ per cent interest for the conversion (a) of the Preference Debt, (b) of a loan of £2,330,000 at 4 per cent raised in 1888 to finance the commutation of Government pensions, and (c) of the Daira Debt whose capital was reduced by 15 per cent. A sum of £E1,300,000 was also earmarked for capital expenditure on irrigation and other public works. The effect of the Conversion was to reduce the service on the foreign debt by £E314,000 p.a. This was more than enough to finance the abolition of the *corvée*. But, in view of the French stipulation that the economies deriving from the Conversion should be put at the disposal of the Caisse, it was necessary to get the permission of the Caisse to use £E150,000 p.a. of this to increase the 'authorised' expenditure. There followed a repetition of the bargaining which had taken place over the previous £E250,000 in 1887. Eventually, after some months of negotiation, the French Government agreed to permit £E150,000 p.a. of the Conversion economies to be used to abolish the *corvée* on condition that a proposed 'Professional Tax,' which had been agreed to by all the Powers and was about to be imposed on Egyptians and foreigners, was abolished. But, in the meantime, 'by a great stroke of luck with tobacco duty,' the Egyptian Government found from its own 'unaffected' resources the £E150,000 p.a. for the abolition of the *corvée*.[57]

Such were the shifts to which Baring and the Egyptian Government were reduced as a result of the international financial regime imposed by the Law of Liquidation and the 1885 London Convention. The most that Baring and Vincent had been able to arrange was to induce the Caisse, in July 1888, to create a Reserve Fund out of surplus 'affected' revenue which could be released to the Egyptian Government, with the consent of the Caisse, for 'extraordinary expenditure.' This was supplemented, two years later, by a second Reserve Fund consisting of accumulated economies from Conversion.

Baring was particularly angry about the French insistence on the 'freezing' of the Conversion economies by the Caisse. Salisbury warned him that there was nothing to be done about it as 'they are undoubtedly on strong ground,' and that 'unless they are softened in some way they will delight in the indulgence of their spite.'[58] Baring accepted this. 'I quite understand that we can put on no pressure about the economies. We must have patience and trust to time to bring them round. I doubt whether they can go on indefinitely keeping unpopular taxation here because they are in a bad humour. Meanwhile the non-concession of the economies retards reforms. It does not do more than this. It does not place us at the mercy of the French or jeopardise financial equilibrium.'[59]

The healthy state of the finances was largely due to the expenditure on irrigation works provided from the loan authorised at the 1885 London Convention, and administered by Scott Moncrieff and his assistants. What had been done by the end of 1890 was summarised by Baring in his Annual Report for that year.[60] 'The Barrage has been completed and placed in a condition to fulfill its original purpose. From upstream of it three main trunk canals irrigate the whole Delta. The outlay on the Barrage since 1884 has been £E460,000. Of the three trunk canals, that on the west, which had been neglected and filled with weeds and sand, has been restored. The eastern canal has been entirely rebuilt since 1886 at a cost of £E372,000. Practically the whole Summer supply of the Nile is diverted by the Barrage into these canals . . . The Barrage has not much increased the area of cultivation, but it has largely increased that of land bearing double crops.' The Report went on to describe various other irrigation works which had been completed over the previous five years —locks and swing-bridges to assist navigation of the canals, desalination and drainage, on which £E140,000 had been spent, and 'minor irrigation works, such as secondary canals, sluices, siphons, escapes, weirs, etc.,' on which £E600,000 had been spent and which 'ensure that even in the worst year the whole of the Nile Valley shall receive its share of mud-charged water.' As a result of the irrigation improvements, the annual Egyptian cotton crop increased from an average of 2,900,000 kantars p.a. to an average of 4,500,000 kantars.[61] This, although to some extent counteracted by a fall in prices, was the principal reason for Egypt's new-found financial equilibrium.

Baring was under no illusions about the limited extent to which the British-inspired reforms had so far benefited the mass of the population. This was partly due to a slump in agricultural prices which, he considered, would in itself have brought Egypt to bankruptcy had the old regime continued. As it was, the reforms 'have enabled Egypt to meet all its financial obligations, in spite of the fall in prices. But they have not done more than this. From a purely pecuniary point of view, the position of the agricultural taxpayer has, by reason of the fall in prices, not been very materially improved.'[62]

There had as yet been no significant reductions in taxation. The state of law and order was still very bad. The National Courts were still dilatory and corrupt. Since it was the masses rather than the classes who had suffered under the kurbash and *corvée*, the masses rather than the classes had benefited from the abolition of these twin engines of oppression. But they still suffered from many of the miseries of arbitrary rule and there was, as yet, nothing much in the way of 'social services'—sanitation, hospitals, schools—to help lift them out of the animal nature of their existence. Such prison reforms as had been effected tended to encourage crime in that they made prison less unattractive.

Because of the limitations so far imposed on the scope of reforms, British officials were not yet very numerous or very costly. In 1890 366 Englishmen were employed in the Civil Administration at a cost of £E150,317 p.a. Of these, 183 were employed in the various inter-national Administrations. Of the remainder, 144 were in 'subordinate employment.' There were 39 high British officials costing £E37,700 p.a. Of these, 2 were in the Ministry of Finance, 3 in the Customs and Coastguards, 2 in the Post Office, 3 in the Lighthouse Administration, 8 in the Police, 9 in the Ministry of Public Works, 1 in the Prisons Administration, 3 in the National Courts, 8 in the Sanitary Department. To these had recently been added a Judicial Adviser, a Judge and a high official at the Ministry of Finance, while 69 British officers and 33 British NCO's were employed in the Egyptian Army.[63]

The dismissal of Riaz and his replacement by Mustafa Fahmy, although it did not lead to any immediate large increase in the number of British officials, led to an immediate and substantial increase in the extent of British control over the Administration. For the first time some effective British control was introduced into the Ministry of the Interior. Kitchener, who had been appointed Inspector-General of Police, as well as being Adjutant-General of the Egyptian Army, started reorganising the provincial police, largely detaching them from the control of the Mudirs and bringing them under his own direct control. Scott, the Judicial Adviser, took the Ministry of Justice in hand. The two principal citadels of Egyptian control, which Nubar and Riaz had succeeded in keeping in Egyptian hands, were effectively taken over. Alfred Milner, at that time Under Secretary in the Ministry of Finance, noted: 'We are now for the first time really responsible for the whole of the country.

Scott is now practically Minister of Justice and Kitchener Minister of the Interior.' But he added: 'Brigandage has not been materially reduced,'and complained that Kitchener was not on the right lines, since 'the proper course is not to diminish the power of the Mudirs over the police but to teach them to use it properly.'[64]

One of the reasons why Baring wanted more control over the Egyptian Administration was to hasten the pace and effectiveness of reforms in order to make the British occupation less unpopular, and to counteract the potential threat from 'ultra-Moslem and Arabist sympathisers who are not defunct but merely quiescent.' 'The more I see of the whole thing the more I am impressed with the inconveniences of the present position and the very great difficulty of getting out of it. It is a mighty difficult thing to govern a Moslem country without the force necessary to give weight to the European foreigners and without the Moslems whose authority might . . . take the place of material force . . . There is no capable Moslem. A sort of paralysis seems to have fallen on the Pasha class. They are quite devoid of elasticity. If they are not allowed to govern according to their own rude methods, which have become not only objectionable but impossible, they cannot govern at all. The only class I see springing up here is exemplified by Tigrane, who sees himself as a future Nubar, Yaqub Artin, another Armenian who is head of the Education Department, Butros Pasha, a Copt, and a few Gallicized Turks who, although Moslem, are in no way representative. All these are much more intelligent than the ordinary Arab or Turk. They want us to go as they feel that the future lies with them . . . But they are all foreigners and most of them are Christians; they are inexperienced doctrinaires wholly out of touch with the general population, not possessed of sufficient knowledge to govern themselves, and too conceited to follow the advice of others.'[65]

At home, Salisbury had by no means ruled out the possibility of an eventual, conditional evacuation as the result of an agreement with France and Turkey. Baring was compelled, reluctantly, to accept this. But his successive elimination of Nubar and Riaz, and his successful insistence on widening the scope of reform, would undoubtedly have increased the problems of evacuation if they ever had to be faced. Instead of buttressing indigenous authority, a policy which he had followed up to the time of the breakdown of the Drummond Wolff negotiations, he proceeded to undermine it, eventually nominating as Prime Minister a man who, as he had admitted to Salisbury some time before, could not survive in office without continual and overt British interference.

Baring knew quite well what he was doing and justified it to Salisbury by arguing that, because of the 'paralysis' which had descended on the

Turco-Egyptians, the 'unrepresentative' and 'doctrinaire' nature of the Copts, Armenians and Syrians, and the 'superstition, rapacity, ignorance and corruption' of the native Egyptians, as exemplified by the membership of the Legislative Council, there was no longer any possibility of a genuinely indigenous Administration working anyway. He hoped to organise his puppet-show without precipitating any crises and, indeed, without anybody realising what was happening. As he had predicted to Salisbury, Riaz' replacement by Mustafa Fahmy had only caused 'a few days' gossip.'[66] In so far as he expected any difficulty, he expected it from the change of Government which was likely to take place in England as a result of the General Election due in 1892. But, in the event, the trouble came from a quite unexpected source.

The precarious structure of indirect British rule in Egypt depended, *inter alia*, on the acquiescence of the Khedive, in whose name Decrees were promulgated, and by whose act Ministers were appointed and dismissed. In addition to being titular Head of State, the prestige of his office still gave the Khedive a certain amount of personal influence, although this had been greatly diminished since Ismail's time by the circumstances of Taufiq's accession, by the Arabi rebellion and by the British occupation. These circumstances, while diminishing Taufiq's personal prestige, more or less ensured his acquiescence in the British occupation, to which he owed his throne and, possibly, his life. He was, moreover, a man of no great energy and no decided personality. Although he sometimes required a little handling, he could, as Baring phrased it, 'always be squeezed without creating any upset' in order to induce him to play his rôle as a figurehead.

From Baring's point of view Taufiq was an almost ideal man for the position. He was neither corrupt, nor cruel, nor rapacious, and his private life provoked no unsavoury scandals. He was neither very intelligent, nor particularly industrious. He was not of the stuff of which martyrs, saints or patriots are made. He was still a comparatively young man and might reasonably be expected to occupy the throne of Egypt for many years to come. But, on 10 January 1892, after a few days' illness, he died, 'undoubtedly killed,' according to Baring, 'by the incompetence of his native doctors.'[67]

He was succeeded by his eldest son, Abbas Hilmi, a youth of eighteen who, at the time of his father's death, was completing his education in Vienna at the Theresianum, known as the Princes' Academy. (He was in fact not yet eighteen according to the solar calendar. But it was agreed between the Egyptian Government and Baring to calculate his age according to the Moslem lunar calendar in order to avoid the complications of a Regency.) Baring was at first favourably impressed. 'He is well-mannered and self-possessed. He did all the ceremonial work, which is rather trying for a boy of eighteen, very well.'[68]

The outward forms of the Sultan's suzerainty were scrupulously observed. Abbas Hilmi was formally called to the Khedivate by the Sultan, but Baring was anxious lest Abdul Hamid should take the opportunity to assert his suzerainty in some more positive way. There was a prolonged comedy over the issue of the Firman of Accession. The Sultan, moved apparently by Mukhtar Pasha, the Turkish High Commissioner whose continued presence in Egypt was the only permanent result of the Drummond Wolff negotiations, caused the Firman to be worded so as to amend, in favour of Turkey, the eastern boundary of Egypt in the Sinai Peninsula. There was some uncertainty about this boundary, which had never been precisely defined, but since 1841 it had always been taken to be a straight line running between el-Arish and the head of the Gulf of Aqaba. In the new Firman it was defined as a line running from el-Arish to Suez, which had the effect of excluding most of the Sinai Peninsula from Egyptian territory. It was all desert, and almost uninhabited, land, and Salisbury was not inclined to make an issue of it. But Baring disagreed. 'I attach more importance than you to the Sinai Peninsula. For the military and strategic arguments I care nothing; there are none. But the Turks are for Egypt troublesome neighbours and I would rather have them not at the hall door but at the porter's lodge.'[69] After a flurry of telegraphic communications between Cairo, London and Constantinople, Baring gained his point. The Firman was amended to his satisfaction and duly promulgated. After its promulgation Baring, in a note to Tigrane Pasha, the Egyptian Foreign Minister, laid down the principle that 'no alteration could be made in the Firmans regulating the relations between the Sublime Porte and Egypt without the consent of Her Majesty's Government.'[70]

Once this little flurry was over, nothing in Egypt seemed to have changed except the occupant of the throne and the style of the British Agent who, in March 1892, was elevated to the Peerage as Baron Cromer. In a letter conveying the offer of the Peerage Salisbury told Baring that it was being offered 'for work done in Egypt which has required very exceptional qualities and the result of which has exceeded all expectations . . . Your removal from Cairo might possibly be promotion for you, but it would not be promotion for Egypt. It would be absurd to recognise your services by destroying in a great measure your special opportunities of rendering them for the future.'[71] Cromer was subsequently created Viscount in 1898 and Earl in 1902.

In spite of advice given to him by Mukhtar and Reverseaux, the French

Consul-General, who urged a change of Ministry, Abbas followed Cromer's advice and confirmed Mustafa Fahmy and his father's other Ministers in their offices. During the early part of the Summer, before he went on his annual vacation, Cromer's main anxiety seems to have been the prospect of a change in British policy as a result of the expected change of Government following the General Election due in July. Locally, everything seemed to be going smoothly. He told Salisbury that the new Khedive had behaved 'very sensibly' over the frontier business.[72] He was complacent about his relations with the new Ruler. 'I am riding my new colt with the lightest of snaffles, but I do not want him to break away altogether or require a stiff pull at the curb to bring him up. By degrees he will acquire confidence in the English Government and, I hope and believe, confidence in me. Not that he shows the least want of confidence, but it must be the work of time and experience. He is frightened of the Turks and especially of Mukhtar, with whom he is unfortunately on bad terms ... As the older man of the two I think the fault lies with Mukhtar.'[73] And a little later: 'I see that the young Khedive is going to be very Egyptian. By that I do not mean so much anti-European, and certainly not anti-English, as anti-Turk, anti-Syrian, etc. His anti-Turkish proclivities have been developed by Mukhtar's injudicious treatment. I endeavour to tone down any too ardent patriotism ... I say to him, "Educate your Egyptians, but don't attempt any heroic remedies," and I daresay I shall bring him round to this view. He wanted to send away his Turkish bodyguard the other day, but Grenfell[74] and I got him to give up the idea; it would create a very bad impression in Constantinople. If I were Khedive I would rather rely on 100 Turks if it came to blows with the same number of fellahin. By giving my French and Russian colleagues plenty of rope they are hanging themselves in the good graces of the Khedive. They offer advice, they try and humiliate him, and they interfere. I am taking the line of non-interference in small things and waiting for him to ask my advice. I feel convinced that by this means I shall soon have him in my pocket without his knowing it or feeling the yoke.'[75] And two months later: 'My poor little Khedive was bandied about like a shuttlecock between rival interests, but he behaved very well ... (and) ... clung to my skirts with a tenacity which is almost greater than I could wish ... (He) is much too European to obtain a real hold over the ultra-Moslem population ... All these diplomatic incidents have pressed me to the front, but I hope soon to retire from the public gaze ... and to take in hand the education of the young Khedive. I cannot make him a good Mohammedan but I shall try and make him appear as if he were one. As it is, he resembles any gentlemanlike and healthy-minded boy fresh from Eton or Harrow—not at all devoid of intelligence but a good deal bored with el-Azhar Sheikhs, Ramadan fasts, etc. I really wish he were not so civilised.'[76]

Reading these letters, it is difficult to escape the conclusion that Cromer was rather enjoying seeing himself in the rôle of a Melbourne teaching the business of constitutional monarchy to a young, inexperienced and not unattractive Sovereign, and assuming that Abbas Hilmi would respond with the same devotion that Victoria showed to Melbourne. Instead, the new Khedive, probably inspired by M. Rouiller, the French-man who had been his tutor in Vienna, and who had accompanied him to Egypt as his Private Secretary, regarded his British mentor in much the same light as Victoria came to regard her humourless, interfering, heavy-handed Uncle Leopold, and determined that he should not be allowed to 'rule the roost.'

8

THE IRON HAND

FOR SOME MONTHS before the General Election held in July 1892 it had been seen as almost inevitable that Lord Salisbury's Administration, dependent as it was on the support of the Liberal Unionists, would be defeated and replaced by a Liberal Administration with Gladstone as Prime Minister. It seemed possible that this change would involve a change in British policy in Egypt of the kind forecast by Gladstone and Morley in speeches made during the Autumn of 1891, when they had expressed themselves as being in favour of evacuation. In spite of the fact that his previous Administration had been responsible for the occupation of Egypt, Gladstone had never really departed from the view expressed by him in an article in the *Nineteenth Century* in August 1877, which events were proving to be prophetic. 'Our first site in Egypt, be it by larceny or be it by emption, will be the almost certain egg of a North African Empire that will grow and grow until another Victoria and another Albert, titles of the Lake sources of the White Nile, will come within our borders, and till we finally join hands across the Equator with Natal and Cape Town—to say nothing of the Transvaal and the Orange River on the south or of Abyssinia or Zanzibar to be swallowed by way of viaticum on our journey—and then, with a great Empire in each of the four corners of the world . . . we may be territorially content but less than ever at our ease . . . My belief is that the day which witnesses our occupation of Egypt will bid a long farewell to all cordiality of political relations between France and England.' If Gladstone had had his way, he would probably have negotiated an evacuation of Egypt with France soon after his resumption of office. The likelihood of this happening caused a certain amount of speculation and unrest in Egypt, of which Cromer had complained to Salisbury, and which Salisbury tried to allay by his Guildhall speech in November 1891.

But Gladstone was not to have his own way. The rich and aristocratic Earl of Rosebery occupied much the same position in the Liberal Party and in the country as Hartington had done twelve years before and, like Hartington, he enjoyed the confidence of the Queen. It would have been almost impossible for Gladstone to have formed a viable Cabinet without him. He was in a position to name his own office and his own terms.

After the Liberals had won the Elections, and after the Queen had unwillingly charged Gladstone with the formation of a Government, Rosebery, with a becoming show of reluctance, accepted the Foreign Office, and soon made it clear to his colleagues that he intended to pursue a foreign policy on the same lines as his Conservative predecessor. With regard to Egypt, he accepted, much more whole-heartedly than Salisbury, Cromer's view that evacuation was impracticable in view of 'the utter incapacity of the ruling classes in the country.' And Cromer's view, first expressed in 1888, about the shift in the centre of gravity of British interests from Constantinople to Cairo as a result of weakening British influence at Constantinople, had been justified by the virtual exclusion of British influence there, resulting from the alliance between France and Russia. Because of this, Rosebery was determined to carry on Salisbury's policy of safeguarding the British position in Egypt by keeping all other Powers out of the Nile Valley. To this end, as we shall see (in Chapter 9), he compelled his reluctant colleagues to accept a British protectorate over Uganda, which even Salisbury had been prepared to abandon as a result of the failure of the British Chartered Company to make good their position there.

But the extent of Rosebery's commitment to a continuance of Salisbury's policy, and of his willingness and ability to enforce this policy on the rest of the Cabinet, were not apparent to Cromer (nor possibly to Rosebery himself) during the winter of 1892–93. Still less were they apparent to the young Khedive and to those politically-minded Egyptians who were beginning to chafe at the increasing pervasiveness of British influence and the apparent permanence of the British military occupation, and who were encouraged by Gladstone's return to office.

When Cromer returned to Egypt in November 1892 he became aware of a change of atmosphere. Nothing much had happened. But the Khedive had acquired a habit of making complaints, mostly frivolous, about various British officers and officials. The Pashas and the Press, taking their tone from the Khedive and realising that criticism of the British would be benevolently regarded at Court, had done likewise. Cliques which were already anti-British were encouraged. Others followed the new fashion set by the Khedive. Cromer 'very soon came to the con-clusion that a sharp conflict was inevitable.'[1] On 13 January 1893 he sent Rosebery what he described as 'the most important despatch I have written since I have been in Egypt.'[2] 'The young Khedive is evidently going to give a great deal of trouble. He is an extremely foolish youth. It is difficult to know how to deal with him. I think he will have to receive a sharp lesson—the sooner the better . . . If the youth gets his head in the air and thinks he can do as he pleases, things in general will go wrong.' He concluded by telling Rosebery: 'I think it possible that a younger and less well-known man would have a better chance of guiding him than I have.' Relations had clearly deteriorated since the year before when Cromer had prophesied that he would soon have Abbas in his pocket and boasted that he had been clinging to his skirts 'with a tenacity which is almost greater than I could wish.' It was also apparent that the Khedive was rather more popular in the country than Cromer had expected and that his estimate of him as resembling 'any gentlemanlike and healthy-minded boy from Eton or Harrow' had been somewhat wide of the mark. Much of the acerbity shown by Cromer in the crisis which followed is probably attributable to personal pique at his failure to win the young Khedive's confidence and at Abbas' refusal to play the part of Victoria to his Melbourne.

The immediate reason for this despatch was that the Khedive had been attempting to assert himself. He had proposed to Cromer that the Prime Minister, Mustafa Fahmy, who was ill, should be dismissed and replaced as Prime Minister by Tigrane Pasha. Cromer had objected, ostensibly on the ground that Tigrane was a Christian, actually because he knew that Tigrane was opposed to the occupation and was encouraging the Khedive in his desire for more independence. Rosebery had agreed with Cromer that a Christian Prime Minister was undesirable, but had advised him not to push his opposition too far.[3]

On 16 January, while Cromer's despatch was on its way to London, the crisis broke. Mustafa Fahmy, the Prime Minister, had been seriously ill and at one time had not been expected to live. By the middle of January he was out of danger although still confined to his room. His subservience to the British was making him objectionable to the Khedive. In view of his state of health there was no reason why the Khedive should not have suggested his resignation to him. There was no established precedent that the British Agent should be consulted before such a suggestion was made. Nubar and Riaz had both been dismissed by Taufiq without Cromer having been consulted. The fact that Mustafa was generally regarded as Cromer's *homme de paille* was not in itself sufficient reason for creating a precedent. At all events, on 15 January, the Khedive sent an emissary to Mustafa to urge his resignation. The Prime Minister, most unwisely, replied to the emissary that the Khedive had better consult Lord Cromer first. Mustafa's words, which were assiduously disseminated throughout the cafés and gossiping-places of Cairo, not only confirmed the general opinion that he was a British puppet, but were also considered disrespectful to the Khedive. Abbas' immediate reaction was to dismiss Mustafa and two other Ministers who were regarded as Anglophile. In Mustafa's place, and without consulting Cromer, Abbas made it known that he intended to appoint as Prime Minister Fakhry Pasha, a close associate of Tigrane who, as Minister of Justice, had previously objected to Scott's law reforms. As soon as he heard the news Cromer saw the Khedive and then sent off a furious telegram to London.[4] 'The last time I saw the Khedive it was fully understood that there was no question of replacing Mustafa as Prime Minister. This morning the Khedive's Private Secretary came to inform me that Mustafa was dismissed and Fakhry Pasha named in his place. The latter is a personal friend of Tigrane. He is an incapable man of bad character. Formerly Minister of Justice and dismissed on my advice because of his opposition to judicial reforms. I have seen the Khedive. He bases the change on the argument that Mustafa's state of health will not allow him to take up his work for some long while. There is no reason why he should be absent for more than about six weeks. The intention to make a change is generally known but the Khedive has promised me to stop the issue of any official notification of it till I could communicate with Your Lordship. I have little doubt that the Khedive has taken this step to show his complete independence.' Cromer then referred to Granville's telegram of 4 January 1884, at the time of the Sudan crisis, laying down the principle that British advice on important matters must be followed as long as the occupation lasted.

'If the Khedive is allowed to act as he has done in this matter, the whole situation both of the Egyptian Government and of the English officials will be changed and great trouble will ensue. It has been clear to me for some while that a struggle with the Khedive was inevitable. The sooner it comes the better. I would take the present opportunity of bringing matters to a head. I have very good reason for believing that the Khedive's present attitude is due in a great degree to his belief that I shall not be fully supported by HM's present Government as I was by the last Government. I do not think it is much use your giving advice. You should send me a telegram which I could show, I would suggest stating distinctly that HMG expected to be consulted about such an important matter as a change of Prime Minister, that no change at present seems necessary or desirable, and that you therefore cannot sanction the proposed nomination of Fakhry. I should be authorised in case of need to take whatever steps are necessary to prevent a change. The Khedive also wishes to change the Ministers of Finance and Justice. To these changes I would offer no objection. I wish to impress very strongly on HMG the importance of the present question. If the Khedive is allowed to carry his point the continuance of the system which I have worked for the past ten years will no longer be possible and we shall very probably have the discussion of the Egyptian question thrust on us prematurely, perhaps in an objection, able form. On the other hand, if the Khedive learns a lesson, he will probably not give much further trouble.'

In two subsequent telegrams[5] sent the same day Cromer told Rosebery (a) that he suspected Mukhtar and possibly Ismail, the exiled ex-Khedive, to be behind Abbas' action, and (b) that the '*coup de main*,' as he described it, was prearranged with the French and Russian Consuls-General. 'I hear also that if the Khedive is successful in his present undertaking the next step will be a wholesale dismissal of British officials. The latter, acting under my instructions, have declined to recognise the new Ministers pending receipt of instructions from London.'

At this point Cromer received Rosebery's reply to his first telegram, which gave him the statement from the British Government which he had suggested. 'HMG expect to be consulted in such an important matter as a change of Ministry. No change appears to be at present either necessary or desirable. We cannot sanction proposed nomination of Fakhry Pasha.'[6] This was immediately followed by another telegram in which Rosebery[7] instructed Cromer to take no measures, other than communicating the contents of his previous telegram, without referring back to London, and asked him: 'What means of pressure do you suggest and what steps do you propose to take in event of Khedive's refusal?'

Rosebery's first telegram gave Cromer exactly what he had asked for. But he may have sensed a certain lack of enthusiasm in the two telegrams taken together in that no general assurance of approval and support had been given. However he determined to force the pace. He immediately replied. 'I will communicate your telegram No. 12 to the Khedive to-morrow morning. In the event of his refusing to submit I propose to request General Walker (C-in-C British troops in Egypt) to take military possession of the Ministries of Finance, Justice and the Interior with instructions to the officers in command that the three Ministers who have been named without our consent shall not be allowed to enter. I would then request Palmer, Scott and Settle (Financial Adviser, Judicial Adviser and Inspector-General of Police respectively) to take charge of the three Departments and to act generally under my instructions until such time as the Khedive had submitted to me the names of Ministers whom HMG could accept. I would also take military possession of the Egyptian telegraph office. I hear that . . . the Khedive proposes to dismiss the Ministers of War and Public Works and to get rid of Scott and Garstin (Under Secretary, Ministry of Public Works in succession to Moncrieff, who had returned to India). He is relying on support from Constantinople and sympathy from France and Russia. I think there will be great difficulty in making him yield but it is absolutely essential that he be made to do so.'[8]

Next morning (17 January), Cromer went to see the Khedive, taking with him a copy of Rosebery's first telegram refusing to sanction Fakhry's appointment. He told the Khedive that, provided Mustafa was reinstated as Prime Minister, no objection would be offered to the proposed changes at the Ministries of Finance and Justice. 'In the contrary event I must reserve HMG's liberty of action with regard to all three Ministries. I said I did not think it would be just for me to press for an immediate answer and that unless he sent for me earlier I would call to-morrow morning to know his answer.'[9] In fact, Cromer wanted to give himself time to receive Rosebery's reply to his proposals for coercion so that he would know how to act in the event of his getting a refusal from the Khedive.

Immediately after telegraphing the result of this audience to Rosebery, Cromer telegraphed[10] asking for expedition of authority to act according to his recommendation in the event of the Khedive's refusal. He told Rosebery: 'It is essential that I be in a position to take prompt action. Delay will do harm. There is considerable excitement here. It is fully understood by all that, if the Khedive is allowed to win the day, English influence here would be completely destroyed.'

An hour or two after sending this telegram Cromer received Rosebery's reply to his recommendations for coercion. It was not what he had hoped for. Rosebery told him:[11] 'We consider the means proposed by you too violent and such as might constitute a breach of International Law. It would be better to inform the Khedive, in case of his refusal, that he must be prepared to take the consequences of his act and that you must refer to HMG for instructions. This would give you breathing time to concert something less violent.' In his next telegram,[12] Rosebery warned Cromer that the adoption of his proposed means of coercion would lead to the intervention of the Powers, 'which indeed may not improbably be the outcome of the present situation,' and asked him whether he could not make some other suggestion.

After receiving these two telegrams Cromer must have realised that he would not be fully supported and that a compromise with the Khedive would be necessary. After seeing Abbas next morning he told Rosebery what had been arranged, in a telegram which did not conceal his bitterness and disappointment.[13]

'I saw the Khedive this morning. In view of the great excitement here and of the fact that your telegrams gave little indication of any intention to act vigorously in support of any representations I may make, it appeared to me essential to settle the matter quietly. I had seen Tigrane previously and told him the conditions I would accept. The Khedive expressed his regret at the recent incident and pointed out that it would humiliate him and make him lose all authority in the country if he were obliged to reinstate Mustafa. He therefore begged HMG not to insist on this . . . He proposed to name Riaz in place of Fakhry . . . (He stated that) . . . his earnest wish was to have the most friendly relations with HMG and that for the future he would willingly follow the advice of HMG in all important matters.[14] I was reluctant not to insist on Mustafa, but at the same time he is ill and will be so for some time. After what has happened it is unlikely that his relations with the Khedive will ever be friendly. Also I think it unwise to humiliate the Khedive too much. The reversal of Fakhry's nomination ought to be a sufficient lesson to him. I therefore took it on myself to say . . . that I would accept the Khedive's proposal as a final settlement of the matter. I trust HMG will approve . . . The matter is thus settled for the time being, but considering the character of the Khedive I can feel no assurance that something of the same sort may not happen again before long. I hope you will consider how to coerce the Khedive if necessary and let me know. I can think of nothing less violent than the measures I have already proposed. I fail to see how the occupation of the Egyptian Ministries constitutes a breach of International Law. With regard to the intervention of the Powers, I can only say that, directly the matter became serious, the French and Russian Consuls-General here were anxious to let everyone know that no French or Russian interest was involved and that they did not intend to interfere. I should be placed to some extent in possession of your views so that I can regulate my conduct accordingly and so that I may do nothing which is likely to be rejected. When a crisis arises it is often difficult to gain the breathing time which one would wish without doing a good deal of harm here.'

Rosebery immediately replied:[15] 'Your conduct approved; I think we may be satisfied with the result. You will tell Khedive that HMG are glad HH has exercised a sound judgement . . . and they note with pleasure his solemn assurance that he desires to work in cordial cooperation with them and to follow their advice in all important matters.' He concluded on a note of mingled rebuke and reassurance: 'I do not understand why you concluded we were not likely to give you vigorous support. I regret such an inference. I agree with you in thinking that we must be prepared for a possible renewal of these outbursts and will communicate my views frankly and without delay.'

The immediate crisis was over. As between Cromer and Abbas honours were about even. Abbas had relinquished Fakhry; Cromer had given up Mustafa and had accepted Riaz who, he told Rosebery at the beginning of the crisis, had advised the Khedive to stand firm.[16] Cromer had undoubtedly over-reacted to the crisis, probably due to a feeling of personal outrage at being defied by a boy of eighteen to whom, as he considered, he had shown every evidence of avuncular goodwill. Had it not been for this personal feeling, he would probably have 'played it cool,' as he had so often done before, and got most of what he wanted without undue fuss.

His telegrams had aroused 'the darkest suspicions of Gladstone and Harcourt when the Cabinet met on 16 March.'[17] Rosebery himself was in general sympathy with Cromer's views about Egypt, but he had to carry the Cabinet with him, and the aggressiveness of Cromer's telegrams made things difficult for him. He told the Queen in a letter that, after making every allowance for the strain to which Cromer was being subjected, 'he cannot think that the tone of his telegrams was judicious.' He went on to attribute this to gout, 'a disease by no means incompatible with statesmanship; there were signs of both in Lord Cromer's telegrams.'[18]

The crisis had an almost immediate sequel. On 19 January Cromer sent the following telegram to Rosebery:[19] 'Yesterday a large number of natives called on the Khedive. The demonstration was made to order. The Khedive is not exactly popular, but it would take very little to place him in the position of an Egyptian patriot opposing foreigners and Christians. The ultra-Moslem masses are very violent and mischievous. General Walker and I both think the British garrison is not sufficiently strong. If we had had to take action a few days ago some risk would have been involved. Heretofore we have always supposed that the Khedive would be with us. He may now be against us, which would make a vast difference. No one can foresee what would be the attitude of the Egyptian Army in case of trouble. The Egyptian garrison is as numerous as the British. They have field artillery. We have none. One of the Egyptian Battalions is commanded exclusively by Moslem officers. There are 700 native police armed with rifles. General Walker will take steps to see that Egyptian Army reserve ammunition is kept under the eye of the British Army. Walker and I recommend that instead of withdrawing one Infantry Battalion and sending more cavalry, the cavalry should be sent without withdrawing the Infantry Battalion and, further, that an additional Battalion should be sent here, making three Battalions in all ... It is quite possible that after a short time we may be able to revert to present strength. Nothing that HMG can do or say would be so likely to prevent further trouble as the prompt adoption of this measure, which I strongly recommend. I should like to make the announcement that the garrison will be increased. I wish to do so before the Khedive or Riaz have time to commit any further folly.'

In a following telegram[20] he told Rosebery: 'I have no doubt that the sympathies of the Egyptian Army are with the Khedive . . . All the young officers are in favour of Egypt for the Egyptians. During the recent crisis the Khedive talked a great deal of being able to rely on the army, etc. Palmer had a long conversation with Riaz to-day . . . (and) . . . was much dissatisfied with his language and came to the conclusion that he meant to throw in his lot entirely with the Khedive. Riaz said that the Khedive had gained enormously in popularity by his recent conduct and that now all Egyptians were with him. As far as the Pasha class is concerned, this is the first time. All this confirms my opinion that reinforcements should be sent not only to act in case of need, but still more to prevent the necessity for action. I shall of course do all I can to avoid another crisis, but with the elements with which I have to deal, I cannot feel certain that a crisis may not at any moment be forced upon me. If it comes it will be more serious than the last . . . The main thing for the moment is that I should, as soon as may be, be put in full possession of your views. If anything serious were to occur I ought to be in a position to act with the greatest decision and promptitude.'

Rosebery was in agreement with the view previously expressed by Cromer to Salisbury in April 1892, and repeated to the Liberal Govern-ment when it came into office, that 'the paramount influence of England . . . (in Egypt) . . . depends mainly on the presence of a British garrison.'[21] It was the first time that Cromer had requested an increase in the garrison in order to assert British authority in Egypt. Such previous increases as there had been were in order to deal with the Dervishes in the Sudan. On receipt of Cromer's telegrams of 19 January, Rosebery minuted to Gladstone: 'Cromer's two telegrams of to-day confirm my impression that it will be necessary to strengthen the Egyptian army of occupation as soon but as unobtrusively as possible. Prevention is better than cure. We have had a significant warning, and if we do not take it, we are at the beginning of a new and alarming phase of the Egyptian question . . . Cromer may possibly take a too gloomy view of the situation. But he does not take a gloomier view than I do. We have only secured a respite by the settlement of yesterday, and though it may be desirable to evacuate Egypt, we cannot be jockeyed or intrigued out of it.'[22] Gladstone was excited and alarmed by Rosebery's proposal to reinforce the Egyptian garrison. He, during the previous few weeks, had been having unofficial conversations behind Rosebery's back with Waddington, the French Ambassador, about the possibility of evacuating Egypt. On receipt of Rosebery's minute, he told Hamilton, his Private Secretary: 'I would as soon put a torch to Westminster Abbey as send additional troops to Egypt. Such proposals make me so fearful about the future. I see nothing for it but for Rosebery to resign.'[23]

Rosebery did not resign. At a stormy Cabinet meeting on 20 January he took the line that 'if they did not agree to Cromer's request they faced the alternatives of leaving Egypt when ordered by the Khedive or sending an army at a later stage.'[24] He was one of a minority of two. After the meeting the following temporising telegram was sent to Cromer:[25] 'We shall be prepared if necessary to increase the British garrison in Egypt but do not think the time propitious for an announcement; request authority before making it.'

This did not satisfy Cromer. On 21 January he sent a long personal telegram of protest to Rosebery[26] in which he told him: 'The system under which Egypt has been governed for the last ten years has broken down. It was always very artificial and unsatisfactory and the wonder is that it has lasted so long. I cannot carry it on successfully any longer. You will have to choose between going backwards or forwards, *i.e.* either asserting yourself more strongly or retiring from the country.' In other words, Cromer presented Rosebery with the classic 'Govern or Go' alternative. Salisbury would not have submitted to this sort of language and Cromer never ventured to use it to him. But it worked with Rosebery. He replied to Cromer in a private telegram:[27] 'There is a Cabinet on Monday, and if you do not receive the powers you ask by Monday evening the Foreign Office will have passed into other hands.' 21 January was a Saturday and there was therefore a weekend intervening between Rosebery's telegram and the Cabinet meeting. On Sunday 22 January Cromer replied:[28] 'I need hardly say that if you should unfortunately leave the Foreign Office I shall follow your example . . . The result will almost certainly be that many of the high English officials here will resign or be dismissed and in fact the whole machine will collapse.'

In spite of Rosebery's virtual isolation in the Cabinet, he won his, or rather Cromer's, point at the meeting on 23 January. On the evening of that day the following official telegrams were sent to Cromer: (1) 'In view of recent occurrences and of the opinion of yourself and of the British GOC, HMG have determined to reinforce the British garrison in Egypt. You should make announcement to Khedive and Riaz but without assigning any reason.'[29] (2) 'The following statement has been issued to the Press: "HMG have determined to make a slight increase in the number of British troops stationed in Egypt. This decision has been arrived at in view of recent occurrences which threatened to disturb public security in that country." '[30]

A Battalion of British infantry which happened to be approaching the Suez Canal on its way to India was landed in Egypt within the next few days.

If, in addition to having had his recommendation for forcible action rejected over the Mustafa Fahmy affair, Cromer had also been refused the immediate reinforcements which he demanded so urgently, he could hardly have remained in Egypt. In view of Rosebery's very dubious reaction to his first recommendation, he can have had no certainty that Rosebery would go to the point of threatened resignation in order to secure Cabinet acceptance of his second recommendation. He was well aware of the weight of opposition to Rosebery in the Cabinet, and he was not yet aware of the extent to which he could rely on Rosebery himself to support his policies. Rosebery's private telegram of 21 March must have come as a great relief to him. But Cromer's victory was by no means a complete one. He no longer had a subservient Egyptian Government. The Khedive, so far from being publicly humiliated, had gained in popularity as a result of his stand against Cromer. For the first ten years of the British occupation the Egyptian Ruler and Government, in appearance and to a large extent in fact, had willingly accepted British cooperation and advice in the administration of the country. They gave no overt, and only occasional covert, encouragement to discontent arising from the British presence. The small British garrison, ostensibly, and in theory, was there to reinforce the Egyptian Army in defending Egypt from external aggression. In reality, its presence was, as Cromer and everyone else recognised, a gage of British determination to maintain their paramountcy in Egypt. But it had never been necessary to brandish it as such in the faces of the Egyptians. And its size had tended to diminish as the danger from the Dervishes grew less.

As a result of the January 1893 crisis all this was changed. Both the Khedive and, to an increasing extent, the Prime Minister, were openly hostile to the British, and encouraged the overt display of what had previously been the covert hostility of others. The hidden weapon of the British garrison had had openly to be used, by its ostentatious reinforcement, as a demonstration that the British position in Egypt rested, not upon consent, which was no longer forthcoming, but on force. Cromer, as he put it to Rosebery in a letter,[31] had been brought out of his hiding place. This was 'enough to shatter' the precarious system of consent by which Anglo-Egyptian cooperation had conducted since the occupation. He went on to develop the theme adumbrated in his 'Govern or Go' telegram. 'We must either go backwards and withdraw from the country or forwards and assert ourselves much more strongly than heretofore. The former means the collapse of all the reforms and the certainty of another Egyptian question; the latter means the risk of European complications. My personal opinion is in favour of the latter as the lesser of two evils. The worst course of all is to drift. It was this which was the cause of all our difficulties when Mr Gladstone was in power before.'

Early in February, Cromer received from Rosebery a detailed appreciation of the situation which, for the first time, gave him insight into the
Foreign Secretary's thinking in the light of the recent crisis.[32] Rosebery
expressed the view that the Khedive's recent action had had the intention
'to change at a stroke the relations between the British and Egyptian
Governments as they have existed for ten years.' 'Such a proceeding, if
successful, would destroy the basis on which the British occupation rests
and the reason for that occupation . . . which was only intended to
restore good order and good government until such time as some degree
of stability has been assured . . . We now have to face a different situation
. . . The Egyptian Army of 12,000 men would, in a crisis of this sort, be
likely to stand by the Khedive . . . The population of Cairo can still be
worked upon to assert a furious hostility to foreigners.' He then provided
a fourfold answer to the question which some of his Cabinet colleagues
may have been asking him—'Why, if we are there against the will of
the country, do we not retire?' (1) It was not clear that the real feeling
of the country was anything but friendly. (2) There was no question of
allowing British policy to be dictated by the whims of the Khedive.
(3) The reforms of the previous ten years could not be precipitantly
abandoned. (4) Retirement would be followed by the reinstatement of
the old abuses. He then set out for Cromer's benefit the international
difficulties of the situation, which he thought Cromer was inclined to
underrate, just as he thought he was inclined to overrate the local
difficulties. 'We must not allow the future of our administration to be
impaired . . . We shall not have much trouble with the Khedive . . . Our
real difficulty will be this; that France, the Porte and Russia know now
that they have in the Khedive an instrument ready to hand for purposes
of annoyance and they will endeavour to provoke incidents to which
they can point as proving that Egypt has become once more a house of
bondage . . . There may come a time when a combination of the Khedive
and hostile Powers may make it necessary for us to appeal either to
Europe, or to the Sultan, or to both . . . If we enter into an arrangement
with the Sultan on the Drummond Wolff lines we shall have HM's
pressure on our side.'

A fortnight later, in another letter to Cromer, Rosebery elaborated this
thesis:[33] 'We should be supported by the Triple Alliance in a Conference
but opposed by France, Russia and Turkey. Therefore we should have a
majority. I should be very anxious to conclude an arrangement with
Turkey which would avoid the evacuation clause of the Drummond
Wolff Convention.' He went on to tell Cromer that most of the Cabinet
were still in favour of evacuation, although there was 'never a moment
when evacuation was less popular in the country.' He asked Cromer to

'endeavour to keep the machine going without outward signs of friction until we can arrive at some understanding with the Sultan which will keep the Khedive in order.'

Cromer was not very enthusiastic about this appreciation. But he told Rosebery that 'falling back on the Sultan' was probably 'the least of many evils' provided that HM did not insist on immediate evacuation,[34] and that 'if we could get into a groove of negotiation with the Turk so much the better.'[35]

In the event, the Liberal Administration's relationships with Constantinople were always very bad and got worse as a result of their unsuccessful attempts, later, to do something about the Armenian massacres. Nothing happened about Rosebery's plan for some settlement over Egypt, either with Turkey or with the other Powers.

Meanwhile the situation in Egypt remained quiet on the surface but, in Cromer's view, fundamentally uneasy. In mid-March he told Rosebery that Riaz, on whose cooperation so much depended, was 'determined to be popular with the ultra-Moslems at any price' and that he had 'taken up a strong patriotic, anti-Christian and anti-European line.' But, as he pointed out, if they got rid of Riaz, the only alternatives were Nubar and Tigrane. 'We should have more civilised people to deal with, less overt hostility, but even more hostility from the ultra-Moslems.'[36] Cromer was evidently trying to follow Rosebery's advice to 'keep the machine going without undue signs of friction,' but he was finding it increasingly difficult. On 24 March he told Rosebery of 'the sullen hostility of the whole Government; British officials are being practically boycotted and so are natives with sympathies with England. The mass of the population are with us but are afraid to say so. The Pashas and the officials are against us . . . The newspapers now in the ascendant are ultra-Moslem and more or less of the Arabist type.'[37]

Early in April the attitude of the Egyptian Government improved, probably as the result of the publication of an official despatch from Rosebery. This despatch stated that the British Government were determined to 'maintain the fabric of administration which has been constructed under our guidance and must continue the process of construction, without impatience but without interruption, of an administrative and judicial system which shall afford a reliable guarantee for the future welfare of Egypt.' After referring to the possibility of 'fresh consultation with the Suzerain and the European Powers,' the despatch warned that, in the event of such consultation leading to some agreement, 'Egypt would in no case be released from European control, which might possibly be asserted in a much more stringent and irksome form than at present.' Referring to the recent crisis, it stated: 'It is impossible not to see how seriously these occurrences impair the security for order and justice and good government which HMG have always declared, and which the Sultan and the European Powers have equally admitted, to be a necessary preliminary to the withdrawal of British troops from Egypt.'[38] On 28 April Cromer reported that Riaz was more friendly 'both in word and deed' and thought that 'on the whole it looks as if we might jog on for some while.'[39]

A few weeks later Cromer departed on his annual vacation and Egypt relapsed into its usual Summer state of political torpor, while most of the principal actors were taking cures or otherwise relaxing in more temperate climates.

When Cromer returned to Egypt in October he found that the situation had again deteriorated. On 29 October he told Rosebery that Riaz was 'bitterly and unreasonably hostile to Europeans in general and to me in particular' and thought that 'a fight with him' was 'almost inevitable.' The Khedive was also being hostile and, between them, they had encouraged members of the Legislative Council to ask questions about evacuation in connection with the cost of the occupation troops which was borne by Egypt. Cromer, although privately in sympathy with Egyptian objections to paying these costs, was furious. 'For the first time an Egyptian Government, backed by the Legislative Council, has publicly and officially declared that they want us to go . . . under the inspiration of an inexperienced and headstrong boy of no particular talent who probably would not be able to maintain himself in power for six months without our assistance . . . The whole business is now more difficult than ever; we may at any moment find ourselves in a position which will oblige us either to go backwards with an appearance of humiliation or forwards with a risk of getting into a serious mess.'[40]

Since Cromer had been told to try to go on working the machine as before, he was driven to his old tactic of inserting a wedge between the Khedive and the Prime Minister, and of reducing them to impotence *seriatim.* On this occasion he succeeded brilliantly. In his own account of the affair, written many years after the event,[41] he tells us: 'I determined to choose my own battleground in the struggle which was obviously impending. It was necessary that the quarrel should be brought to a head over an issue which would be comprehensible to the British public and would afford no just ground for the intervention of any foreign Power . . . I felt convinced that, if I had the patience to wait, the folly of my opponents would afford me a suitable opportunity for striking a decisive blow.'

He had not very long to wait. The Khedive, ever since his accession, had been sensitive on the subject of British control of the Egyptian Army.

He had shown himself particularly sensitive about the outward forms of respect shown to him by British officers in the Egyptian Army. He had insisted on receiving reports about the Army through the Egyptian War Ministry instead of through the British Sirdar. In the Summer of 1893, while Cromer was in Europe, he had appointed Maher Pasha, who was in his confidence, as Under Secretary at the War Ministry. In January 1894, accompanied by Maher Pasha, and by Kitchener, the Sirdar, he went on a tour of Upper Egypt to inspect the Egyptian Army units on the Sudanese frontier.

Kitchener had been one of the first British officers to be seconded to the Egyptian Army in 1883. He had taken a prominent and distinguished part in the Gordon relief expedition, operating forward of the expedition in Dongola and acting as its principal source of intelligence. Afterwards he had served as Military Governor of Suakin, as Adjutant-General of the Egyptian Army, and as Inspector-General of the Egyptian Police. In 1892 he had been appointed Sirdar in succession to Sir Francis Grenfell. He was an extremely able and ambitious soldier, but overbearing, tactless, very much aware of his own importance, and without very much sense of humour. The inspection tour was a disaster. The Khedive, egged on, as it appears, by Maher Pasha, made continual criticisms about the drill and bearing of the Army, in spite of the fact that he knew nothing about military matters. He particularly went out of his way to criticize the competence of various British officers. It seems probable that he was simply continuing his previous petulant practice of 'taking it out on' the British and that he had no fixed intention of bringing about a crisis.

The incident seized on by Cromer as 'a suitable occasion for striking a decisive blow' took place at Wadi Halfa on 19 January 1894. It was described in a telegram sent that evening by Kitchener from Wadi Halfa to Cromer and to General Walker, the British GOC.[42] 'On parade this afternoon Khedive made various disparaging remarks to British Commanding Officer and subsequently told me that he considered it disgraceful for Egypt to be served by so bad an army. I thereupon respectfully tendered my resignation. Since the Khedive arrived on the frontier it has appeared to me and to others that he has consistently spoken with dislike of almost every English officer and his remarks this afternoon were rather a culmination of a series of uncalled-for instances which in this case I did not feel myself able to pass without some definite protest for the honour and credit of the Egyptian Army. Khedive became immediately very cordial and repeatedly begged me to withdraw my resignation. I pointed out that the position of English officers in the country would become almost untenable if they were so publicly rebuked and that it would be impossible for me to obtain the services of good officers in the Egyptian Army if this continued. Khedive assured me of his complete confidence and although I did not absolutely withdraw my resignation I gave him to understand I would not persist in it. Khedive did not attend dinner given by officers on plea of indisposition. I hope you approve of my action.'

Cromer, in his own words,[43] 'resolved to insist on adequate but not on unduly humiliating reparation.' He replied immediately to Kitchener: 'I entirely approve your action. If you think it advisable you may inform Khedive that I greatly regret to learn the language he has used in respect of the army, as to the efficiency of which there can be no doubt, and that I have reported the circumstances to London.' At the same time, he transmitted Kitchener's telegram to Rosebery with the recommendation that HMG should insist on the removal of Maher Pasha and the issue by the Khedive of an Order of the Day in commendation of the Egyptian Army and the British officers in it. If this were refused he recommended, 'as a last resource,' that the Egyptian Army should be put under the command of the British GOC.[44] Rosebery replied immediately:[45] 'I regard this as very serious and so you may tell Khedive. It has become a deliberate practice of his to insult British officers. This we cannot allow and if we could the nation would not. I think that the only reparation he can make is to issue an Order of the Day in commendation of the Egyptian Army and the British officers and that he should remove Maher Pasha, who is a bad adviser and a cause of strife, and an obstacle to harmonious co-operation. Should HH refuse just satisfaction we must consider stringent measures which will place the Egyptian Army under more direct control and protect British officers from injurious treatment. I should also at once publish the various instances of insult which have occurred of late so that the country may realise the situation.'

All this was in accordance with Cromer's recommendations telegraphed to Rosebery with Kitchener's report. He transmitted the contents of Rosebery's telegram to Kitchener, who was still in Upper Egypt. But the Khedive had left before Kitchener had an opportunity of communicating them to him. Meanwhile Cromer, in Cairo, saw Riaz and Tigrane, the Foreign Minister, informed them of the contents of Kitchener's report and of Rosebery's demands, and pointed out to them 'how difficult it would be to maintain discipline in an army of Moslems commanded by Christians if the Head of State, being himself a Moslem, fomented discord.' Cromer told Rosebery that 'the Ministers manifestly recognise the gravity of the incident and will I think give the Khedive prudent advice.'[46] Riaz, of course, had good reason to know all about the implications of an undisciplined army.

Cromer had chosen his ground well. He had made it almost impossible for Riaz to support the Khedive on this issue. The European colonies, remembering Arabi, were terrified at the prospect of a mutinous and xenophobic army. Reverseaux, the French Consul-General, told Cromer that he would urge moderation on the Khedive and his Ministers, and Cromer was able to tell Rosebery that 'the French and Russian Consuls-General do not want to provoke a serious crisis.'[47] There had also been a great movement in British public opinion over the previous year. The publication of Milner's book *England in Egypt*—a eulogistic, not to say euphoric, account of the very moderate benefits which the British occupation had brought to the people of Egypt—at the end of 1892 had contributed to a great access of interest and pride in the British achievement in Egypt, combined with a growing irritation towards the French on account of the difficulties, luridly described by Milner, which they had put in the way of that achievement.[48] Cromer himself had always had a lively appreciation of the uses of publicity and was acutely aware of the extent to which British public opinion could make or mar his task in Egypt. In his early days as British Agent he had suffered from the climate of British public opinion; now that this climate had changed —as Rosebery told him, there had never been a moment when evacuation was less popular—he was determined to take advantage of it. He had himself to some extent contributed to the change. He had persuaded Salisbury to start publishing his Annual Reports. He had encouraged Milner to write his book. He was forthcoming with friendly Press correspondents. The voluminous Press coverage given in England to the 'frontier incident,' as it was called, the denunciation of the Khedive, the demands for British firmness, were not altogether fortuitous.

This climate of opinion greatly influenced the Cabinet and helps to explain the very full support given to Cromer over the 'frontier incident' compared with the hesitancy displayed over the Ministerial crisis a year previously.

After Cromer's interview with the Ministers, and after he had addressed to them 'an earnest personal appeal that the Khedive and his Ministers should yield at once on the two points demanded in order to avoid ultimate consequences which might be serious,' Riaz left for Upper Egypt to meet the Khedive on his way back to Cairo. Cromer felt confident that Riaz would 'do his best to arrive at a solution.'[49]

On 26 January Cromer was able to tell Rosebery that the Khedive would publish an Order of the Day as demanded and that Maher Pasha would be transferred as soon as a suitable position could be found for him. The Order of the Day was duly published and, after a week or two, Maher was appointed Governor of Port Said. He was replaced at the

Ministry of War by a nominee of Kitchener's. The 'frontier incident' was over.

The British Government marked their sense of the occasion by recom-mending Kitchener for a KCMG. Rosebery told him: 'It would be idle to deny that I have chosen this particular moment for the recommendation in order to make it clear . . . that I feel the warmest sympathy for you in the very difficult circumstances in which you have been placed for some time past and which have recently come to a head.'[50]

Riaz who, Cromer reported, had 'behaved well,' who was 'believed to be the only person who has any influence with the Khedive,' and on whom Cromer relied in order to persuade the Khedive to yield,[51] was less lavishly rewarded. His influence with the Khedive was destroyed by his insistence on yielding to the British Government's demands. On 10 April Cromer told the British Government that the relations between the Khedive and his Ministry were 'very strained.'[52] But, as he wrote later,[53] he 'did not consider that one friendly step, taken under com-pulsion, was enough to justify me in condoning a long course of previous enmity.' So, when Riaz resigned a few days later, Cromer advised the Khedive to accept his resignation and send for Nubar. 'He was reluctant to accept and suggested Mazloum or Fakhry. I rejected them. He asked for time to decide. Our conversation was very friendly.'[54] A few hours later Cromer reported: 'The Khedive has sent a message to tell me that he has sent for Nubar.'[55] Nubar was by this time an old man, anxious for office, but not anxious for power, and more or less willing to act as Cromer's obedient servant.

By his exploitation of the frontier incident, Cromer had killed two birds with one stone. He had got rid of Riaz and he had brought the Khedive to heel. He had done so just in time. For, in March 1894, Gladstone had at last resigned, being succeeded as Prime Minister by Rosebery, who was himself replaced at the Foreign Office by the Earl of Kimberley. Rosebery, as Prime Minister, was, paradoxically, in a less powerful position over Egypt than he had been as Foreign Secretary since, as Prime Minister, he had to take more account than before of the opinions of his colleagues, some of whom, like Harcourt and Morley, carried on the Gladstonian tradition of anti-Imperialism and freedom for subject peoples.

The outcome of these two trials of strength with the young Khedive, the details of which were reported, round by round, in the British and European Press, confirmed Cromer, *urbi et orbi*, in his position as the real ruler of Egypt and as something like a public hero in England. He had, as he had prophesied, 'come out of his hiding place.' The result was not altogether advantageous to British interests and, although approved by public opinion, was regarded less enthusiastically by informed people in England. Salisbury was said to have expressed his anger at Cromer's clumsiness and to have opposed a suggestion that he should be appointed Viceroy of India.[56] There were obvious possibilities of difficulties with the Powers. There was the possibility of having to keep on reinforcing the British garrison. Evacuation was no longer a viable diplomatic bargaining counter. The old concept of occupation in the name and at the request of the Khedive had disappeared. Henceforward, whatever the formal position, and however circumspect his personal behaviour, the Khedive would almost inevitably form a nucleus of opposition to British rule, around which would become organised the various potential and still more or less incoherent and disparate elements of that opposition —the disgruntled Turkish Pashas who disliked their exclusion from power, the Armenian and Syrian Christians who considered themselves as more intelligent than the British and just as capable of running the country, the fanatical Moslems who hated all Christians, the Islamic Modernists and intellectuals who were influenced by currents of national- ism drifting in from Syria, from Turkey and from countries farther west, and the Arabists, who still dreamed of a distinctively Egyptian nation, purged of Turks, Syrians and Europeans. The political vacuum created by the collapse of the Arabi rebellion was beginning to fill up. The clash between Cromer and the Khedive, and Cromer's emergence from his 'hiding place,' hastened what was probably an inevitable process.

Cromer's first ten years in Egypt had imbued him with four principal convictions which were henceforward to dominate his policy. (1) There must be no British commitment to evacuate Egypt until there was a reasonable certainty that the stability, solvency and security which the British occupation had brought about could be maintained after that occupation had come to an end. (2) The international restrictions on the Egyptian Government's internal administration must be got rid of or, at all events, greatly diminished. (3) The development of representative institutions was premature and dangerous and must not be allowed to proceed beyond the rudimentary level established as a result of Dufferin's recommendations. (4) The policy of a partnership in government between the British and independent-minded indigenous statesmen such as Riaz and Nubar had only been a *pis aller* and was no longer viable (a) because of the attitude of the Khedive and (b) because of the lack both of governing capacity and willingness to cooperate with the British amongst the native ruling class.

Because of these convictions Cromer, by the end of the 1894 crisis, had come to the conclusion that Egypt must be ruled for an indefinite period by a benevolent, British-directed despotism, exercised behind the

more or less transparent façade of an entirely subservient Egyptian Govern‑
ment. He recognised that such an Administration could not hope to
secure the cooperation and support either of the Khedive, or of the rising
intelligensia, or of the Pasha class generally, and might provoke their
active opposition. But he calculated that the lack of this cooperation and
support might be counterbalanced by an increasing popularity among
the peasants, the merchants and the salaried and wage‑earning classes by
concentrating on efficient, just and economical administration which
would reduce taxation, improve the machinery of justice, and promote
prosperity. He considered that any overt opposition could be overawed
by actual or threatened increases in the army of occupation and by
periodical firm declarations from the British Government.

'If we are to stay here,' Cromer told Kimberley, 'we ought to try and
make ourselves popular.' Since he ruled out political concessions which
might have earned popularity with what he called 'the talkative classes,'
he concentrated on economic amelioration. One of his most cherished
beliefs, and perhaps the only tenet of Gladstonian Liberalism to which
he remained faithful, was that 'low taxation is the most potent instrument
with which to conjure discontent. This is the policy which will tend
more than any other to the stability of Imperial rule.' In pursuance of this
policy, he not only concentrated on projects such as irrigation, which
increased the productivity of the country, to the virtual exclusion of
'social services' which did not. He also waged continual, and mainly
unsuccessful, war with British Chancellors of the Exchequer to relieve
Egypt from as much as possible of the financial burden of the occupation
expenses, and those of the Sudan, and to get the British taxpayer to take
over some of this burden. He also made continual, and ultimately success‑
ful, efforts to free Egypt from some of the worst financial consequences of
her international servitude.

Such a policy also necessarily involved either the submission of the
Khedive or continued opposition from him. Although Abbas never
again openly challenged Cromer, he never acquiesced to the rôle in
which he was cast. Since direct action had proved unsuccessful, he
resorted to intrigue—with the nationalists, with the Sultan, with the
European Consuls, with whoever seemed likely to be able and willing
to embarrass the British occupiers. Cromer was bothered about these
intrigues, and tended to overestimate their importance. He told Salisbury
that 'the Khedive, if he knew it, is in reality much more master of the
situation than he imagines,'[57] and came to see the Khedive's hand behind
almost every manifestation of discontent in Egypt. He frequently con‑
sidered the possibility of his deposition. In February 1895, in a letter to
Kimberley, he referred to 'anti‑foreign agitation,' blamed the Khedive,

and expressed the view that 'his deposition sooner or later is inevitable.'[58] He used the implied threat of deposition as his 'ultimate deterrent' in his dealings with Abbas. He told Salisbury in 1898 that 'deposition is at present the *ultima ratio* in Egyptian affairs and it is as well constantly to bear in mind . . . that a moment may come when we will be obliged to resort to it.'[59] He received little encouragement over this from Salisbury, who came to take Cromer's irate references to Abbas—'a true successor of Ananias,' 'a self-opinionated boy,' 'a foolish youth' with a pinch of salt. But Rosebery was more responsive. At the beginning of 1895, when Abbas was trying to get rid of Nubar (who went of his own accord a little later), Rosebery authorised Cromer to tell him that, 'if there is a change HH must be prepared to take the consequences, which may be of a more serious nature than he imagines.'[60]

In the early years of the twentieth century, new currents of nationalism, the Entente with France, and Abbas' own efforts at self-enrichment, which alienated nationalist sympathies, eroded almost to nothing the Khedive's potentiality for effective opposition. This deprived Cromer's vendetta of most of its *raison d'etre* and, as time went on, his opposition to Abbas' political ambitions became translated into opposition to his financial venality. In this opposition Cromer had to some extent the support of the more moderate nationalists, such as Mohammed Abdu. Abbas had ceased to be a rival. He was, as Cromer saw it, merely fulfilling his own earlier prognostications of inherent unworthiness. 'Cromer had never seen Abbas in his true light, as a young man eager to try his wings, but who saw himself baulked at every turn by a domineering foreigner. Too early in his reign Abbas had been shown the iron fist in the velvet glove by Cromer; but ten years of experience with Taufiq had worn the velvet thin, so that too much iron showed through.'[61]

9

THE RECONQUEST
OF THE SUDAN

WHEN THE DECISION to abandon the Gordon relief expedition was taken in May 1885 it was decided to withdraw the Egyptian frontier to Wadi Halfa and to retain for Egypt the Red Sea port of Suakin and the area immediately around it. This latter decision was in order (a) to retain some control over the export of slaves from the Sudan; (b) to avoid the possibility of interruption to maritime communications via the Red Sea as a result of Mahdist piracy; and (c) to keep a convenient point of re-entry for a possible future reconquest of the Sudan.

The rest of the Egyptian possessions on the Red Sea and the Gulf of Aden were partitioned, in a somewhat haphazard manner, among the Powers. The port of Massawa was occupied by the Italians, who immediately began pushing forward from there into the highlands of Eritrea with a view to forming a colony for Italian settlement. This occupation was connived at and, at first, viewed with benevolence, by the British, who wanted the Italians to guard the Egyptian left flank on the Red Sea against the Dervishes and the Abyssinians. The port of Obok (later known as Jibuti) and its immediate hinterland were occupied by the French, who wished to establish a *point d'appui* on the Red Sea and to open up a trade route to Abyssinia. This was viewed with less benevolence, but without much alarm, by the British, who were perennially suspicious of any French activity in this area. The coast of Somaliland along the Gulf of Aden was occupied by the Government of India, who attached importance to it as a means of provisioning Aden.

The inland boundaries of these colonies, marching with Abyssinian territory, were left undefined, but only the Italians had serious expansionist designs in that direction. The Sultan of Turkey, the nominal Suzerain of all these lands, raised various objections and the Egyptian Government had, for many years, to go on paying tribute to him in respect of Zeila, part of what became known as British Somaliland, which had been occupied by the Government of India. Various proposals were considered by the British and Egyptian Governments for handing Suakin back to Turkey, in order to avoid the expense of administering it. But they all came to nothing and the idea was abandoned soon after the non-ratification of the Drummond Wolff Convention. Afterwards, as the financial situation improved, and as the reconquest of the Sudan began to become a possibility, there was no more question of relinquishing Suakin.

In the Nile Valley, any immediate danger of a Dervish invasion of Egypt was extinguished on 30 December 1885, when an advancing Dervish force was defeated at Ginnis, a few miles south of Wadi Halfa, by a mixed British and Egyptian force under the command of General Stephenson, GOC British troops in Egypt.

After the battle of Ginnis the area between Wadi Halfa and Aswan was made into a military district under the Governorship of Colonel Woodhouse of the Egyptian Army, which became entirely responsible for the defence of the southern frontier. There were a few skirmishes with the Dervishes, notably one at Sarras, near Wadi Halfa, in April 1887, which served to blood the new Egyptian Army, but there was no attempt to invade Egypt until the Summer of 1889, when Wad el-Nejumi, the bravest and best of the Dervish leaders, advanced northward through the desert to the west of the Nile, by-passing Wadi Halfa and intending to join the river somewhere between there and Aswan. Wad el-Nejumi commanded a somewhat motley force of about 5,700 fighting men and 8,000 camp followers, which represented no very serious threat unless the invaders were joined by the indigenous population. Wad el-Nejumi's force, from the moment of its crossing the frontier, was harassed by a flying column of about 2,000 Egyptian troops under Colonel Woodhouse and eventually, on 2 August, was attacked by the main body of the Egyptian Army, commanded by the Sirdar, Sir Francis Grenfell, at Toski, a village on the west bank of the Nile between Halfa and Korosko. The Dervish force was completely defeated and Wad el-Nejumi killed. This was the end of any offensive activity by the Dervishes in the Nile Valley. From then on the emphasis was not on the defence of Egypt, but on the eventual recovery of the Sudan.

The defence of Suakin had also been entrusted to the Egyptian Army, and a British officer of the Egyptian Army was appointed as military governor. The territory held consisted only of the immediate hinterland around Suakin. In 1888, after three years of comparative quiet, Osman Digna, the Dervish leader in the Eastern Sudan, laid siege to Suakin. Reinforcements of the Egyptian Army were sent by sea from Egypt and, on 20 March 1888, the Dervish forces were attacked and forced to raise the siege. There followed another three-year period of comparative quiet.

The Egyptian Government had neither the money nor the means to undertake offensive operations.

By the end of 1886 all the Egyptian garrisons in the interior of the Sudan had either been evacuated, or overwhelmed, or had surrendered, with the exception of the Equatoria garrisons under the German Governor, Emin Pasha who, with a small body of Egyptian troops, remained in precarious control of a strip of territory about 180 miles long between Lado and Lake Albert. After the fall of Khartum Emin was completely isolated from the north and had neither the means, nor apparently the wish, to withdraw to the East African coast. In February 1886 he received his first communication from the Egyptian Government for some time, informing him that they had decided to abandon the Sudan, that they were unable to afford him any assistance, and authorising him to take such steps as he could to leave the country. But he decided to stay on with the Egyptian garrison, most of whose members had acquired local wives and had settled down more or less happily in a not-unpleasant exile.

Equatorial Africa was beginning to attract great interest in Europe as a result of the recent journeys of exploration and the discovery and mapping of the Great Lakes. Apart from missionary endeavour, five Powers—Great Britain, Germany, France, Belgium and Portugal—were displaying interest in the trading possibilities of the African interior. On the east coast, the mainland coastal area between the Juba river in the north and the Rovuma river in the south was included in the territory of the Sultan of Zanzibar, whose independence had been recognised by Great Britain and France in an Agreement signed in 1862. At that time, British interest in Zanzibar was limited to attempts being made to suppress the slave-trade flourishing in the Sultanate, which was a principal entrepôt for the collection and export of slaves from the African interior. Control of the slave-trade involved an ever-increasing control over the affairs of the Sultanate. Some legitimate trading with the interior was developed by British private enterprise, but the British Government were wary of giving it more than cautious support. The Germans were much more enterprising. They occupied Dar-es-Salaam, a port on the coast which was part of the Sultan of Zanzibar's dominions, and a German concessionary Company, with the support of the German Government, pushed inland from the coast towards Lakes Tanganyika and Victoria and induced the German Government to take the territory they acquired under German jurisdiction. In October 1886, the British Government, who were anxious to secure Bismarck's benevolence in Europe and in Egypt by making colonial concessions to Germany in places where they were not as yet particularly interested, made an Agreement with the

German Government by which the dominions of the Sultan of Zanzibar were held to be confined to a ten-mile strip along the coast, leaving the hinterland open for competitive British and German penetration.

Meanwhile, penetration of Central Africa from the west coast by way of the Congo river had been proceeding vigorously under the aegis of l'Association Internationale du Congo, a Belgian commercial enterprise founded in Brussels in 1879 by King Leopold of the Belgians. This Association established a chain of armed posts and trading stations along the length of the Congo and its tributaries. By 1884 the Association's agents had penetrated as far inland as what are now known as Stanley Falls. The two principal instruments of the Association were the explorer Stanley, who was acting as King Leopold's principal agent, and the French explorer Brazza, who was primarily an agent of the French Government and concerned, on its behalf, to keep the hinterland of the French Congo—on the west coast of Africa north of the Congo mouth and between that river and the German Cameroons—open for possible future French penetration from the coast.

One difficulty faced by the Congo Association was the fact that the mouth of the river was in Portuguese hands. In 1884 the British Government, in an attempt to counteract the influence of the French and Belgians in the Congo Association, and to revive British trade in the area which had been damaged by the existence of the Association, made a Treaty with Portugal which recognised Portuguese claims to the Congo Basin and obtained in return certain trading concessions there. The signature of this Treaty led to immediate protests from the Association and from the French Government. Bismarck, who was quarrelling with the British Government at the time over a colonial question in South-West Africa, supported the protest. The Anglo-Portuguese Treaty remained unratified and, at a Conference convened in Berlin, the Congo Association was converted into 'l'Etat Independent du Congo,' recognised by the Powers, with (more or less) defined boundaries.

In March 1887 Stanley, one of the principal architects of the Congo Free State, set out from Banana, at the mouth of the Congo, on his much-publicised expedition to 'rescue' Emin. The expedition set out with the knowledge and approval of the Egyptian Government who, on Cromer's advice, contributed £10,000 towards its expenses and gave Stanley a letter to Emin from the Khedive telling him that he was at full liberty either to remain where he was or to evacuate, but warning him that he could expect no further help from the Egyptian Government. The expedition, and the contents of the Khedive's letter to Emin, were known to the British Government and approved by them, but there is no evidence that Stanley was, in any sense, their agent. Ostensibly, the purpose of the expedition which, apart from the Egyptian Government's contribution, was financed out of public subscriptions, was for the charitable purpose of rescuing Emin and his garrisons. But Stanley was also interested in trading possibilities and, apart from being in close touch with the Congo Free State, was also in communication with Sir William Mackinnon, founder of the British East Africa Association, which had been formed for the development of British trading interests in the hinterland of East Africa and was at that time seeking a Charter from the British Government.

After an adventurous journey between the Congo and Nile basins, Stanley met Emin on the shores of Lake Albert in April 1888. Stanley gave Emin the Khedive's letter and, at the same time, suggested three alternatives to him: (1) evacuating and returning to Cairo; (2) staying on to govern Equatoria in the name of the King of the Belgians and with support from the Congo Free State; (3) staying on as Representative of Mackinnon's East Africa Association. Stanley was patently anxious to get Egyptian sovereignty out of the way and open up a field for European colonisation. Emin, after consultation with his Egyptian officers, rejected all these alternatives and decided to stay on in the service of the Egyptian Government, as he had been authorised by the Khedive to do. There followed a confused period of mutiny, intrigue, argument, persuasion and threats. Most of Emin's Egyptian officers, for whatever reason, wished to stay on in Egyptian service. A minority wanted to evacuate. Eventually, in April 1889, Emin, his local influence almost destroyed by Stanley's intrigues and by mutinies among his troops, half unwillingly agreed to withdraw in company with Stanley and make for the east coast with such few of his men as were prepared to accompany him. The rest stayed on in Equatoria. When he arrived on the east coast, Emin joined his German compatriots and, soon afterwards, went back with a German expedition into the interior, where he was murdered in March 1892.[1]

Emin's departure from Equatoria set in train a process of attempted penetration of the area by the four interested Powers—Great Britain, Germany, France and the Congo Free State—and provided the setting for a series of complicated and embittered international rivalries and disputes, centring on Egypt.

The Emin rescue expedition coincided approximately with the beginnings of a British African policy based on fencing the Nile Valley off from the incursion of any other Great Power, in order to prevent such a Power from exerting pressure on the British position in Egypt by threatening the water supply. As we have seen, this policy seems first to have been adumbrated by Cromer in a letter to Goschen in December 1888 in which he had told him that, although there could be no immediate question of a reconquest of the Sudan by Egypt, 'it would be most menacing to Egypt that a European Power should hold the headwaters of the Nile.' A year later Cromer indicated, in a letter to Salisbury, that he was thinking in terms of the Atbara rather than of the White Nile and that he was immediately worried by the prospect of an Italian occupation of Kassala, giving them access to the waters of the Atbara, the principal tributary of the Nile below Khartum. The Atbara, together with the Blue Nile, provided Egypt with most of its flood water. 'I had always looked on the question of Italian expansion from Massawa as not very important to us or to Egypt . . . (but) . . . I always imagined that the main line of their wild colonial enterprise would be towards Abyssinia and that Abyssinia would be a sufficiently hard nut for them to crack. But they are now evidently making serious advances towards the Sudan. If they are allowed to do that they will soon clash with our Egyptian policy,' since, if they took Kassala, 'they would soon strike at the valley of the Nile.'[2]

Cromer, at all events until 1894, took very much more interest in blocking the Italians on the Atbara than he did in keeping other Powers out of the White Nile which, from the point of view of the threat to Egypt's water, was much more important. His backing of the Emin rescue expedition seems to have been entirely due to a desire to liquidate the Egyptian position in Equatoria and he took no immediate interest in what happened there afterwards. But his interest in the Atbara was not entirely due to his fears about water, which he probably (although not certainly) realised were chimerical. Once he had determined that evacuation was impracticable—that is to say after the non-ratification of the Drummond Wolff Convention—he always had in mind an eventual reconquest of the Sudan, as soon as Egypt's military and financial circum-stances might permit this. It is probable that he thought of this reconquest in terms of an advance from Suakin to Berber across the desert, accom-panied by the construction of a railway, rather than the alternative route via the Nile Valley followed by the Gordon relief expedition. He had favoured the Suakin–Berber route at the time of the Gordon relief expedition; he regarded it as the natural channel of Sudan trade after its reconquest, provided that a railway were built; and he realised that the best way of getting a railway built would be as part of military operations for reconquest. He also realised that unlimited Italian expansion in the direction of Kassala might well put the Italians between Suakin and Berber and thus jeopardise both the reconquest and the subsequent rehabilitation of the Sudan under British auspices. As he put it to Salisbury: 'I do not want to have Crispi's bersaglieri running all over the Eastern Sudan, nor do I want them to influence the tribes between

Suakin and Berber which, rather than the Nile route, will form the commercial route for the Sudan.'³

This, rather than any fears about Nile water, explains Cromer's per- sistent opposition to Italian expansion towards Kassala, which was manifested between 1889 and 1891. It also explains his prolonged, and eventually successful, attempts to persuade Salisbury to agree to the recapture of Tokar, since this extension of the Suakin 'bridgehead' formed some sort of barrier against Italian expansion towards the Suakin– Berber line and provided a more secure base for an eventual campaign of reconquest based on Suakin.

Salisbury, whether because of better technical information, or for some other reason, was much more interested in keeping other Powers off the White Nile. At the beginning of 1890 Cromer was complaining that Salisbury was not taking Italian expansion towards Kassala seriously enough. On 23 February he told him: 'I wish I could persuade you to do something about the Italians in the Red Sea. If we cannot come to terms about the limit of Italian expansion inland, which is what I would like, surely we may ask them to confine their operations on the west to their own territory.'⁴ He also continued to urge the occupation of Tokar, which Salisbury had just turned down. 'I regret the decision not to go to Tokar. The Dervish movement is going downhill⁵ and the risks are infinitesmally small. There is no danger of financial embarrassment . . . I feel sure I can keep my soldiers in hand. I have done so before and I think I could again.' He even thought that a 'slight push' to Mahdism at Tokar 'might knock it over.'⁶

Salisbury was not very forthcoming. He was engaged in delicate negotiations with Germany about the Upper Nile, which he thought far more important than the Red Sea and the Atbara, and, in order to keep Germany sweet, it was necessary to keep Italy reasonably happy. And, so long as the fire-eating Crispi was in office, Italy could not be kept happy if her plans for colonial expansion were too directly opposed. He had told Cromer at the end of 1889: 'The Italians are very tiresome with their misplaced and suicidal African ambitions,' and that he had 'no wish that their aspirations should be gratified at the cost of any solid sacrifices by us.'⁷ But he did nothing about it. As he explained to Cromer a few months later,⁸ 'The Italian alliance is valuable to us chiefly because it is essential to Germany, and the friendship of Germany is important to us because she keeps Russia and France in order.'

Salisbury also objected to the idea of reoccupying Tokar. 'The argument that you have used over Kassala, that it gives to the Power occupying it a command over one of the main affluents of the Nile and therefore the power of diverting part of the Nile water supply vital to Egypt does not apply to the east coast. Tokar has nothing to do with the Nile Valley. The doctrine of the military that it is necessary to possess the territory round Suakin in order to protect Wadi Halfa, which is 300 miles off, is too abstract for civilian comprehension . . . Public opinion shrinks instinctively from any proposal to advance into the Egyptian desert . . . Until you have enough money to justify you in advancing to Berber you had better remain quiet. When that time has arrived you may possibly go to Khartum and you may contemplate a railway from Suakin to Berber. Such measures may be necessary to protect the Nile Valley against outside Powers. And, if you have any money to throw away, the operation may not be without profit. Then, when you are masters of the Nile Valley, you may extend your dominance to the Red Sea. But I look with apprehension on a reversal of the process.'[9]

However, Salisbury consented to Cromer's trying to negotiate an agreement with the Italian Government in Naples in September 1890 on his way back to Egypt from his annual vacation.

In his instructions to Cromer for the negotiations in Naples, Salisbury, whose attitude towards Italy had stiffened during the Summer, probably as a result of his successful conclusion of the AngloGerman Agreement over East Africa and the Upper Nile on 1 July, told him: 'We should insist on command of all affluents of the Nile as far as Egypt formerly possessed them, (but) there are no such imperious interests to safeguard on the Red Sea slope. Our interests there require the magnifying glass of military theory to be visible at all.' Salisbury thought that no agreement was likely while Crispi was in office and he told Cromer: 'I do not think that England will lose by delay.' He also indicated that the value of the Italian alliance had somewhat diminished. 'I do not put the friendship of Italy so high as some other objects of political desire. It is desirable, but it is not worth a great price even in terms of African square metres. We are negotiating these African matters with somewhat greater ease now that we have agreed with Germany and France.'[10]

In the event no agreement was arrived at in Naples. But, in April 1891, after Crispi had gone out of office and been replaced as Prime Minister by di Rudini, who was less enthusiastic about colonial affairs than Crispi had been, an Agreement was arrived at in Rome between the British Government, represented by Lord Dufferin, the British Ambassador, and the Italian Government, by which the British recognised an Italian 'sphere of influence' in East Africa west of longitude 35 E and between latitude 6 N and latitude 17 N. This kept the Italians well away from the Nile Valley and, in return, conceded to them the right of expansion, more or less at will, into the Abyssinian territories of Tigre, Harrar and Ogaden and along the Indian Ocean coast between Cape

Guardafui and the Juba river.[11] This Italian 'sphere of influence' was further defined in a second Agreement signed in 1894 by which the Italians were allowed to occupy Kassala on condition that it was returned to Egypt as soon as Egypt should be in a position to occupy it. By the time of this second Agreement, the anxieties of Cromer and the British Government had, as a result of subsequent events, been switched decisively from the Atbara to the White Nile.

Salisbury still showed himself very reluctant about the reoccupation of Tokar. In November 1890 he asked Cromer: 'Why do you want to go to Tokar? . . . Surely, if you are not ready to go to Khartum, these people (*i.e.* the Dervishes) were created for the purpose of keeping the bed warm for you until you can occupy it. If you were to advance on Tokar and take it and the authority of the Khalifa were to vanish, what would happen in the Nile Valley? Would it want mastership and ownership till your finances enable you to govern it without asking for resources from France and from the Caisse? I imagine not.' He went on to explain that Italy was claiming that Egypt's right to the Sudan had lapsed and that it was now, in international law, *res nullius*. 'Ever since Italy first formed that doctrine to justify her claim to the occupation of Kassala I have felt that we must reconsider our Egyptian enmities and friendships. The doctrine that Egypt has lost all claim to the places evacuated five years ago and that Italy will acquire a claim if, in process of self-defence, she is called on to occupy these places, makes it evident that Italy is the most formidable enemy Egypt has to fear. If that be so the Dervishes are rendering a service in keeping Italy out, and we should think twice before we starve them out and try and bring their domination to an end. This is on the assumption that you are not financially ready to go to Khartum. Whenever you are ready to do so, this will cease to have any application.'[12]

But Cromer, although he expressed his agreement with Salisbury's argument about the Dervishes 'keeping the bed warm,'[13] persisted. 'Tokar is a small local question. Nothing very dreadful will happen if we don't take it. On the other hand the local advantages are considerable.'[14] So Salisbury reluctantly agreed and Tokar was taken against rather more severe resistance than Cromer had been led to expect. He told Salisbury: 'If I had known the Dervishes were so strong I should have hesitated to recommend an advance. Wo Intelligence reports were quite valueless.'[15] Salisbury was generous and replied that 'all seems to have gone well with the Tokar expedition,' that the Queen was pleased about it, and that the general public had taken very little notice of it as they were 'thinking of nothing but strikes and the later cantos of the epic of Kitty O'Shea.'[16]

The revelation of Dervish strength at Tokar caused Cromer to discount any immediate prospect of a reconquest of the Sudan. After the signature of the Anglo-Italian Agreement in April 1891, and for the next four years, he appears to have adopted Salisbury's view about the Dervishes 'keeping the bed warm' for him and no longer to have regarded the Sudan as a matter of urgency.

Salisbury, after he had been inspired by Cromer with the necessity for fencing off the Nile Valley from the incursion of any other great Power, concentrated his attention on the Upper Nile which now lay masterless as a result of Emin's retirement. It is not clear how seriously he regarded the water argument as advanced by Cromer. There was undoubtedly something in it, and Salisbury may have taken competent technical advice and satisfied himself that the danger alluded to by Cromer was chimerical as regards the Blue Nile and Atbara but a real one as regards the White Nile. The determination which he formed that England must herself control the waters of the Upper Nile may have been inspired by two alternative considerations at a time when he had not yet abandoned the possibility of using the evacuation of Egypt as a bargaining counter with the Powers. So long as England remained in Egypt it was necessary that she should not be jockeyed out of it by some other Power being in a position to threaten Egypt's water supply. Alternatively, if the British evacuated Egypt, it was desirable that they should be in a position to pose a similar threat to any other Power, or combination of Powers, which might occupy, or threaten to occupy, it. In other words, on the assumption of the validity of the water threat, English possession of the Upper Nile was an essential factor, whether or not England continued in occupation of Egypt. It is this double consideration which seems to be the explanation for the singlemindedness with which Salisbury pursued his policy of not merely fencing off the Upper Nile from the incursions of other Powers, but of trying to secure uninterrupted British access to it.

After Emin's withdrawal this uninterrupted access was principally menaced by German activity in East Africa. Since the 1886 Agreement the Germans, through their Chartered Company, Deutsche Ostafrikan- ische Gesellschaft, directed by Carl Peters, had made much more progress in opening up the interior than the British East Africa Company under Mackinnon, which received its Charter in 1888. It seemed likely that the expansion of the German Company would end by sealing the British off altogether from access to the Great Lakes and the headwaters of the Nile. Salisbury was prepared to make very considerable sacrifices else- where in order to avoid this. Assisted by the fall of Bismarck in the Spring of 1890, he succeeded, on 1 July 1890, in concluding with the German Government a Convention by which Germany, in return for the cession by England of the island of Heligoland in the North Sea, conceded to England: (1) a British Protectorate over the island and dependencies of

Zanzibar; (2) a line of demarcation between British and German territory in East Africa running from Wanga on the coast north-westward to a point midway along the east shore of Lake Victoria and prolonged due west from there across Lake Victoria to the east border of the Congo Free State. This line of demarcation left the whole of Uganda and the headwaters of the Nile in the British sphere and gave England un-interrupted access to the Upper Nile valley from the east coast; (3) recognition that the British 'sphere of influence' extended 'to the borders of Egypt (which were left undefined), to the Congo Free State, and to the western watershed of the Upper Nile.'[17]

In an endeavour to appease the French Government, who had not been consulted over the Anglo-German Convention, which altered the status of Zanzibar and consequently nullified the 1862 Anglo-French Agreement, Salisbury then proceeded to the negotiation of an Anglo-French Agreement, which was signed on 5 August 1890, by which England, in return for French recognition of the British Protectorate over Zanzibar, recognised a French Protectorate over Madagascar and also recognised large and mainly desert areas in West and North Africa as French 'spheres of influence.'

By the Agreements with Germany and Italy Salisbury had sealed off the approaches to the Nile Valley from the east and south. But they still lay open from the west in the line of a potential French advance through the hinterland of the French Congo. In 1890 this was only a distant threat, although Brazza, now Governor of the French Congo, already seems to have been thinking in terms of pushing inland to the Nile Valley.[18] Salisbury concentrated on trying to consolidate the British position in Uganda, round the headwaters of the Nile, as a preliminary to a future advance northward along the line of the Upper Nile to occupy the territory evacuated by Emin. The instrument he attempted to use was Mackinnon's British East Africa Company, which proved to be a broken reed. The great limitation on British Imperial policy at this time was the extraordinary parsimony displayed by Parliament over the expenditure of money on Imperial adventures and the great reluctance shown by successive Governments in asking Parliament for money for these pur-poses. In Egypt British Imperial policy was largely financed by the Egyptian taxpayer. In East Africa this resource was not available and the attempt to finance it by commercial enterprise was not a success. In order to save the Chartered Company, to colonise Uganda, and to use it as a jumping-off point for an occupation of the Upper Nile, a railway from the coast to Lake Victoria was an urgent necessity. But the most Salisbury could get from Parliament was a vote of £20,000 for a pre-liminary survey.

Missionary activity in Uganda had resulted in endemic civil war between Moslems, Catholics and Protestants. Sir Frederick (afterwards Lord) Lugard, sent there by the East Africa Company, succeeded in patching up a settlement in 1892. But, by that time, the Company was on its last legs financially and announced its intention of withdrawing from Uganda altogether. It was clear that the result would be a renewal of chaos and a probable massacre of missionaries. In face of the latter possibility, the Liberal Government, with Rosebery as Foreign Secretary, which came into office in August 1892, agreed to subsidise the Company to enable it to stay on for a few months and cover the withdrawal of the missionaries, most of whom refused to leave. But something more per/ manent was needed if the Nile Valley policy, which Rosebery had taken over from Salisbury and which had become the cornerstone of British African policy, was to remain valid. Therefore, in November 1892, Rosebery, who was having continual difficulties with the Liberal Cabinet over his African policy, managed to get Cabinet agreement to send Sir Gerald Portal who, a few years before, had worked with Cromer in Cairo, to Uganda as 'Imperial Commissioner,' ostensibly to 'enquire and report,' but actually to take over the affairs of the territory from the Company. In December 1893, after a year in Uganda, Portal reported to Rosebery in favour of 'the maintenance of some form of British pre/ ponderance.' He based his recommendation on the ground that the interests of the missionaries there would certainly justify the intervention of some other Power if England abandoned it, and argued: 'It is hardly possible that Uganda, the natural key of the whole Nile Valley . . . should be left unprotected and unnoticed by other Powers because an English Company has been unwilling to hold it and because HMG has been unwilling to interfere.'[19]

By this time news had been received in London of a projected French advance on the Nile Valley through the hinterland of the French Congo. The Belgians were also infiltrating into Equatoria Province from the Congo Free State. In May 1894, Lord Kimberley, the Foreign Secretary,[20] with Rosebery's support, but in face of considerable opposition from Harcourt and others, obtained Cabinet agreement to the declaration of a British Protectorate over Uganda. In the House of Commons on 30 May Sir Edward Grey, the Under Secretary at the Foreign Office, obtained Parliamentary approval for a credit to cover the cost of administering Uganda in accordance with Portal's recommendations. The next neces/ sary step was the construction of a railway connecting Uganda with the east coast. But this was not started for another two years, when Salisbury was again in office.

The French plan for an advance on the Nile Valley through the hinterland of the French Congo had its inception in May 1893 when Commandant Monteil received orders to lead an expedition from the west coast to Fashoda, near the confluence of the White Nile and the Sobat, and to plant the French flag there. It appears[21] that this was the result of a decision taken by the French President, Sadi Carnot, who had been influenced by a recent public statement by M. Victor Prompt, a French hydraulic engineer (who also happened to be an old schoolfellow of the President's), about the possibilities of controlling the flow of the Nile.

Prompt was a member of an international commission which had gone to Egypt to advise the Egyptian Government about the location of the proposed reservoir in Upper Egypt, on which Cromer had set his heart. In the course of a lecture on the Nilotic Sudan, given in January 1893 to the Institut Egyptien in Cairo, he allowed himself the following rather indiscreet speculations. 'If a barrage three metres high were constructed at the outlet of Lake Victoria, at the head of the Ripon Falls, the level of the lake, which is fifty milliard square metres in extent, would be raised by about 0·3 metres per annum. It would thus take ten years to raise the water to the height of the barrage. In this way Egypt, during the period of low Nile, would only receive 250 cubic metres of water a second instead of 455. A similar effect would be produced by the erection of barrages at the seventh and eighth cataracts. By such means one could reduce the flow of water at Cairo, during an exceptionally low Nile, from 200 cubic metres a second to 80/100 cubic metres, which would mean complete ruin for Egypt.'[22]

It is unlikely that the French had any intention of building such a barrage, or series of barrages. In any case, there was no stone within hundreds of miles of Fashoda, which was the intended destination of the Monteil expedition. And, so far as is known, no irrigation engineers were detailed to accompany Monteil. They may not have been unwilling to focus British attention on a latent, theoretical possibility. But what they really wanted was to create some sort of *fait accompli*, in the form of an actual French presence on the Upper Nile, which might induce the British to come to the negotiating table and discuss terms for the evacuation of Egypt.

Ever since the formation of the Congo Free State and the definition of its boundaries in 1885, there had been continual disputes between the French and the Free State about its northern boundaries. The French had been concerned lest Free State expansion northwards should block their line of approach to the Nile Valley. The territory in dispute was the basin of the Ubanghi, a tributary of the Congo flowing into it from the north-east. The French were interested in securing for themselves possession of this river and its northern tributaries as providing the only practicable line of advance into the Bahr el-Ghazal and the Nile Valley. The matter was a complicated one since there were no accurate maps. It had not been settled by the time Monteil received his instructions.

Monteil's expedition was supposed to be secret but became known to the British Government early in 1894 while Monteil was still in France. The British Government's reaction was threefold. First, as we have seen, they declared a Protectorate over Uganda. Secondly, they attempted to block the French advance by agreeing with the German Government that the hinterland of the German colony of the Cameroons, to the north of the French Congo, could be extended eastwards to the Nile basin. This move was countered by a Franco-German Agreement signed in February 1894 which delimited the frontier between the Cameroons and the French Congo so as to allow a clear line of French expansion inland. Thirdly, the British Government entered into negotiations with the Congo Free State which led to the Anglo-Congolese Convention of May 1894. By the terms of this Convention the British Government leased to the Congo Free State (a) the west bank of the Upper Nile between Lake Albert in the south and latitude 10' N in the north, and between the river and longitude 29' E to the west for the period of King Leopold's lifetime, and (b) the area known as the Bahr el-Ghazal, bounded by latitude 10' N to the north, the existing boundaries of the Free State to the south, latitude 29' E to the east and latitude 25' E to the west, during the lifetime of Leopold 'and his successors.'[23] These leases were designed to erect a barrier between the French and the Upper Nile along the line of Monteil's proposed advance. The only 'right' which the British Government possessed in order thus to dispose of territory which was theirs neither by right of sovereignty nor of conquest, was the German acknowledgement of this territory as part of a British 'sphere of influence' under the terms of the 1890 Convention. The Anglo-Congolese Convention also provided for a lease by the Free State of a strip of land along Lake Tanganyika, on the eastern border of the Free State and adjacent to German East Africa, which would have linked the new British Protectorate of Uganda with the territory administered by Rhodes' Chartered Company south of Lake Tanganyika, thus providing for the eventual realisation of Rhodes' dream of an all-British route from Cairo to the Cape.

The German Government objected to the lease of this strip and, as a result of their representations, the British Government agreed to give it up. The French Government's reaction was more violent. They denounced the whole Convention as contrary to the international status of the Congo Free State as laid down in Berlin in 1885, and to various Ottoman

Firmans forbidding the cession of Egyptian territory. (During the subsequent course of the Upper Nile dispute both the British and French
Governments alternated impartially, as it happened to suit their immediate purposes, between professing to regard the Upper Nile as *res
nullius*, and thus open to the first comer by right of conquest, or as
Egyptian territory and so inalienable from Egypt without the Sultan's
consent.) The French Chamber voted a credit of Frs 1,800,000 for the
'protection of French interests in Africa.' Monteil was appointed Governor
of the newly formed Province of Haut-Oubanghi, covering the area
disputed with the Free State in the hinterland of the French Congo.
Leopold intimated to the British Government that he could not ratify
the Convention unless the British undertook to protect him against
French reprisals. The British Government thereupon released Leopold
from the Convention and, in August 1894, a Franco-Congolese Convention was signed in which the Free State (a) abandoned the leases
which had been granted to it under the terms of the Anglo-Congolese
Convention, and (b) agreed to a delimitation of the frontier between the
Free State and the new French Province of Haut-Oubanghi which
ceded most of the disputed territory to the French and left them with a
clear road between the coast and the Upper Nile. British diplomacy had
met with an unmitigated defeat and the dispute with France over British
claims to the Upper Nile had been brought out into the open.

In retrospect, it is clear that the British Government over-reacted to the
news of the Monteil expedition and behaved clumsily. By doing so they
encouraged the French to think that the British tail could be twisted by
occasional forays and rumours of forays in the direction of the Upper
Nile.

Nothing much happened about the Monteil expedition. Monteil did
not reach Haut-Oubanghi until March 1894 and, a few months later,
was transferred to the Ivory Coast and replaced as Governor of Haut-
Oubanghi by Liotard, a civilian, who was instructed to take over
Monteil's task of pushing forward to the Upper Nile.

In March 1895 British suspicions about French activities were again
aroused by speeches made by members of the colonial 'lobby' in the
French Chamber and by a newspaper interview given by Brazza, the
Governor of the French Congo, on the subject of the Franco-Congolese
Agreement, in which he stated that the Agreement would assure France of
access to the Nile Valley, which access would in due course enable France
to settle the Egyptian question in accordance with her own interests.[24] This
led to questions in the House of Commons and eventually to a statement
in the Commons by Sir Edward Grey on 28 March 1895. Grey stated
that the British claim to the Upper Nile had been formally recognised

by Germany, Italy and the Congo Free State and was 'well known to all the other Powers.' There was also the claim of Egypt which France, in her protest against the Anglo-Congolese Convention, had not only admitted but emphasised. Taken together, 'the British and Egyptian spheres of influence covered the whole of the Nile waterway.' He urged that rumours about French expeditions to the Nile should be treated with great reserve; the Foreign Office had 'no reason to suppose' that they were true. 'I cannot think it possible that these rumours deserve credence, because the advance of a French expedition under secret instructions, right from the other side of Africa, into a territory over which our claims have been known for so long, would not be merely an inconsistent and unexpected act, but it must be perfectly well known to the French Government that it would be an unfriendly act, and would be so viewed in England.'[25]

In Cairo, Cromer reacted strongly to rumours about a French expedition. For nearly four years he had put the Sudan at the back of his mind and had determined that, for financial reasons, any question of its reconquest must wait until after the construction of the Aswan reservoir, on which he had set his heart. He was extremely annoyed that what he termed 'this abominable Sudan business' should have come to the front again. He realised that a forward move might be forced on him and, on 8 March 1895, he told Kimberley that he was arranging for the Nile Valley railway to be prolonged south as far as Aswan and for the telegraph to be extended south from Korosko across the desert route towards Abu Hamed. 'I look upon both these measures as steps which will facilitate the ultimate reconquest of the Sudan.'[26] On 29 March, the day after Grey's declaration in the Commons, he wrote again to Kimberley: 'Surely it is impossible to leave the Sudan for all time in its present condition. If Egypt does not retake it, the French or Italians will . . . The activity of the French may force a premature consideration of the issue.'[27] In June, Kimberley told Cromer that he did not believe that the French had any considerable force in Bahr el-Ghazal, but thought that there might be 'some sort of roving detachment which is probably employed in trying to make alliances with the natives.'[28] By this time Kimberley was a 'ministre demissionaire,' since the Liberal Government had just been defeated at the Elections, and he probably took a detached view of the situation on the Upper Nile.

Cromer had also taken up the question strongly with Rosebery, the Prime Minister. In April he told him that the Egyptian Ministers were very agitated about the rumours of French activity but were powerless to do anything themselves and hoped that the British Government were looking after the matter. 'The anglophil Press argues that it is incumbent on England to stop the advance of the French; the opposition newspapers dilate on the generosity of the French in wanting to hold the Upper Nile for Egypt and thus save them from British rapacity . . . We had better speak less of the "British sphere of influence" and more of "Egyptian territory" . . . There cannot be a shadow of doubt that the Egyptians generally would like to reconquer the Sudan . . . Wingate (Major, later Sir Reginald, Wingate, at that time Chief Intelligence Officer of the Egyptian Army) tells me that the power of the Khalifa remains much as it has been for the last four years, or rather weaker if anything . . . He has no doubt that the Khalifa would be unable to stop the French on the Upper Nile but that he would not give up Khartum without a fight. He does not think that the French would have any difficulty occupying Bahr el-Ghazal.' He went on to tell Rosebery that he had always been in favour of an eventual reconquest of the Sudan. 'It is now more than probable that the question will be forced on us prematurely. The presence of the French on or near the Upper Nile entirely alters the situation. If they are allowed to establish themselves there is an end of all idea of an Egyptian reconquest . . . If any civilised Power holds the waters of the Upper Nile it would be in a position to exercise a perilous influence on the fate of Egypt.'[29] 'In Egypt we are continually faced with the alternatives of giving way to the French or risking a serious quarrel with them.'

He recognised that a decision to reconquer the Sudan 'involves the possibility of war with France,' but pointed out that this was 'a direction in which we have been drifting for some time in connection with Egypt.' He went on to refer to the financial difficulties of reconquest and to the desirability that the reconquest should be made by Egypt under British supervision. 'It would be perfectly useless for the Egyptian Government to ask the Powers (*i.e.* the Caisse) for the money unless they were assured of strong British support. It would be worse than useless for us to encourage them to put forward any such demand unless we were quite determined to carry our point in spite of French opposition.' He asked Rosebery whether the other Powers would be prepared to abstain from protest if, in spite of French dissent, the money were taken. He also asked whether the Navy was strong enough 'to hold our own with the French fleet.' 'I am more convinced each day of the inadvisability of drifting on without a comprehensible Egyptian policy . . . I do not believe that the Sudan question can be solved by any means other than effective possession . . . Eleven years ago I said that the ultimate solution of the Egyptian question would depend on the relative naval strengths of England and France. The force of circumstances . . . has driven us into a situation which makes war a not improbable solution of the whole mess.'[30]

This was very bellicose stuff, and it can be seen in retrospect as an over-reaction to French pinpricks on the Upper Nile and in Egypt itself. Correspondence with Rosebery frequently had the effect of bringing Cromer to the boil. He would never have written in these terms to Salisbury, whose massive calm, so different from Rosebery's immature exuberance, had a soothing effect on his irascibility.

In reply Rosebery made it clear that 'no instructions will come from this country for a reconquest of the Sudan' and that 'the initiative should come from Egypt.' 'I myself should not be disposed to discourage a not too distant proposal . . . (but) . . . if we are to wait for two years after letting our intentions be known . . . every Frenchman would feel it his duty to press forward to the Nile . . .' With regard to the international situation Rosebery told Cromer that he was happy about British naval strength as compared with France, but that 'both Russia and Germany are disgusted with us . . . we could confidently calculate on a very tangible amount of ill-will among the Powers . . . Even if I received an urgent request from the Egyptian Government for a Sudan expedition I could not bring the present Government to agree to it.'[31]

A few weeks after writing this letter Rosebery was out of office and Salisbury was once more Prime Minister and Foreign Secretary, head of a Conservative-Unionist Administration with a clear majority in the House of Commons.

In the Autumn Cromer, after his Summer vacation and, as always, feeling more at ease with a Conservative Administration, had calmed down over the Sudan. Absorbed in the Nile reservoir scheme, for which he was planning the finances, he expressed himself as being in agreement with Salisbury's view that there should be no forward movement into the Sudan until the completion of the Uganda railway from the coast which, at long last, had just been started. Salisbury's idea, once the railway had been completed, was that any forward French movement could be frustrated by a converging advance by the Egyptians up the Nile from the north and by the British down the Upper Nile from Uganda. But it would be impossible to organise an advance from Uganda in sufficient strength until the railway had been completed, which would not be for another two years. Meanwhile, any movement from Egypt alone would immediately provoke a forward French movement which could not be stopped from Uganda.[32]

In the event, the 'forward movement' from Egypt took place, within the next few months, long before the Uganda railway had been completed, against Cromer's wishes, and on the insistence of the British Government, as the result, not of any French movement towards the Upper Nile, but of an Italian defeat at the hands of the Abyssinians.

The Italian attempts to use Massawa as a base for expansion into the highlands of Eritrea and Abyssinia had met with almost continual trouble. In 1887 an Italian expedition was annihilated by the Abyssinians at Dogali, almost within sight of Massawa, and Gerald Portal, Cromer's assistant in Cairo, was sent on a mission to King Johannes' Court to try to obtain for the Italians by negotiation what they had failed to obtain for themselves by force. The mission was a total failure and it was the Dervishes and not the British who, unwittingly, saved the Italians from their predicament. In January 1888, as a result of a Dervish invasion of Abyssinia, King Johannes was compelled to withdraw most of his army from around Massawa and the Italians were able to make some advance on to the Eritrean plateau. In March Johannes was killed in battle with the Dervishes. The usual struggle for the succession followed. The Italians backed Menelik, Prince of Shoa, with whom they had already a friendly relationship. They made the Treaty of Ucciali with him in May 1889 and, with supplies of arms and ammunition, helped him to defeat Mangasha, the illegitimate son of Johannes, who was his principal rival for the throne. They also improved the occasion by extending their frontiers further into Eritrea, occupying Keren and Asmara. 'From Keren, perched on the westernmost bastion of the *antiplano*, the Italians looked down over the foothills to Kassala and the valley of the Nile beyond.'[33]

It was this expansion which caused Cromer all the alarm which has been described, and which led eventually to the conclusion of an Anglo-Italian Agreement in 1891 delimiting 'spheres of influence' and in effect, giving the Italians a free hand in Abyssinia. But, from then on, the Italian position deteriorated. Menelik got tired of their exigencies, and their approaches towards Kassala (which, in 1894, with the agreement of the British, they occupied as 'caretakers' for Egypt) embroiled them with the Dervishes.

In the Autumn of 1893, after Monteil had received his instructions, the French, thinking in terms of a possible converging French advance on the Upper Nile from the French Congo via the Ubanghi on the west and from Jibuti via Abyssinia on the east, began to cultivate friendly relations with Menelik who, harassed by Italian ambitions, was anxious for another European alliance and for an alternative source of European arms and ammunition. He therefore welcomed the French approaches and the supplies of French arms and ammunition which soon started to arrive via Jibuti, by this time Abyssinia's principal port of access to the sea. It was with the assistance of French arms that Menelik, in January 1896, inflicted a defeat on the Italians at Amba Allagi. It seemed likely that the Dervishes would take advantage of the Italian discomfiture by attacking them in Kassala. Immediately the question arose as to whether and how the British could relieve the Italians from their embarrassment.

International circumstances—the desirability of keeping Italy happy in order to keep Germany sweet—combined with local considerations—the undesirability of allowing the Dervishes to win a victory over a European enemy and, perhaps, once more pose a threat to Tokar and Suakin—suggested that something ought to be done. Cromer did not want to let Kassala fall into Dervish hands 'while the Italians are being beaten as I suspect they will be.' But, for financial reasons, he did not want a major expedition. 'We are tied hand and foot by international fetters and, if we again get into financial difficulties, we shall be more or less at the mercy of the French.'[34] He expressed himself as being in favour of a limited advance from Suakin to relieve the pressure on the Italians. The British Government suggested a demonstration south of Wadi Halfa. Cromer insisted that, wherever they advanced, any territory taken by Egyptian troops and with the expenditure of Egyptian money must be held for the benefit of Egypt. Egyptian resources could not be used merely to save the Italians from the consequences of their folly or to satisfy the German Government. Any effort made at Egypt's expense must seem to be for Egypt's benefit. Eventually London decided that it would be best to wait and see what happened at Kassala. Then, on 2 March, came news of a second, and much more serious, defeat of the Italians by the Abyssinians at Adowa. 'For a moment it seemed that Adowa had put a match to all the combustible material generated by Italy's chronic social and economic discontents, and had precipitated a revolutionary situation. Italy might be driven not only out of Africa . . . but out of the Triple Alliance as well.'[35]

One result of the defeat at Adowa was to overthrow the Government of the fire-eating Crispi and to replace it by one headed by the more accommodating di Rudini. On 10 March the Italian Ambassador in London made an official request for a diversion in favour of Italy '*du côte du Nil*' in order to prevent the Dervishes from attacking the Italian flank.[36] There also appears to have been a personal appeal by the German Kaiser to Lascelles, the British Ambassador in Berlin.[37] At all events, Salisbury's decision to meet the Italian Ambassador's request was due to his almost traditional policy of picking Italian chestnuts out of the fire in order to placate Germany. The method chosen—a demonstration up the Nile rather than a limited advance from Suakin—was almost certainly due to the advice of Wolseley.[38] At a Cabinet meeting on 11 March an advance up the Nile 'as far as and no farther than we can go without any undue effort on the part of Egypt' was approved. On the following day—12 March—there was another Cabinet meeting at which Wolseley was present. It was then agreed that there should be two separate operations: (1) The immediate occupation of Akashe, a village some thirty miles south of the Egyptian advanced post at Sarras; and (2) a demonstration

towards Abu Hamed across the desert from Wadi Halfa. It was considered 'most important' that these operations should be carried out at
once.[39]

All these decisions were taken without any reference to Cromer, or to
the Egyptian Government, although the operations were to be carried out
by Egyptian troops at the expense of the Egyptian Government. They
were communicated by the War Office to General Knowles, GOC
British troops in Egypt, on the evening of 12 March. Rennell Rodd, at
that time Cromer's First Secretary in Cairo, recorded: 'There was no
preliminary discussion of ways and means. The contemplated movement
was told to the British Press with barely time for us to tell the Khedive.
The news was announced in *The Times* on 13 March disguised as a
Reuter message from Cairo . . . Wolseley was responsible . . . The
decision, involving the initiation of the reconquest of the Sudan, four or
five years before we were ready for it, was taken in London by Ministers
one of whom was said to have admitted that he did not know where
Kassala was. No details were examined and no provision made for
expenditure. We had not long to wait before learning that Egypt was
to pay for all. The French Press proclaimed that the advance was a pretext
for prolonging the occupation. The Khedive . . . assumed that the
action had been taken exclusively for the benefit of Italy . . . Cromer's
advice had not been followed and the chief military authorities at home
had rushed the Government into an alternative plan . . . There were two
points on which Cromer and Kitchener were agreed: (1) We must
either retake and hold Dongola or not move up the Nile at all; (2) There
must be a backing of British troops.'[40]

Cromer was informed of the position in a telegram from Salisbury sent
on the evening of 12 March—about the time of the War Office telegram
to Knowles—which was not in accordance either with the Cabinet
decision or with the instructions given to Knowles. 'The Italian
Ambassador has pressed me urgently to take some steps against the
Dervishes . . . After consulting the military authorities HMG are of opinion
that the occupation of Dongola would be the most effective demonstration,
will be greatly in the interest of Egypt, and a charge she may fairly be asked
to bear. It will also tend to repel any disposition to attack Egypt which
the recent victories may have created among the Dervishes. Of course it
is intended to keep Dongola.'[41]

The following day Salisbury sent a private telegram to Cromer in
which he tried to explain matters more fully: 'The Cabinet decision was
inspired especially by a desire to help the Italians at Kassala and prevent
the Dervishes winning a conspicuous success which might have far-
reaching results. In addition we desired to kill two birds with one stone

and to use the same military effort to plant the Egyptian foot farther up the Nile. Also we wished to avoid crossing swords with the Abyssinians. But the main reason was to relieve the strain on Kassala. For that reason publicity was essential. I have told Ambassador that we have sanctioned advance to Dongola. We are not bound to go so far if the difficulties are serious. We do not wish to have to send more British troops to Egypt if we can help it because this will involve diplomatic explanations. But if necessary it can be done. At present orders are being drawn up for the immediate advance of Egyptian troops some way up the Nile. But we shall avoid any absolute undertaking to go to Dongola. I could have wished that the Italians had less capacity for being beaten and let us wait for 2/3 years until we were quite ready. But it would not have been safe either from the African or European point of view to sit still while they were being crushed.'[42]

Salisbury's point about planting Egypt's foot farther up the Nile was probably an *ex post facto* rationalisation of Wolseley's objection to operations based on Suakin. And the confused vagueness about the expeditions's ultimate destination was due to Cromer's previous insistence that any territory taken must be held for the benefit of Egypt.

Cromer was very annoyed indeed. Without having been consulted in any way, he had been jockeyed into an expedition before he was ready for it, for what he considered inadequate reasons, and by the wrong route. He had been placed in a position of embarrassment vis-à-vis the Khedive and the Egyptian Government by the British action in ordering the employment of Egyptian troops for warlike operations without any pretence of prior consultation and without any reference whatever to Egyptian interests. He sent off a series of furious telegrams. He asked Salisbury to take steps to 'stop the War Office from issuing orders involving movements of Egyptian troops and expenditure of Egyptian money as if no such thing as an Egyptian Government existed . . . Unless the business is worked through me the utmost confusion will arise.'[43] It even seemed possible that Cromer might resign if he were not appeased. That would have been awkward. A Cabinet meeting was held on 15 March to discuss the situation. It was decided, in effect, that Cromer was to take charge of the expedition which the War Office had initiated, that Kitchener, the Sirdar of the Egyptian Army, should be responsible to Cromer and not to the War Office, and that Cromer himself should receive his instructions about the expedition from the Foreign Office and not from the War Office.[44]

Cromer was somewhat mollified. But he expressed his regret that his 'comparatively humble Sudan proposal,' *i.e.* for a limited advance from Suakin, had not been adopted, and made it clear that Dongola, and not the 'demonstrations' ordered by the War Office, must be the objective of the expedition. For local reasons it had to be represented that the expedition was for an Egyptian and not for a European objective. But, as he told Salisbury, 'it will be a serious business from a military point of view to get to Dongola. I doubt whether it can be done without employing British troops. And, if we get to Dongola, it will not be easy to stop the move, ment there. But the financial side is even more serious and, if Egypt is to pay the whole thing, the question of Egyptian financial liberty must be faced. Otherwise I do not see how we are to get on. Directly we get into financial difficulties we are at the mercy of the French . . . In some form or another we must get the Egyptian Government out of the mess into which, through no fault of their own, they must necessarily fall unless preventive measures are taken betimes. Goschen knows all about it.'45

The financial difficulties began almost immediately. A few days after the expedition had been ordered, official application was made to the Caisse for a sum of £500,000 from the Reserves as 'extraordinary expenditure' to cover its cost. The British, German, Austrian and Italian Commissioners agreed, and the French and Russian Commissioners dissented. The money was therefore advanced. But the French and Russian Commissioners immediately instituted a suit in the Mixed Courts against the Egyptian Government demanding the return of the money on the ground that, under the terms of the London Convention, a decision to advance money from the Reserves for extraordinary ex, penditure had to be unanimous.

There were other difficulties. The Sultan objected officially to the Khedive that 'any despatch of Egyptian troops, especially against Moslems, depends absolutely on the will and permission of H.I.M. and it is impossible that he can sanction this expedition.'46 This was awkward, since the Khedive was already, with some justification, annoyed about the way in which he had been treated over the expedition. Cromer had already apologised to him for 'the manner in which proceedings had been conducted,' for which, he considered, 'he had some cause for complaint,' and impressed on him the necessity of keeping to himself such hostility as he might feel towards the expedition.47 The position was not improved by a statement by Salisbury in the House of Lords that the expedition was in order to 'satisfy Egyptian opinion.'48 But matters were somehow arranged. The Khedive sent a respectful reply to the Sultan telling him that the expedition was the result of his agreement 'with the views and proposals of HMG,' and Cromer reported that he was 'behaving well' as far as his public conduct was concerned.49

By the end of March Cromer felt that he had got the situation in hand.

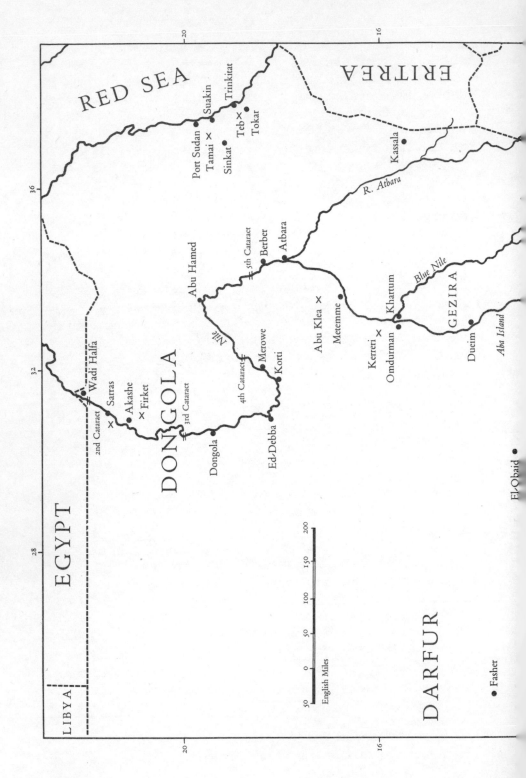

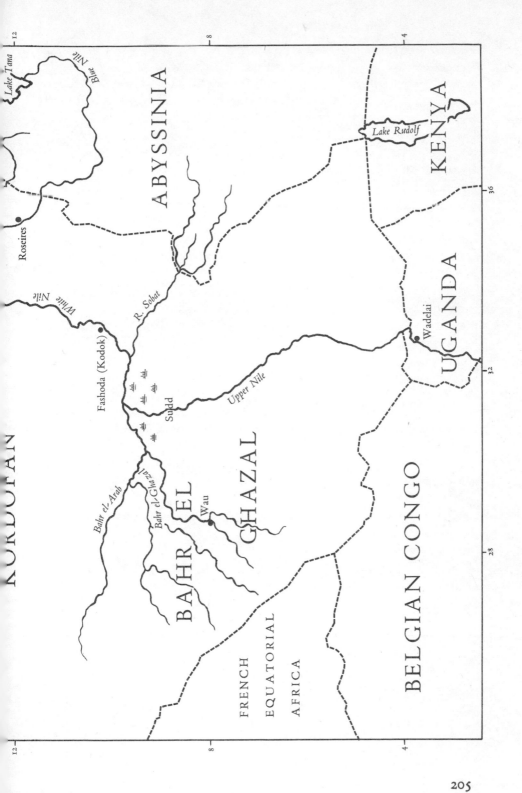

Lake Tana

Blue Nile

ABYSSINIA

KENYA

Lake Rudolf

Roseires

White Nile

R. Sobat

Fashoda (Kodok)

UGANDA

Wadelai

Upper Nile

Sudd

Bahr el-Arab

Bahr el-Ghazal

Wau

BAHR EL GHAZAL

KORDOFAN

BELGIAN CONGO

FRENCH

EQUATORIAL

AFRICA

He had wrested control of the campaign out of the hands of the War Office. He was getting on well with Kitchener who, he told Salisbury, 'is cool and sensible and knows his job thoroughly and is not at all inclined to be rash.'⁵⁰ The Khedive was behaving himself. The Sultan had been silenced. And, for the time being, he had the support of three out of the five foreign Powers represented on the Caisse. He told Salisbury what he regarded as the objective of the expedition. 'What we want to do is (i) to get to Dongola and (ii) to resist the almost inevitable pressure to go further. There can be no question of stopping short of Dongola, and Dongola cannot be the final halting place. Khartum will have to be recovered. But the Egyptian Government, for military and financial reasons, cannot go further than Dongola at present.'⁵¹

Cromer still thought that British troops might be necessary in order to capture Dongola and he reluctantly agreed to Kitchener's request to ask for Indian troops to garrison Suakin in order to enable the Egyptian garrison there to be transferred to the Nile Valley. (After the Indian troops had arrived he grumbled continually about their extravagance— 'hecatombs of doctors and donkeys'—and the size of the bills the Government of India kept sending to the Egyptian Government for their maintenance.) Salisbury was haunted by the fear lest British troops would have to be sent to the Sudan to rescue the Egyptian Army, a course which would lead to endless Parliamentary and international complications. He told Cromer that he wanted to avoid the use of British or Indian troops for 'as long as I safely can,' and expressed the fear lest Kitchener should break loose and go beyond Dongola. 'I feel some disquietude that he has bought 5,000 camels. I had much rather see him without them; if he is entirely supplied by rail and river at Dongola they are unnecessary.'⁵² Cromer assured him that Kitchener, 'although, like other soldiers, he would like to reconquer the Sudan, is not inclined to do anything rash.'⁵³

In the event British troops were not required to assist in the capture of Dongola apart from one battalion (the North Staffs) which was already in Egypt. The first major engagement of the campaign was on 6 June at Firket, on the east bank of the Nile about 100 miles south of Wadi Halfa and 16 miles south of the railhead, which had been pushed forward to Akashe. The Egyptian troops conducted themselves well. The Dervishes were attacked after a surprise night march and decisively defeated. Cromer told Salisbury that the victory had been won 'in spite of the incubus of War Office advice and interference.'⁵⁴ He afterwards reported that 'the blacks can both march and fight' and that 'the fellahin can undergo fatigue and march well and Kitchener has a fair degree of confidence in their fighting qualities when commanded by British officers.'⁵⁵

At the beginning of July Cromer left Egypt for his annual vacation, after instructing Kitchener to drive the Dervishes out of Dongola Province and 'absolutely vetoing any further advance.'[56] Dongola town was captured without any further major engagement on 23 September, while Cromer was still on holiday.

On his return to Cairo in the Autumn, Cromer, having received reports from Kitchener about the campaign to date, began to think, for the first time, that the Sudan could be reconquered without having to call on the British Army for help. He told Salisbury: 'The further reconquest of the Sudan must be made by the Egyptian army, and they are capable of doing it if they are well handled and not tried too high. I am confident that the decision not to advance any further at present is wise on financial and military grounds . . . Abu Hamed might be taken next year.'[57] This was a considerable advance on his previous thinking, when he had refused to contemplate any immediate move beyond Dongola.

Kitchener went to London to discuss the military and financial future of the campaign. He had satisfied himself, erroneously as it turned out, that the Dervish strength was less than had been expected, and was anxious to push straight on to Khartum. Both he and Cromer were convinced that the real difficulty was not military but financial. The French and Russian Commissioners' suit against the Egyptian Govern-ment had been decided in the Commissioners' favour; the appeal still had to be heard, but it seemed likely that the £500,000 would have to be repaid. In that event, this sum, plus some additional money for the continuance of the campaign, would have to be found by the British Treasury. (The Egyptian Government's appeal was lost early in December. By that time, the Egyptian Government was assured of an advance from the British and immediately repaid the whole sum to the Caisse.) For this financial purpose Kitchener's visit to London was a great success. On 27 November Salisbury wrote to Cromer: 'Kitchener's campaign against the Chancellor of the Exchequer was not the least brilliant and certainly the most unexpected of all his triumphs. But all his strategy is of a piece—the position was carried by a forced march and a surprise.'[58] In fact the Treasury agreed to advance to the Egyptian Government the sum of £800,000 at 2½ per cent interest[59] which, according to Kitchener's estimates, would get the expedition as far as Berber, and the railway as far as Abu Hamed, during the course of the following year. Salisbury told Cromer: 'My impression is that when you get to Berber you will stay there for some little time . . . But your steps may be hastened by the advance of some other Power towards the Upper Nile.'[60]

On 5 February 1897 Hicks Beach, the Chancellor of the Exchequer, advising the House of Commons of the financial arrangements made, said that Egypt would never be permanently secure if a hostile Power were to take possession of the Nile Valley and that Kitchener had been authorised to advance 'in the first place to Abu Hamed and afterwards possibly beyond.' The last part of his announcement was greeted with loud cheers. 'The Dongola campaign had charmed the British nation, and 1897 was the year of Queen Victoria's Diamond Jubilee. That was a great Imperial occasion and, to those who celebrated it, war can seldom have appeared to be more delightful and rewarding or less dangerous and expensive.'[61] There were unlikely to be any further House of Commons' objections to the advance of money for the reconquest of the Sudan and for keeping the French out of the Upper Nile.

The possibility of a French advance to the Upper Nile had taken on a new lease of life as the result of the appointment, in February 1896, of Captain Marchand to join Liotard in Haut Oubanghi and to lead an expedition to Fashoda, on the west bank of the White Nile on latitude 10 N, just north of the marshy Sudd area and a little upstream of the junction of the White Nile and Sobat rivers. The political object of the mission was stated to be the creation for France 'in the region of the White Nile serious alliances and indisputable titles of possession against the day when the future destiny of these Provinces will have to be decided.' Marchand, who had taken the initiative in securing this mission for himself, had earlier described its object as being 'to compel England by peaceful but sure means to accept, or even to propose the meeting of, a European Conference to discuss the future of the Egyptian Sudan, that is to say the Nile Valley. Apart from the importance of such a result for French colonisation in Africa, the future of which is gravely threatened by British ambitions, may we not hope that the question of the evacuation of Egypt will arise quite naturally from that of the Egyptian Sudan and will impose itself with a new force at the deliberations of the Conference?' These ideas, as expressed by Marchand, seem to have been accepted by the French Government and would appear to have been their reason for sanctioning the expedition.[62] Marchand arrived in the French Congo in July 1896, but only started from the Haut Oubanghi on his journey towards the Nile Valley in April 1897.

Rumours of this new expedition, together with news of the presence of a French mission in Abyssinia, which was believed to have plans for sending an expedition westwards down the Sobat to join hands with Marchand, go some way towards explaining the Cabinet's acquiescence in an immediate further move forward by Kitchener.

The French in Abyssinia, apart from this supposed activity, were also trying to block the Anglo-Egyptian claims to the Upper Nile by encouraging Menelik to put forward his own claims in that area. And there was a suspicion that Menelik was in friendly relations with the Dervishes as a result of their common hostility to the Italians. For all these reasons, Mr (afterwards Sir Rennell) Rodd, Cromer's First Secretary in Cairo, was sent to Addis Ababa with a mission early in 1897 to try to arrive at some understanding with Menelik. He was unable to accomplish much. The British Government were prepared to give nothing away to Abyssinia, either on Egypt's account or their own, in the Nile Valley; Menelik was furious with the British for what he regarded as their consistent support of Italy in East Africa and for their refusal to allow arms to be imported into Abyssinia through Zeila. Rodd decided that nothing could usefully be done about fixing a boundary between the Sudan and Abyssinia until Egyptian, or Anglo-Egyptian, forces had reached Khartum, but he managed to secure, for what it was worth, an undertaking from Menelik not to supply arms to the Dervishes. He then left Addis Ababa with his mission.

That Summer, Rodd, in an interview in London with the Prime Minister, found that Salisbury was not seriously concerned about Abyssinia. He thought that 'the French advance towards the Nile was a more serious matter.' Rodd, who had probably been primed by Cromer, urged that the British forces then in Uganda should 'move downriver as quickly as possible' and try and reach Fashoda before Marchand. 'Salisbury said, "Let's hope he won't get there." '63 In fact, there were in Uganda only a few British officers and some unreliable native troops. The railway from the coast had not yet been completed and there was no way of provisioning anything like a major expedition. There were a few half-hearted and abortive advances down the Upper Nile, which led to nothing, and which had no effect either on the progress of the campaign farther north, or on the progress of Marchand's difficult but determined advance on Fashoda from the west.

Cromer, in Cairo, does not appear to have been very worried over the rumours about Marchand. In April he told Salisbury that he thought Kitchener would take Abu Hamed without difficulty, but that he might have to ask for British troops 'for a winter to take Khartum later.' But 'I do not want assistance from England until I ask for it, and I shall be chary of putting myself in a position in which I have to ask for it.'64

Abu Hamed was taken on 29 July 1897 as the result of a march of 130 miles upriver from Merowe, the farthest point of advance the previous year. A month later Berber was taken without fighting. The railway between Wadi Halfa and Abu Hamed was completed and the desert route between Suakin and Berber opened as an additional channel of supply. The objectives of the 1897 campaign had been achieved with very little fighting and both Kitchener and the War Office were keen to send in British troops and to finish off the campaign with the capture of Khartum as soon as possible.

It seems that the War Office regarded this as the occasion to try to reassert their control over the campaign which Cromer had successfully wrested from them in March 1896. They appointed Sir Francis Grenfell, previously Sirdar of the Egyptian Army, as GOC British troops in Egypt and seemed to intend that, as soon as Kitchener and Cromer asked for British troops, Grenfell should be appointed over Kitchener's head to command what would then be an Anglo-Egyptian expedition.

Kitchener was suspicious about Grenfell's appointment, apprehensive of being superseded, and nervous over the possibility of a Dervish attack which he would not be able to withstand without British troops. But a request for British troops might mean his own supersession. And, if he did not ask for British troops, it might lead to a disaster. There in the desert, he worried himself to the point of a nervous breakdown. In Cairo, Cromer, as usual, was worried about money. The campaign was proving more expensive than he had expected. There were quarrels between Kitchener and Palmer, the Financial Adviser. His enthusiasm for going forward to Khartum diminished as he came to realise that it would probably mean a campaign conducted by the War Office with Egyptian money. In October 1897, after he had returned from his annual trip to Europe, he told Salisbury that there was not 'the smallest question of any further advance at present,' since the recapture of Khartum was 'beyond the military and financial resources of the Egyptian Government.' He indicated that Kitchener had had a nervous breakdown and complained that 'in moments of retrospection I tear my hair over the hurried decision of March 1896. It has upset all my calculations and introduced an entirely new element into Egyptian politics.'

What he appears to have meant by this is that he disliked having to spend Egyptian money on what was not really an Egyptian interest at all at a time when nationalist feeling was making it all the more necessary to demonstrate the benefits of the British occupation to the masses. Arguing against the use of British troops, he went on: 'My own opinion is that there is no sufficiently important British interest involved to justify the loss of life and money involved in the capture of Khartum. The only possible justification is that HMG have placed the Egyptian Government in their present position and must help them, but this argument does not apply unless it is shown that the Egyptian Army must either advance or fall back. And I am not convinced of either necessity.'[65]

For the next two months Cromer continued to argue against any further advance on the assumption that the Egyptian Army would be able to maintain themselves in their existing positions. He told Salisbury that the main argument advanced by the War Office in favour of an immediate advance was 'the alleged necessity of not being forestalled by the French in the Nile Valley.' He proceeded to dispose of this argument. 'Although I should prefer that the French did not establish themselves on the Upper Nile . . . (I do not think) it is absolutely necessary to prevent them from doing so. What do we want in Africa? We do not want to acquire on our own or on Egypt's account large tracts of useless territory . . . What we want is trade with Central Africa. It would be preferable that no part of the Nile Valley should be in the hands of a European Power. Let us therefore do all that can be done by diplomacy, by negotiations with Menelik, by affording some reasonable assistance to Egypt, to prevent any such consummation. But whether it is desirable, merely to forestall the French, to send a large expedition to Khartum, with the possibility . . . of being drawn by public pressure and military argument into further and more remote enterprises appears to me to be very questionable. We can always get to Khartum before anyone else whenever we choose and we now hold Berber and can connect the Nile Valley with the Red Sea by rail. This will have to be considered before long . . . For all important commercial purposes the French are already forestalled . . . (and) . . . the importance of the trade in question is not so great as is often supposed.' He concluded that 'HMG should not be hurried by fear of French activity,' that no expedition should be sent to Khartum that Winter, and that future policy should remain in suspense, 'subject always to the Egyptian Army being able to maintain itself in its existing positions.'[66]

It is impossible to reconcile the views expressed in this letter either with Cromer's willingness to go to war with France over the Nile Valley in 1895 or with his oft-repeated thesis that the presence of a European Power in the Upper Nile Valley would be fatal to Egypt's interests. The truth seems to be that he never took the 'water' argument very seriously and used it in the first instance merely as a convenient argument for keeping the Italians out of Kassala and for keeping open the Suakin–Berber route of re-entry to the Sudan. Later, his explosion to Rosebery about rumoured French moves towards the Upper Nile was due more to his accumulated exasperation at what the French had been doing in Egypt for the past ten years than anything which they might have been contemplating, 3,000 miles up the Nile. In the Autumn of 1897 his fears of the effect of an advance to Khartum on Egyptian finances, and consequently on the whole of his Egyptian policy of commending the British occupation to the masses, were much more important and more immediate than what he must have felt to be the rather theoretical 'water' fears. These were, in any case, his own copyright, so to speak; and now the War Office was having the impertinence to exploit them for the furtherance of its own nefarious schemes.

In November, still sticking to his point, Cromer told Salisbury: 'Financially Egypt has come absolutely to the end of its tether which, so long as the present international regime lasts, is a very short one. If an advance takes place, the whole expense, both English and Egyptian, will almost certainly have to be borne by the British Treasury.' He pointed out that, by the terms of the London Convention, Egypt could only borrow up to £1 million and had already borrowed £800,000 to pay for the campaign so far.[67]

But, in the end, the ground was cut from under Cromer's feet. 'During the third week of December 1897 a tremendous event occurred. On leaving Cairo a month earlier Kitchener had visited Massawa in order to confer with the Governor of the Italian colony of Eritrea about the change-over at Kassala. On his return to Wadi Halfa on 18 December, Kitchener was informed by Wingate that the Khalifa was about to march immediately on Berber at the head of his entire host. Kitchener at once informed Cromer that the Egyptian Army would not be able to resist that onset unaided and that the position was serious; and Cromer alerted Lord Salisbury. On 23 December, accordingly, the British Cabinet decided to give Cromer and Kitchener a free hand in dealing with the emergency and to send them any reinforcement for which they might ask.'[68] Just before the end of the year Kitchener who, when it came to the point, proved unwilling to ask for British troops because he feared it might lead to his own supersession, gave way to Cromer's insistence, and British troops were officially asked for. Now that Cromer was satisfied that the position was not secure without them, he was anxious to get them as soon as possible, and in such strength as was necessary to reach Khartum and finish the job without delay.

Wingate's information was, in fact, incorrect. And Kitchener's behaviour, for the past several weeks, had been impulsive and inconsistent. As a result, Cromer's references to Kitchener, both in his letters to Salisbury and elsewhere, are a good deal less enthusiastic. He complained that 'it is sometimes difficult to extract the whole truth from him,' and that 'he generally has some personal interest behind the view which he puts forward in public matters.' He also complained that Kitchener had put him in a most difficult position by compelling him to act prematurely, and that he was 'very unpopular.'[69]

But, essentially, Cromer got what he wanted in that he avoided a War Office 'take-over' and in that he got the British Treasury to pay most of the cost of the new campaign. So he accepted the situation philosophically.

He wrote to Salisbury on Christmas Day, just after he had heard of the Cabinet decision to agree to British reinforcements, stating that he greatly feared an expedition to Khartum in 1898 was unavoidable. 'It is no longer a question of anticipating the French on the Upper Nile. The real question is . . . whether the Egyptian Army can hold the territory they have acquired. The difficulties that arose as soon as there were reports of a Dervish advance have brought home to me the precariousness of the situation. I do not at all like the idea of a British expedition, but it will not be prudent to allow the present situation to continue . . . If you decided to make Egypt a present of the £800,000, and if we sell the railway[70] we can then pay for the Khartum expedition, if it does not cost more than £$\frac{3}{4}$ million, and at the same time preserve our borrowing powers unimpaired. But control over the expedition should be exercised here and not by the War Office . . . In fact there would be no British expedition but an Egyptian expedition aided by England.'[71]

In the middle of January Cromer told Salisbury that he had no serious anxieties about the Sudan. 'At one time I feared that Kitchener might be attacked before he was ready, but that danger is over . . . The first of the English troops have reached Abu Hamed and three British battalions are on their way.'[72]

He was soon thinking of the political implications of the capture of Khartum. 'Once Khartum is reached our main military and financial difficulties are over. I presume that sooner or later we shall have to put up an Egyptian flag at Fashoda. And then we shall pass into the stage of diplomatic bickering . . . The thing to be avoided above all things is a collision with the Abyssinians. I hope we shall administer the conquered Provinces without making any call on the Chancellor of the Exchequer.'[73]

Cromer's principal reason for shrugging off the French on the Upper Nile was financial. He had no intention of getting Egypt involved in military operations or administrative expenditure south of Khartum. Any French presence on the Upper Nile could be dealt with by 'diplomatic bickering.' He clearly dismissed as moonshine any idea that such a French presence might represent a menace to the British position in Egypt.

Salisbury, in reply to Cromer's Christmas Day letter, indicated that the Cabinet might be forthcoming in the matter of finance for the Sudan campaign. He asked Cromer for an estimate of the financial aid the Egyptian Government would require for the capture of Khartum, explaining that it would probably be necessary to ask for a vote in the Commons. 'If we granted £$\frac{1}{2}$ million, we might subsequently remit so much of it, together with the existing loan, as might be necessary to restore to Egypt sufficient borrowing powers.'[74] In the event, in June 1898, the Commons agreed to treat the loan of £800,000 advanced to the Egyptian Government in November 1896 as a gift, and to advance another £750,000 to finance the rest of the campaign.

The reason for this change of attitude on the part of the British Government was not far to seek. By making this financial contribution, Salisbury was determined to establish the British claim to make a political settlement in the Sudan in accordance with the Nile Valley policy which had been the cornerstone of his diplomacy in Africa for the previous ten years, and to which he now saw the opportunity of applying the finishing touches. Cromer was not disposed to look a gift-horse in the mouth, and the effect of the British Government's comparative generosity was to transfer the initiative in deciding on the political future of the Sudan from Cromer to Salisbury. Cromer's idea, in so far as he had formulated one, seems to have been to restore Egyptian sovereignty along the Blue and White Niles approximately up to Roseires on the Blue Nile and possibly, after some 'diplomatic bickering,' to Fashoda on the White Nile, and to administer this area so economically as possible with such financial assistance as might be squeezed out of the British Government. If the British Government wanted to occupy the Upper Nile Valley south of Fashoda, they could do so from Uganda. But Salisbury had quite other ideas.

The long process of retreat from Constantinople which had been going on in Salisbury's mind from the time of the Berlin Congress in 1878 had ended in 1895, when the futility of the previous Government's attempts to put pressure on the Sultan to stop the Armenian massacres had become apparent. In October 1897 he wrote to Sir Philip Currie, the British Ambassador in Constantinople; 'Since two years back when the Cabinet refused me leave to take the fleet up the Dardanelles I have regarded the Eastern Question as having little serious interest for England. We have no other way of coercing the Turk . . . We really have no hold on and no interest in any of the Sultan's territories except Egypt. On the other hand, our interest in Egypt is growing stronger . . . The only policy left to us . . . (is) . . . to strengthen our position on the Nile and withdraw as much as possible from all responsibility at Constantinople.'[75]

The change in the centre of gravity of British Near Eastern interests from Constantinople to Cairo was, in Salisbury's mind, complete by the beginning of 1898. And his policy of 'strengthening our position on the Nile' involved not only Egypt but the whole of the Nile Valley.

One of the diplomatic difficulties about dealing with the Upper Nile arose from the fact that it had suited nobody to try to define exactly how far south Egyptian sovereignty could be said to extend. Salisbury, writing to Cromer in October 1897, had referred to 'whatever, in the valley between Lado and Khartum, is not Egyptian.' The British position was that they claimed for themselves anything in the valley that was not Egyptian. But this claim was only based on assertion and, in international law, any territory in the valley that was not under Egyptian sovereignty was *res nullius* and open to the first comer. On the other hand, admission of Egyptian sovereignty involved all the complications inherent in Ottoman suzerainty, including the necessity for consultations with the Powers.

On 3 June Salisbury wired to Cromer proposing that the whole of the Sudan 'from Halfa to Wadelai' should be treated, neither as *de jure* Egyptian territory temporarily dominated by rebels, nor as *res nullius*, but as an independent and sovereign 'Mahdi State.' 'We might treat Khartum as the capital of the Mahdi State, and our capture of Khartum would deliver by right of conquest the whole of the Mahdi State from Halfa to Wadelai into the power of the capturing army. That army consists of two allied contingents . . . At Khartum, when it was captured, the British and Egyptian flags would fly side by side as a symbol of the juridicial equality of the two conquerers, who would jointly claim possession of the Mahdi State from Halfa to Wadelai by right of conquest.'[76]

At first, Cromer was not very happy about the 'two flags' idea, although, on 11 June, he told Salisbury that 'the more I think it over the more I like it.' On 9 April the battle of the Atbara had been fought and won by the Anglo-Egyptian forces in the Sudan and Marchand was known to be approaching his destination at Fashoda. On 15 June Cromer sent Salisbury a long and detailed memorandum on the Sudan.[77] 'It seems quite clear that we are pledged to the occupation of Egypt for an indefinite period. It is also certain that, so long as the occupation lasts, the Khedive and the small but influential class which looks to the Khedive for guidance will maintain a position of irreconcilable hostility . . . It is almost a political necessity that the mass of the people should be in such a condition of material prosperity as to render them proof against appeals made to sentiments of race hatred and religious fanaticism. Therefore I am anxious to revert as soon as possible to a policy of fiscal reform.' As always, Cromer's attitude towards the Sudan was that it should not, if he could help it, become a financial burden upon Egypt. With regard to the future administration of the Sudan, he laid down two principles: (1) to avoid hostilities with Abyssinia; (2) to use the 'two flag' policy to emphasise that 'the Khedive is not free to act in the Sudan without the consent of his senior partner' and to give 'a salutary warning to the Sultan . . . and a clear indication to the French and Abyssinians that the control of the Nile is more a British than an Egyptian question.'

He suggested that, after Khartum had been captured, the Sirdar should administer the whole of the Sudan from Khartum for the time being under conditions of martial law. With regard to the two immediate problems after the defeat of the Dervishes—the Abyssinians and the French: 'I would propose that two flotillas should be despatched from Khartum, a relatively large one up the White Nile and a smaller one up the Blue Nile . . . The Sirdar should take command of the White Nile one . . . They should defend themselves if attacked but should not take the offensive.' He proposed that the Blue Nile flotilla should proceed as far as Roseires, hoist British and Egyptian flags there, and tell the Abyssinian commander that the frontier would be established later by negotiation between the British and Abyssinian Governments. With regard to the White Nile flotilla, Cromer proposed that, 'if the French flag is found flying,' the Sirdar should 'protest against the presence of a French force and formally lay claim to the territory and establish posts up and down stream of the French post.'

This memorandum was circulated to the Cabinet and discussed at a Cabinet meeting on 25 July at which Cromer, who had arrived in England earlier in the month, was present. As a result of the meeting instructions were sent to Kitchener about the two flotillas on the lines set out in Cromer's memorandum. At the same meeting the 'two flag' policy for the Sudan was formally agreed upon and officially communicated to Cairo. 'In view of the substantial military and financial cooperation which has been afforded by HMG to the Government of the Khedive, HMG have decided that at Khartum the British and Egyptian flags shall be hoisted side by side. You will explain to HH the Khedive and his Ministers . . . that HMG consider that they have a predominant voice in all matters connected with the Sudan and that . . . any advice which they may . . . tender to the Egyptian Government in respect to Sudan affairs will be followed.'[78]

On 2 September, the Anglo-Egyptian force defeated the Dervishes at Kerreri, just outside Omdurman, and occupied the Dervish capital, and the former capital of Khartum on the other side of the river. All organised Dervish resistance was at an end.

Marchand, now promoted to Commandant, had arrived at Fashoda with a small force of about 120 men on 10 July. He had been led to expect that there would be a French force from Abyssinia on the other bank to join hands with him. There was no such force there. Marchand sent his steamer *Faidherbe*, on which his party had made the trip across Africa, some 150 miles up the Sobat river, to find out what had happened. It was learnt that two small French parties which had set out from Abyssinia had failed to reach the Nile, and that an Abyssinian force,

accompanied by a French and a Russian officer, had reached the confluence of the White Nile and Sobat, a little upstream of Fashoda, on
22 June, some three weeks before Marchand's arrival at Fashoda. But,
after having planted the Abyssinian flag on the east, and the French
flag on the west bank of the White Nile, the party, short of supplies and
ravaged by fever, had departed by the way they had come. Marchand,
with an inadequate force, and with inadequate provisions, was left to
make the best he could of his isolated position at Fashoda. He made a
treaty with a local chieftain who recognised a French protectorate over
the area. He repulsed an attack from a Dervish steamer which had been
sent upriver from Omdurman to investigate his movements. He sent
messages to Paris via the West coast and via Abyssinia, reporting his
arrival, enclosing copies of his treaty, and asking for instructions.

Immediately after his victory at Kerreri, Kitchener obtained news of
Marchand's presence from the crew of the Dervish steamer which had
just returned to Omdurman after its encounter at Fashoda. He left
Omdurman for Fashoda in accordance with his instructions on 10
September in a flotilla of five gunboats, with Wingate, his Chief
Intelligence Officer, two battalions of Sudanese troops, a battery of
Egyptian artillery, a detachment of 100 Cameron Highlanders, and some
Maxim guns. Marchand's party had been reduced to seven French
officers and NCOs and 120 Senegalese troops. He had no artillery nor
automatic weapons and he was short of ammunition and food.

Kitchener met Marchand on 19 September. In order to avoid wounding
French susceptibilities his flotilla flew only the Egyptian flag and he
met Marchand in the uniform of an Egyptian General. He spoke French
fluently and the two soldiers took a liking to one another. He later told
Cromer that he had formed 'the highest admiration' for Marchand, and
expressed his astonishment that 'an attempt should have been made to
carry out a project of such magnitude and danger by the despatch of so
small and ill-equipped a force which . . . was neither in a position to
resist a second Dervish attack nor to retire.'[79] After Marchand had told
Kitchener that he could not quit Fashoda without orders from his
Government, Kitchener landed one Sudanese battalion and the Egyptian
artillery at Fashoda, hoisted the Egyptian flag, established a second post
south of Fashoda at the mouth of the Sobat, and told Marchand that
he would leave him and his party undisturbed until the matter had been
settled through diplomatic channels. He then sailed back to Omdurman,
after securing the cancellation of Marchand's treaty, and after warning
Marchand that 'all transport of munitions of war on the Nile is absolutely
prohibited.'

Cromer had little or nothing to do with the subsequent diplomatic crisis over Fashoda which, amid mounting popular hysteria on both sides of the Channel, seemed at one time likely to end in war between England and France. The two decisive factors in the situation were (a) that, in this matter, France received no support from her Russian ally nor from any other European Power, and (b) that the British naval forces in the Mediterranean and the Channel were greatly superior to those of the French. Salisbury stood absolutely firm, refused any concessions whatever, instructed HM's Ambassador in Paris to use the most intransigent language and, in the end, secured the unconditional withdrawal of Marchand from the Upper Nile Valley and the abandonment of all French territorial claims there.

In October, in the midst of the crisis, Cromer, back in Cairo, suffered an agonising personal bereavement. His wife, Ethel, to whom he had been married for twenty-two years, and who had borne him two sons, died after a long illness. Two years later he married, as his second wife, a daughter of the Marquis of Bath, by whom he had one son.

What Cromer would have liked to achieve out of the Fashoda crisis was the financial freedom, the release from the bonds of various international financial settlements, which he had been trying to arrange ever since he had been in Cairo. In the middle of November, while the crisis was still smouldering in London and Paris, he wrote to Salisbury about French obstruction in Egypt: 'Has not the time arrived when we might tell the French that the constant heckling we have had to endure from them in Egypt will no longer be tolerated? No one who has not been behind the scenes can realise fully the annoyances to which we have been exposed.' He went on to explain how the financial restrictions imposed by international agreements were maintained and used by the French 'for the purposes of obstruction and for nothing else.' 'I do not propose that we should establish a Protectorate . . . nor do I propose that we should annex the country; a course which would solve everything, but which is open to obvious objections. But surely we have a right, on the precedent of the French in Tunis, to insist that we are no longer hampered by all the obsolete restrictions by which we are at present bound, e.g. could we not demand that their hold on the economies resulting from debt conversion, which now amount to over £3 million, be released and that the Caisse be confined to its proper functions? . . . British public opinion is favourable. It seems also pretty certain that, if it came to the risk of war, although I disbelieve in the possibility, we are stronger than they. Would it not be advisable to take advantage of such an exceptionally favourable combination of affairs?'[80] This letter was circulated to the Cabinet but, perhaps because other Powers beside France were involved, nothing was done to meet Cromer's wishes.

The proposal, adumbrated in the 'two flag' policy, of a Sudan effectively controlled by himself and relieved from all the 'top hamper' of
internationalism which bedevilled the Egyptian Administration, must
have seemed to Cromer a very poor second-best compared with what he
really wanted. And he was still nervous lest the Sudan, with its new
status, might become a permanent drain on the Egyptian Treasury. He
had no desire to see money which he hoped to devote to the remission
of taxes in Egypt disappearing somewhere in the 'useless territories' of the
Upper Nile. For this reason he was determined to keep as tight a hold
as he could on Sudanese finances, and to try and ensure that the Sudan
was administered economically.

It had been decided that the 'two flag' policy was to be set out in the
form of a Convention between the British and Egyptian Governments.
On 10 November, Cromer sent Salisbury a draft Convention which
formed the basis of the Anglo-Egyptian Condominium Agreement
signed on 19 January 1899. Such alterations as were made to Cromer's
draft were the result of discussions between Salisbury and Kitchener, who
was to be the first Governor-General of the Sudan, and who objected
to the extent to which Cromer was putting him into leading-strings.
Salisbury wrote to Cromer suggesting that Kitchener was right in not
wanting too much centralisation and warned him against 'that mania for
paper piling which is the endemic pest of the British Departments,'
leading to 'endless temptations to pedantry and circumlocution.'[81] Cromer
was not a great admirer of the methods of the 'British Departments'; what
he wanted in the Sudan was sufficient financial control to ensure that
Kitchener, or some future Governor-General, would not be able to pile
up overdrafts in their current account with Egypt.

In its final form the Agreement, known as the Sudan Convention of
1899, and signed by Cromer for the British Government and Butros
Ghali, the Egyptian Foreign Minister, for the Egyptian Government,[82]
formed the 'constitution' by which the Sudan was governed for the next
fifty years. It provided, *inter alia*; 'that the supreme military and civil
command in the Sudan shall be vested in one officer, termed the Governor-
General of the Sudan. He shall be appointed by Khedivial Decree on
the recommendation of HBMG and shall be removed only by Khedivial
Decree with the consent of HBMG'; (Article 3); that 'laws may from time
to time be made, altered or abrogated by proclamation of the Governor-
General . . . all such Proclamations shall be notified to HBMG's Agent and
Consul-General in Cairo and to the President of the Egyptian Council
of Ministers and to HH the Khedive (Article 4); that 'no Egyptian law
or other enactment shall apply to the Sudan save insofar as the same
shall be applied by Proclamation of the Governor-General' (Article 5)

that 'no special privileges shall be accorded to the subjects of any one or more Powers'; (Article 6); that 'import duties shall not be leviable on goods coming from Egyptian territory . . . but (in the case of other territories) they shall not exceed the corresponding duties . . . leviable on goods entering Egypt from abroad' (Article 7); that 'the jurisdiction of the Mixed Tribunals shall not extend . . . to any part of the Sudan, except in the town of Suakin' (Article 8);[83] that 'no Consuls, Vice-Consuls or Consular Agents shall be allowed to reside in the Sudan without the previous consent of HBMG.'

The boundaries of the Sudan were defined in the first Article of the Convention as 'all the territories south of latitude 22 N which had either been retained by or lost to the Egyptian Government since 1882' plus any 'which may hereafter be conquered by the two Governments acting in unison.' This left the British Government with a fairly wide discretion. In the event: (a) a Convention was signed with France in March 1899 by which the frontier between the Sudan and the French possessions in West Africa was drawn along the watershed between the Nile and Congo basins; (b) an Agreement was signed with Abyssinia in 1902 which provided, *inter alia*, that Abyssinia should not 'construct or allow to be constructed any works on the Blue Nile, the Sobat or Lake Tana which could obstruct the flow of their waters to the Nile except by agreement with HBMG and the Government of the Sudan';[84] (c) an Agreement with Italy in December 1899 delimited the frontier between the Sudan and Eritrea; (d) an Agreement with the Congolese Free State in 1906 provided for the lease to the Free State of a narrow strip of land on the west bank of the Nile between Lake Albert and Lado, known as the Lado Enclave, which was to revert to the Sudan on the death of King Leopold; (e) an Agreement with Uganda in 1913 delimited the frontier between the Sudan and Uganda approximately along the line of latitude 4 N.

Thus ended the campaign for the reconquest of the Sudan. It had been undertaken on British initiative, but mainly with Egyptian money and lives. The total cost of the Sudan campaign was £E2,354,000. Of this, £E768,000 was paid by the British and the rest by the Egyptian Government. Total British casualties were something under 1,000, fewer than those incurred in the unsuccessful Gordon relief expedition twelve years before. The attempted British military contribution from Uganda had been nugatory. Apart from the expenses of the campaign, Egypt had to make good annual Sudanese deficits, amounting to an average of about £¼ million a year, during the first fourteen years of the Condominium. The Egyptian Treasury also had to finance the Sudan Government's capital expenditure. The benefits accruing to Egypt from the reconquest were theoretical from the point of view of security, minimal from that of trade. The 1899 Convention was unpopular in Egypt and made a considerable contribution to the nationalist discontents which were beginning to make things difficult for the British authorities.

Cromer dictated neither the timing nor the terms of the reconquest and had little influence on either. Both were decided more in terms of British than of Egyptian interests. By 1898 the question of keeping the French out of the Upper Nile was more a question of British prestige than of Egyptian security. Cromer would rather have had the Caisse cut down to size in Cairo than the French excluded from the Bahr el-Ghazal.

But the reconquest did have two important and, from Cromer's point of view, favourable results. First, it was made clear to everyone concerned that there was no question of the British evacuating Egypt within the foreseeable future. In February 1899 Salisbury told Cromer that, in an interview with the Turkish Ambassador, 'I refused to reiterate the promises of evacuation at some unknown date which, on previous occasions, we had freely given.'[85] Secondly, the French humiliation over Fashoda did much to discredit the old anglophobe French colonial school of thought, represented by the Comité de l'Afrique Française, which could never forget how the British had 'usurped' French 'rights' in Egypt, and to encourage a newer form of 'business' colonialism, represented by l'Union Coloniale, which was more interested in the future than in the past, and less concerned with old grievances than with new opportunities in Morocco and elsewhere.

10

THE POWER
AND THE GLORY

THE TWO KHEDIVIAL crises, in 1893 and 1894, revolutionised Cromer's conception of his rôle in Egypt, which had undergone a process of evolution since his arrival in Egypt in 1883. At first, and for a very brief period, he had regarded his assignment as a short-term one, leading to a rapid evacuation after the establishment of a few 'instant' reforms. He had soon discarded this conception and, after the Sudan had been evacuated and the London Convention signed, had devoted himself to a rehabilitation of Egyptian finances, leaving most of the internal administration of the country to Nubar and the Egyptian Government, in the expectation of an evacuation of the country within a few years. By the end of 1887 he had become convinced of the undesirability, if not of the impracticability, of evacuation by reason of the incapacity of Egypt's ruling classes, and began gradually working towards the creation of a puppet régime, headed by a *fainéant* Khedive, behind which the British would exercise an increasingly comprehensive control, but in which the overt executive authority, and the outward trappings of power, would be wholly Egyptian. Such a regime was, to all intents and purposes, in existence when Abbas came to the throne at the beginning of 1892 and, almost immediately, showed his unwillingness to play the rôle which Cromer had written for him. His recalcitrance completely upset Cromer's calculations. Because of his overt objection to being a puppet, it proved impossible to go on with the puppet show as originally devised. Henceforward, there were two openly competing powers in Egypt—the Khedivial Court and the British Agency. The Pashas, the nationalists and the malcontents generally—all those whom Cromer was wont to refer to as 'the talking classes'—tended to gravitate to the Court, and the British Agency was forced into the position of competing with the Palace and the 'talking classes' for the favour of the rest of the country—the fellahin (by which Cromer meant not the landless labourers but the medium and small landowners), the merchants, the foreign communities and the

masses. This necessitated, both a denial of political advancement in order
to contain the opposition of the one side, and a concentration on economic
improvement and administrative reform in order to secure the favour of
the other. The denial of political advancement involved opposition to,
and from, the 'talking classes,' and the concentration on economic improvement and administrative reform led to increasing British control of
the administration. Thus political opposition increased the urgency of
economic improvement and administrative reform, whilst these in turn
increased the intensity and bitterness of opposition. This situation explains
the dichotomy between political repression and administrative achievement characteristic of Cromer's last fifteen years in Egypt.

Some writers have tried to explain this dichotomy in terms of Cromer's
personal character and predilections. This is valid in so far as his personality prevented any serious attempt at coming to terms with the
Khedive, and arriving at a *modus vivendi* of the kind achieved with Nubar
in 1884. But Cromer, who had already convinced himself of the
incapacity of Egypt's ruling classes, was not prepared to go into reverse
to this extent, or indeed at all. Given his assumption that a puppet
Khedive was a political and administrative necessity, and given Abbas'
character and ambitions, there was really no alternative to the situation
which developed. It is characteristic of Cromer that, once he had satisfied
himself of its inevitability, he entered into it clear-sightedly and whole-
heartedly, with a keen eye for essentials, and with an acute appreciation,
at all events in the short term, of its possibilities and limitations. There
was no point in appeasing either the Khedive or the nationalists, since
almost any act of appeasement would have retarded the economic improvement and administrative reform through which he pursued the
political aim of creating a broad base of acceptance of the British
occupation. He appealed directly and openly to the pockets and bellies
of the non-political classes and masses for support against the opposition
of the 'talking classes.' There was no point in his remaining in his 'hiding
place,' as he had done in Taufiq's time. It was the essence of his policy
that the British should get the credit for what was being achieved in the
economic and administrative fields, and that it should be made apparent
that these achievements were being jeopardised by the personal ambitions
of the Khedive and the political ambitions of the nationalists.

The pursuit of this policy necessarily involved a greater reliance than
before on the presence of the British garrison in Egypt. Although its
strength was not permanently increased during the last fifteen years of
Cromer's term of office, it was, on several occasions, temporarily reinforced
as an ostentatious reminder of its real purpose in Egypt. (It had never been
reinforced for internal reasons between 1882 and 1893.) Units of the

British garrison were also sent through the Provinces on several occasions to 'show the flag' and demonstrate the coercive force at the disposal of the British Agent.

This policy also implied a subservient Council of Ministers, a progressive increase in British control over the various Departments of State and, consequently, in the number of British officials. In March 1893, soon after the first crisis with Abbas, Cromer insisted on a change in the procedure regarding attendance of British Advisers at Cabinet meetings. Previously, only the Financial Adviser had the right to attend all Cabinet meetings; other Advisers attended by invitation when the affairs of their own Ministry were being discussed. Under the new procedure, Cromer successfully insisted that Ministers must show their British Advisers any proposal which they intended to discuss in Cabinet and that these Advisers must have the right, if they wished, to attend Cabinet meetings at which these, or any other proposals concerning their Ministries, were being discussed. Cromer told Rosebery: 'I should be obliged to condemn . . . as null and void' any decision taken without the concurrence of the British Adviser concerned.[1] This, in effect, meant that Egyptian Ministers became entirely subordinated to their British Advisers and, through them, to Cromer himself.

After Nubar's resignation, because of ill-health and old age, in November 1895, Mustafa Fahmy became Prime Minister and remained as Cromer's obedient servant until Cromer's own retirement in 1907. During Nubar's term of office, a British Adviser (Eldon Gorst) was appointed to the Ministry of the Interior and the affairs of this Ministry, which Cromer once described as 'the centre of Egyptian misgovernment . . . the very citadel of corruption, the headquarters of nepotism, the cynosure of all that numerous class who hoped to gain an easy, if illicit, living by robbing either the Treasury or the taxpayers,'[2] were subjected to more or less effective British control, exercised through the British Adviser and a number of British Inspectors in the Provinces who reported to him.

Although Cromer's policy continued to be one of 'using native agency to the utmost possible extent' in the administration of the country, and although most of the British-inspired reforms were carried out by means of 'advice' which was recognised to be, and generally accepted as, mandatory, the number of European (mostly British) officials showed a constant tendency to increase, as indeed did the total number of officials in Government service. The mania for 'paper piling' which Salisbury once stigmatised as 'the endemic pest' of British Government Departments was, partly as a result of the British occupation, caught in a virulent form by Egyptian Government Departments. In 1906 there were 1,252

European and 12,027 Egyptian officials in Egyptian Government service as compared with 690 Europeans and 8,449 Egyptians in 1896.[3]

The main obstacle in the way of economic improvement and administrative reform was financial, at all events until the Anglo-French Agreement of 1904. In the early years of Cromer's term of office his efforts and those of the Financial Adviser had been directed to the achievement of solvency and the consequent avoidance of increased international supervision. By 1889 solvency had been achieved and deficits converted into surpluses. Thereafter the problem was one of using increased revenues to reduce taxation and to finance reforms, as part of Cromer's policy of offsetting political frustration by economic and social satisfaction. This policy was hindered, both by the financial restrictions imposed by the 1885 London Convention, and by the threat of open-ended commitments to expenditure in the bottomless pit of the Sudan. These restrictions and this threat advanced and receded, but were never entirely exorcised, and explain Cromer's repeated and eventually successful insistence (a) on financial 'freedom' for Egypt, and (b) on personal control, first of the military expenditure for the reconquest of the Sudan, and then of the civil expenditure for its administration.

At the beginning of the occupation, all the Englishmen concerned with the problem of Egypt's finances—Dufferin, Cromer, Vincent—had been convinced that the only way in which Egypt's indebtedness could be met without placing an intolerable burden on the British taxpayer, and the only way in which the twin objectives of financial stability and lighter taxation could be achieved, was by the development of the country's agricultural resources through improvements to the irrigation system. One of Dufferin's first acts was to bring Colonel Scott Moncrieff from India to act as Irrigation Adviser to the Egyptian Government. Cromer successfully insisted on a sum of £1 million for irrigation works being included in the internationally guaranteed loan in 1885. The improvements carried out by Scott Moncrieff, including the activation of the Delta Barrage, were a major factor in converting Egypt's annual Budget deficits into surpluses. After the repairs to the Barrage had been completed in 1890, optimum use was being made of all the available Summer water. But most of the flood water was still going down to the sea because there was no means of storing it. If some of the flood water could be stored in a reservoir behind a dam it would be possible to use it during the Summer to increase the amount of water available during the season of low Nile. From 1892 onwards the attention of the British irrigation engineers was concentrated on this possibility, and one of them, Mr (later Sir William) Willcocks, was employed on a detailed study of possible sites for a dam and reservoir. Since it was probable that an application to the Caisse for an advance from the Reserves to finance the construction would be necessary, an International Commission, with members from all the countries represented on the Caisse, was also appointed to study the project. This resulted in the usual diplomatic obstructions but, from the technical point of view, the consensus of opinion was in favour of a plan drawn up by Willcocks for a dam and reservoir at Aswan, in Upper Egypt, about 600 miles upstream of Cairo, where a granite rock formation formed the bed of the river and so was able to provide both a foundation for the dam and some of the material required for building it. By the end of 1895 Cromer had satisfied himself that it would be possible to go ahead with the project, provided that the reconquest of the Sudan was postponed until after its completion.[4]

One of the reasons for Cromer's anger at the British Government's committing Egypt to a Sudan campaign in March 1896 was his realisation that this would necessitate the postponement of the construction of the reservoir. But Cromer continued his efforts, trying to get the Treasury to assist by guaranteeing a loan on the London money market. In reply to Treasury objections that the Egyptian Government should not incur expenditure on the reservoir simultaneously with expenditure on the Sudan campaign, he told Salisbury: 'The longer we delay, the longer we postpone the time when some benefit will be derived from it . . . I am continually hearing complaints of want of water. We have been able to find a financial combination which postpones any demand on the Egyptian Treasury for five years, and by that time we shall have seen the end of the Sudan business and we shall have begun to drive some benefit from the reservoir.'[5] Salisbury was unsympathetic and replied that the Cabinet upheld the Treasury's adverse decision.[6] But Cromer persisted. In December 1897 he put up a plan to London by which Messrs Aird & Co., the contractors, agreed to construct the dam and reservoir in five years and to accept payment by instalments from the Egyptian Government over a period of thirty years from date of completion. Cromer told Salisbury: 'I am convinced not only that the financial operation is sound, but that the risk here is delay rather than immediate action. If we are to bear the Sudan burden we must increase the revenue, and the only way to do so is to improve the water supply. It is of great importance . . . I hope you will be able to give an answer before 3 January.'[7]

Cromer, who was an excellent bargainer, was now using the reconquest of the Sudan, which the British Government had forced on him, as a reason for getting the Cabinet's approval for the construction of the reservoir on the ground that the additional responsibility for the Sudan necessitated a permanent increase in the Egyptian revenue which could only be achieved by the construction of the reservoir. This time, the Treasury and the Cabinet gave way and, on 20 February 1898, a contract was signed between the Egyptian Government and Messrs Aird by which the contractors undertook to complete the dam and reservoir by 1 July 1903 and by which the Egyptian Government agreed to pay the cost of approximately £2 million by instalments spread over thirty years from date of completion.[8]

The dam and reservoir were completed on time. The total cost, including that of the satellite barrage at Asyut, some 250 miles upstream of Cairo, which helped to control the release of the stored water, was £E3,439,864, of which £E1,346,699 was provided by the Caisse out of the General Reserve, £E143,165 by the Egyptian Treasury out of their Special Reserve, and the balance of £E1,950,000 financed by the contractors against an undertaking of repayment by the Egyptian Government in sixty six-monthly instalments of £E76,648 starting from the time of the completion of the work.[9]

As a result of the construction of the dam and reservoir, a quarter of a million acres of land in Upper Egypt had been converted from basin to perennial irrigation by the end of 1905, thus enabling two or three crops a year to be grown instead of one.[10] The gain to the revenue in increased land-tax as a result of the dam and reservoir was estimated at £E380,000 p.a., which was much more than sufficient to cover the repayments to the contractors, and the addition to the country's gross income was estimated at £E2,600,000 p.a.[11]

The Aswan dam and reservoir, at their original height and storage capacity (the dam was heightened in 1912 and again in 1934, increasing the capacity of the reservoir correspondingly), was the first stage in the process by which the whole of the Nile flood water came to be stored for irrigation purposes instead of being allowed to flow into the sea.

Long before the completion of the Aswan dam Cromer was universally recognised, both in Egypt and abroad, as the real ruler of the country. After 1898 there was no more question of evacuation. The British Government, provided they were not asked to contribute financially, interfered less and less with his proceedings, but remained deaf to his demands that they should make some contribution both to the costs of administering the Sudan and to the costs of the occupation forces in Egypt. In spite of the growing volume of opposition, the strength of these seldom exceeded 4,000 men. The threat of force was in the background, but was never overtly used. There was, as yet, nothing like a mass movement of discontent. The Khedive had none of the qualities of a popular leader. He was mistrusted and disliked by the new generation of educated nationalists, and neither he nor they made much appeal to the masses.

Opposition, whether inspired by the Khedive or the nationalists, consisted mainly of abusive anti-British articles in the Press, or criticisms in the Legislative Council, or attempted intrigues with foreign Consulates-General and an assiduous courting of the Sultan, whom both the Khedive and the nationalists disliked and mistrusted almost as much as they did each other. None of this was very formidable for the time being. Cromer ignored the Press and the Legislative Council and kept the Khedive in order by an occasional admonitory raising of the forefinger. He never, or hardly ever, had to uncork the 'bottled thunder' which, in the form of an official declaration of support from the British Government, he usually had in reserve.

During the long and turbulent history of Egypt, rival potentates have frequently fought one another for the privilege of ruling the country. Sometimes two or more potentates have simultaneously claimed to be the real ruler. In the light of this experience, the Egyptians have developed a sure instinct for recognising where the real seat of power lies. Time and again this recognition has had the effect of confirming and consolidating the power of the victor in a struggle which has already been fought and won. The struggle between Cromer and the Khedive in 1893 and 1894 was a repetition of a process which had taken place many times before in Egypt's history, and Cromer's victory was thus followed by popular recognition. This did not imply popular approval or esteem. It was simply the recognition and, in consequence, the confirmation of a *fait accompli*. Henceforward the destination of petitions and complaints—in Egypt always a sure sign of the location of the real seat of power—tended increasingly to be the British Agency rather than the Khedivial Palace. It was the man in the street's recognition of Cromer as the man who could get things done, the man who could give orders that were obeyed, the man who could cut red tape and circumvent the 'usual channels,' the man whose word was law.

The Egyptians are a docile people, with an instinctive respect for government, and particularly for personal government, and the man whose authority has been confirmed in this way by popular opinion soon accumulates an immense fund of prestige. Such prestige is ephemeral and perishes with its owner. A system cannot be built upon it. It carries with it the virtual certainty of ultimate reaction. But, while it lasts, it can be immensely potent.

During the thirteen years from 1894 to 1907, Cromer became an increasingly powerful and prestigious figure among the Egyptians. When he drove abroad in the streets of Cairo, his carriage was preceded by uniformed escorts clearing a way for him. His periodical formal visits to the Khedive, usually with a message of admonition or rebuke, were reminiscent of those once paid by some all-powerful Mamluk Shaikh el-Balad to a *fainéant* Turkish Governor, bearing an ultimatum or sentence of dismissal. His intervention and arbitration were sought both by Egyptians and by foreigners in all sorts of matters quite outside the administration of the country, quite apart from cases of alleged govern-mental injustice and oppression. He intervened to prevent the Khedive from dismissing Mohamed Abdu from his post of Mufti,[12] and supported Mohamed Abdu in a dispute with the Khedive about Moslem religious trusts.[13] He appeased the wrath of the wives of some foreign Consuls-General who were outraged at the Khedive having been accompanied by his Hungarian mistress at a Court ball.[14] He patched up a com-plicated quarrel in the Khedivial family over the imprudent marriage of one of its members.[15] He successfully objected to some of the Khedive's more disreputable financial transactions and, according to Blunt, told him that he must choose between being the Khedive or a tradesman.[16] In dealing with all these multifarious and relatively trivial matters, Cromer won general respect, even from his opponents, for propriety and good sense, and for his refusal to be used as a means of forwarding particular financial or other interests, whether Egyptian or European.

Cromer's reputation in England increased *pari passu* with his prestige in Egypt. Mention has already been made of the growing interest being manifested in England in the British administration of Egypt. English Winter visitors to Egypt returned with glowing accounts of the efficiency and benevolence of British rule and of the enlightened dictatorship exer-cised by Lord Cromer. Cromer was very careful to cultivate the Press, both in England and in Egypt. David Rees, Reuter's agent in Egypt, was very much Cromer's man, possibly because Cromer had helped him over financial difficulties.[17] Several Egyptian newspapers, including *el-Muqattam* and the English language *Egyptian Gazette*, were subsidized by the British Agency.[18] Journalists, including Liberals who might have been expected to be critical, were, almost without exception, favourably impressed. Blunt complained that Cromer had told Harold Spender, of the *Daily News*, that 'he wants the whole army of occupation withdrawn, that he can depend for order on his native police, that he would like a native administration, but cannot find Egyptians fit for responsibility,' and that Spender had 'swallowed it all' and admitted that England was in Egypt to stay.[19] Since 1892 Cromer's Annual Reports, consisting mainly of eulogistic accounts of his administration, had been published both in England and Egypt, and were widely read and admired in Britain. Blunt described them as being in the style of the First Chapter of Genesis.

The effect on Cromer's character of all this power and adulation was not altogether favourable. Rennell Rodd, who was First Secretary at the British Agency from 1894 to 1901, gives the following picture of him during this period: 'Circumstances developed the autocratic character to which (he) was temperamentally disposed. The success which attended his efforts to produce order from chaos, and the eventual elimination of all interference from home, increased his sense of absolute self-dependence, and made an authority which became too exclusively personal and tended to diminish the sense of responsibility in those who worked under him. It was curious, when he adopted a suggestion made to him which proved successful in its effects, in how short a time he convinced himself that the measure was due to his own initiative. He had always been handi-capped by the absence of any definite policy . . . and the obligation to carry on with no avowed goal in view. The objects to be attained during the earlier years of a terminable occupation were purely material. It could not well be otherwise. But it is the exclusively material character of our achievement throughout, to the exclusion of moral development, which might offer ground for criticism. Cromer's positive mind, though it had a humanistic side, was disposed to pass by the things of the soul. Under his regime, with a constantly renewed pressure of obstacles difficult to surmount, administrative conditions, which were only designed to be provisional, gradually hardened into permanence with no considered scheme of expansion to meet the changes they were destined to effect . . . History and the great Greek and Latin authors were Cromer's constant resource . . . Philosophy did not seem to have the same attraction for him. Nor could he be induced to read modern poetry. He had stopped short at Dryden . . . It was evident that the suggestive and imaginative made no appeal to him . . . Nor could I discern any real interest in art or architecture. To admire a primitive was to him so incomprehensible as almost to seem an affectation. Though he was never intolerant towards the tastes and inclinations of others, his own mind seemed only receptive of the positive and concrete.'[20]

Before he left Egypt in 1901 Rodd recorded: 'I could not help feeling that elements of permanence and continuity were wanting and that there was a growing danger in the indeterminate character of a regime which we were neither disposed to regularise nor to terminate in a measurable time.' He went on to describe relations between Cromer and the Khedive as 'those of pupil and schoolmaster' and realised and regretted that the antagonism between the two was 'irremediable.'[21]

Cromer himself suffered from no such doubts. With advancing years he had become less brusque but more obstinate, less inclined to argue a case and more determined to reiterate a prejudice. Even in his earlier years in Egypt, Vincent, who had been Financial Adviser until 1889, described

him as 'not subtle or mentally agile, but endowed with that curious combination of character which lends authority even to doubtful decisions,
and makes those who possess it respected in counsel and obeyed as
rulers.'[22] With advancing years, his mental agility decreased *pari passu*
with increased authority and the increased respect deriving from it.

With senior British officials established in all the Ministries, and with
Financial Advisers in whom he reposed great confidence (first Sir Elwin
Palmer and later Sir Eldon Gorst, who succeeded him in 1898) dealing
with the Khedive and Prime Minister in all routine matters, he gradually
became less in touch with what was happening and with what people
were thinking and saying. In his earlier years he had done almost everything himself, while remaining behind the scenes. Later, when in the
centre of the stage, he tended more and more to rely on those British
Advisers in whom he had particular confidence. Palmer, the Financial
Adviser, was very much his right-hand man at the time of the first
Khedivial crisis in January 1893 and continued as such until his retirement in 1898. Gorst, who was appointed Adviser to the Interior in
1894, also enjoyed his confidence. In December 1894, a few weeks after
his appointment, Cromer told Kimberley: 'I no longer hear anything
about the affairs of the Interior.'[23]

But Cromer was by no means indiscriminate in the confidence which
he extended towards senior British officials in the Egyptian Government.
He seems to have disliked Moncrieff, the pioneer of the Egyptian
irrigation reforms. He had a low opinion of most of the English judges
and police officers and expressed himself uninhibitedly about some of
them in his private correspondence. During his last year in Egypt he told
Grey that Sir William Garstin, Moncrieff's successor as Under Secretary
at the Ministry of Public Works, was the only British official 'who is not
departmentalised in the narrowest sense.'[24] But it seems likely that
Cromer's view of the competence or otherwise of British officials was
influenced by the extent to which they fell in with his ideas about the
government of Egypt. Officials like Money, the British Commissioner of
the Caisse, and Willcocks, who subscribed £10 to an Egyptian
nationalist newspaper, were visited with his displeasure, the one being
dubbed as a fool and the other being threatened with dismissal.

The attitude of the British officials towards Cromer was one of great
respect, verging on fear. Even the redoubtable Kitchener went in awe of
him.[25] Dawkins, Milner's successor as Under Secretary at the Ministry
of Finance, told Milner that 'one is not able to talk directly to Cromer.'[26]
Willcocks, the irrigation engineer, who was responsible for the planning
of the Aswan dam and reservoir, and who did not get on with Cromer,
complained that 'all the officials who enjoyed working under him seemed

to lose their backbones.'[27] Many of the British officials were quite ready to criticise Cromer behind his back. Milner invariably wrote highly of him, even in private. But Dawkins commented that 'a man loses some' thing of his best when he begins to consider himself indispensable, and he is certainly not inclined to take trouble and use his own eyes as he used to do.'[28] He considered that he had 'an odd vein of laziness which is combined with his great energy,' which caused him 'to work through some one agent and to hear everything through him alone.'[29]

Through necessity, Cromer controlled Egypt much more through the senior British officials in the Egyptian Government than through his own staff at the British Agency, among whom were numbered several— Portal, Hardinge, Rumbold, Rodd, Nicolson—who subsequently had very distinguished careers. Two of these—Nicolson and Portal—were named by Cromer to Rosebery as being among the only three—the third being Milner—who, in 1893, seemed to him to be possible successors to himself.[30]

The man on whom Cromer came to rely more and more for information on the state of local opinion was Harry Boyle, his Oriental Secretary. Boyle, of the Levant Consular Service, had come to the British Agency as a young man in 1885 after a short period of pupilage in the British Embassy in Constantinople. He was an excellent linguist and soon attained a mastery of the Arabic language, as well as of Turkish. In 1888 Cromer created for him the post of 'Oriental Secretary' in the British Agency, which meant that he was the Agency's principal contact with unofficial local opinion. He appears to have fallen greatly under the influence of the prosperous and influential Lebanese community in Egypt, and particularly under that of Faris Nimr, the owner and editor of the newspaper el-Muqattam. This Lebanese colony consisted of Christians from the Lebanon who had come to Egypt over the previous twenty or thirty years to share in the economic opportunities and to benefit from the relatively liberal political conditions which Egypt had to offer as compared with Ottoman rule in Syria. Many of them, by reason of their superior education and quick wits, had obtained responsible positions, in journalism, in Government administration, and in business. They were unpopular with Egyptians, and particularly with Egyptian nationalists, who regarded them in much the same light as Arabi and his associates had regarded the Circassians. Unlike the Circassians, they spoke Arabic as their mother-tongue; but, also unlike the Circassians, they were Christians. They were well-regarded by the British, who found their qualities useful, and they, in return, tended to regard the British as their protectors.

It was from these people that Boyle seems to have derived most of his information and opinions about local affairs. In addition, his political views appear to have been those of a crusted Tory. Both his local sources and his political prejudices influenced the information and advice which he gave to Cromer. The nature of that information and advice can be judged by a letter which he wrote to Rodd in April 1907, just before Cromer's final departure from Egypt. 'The political situation here is simply damnable. The nationalists are very active and intensely virulent, with the Khedive practically openly with them, with a strong party in the House of Commons ready to back them up in any madness they project. Their insolence and vehemence exceed all bounds of reason and decency . . . They even insult openly in the streets all whom they think well-disposed to us, and they have succeeded in establishing such a reign of terror as few Egyptians have the courage to resist . . . Our power is moribund and only the adoption of a very vigorous remedy . . . can set things to rights. So much for the fruits of the policy of dealing with the Egyptians otherwise than by the time-honoured and effective instrument of our predecessors in rule . . . This is no country for a gentleman in these times.'[31]

Boyle's views on Egyptians in general can further be gathered from a memorandum which he wrote for Cromer in 1905, which was intended for circulation to newly-joined British officials in the Egyptian Govern-ment. (Cromer wisely did not have it circulated for fear lest it should be 'leaked' to the Egyptian Press.) In this memorandum it was stated that the original policy of employing only a few Englishmen in the Administration had proved 'incompatible with the true interest of the country,' since 'experience showed that the native officials, considered as a class, however gladly he might welcome or intelligently receive the advice and instructions of his English superior, had not reached either the stage of intellectual development which would enable him to carry out those instructions with efficiency, or of moral courage enough to face the terrors of un-supported responsibility . . . Hence it is that the backbone of the Egyptian administrative body has been strengthened in recent years by a com-paratively large number of young Englishmen, carefully selected for their character and attainments . . . It is hardly to be hoped that a nation which has remained for many centuries under foreign domination will be able to develop to any considerable extent the virile qualities of courage and independence or the higher moral attributes which are the heritage of more favoured peoples . . . It would obviously be unfair to expect from the Egyptian qualities which he has never had a chance of developing or to feel disappointment if he fails to come up to our standard of moral courage, justice and truth . . . These defects are not to be set right in one generation . . . (but) . . . it does not seem to me too much to hope that the force of healthy example, constant watchfulness, and strict but kindly discipline on the part of the British officials ought in time to develop a higher standard of honour and truth in the Egyptian character.'[32] There was much more of the same nature. It is not easy to judge whether Cromer derived these views from Boyle or Boyle from Cromer. They are more or less indistinguishable from the views which Cromer was wont to express himself. According to Wingate's son and biographer Cromer trusted Boyle but was not over-influenced by him.[33]

Although he was a harsh judge of his subordinates, Cromer seems to have had a high opinion of Boyle. He was impressed by his knowledge of Arabic (of which Cromer only learnt to speak a few words) and liked him personally. He was particularly intimate with him during the two years between his first wife's death and his second marriage. They frequently walked together by the banks of the Nile and dined alone together at the British Agency, quoting the classics to each other. Cromer was not a man with intimate friends, and Boyle seems to have been a queer choice for someone of his outlook and temperament. It seems probable that it was more of a relationship between master and trusted servant than a friendship between equals. Boyle, in his letters[34] showed himself very proud of what he regarded as his position as Cromer's *eminence grise*, and of the local reputation which he enjoyed as such; but there is a whiff of the servants' hall in his attitude.

By temperament and as a result of his Indian training, Cromer was antipathetic to the political aspirations of subject races. Boyle's information and views tended to confirm rather than to correct his prejudices in this direction, which became more and more deeply rooted, and more and more divorced from reality, as time went on.

But, so long as he remained in Egypt, and so long as he had the unquestioning support of the British Government, there was no serious trouble. The slightest movement of his forefinger raised in admonition was enough to keep the Khedive and the country in order. He made no concessions whatever to the Khedive's desire to choose his own Ministers, to the Legislative Council's demands for an extension of their powers, to nationalist demands for the replacement of British by Egyptian officials. He had convinced himself that the Egyptians were unfit for self-government and he was determined to offset the discontent of the politically-minded minority by providing good government, remission of taxes, and even-handed justice for the apolitically-minded majority. This, in his view, inhibited any move either towards representative government or towards the replacement of senior British by Egyptian officials. On the contrary, it necessitated a continued movement in the opposite direction. He was prepared to welcome the cooperation of any politically-minded Egyptians who, in the general interest, were prepared, for the indefinite future, to sacrifice their own political aspirations to the economic and social betterment of their fellow-citizens. But he was not prepared to make any political concessions to them. The furthest he would go was to arrange for the up-grading of the Department of Education to a Ministry and to have appointed as Minister Saad Zaghlul, a moderate nationalist politician, who was a son-in-law of Mustafa Fahmy. And it seems likely that his relationship with Mustafa Fahmy, rather than his nationalism, was the principal reason for his appointment. In the event, Cromer's expectations of Saad Zaghlul's willingness to cooperate with the British proved to be somewhat exaggerated. But that is another story.

In the Sudan, where the defeat of the Dervishes and the collapse of the Mahdist State had created a *tabula rasa*, where the Condominium Agreement had swept away all the international restrictions with which Egypt was encumbered, and where there were hardly any foreign residents and an unsophisticated native population with no contact with European ideas, Cromer's recipe of a benevolent administrative autocracy combined with a *laissez-faire* economy, with low taxation and minimal government expenditure, excited little opposition and was probably the regime best fitted for what was still an extremely primitive and poverty-ridden country. Cromer's general ideas, which were perhaps motivated more by a determination to spare the Egyptian Treasury (which had to make good any deficits in the Sudan) than to benefit the Sudanese people, were followed faithfully by Wingate, who succeeded Kitchener as Sirdar and Governor-General towards the end of 1899, when Kitchener went to the South African War as Chief-of-Staff to Roberts. As in Egypt, the recipe followed was economical administration, with a minimum of 'prestige' expenditure or 'social services,' generous capital expenditure, financed by Egypt, for development purposes, and no concessions what-ever to any theories about preparing the people for self-government. One important item of capital expenditure was one in which Cromer had been interested ever since his arrival in Egypt twenty years before—the construction of a rail link between the Red Sea and the Nile Valley as providing the most economical means of developing the Sudan's import and export trade. This was completed in 1906 and had the incidental, and perhaps not unintended, effect of channelling the Sudan's trade away from Egypt and of making the Sudan less dependent on Egypt.

And so the years went by, to all appearance a triumphal progress whose achievements were recorded in the statistical returns and official prose of Cromer's Annual Reports. In his Report for 1897 Cromer stated: 'What Egypt most required and for many years to come will require is honest, just and orderly administration and the establishment of the supremacy of the law on so firm a footing as to render impossible any return to that personal system of government which, twenty years ago, was well-nigh the ruin of the country. At some future date the Egyptian question may pass from the administrative to the political stage . . . However, that moment would appear to be distant.'[35] As if to underline the point, the same Report announced the appointment of an Englishman as Procureur-Général of the National Courts in place of an Egyptian. In his Report for 1898 Cromer announced remissions of taxation amounting to £E1,275,000 p.a. since 1890,[36] and in his Report for 1899 he wrote that 'during no previous period in recent years has the cordial cooperation of the Egyptian element in the Administration and the European element been more marked.'[37] In his Reports for 1900 and 1901 he announced revenue surpluses of £E560,000 and £E864,000 respectively, the abolition of octroi duties everywhere except at Cairo and Alexandria, and the cutting of the Sudd in the Sudan, thus facilitating navigation and increasing the supply of Summer water in Egypt.[38] In his Report for 1902 he announced the abolition of octroi duties in Cairo and Alexandria and calculated that the incidence of taxation over the twenty years of the British occupation had decreased from £E1.030 to £E0.789 per head, 'in spite of the extra cost of the Sudan,' and in spite of extraordinary expenditure amounting to £E29 million devoted to drainage and irrigation over that twenty-year period.[39] He went on to announce that 'the main items of fiscal reform and reduction of taxation have now been completed' and that, with the completion of the Aswan reservoir, 'the main objects of the Government programme will have been accomplished.' 'It may now be hoped that administrative reform may occupy a more prominent place in the Government programme.' In the same Report he indicated that this administrative reform would include reforms in the Departments of Police and Justice and in the field of sanitation. He continued on a cautiously liberal note: 'It cannot be said that the Departments of Justice and the Interior have as yet settled down into a normal and steady rate of progress . . . It may be that a few more British officials will be found here and there to be necessary, either as Inspectors or in some other capacity. But the main policy remains unchanged. That policy consists in using native agency to the utmost possible extent . . . I can conceive of nothing more unjust or more impolitic than to educate the Egyptian and then to close all the principal doors which lead to a public career . . . There is no intention whatever of adopting it.'[40]

In his 1903 Report, apart from announcing the completion of Aswan dam and his intention of not extending the powers of the Legislative Council, although it 'has occasionally performed some useful functions,'

Cromer set out the policy of the Government towards the fellahin. 'Without resorting to any protective measures, all that is possible should be done to maintain in existence peasant proprietorship and to encourage its growth . . . The large reductions in land tax, the increase in pro-ductivity from improved irrigation, the establishment of an Agricultural Bank, the partition of Government land, when sold, into small plots, the abolition of octroi dues etc., have been to this end. The peasant proprietor is not only holding his own, but showing a slight tendency to increase.'[41]

In his 1904 Report, after giving details of the implications for Egypt of the Anglo-French Agreement concluded in April of that year (see Chapter 11), Cromer gave details of a long-term programme of irrigation development for Egypt and the Sudan prepared by Sir William Garstin, Under Secretary for Public Works, costing £E13 million for Egypt and £E8.4 million for the Sudan, to be financed partly out of the accumulated reserves in the Caisse which had been handed over to the Egyptian Government as a result of the Anglo-French Agreement, and partly out of future surpluses which, also as a result of that Agreement, would henceforth be entirely at the disposal of the Egyptian Government. This programme included the completion of a main irrigation canal in Middle Egypt so as to convert the whole of the area between Cairo and Asyut to perennial irrigation, and the raising of the Aswan dam. He also announced a proposal to spend £E1 million p.a. on the railways to bring them up-to-date now that they had been released from international control as a result of the Anglo-French Agreement.[42]

In his 1905 Report, after describing his proposal for a Legislative Council of foreign residents which would have the power to approve legislation initiated by the Egyptian Government (see Chapter 11), Cromer announced a revenue surplus of nearly £E1,500,000 and tax reductions amounting to £E332,000 p.a., including the abolition of the salt monopoly.[43]

The advent of a Liberal Administration in England at the beginning of 1906, in place of the Conservative Administration which had been in office for the previous eleven years, marked the beginning of the end of Cromer's triumphal progress.

11

THE ANGLO-FRENCH AGREEMENT

ON 4 JANUARY 1883, the British Government had moved the Egyptian Government to abolish the Anglo-French Dual Control and to appoint instead a British Financial Adviser. M. Duclerc, the French Foreign Minister, who had conducted for several weeks a somewhat acriminious negotiation on the subject with the British Government, informed Lord Granville that the French Government would 'resume their liberty of action' over Egyptian affairs. This 'liberty of action' resolved itself into an official French hostility towards the British occupation of Egypt, expressed both locally and internationally, which only stopped just short of war, and which lasted for twenty-one years.

No European country, other than France, had an interest in Egypt comparable with that of England. For exactly eighty years—from the invasion of Egypt by Bonaparte in 1798 to the Congress of Berlin in 1878 —rival British and French interests in Egypt had been a constant cause of tension between the two countries and, on one occasion—in 1840— had nearly led to the outbreak of war between them. The Suez Canal had been opposed by the British Government mainly because it was a French-sponsored scheme, and Egypt's profligate foreign indebtedness was, in part, the result of competitive lending by nationals of the two countries who were encouraged by their Governments to obtain influence over the Egyptian Government in this way.

As the result partly of joint arrangements forced on them by Egypt's bankruptcy, and partly of informal arrangements made between Salisbury and Waddington at the Congress of Berlin, this rivalry was, so to speak, 'cartelised' into an agreement to manage Egyptian affairs on a joint and equal basis and to keep any other Power from interfering. This, as far as England and France were concerned, made Egypt a *régime d'exception*,' differentiated from the rest of the Ottoman Empire whose affairs, since the Treaty of Paris in 1856, had been regarded as the joint concern of all the great European Powers.

The British occupation and the subsequent abolition of the Dual Control were regarded at the time by French official and public opinion as the culmination of a deliberate plot to oust the French from Egypt and to establish a preponderance of British influence there.

There was a long history of envenomed rivalry which appeared to the French to justify this accusation—Palmerston's activities in isolating France in the Concert of Europe in 1840, his later attempts to frustrate the building of the Suez Canal, Disraeli's purchase of the Khedive's Suez Canal shareholding. From the British point of view, there was also a long history of what appeared to them to be French jealousy and an overweening regard for exclusive French interests in Egypt—the inordinate claims of the Suez Canal Company, the extreme view which the French had always tended to take of Capitulations privileges, the obstruction shown by the French Government in the negotiations leading up to the inauguration of the Mixed Courts.

There was also a long history of rivalry between the British and French communities in Egypt. The French community was much the more numerous of the two (in 1883 there were about 15,000 French and 6,000 British residents), much more bound up with the country's economic life and fortunes, and much more influential, both locally and with their home Government. Such Western culture as there was was mainly French; for long after the British occupation French was the second language of administration after Arabic, and conversations and correspondence between Europeans and Egyptian Ministers and high officials were invariably conducted in French, a good knowledge of French being a necessary qualification for British officials in Egypt. The legal and educational systems were based on French models; most of the European language newspapers were published in French (and often directed by Frenchmen). The whole ambience of the administrative, business and social life of Cairo and Alexandria seemed to suggest that the British, by their occupation, had usurped a rightful French heritage.

The influence of the powerful French community, which was usually sufficient to break any French Consul-General who showed weakness in supporting their views, was important in its effect both on public opinion in metropolitan France and on the policy of successive French Governments.

Apart from these historical, sentimental and local matters, there was a very real interest at stake. The French, almost as much as the British, considered it vital that Egypt should not fall under the exclusive control of any other European Power. As in the case of the British, there was a certain element of paranoia in this. But there was also a certain amount of reason. The French, as well as the British, had their possessions and their interests all around the Indian Ocean—Madagascar, Indo-China,

Jibuti, Réunion, New Caledonia. Even more than the British, they were interested in the balance of power in the Mediterranean, and the British possession of Egypt, added to Gibraltar, Malta and Cyprus, tilted the balance heavily in the wrong direction.

For all these reasons it was inevitable that the French should use every diplomatic weapon to hand to compel the British to bring their military occupation to an end. For the French took the view, shared by Cromer, that the special British position being built up in Egypt—British Advisers and Inspectors in all the Ministries, British officers commanding the Egyptian Army, British control of Egyptian finances, British reorganisation of Egyptian irrigation, law, et cetera, was maintained and guaranteed only by the continued presence of a British garrison and that, if the garrison went, British preponderance would go with it.

There were many diplomatic weapons, both international and local. The international ones were mostly double-edged in that Anglo-French rivalry over Egypt provided other Powers with the opportunity of exploiting both England and France in their own interests. Since the other Powers had a similar, although—compared with France—less imperious interest in preserving international control in Egypt, England tended to be the victim and France the beneficiary of this exploitation. But this was not always the case, since, in these matters, local Egyptian interests were often dwarfed by wider considerations. Local weapons, on the other hand, were single-edged and very effective by reason of the complicated system of foreign privileges, mixed jurisdictions and international debt settlements which had been imposed on Egypt as a result both of the Ottoman connection and of national insolvency.

Successive French Governments adopted a deliberate policy of exploiting these restrictions on Egyptian sovereignty to the maximum possible extent, with the object of so embarrassing the British occupiers as to compel them to put a term to their occupation. Even if this policy failed, as it did, in its primary object, it could not fail to have the secondary effect of maximising international, and of minimising purely British, influence in Egyptian affairs.

This was a perfectly comprehensible policy and, in terms of international politics, it would have been absurd for the British to feel either surprise or shock at the vigour and virtuosity with which it was pursued by the French. The British had played much the same game with the French over Mohamed Ali in 1839–40 and over the Suez Canal between 1856 and 1864. It was part of the accepted cut-and-thrust of international diplomacy, and it only got out of hand when the French supplemented the manipulation of International Conventions by the despatch of military expeditions across the centre of Africa.

When Cromer took over in Egypt in September 1883 he had at first the optimistic idea that the British Government would either be able to negotiate, or be prepared unilaterally to underwrite, an almost total abrogation of the international servitudes which limited the Egyptian Government's freedom of action. Amongst other things, he wanted the abolition of the criminal jurisdiction of the Consular Courts, the restriction of the jurisdiction of the Mixed Courts over the acts of the Egyptian Government, and an end to the virtual ban, imposed by the Capitulations and upheld by the Mixed Courts, on any legislation affecting foreign residents in Egypt without the prior unanimous consent of all the fourteen Capitulatory Powers. But, after some years of bitter experience, during which little or no progress had been made in any of these matters, he became less ambitious and concentrated on what he termed 'financial freedom' for the Egyptian Government—that is to say, release from the various budgetary controls and restrictions imposed by the Law of Liquidation of 1880 and the London Convention of 1885, and freedom for the Egyptian Government to frame its Budgets and to apply its revenue according to its discretion and subject only to the punctual payment to the Caisse of the sums required for the discharge of the various foreign debt coupons.

In 1889 increasing financial stability enabled the Egyptian Government to convert part of its foreign debt, which resulted in a considerable saving on the annual charges on this debt. About the same year, Egypt's annual Budgets started to show a surplus. But, owing to the provisions of the London Convention, none of the economies deriving from the conversion operation, and only part of the budgetary surpluses, were at the disposal of the Egyptian Government. The rest had to be paid over to the Caisse for the redemption of the debt. In the same year—1889— arrangements were made for the creation of a Reserve consisting (a) of conversion economies and (b) of budgetary surpluses accruing to the Caisse under the terms of the London Convention, from which loans or grants could be made to the Egyptian Government for 'extraordinary expenses' on the application of the Egyptian Government and with the unanimous consent of the six members of the Caisse. But a treasure-chest which could only be opened by six keys, one of which was held by the French Government, had something of the disadvantages of a tantalus.

The locking up of all these economies and surpluses in the Caisse strong-box meant that the benefits of Egypt's improved finances could not fully be passed on to the people in the form of reduced taxation or increased public services. The Egyptians were being deprived of part of the material benefit which they might otherwise have received from the British presence. This became tremendously important to Cromer from about 1893 onwards, when the hostility of the Khedive and incipient nationalist discontent made it increasingly necessary for him to commend the benefits of the occupation to the mass of the people and to counter-balance political repression by material amelioration.

Naturally, these considerations made the French all the more determined to insist on evacuation as a *quid pro quo* for any relaxation of the financial provisions of the London Convention, and ensured their objection to providing money from the Reserve for any purpose designed to con-solidate the British position in Egypt, *e.g.* the Aswan reservoir and the campaign for the reconquest of the Sudan.

Cromer eventually came to realise that no British Government would be prepared to underwrite a denunciation by the Egyptian Government of the terms of the London Convention. Salisbury told him that he must 'make love to the French' if he wanted to get the terms of the Convention relaxed, and Rosebery made it clear to him that he would not support any proposal to 'take' from the Caisse the money required for a Sudan campaign. Even in November 1898, after Fashoda, Salisbury was not prepared to pile on the agony for France by accepting Cromer's suggestion that 'the time (had) arrived when we might tell the French that the constant heckling we have had to endure from them in Egypt will no longer be tolerated.' It was made clear to Cromer, time and again, that, if release were to be obtained, it would have to be obtained by way of negotiation. And the French price was always the same—evacuation.

For Cromer, this was not negotiable. He was no longer interested in preparing Egypt for evacuation. He wanted 'financial freedom' in order to make the occupation more acceptable to Egyptians. With Salisbury, right up to, and including, 1896, and possibly into 1897, some form of conditional evacuation, on the general lines of the abortive Drummond Wolff Convention, would probably have been negotiable. The occupation still hampered his freedom of manoeuvre in European affairs and he may have calculated that the increasingly important British lever in Egypt might yet be manipulated without a British military presence by remote control from the Upper Nile Valley.

In February 1896 de Courcel, the French Ambassador in London, approached Salisbury about Egypt. He indicated in general terms that the French Government had no desire to be obstructive, that they were actuated by no unfriendly intentions towards the British in Egypt, and that they would be satisfied with the fixing of a definite date for evacuation and with the appointment of a rather larger proportion of Frenchmen in Egyptian Government service. Salisbury communicated the substance of de Courcel's remarks to Cromer,[1] in a letter which invited Cromer to state his reasons for regarding the continued presence of a British garrison as a vital safeguard for the maintenance of those conditions of stability, solvency and security which Cromer had succeeded in bringing about. Salisbury realised that the weakest point in the British bargaining position vis-à-vis the French was the simultaneous assertion (a) that the British had fulfilled their stated objectives in occupying Egypt and (b) that, in spite of this, a continuance of the occupation was necessary.

Cromer replied to Salisbury with a long letter[2] in which he stated his reasons for believing that the maintenance of a British garrison in Egypt was necessary. (1) 'Elements of disorder and confusion abound.' (2) The incapacity of the Egyptian governing classes. (3) The arbitrary disposition of the Khedive. (4) The unreliability of a Moslem army officered by Christians. (5) The existence of a 'very ignorant and credulous population which have learnt that they possess rights, *e.g.* over the distribution of water, and will not allow them to be infringed.' (6) 'A host of incompetent and corrupt place-hunters.' (7) 'A debased and unreasonable European population influenced by international rivalry and under no proper legal control.' (8) 'A formidable foe on the frontier.' He went on: 'If the Army is withdrawn you will have to rely entirely on two individuals —the Khedive and the British Consul-General. The British officials, excellent as many of them are, would act as breakwaters, but they are themselves to some extent lacking in judgement; they are certain to look only at the departmental aspect of problems and they necessarily derive all their powers from the support of the Consul-General, that is to say of HMG. The Khedive, even allowing for childish ebullitions of temper, does not possess any of the qualities necessary for the efficient ruler of this or any other country; he is wholly ignorant of public affairs and has no desire to learn. He is also very unpopular. An anti-Khedivial movement based more or less on Arabist principles would follow very shortly on the evacuation of the British garrison. None of the Khedivial family possess qualities superior to his own. Will the authority of the British Consul-General, backed by HMG, be sufficient to ensure the working of the machine without the weight of some British troops? My belief is that personal authority on the spot backed by moral support from London will not be sufficient to prevent either immediate collapse or, more probably, gradual disintegration of the reformed government of Egypt.'

But Cromer realised that these arguments would not prevail with Salisbury if he saw some real chance of an agreement with France which would enable him to keep his options open on the European chessboard. He had to face the possibility that, in terms of European politics, his work in Egypt might have to be regarded as expendable. So he told Salisbury: 'If the risk (of evacuation) is to be run, I think we should adopt the general line of the Drummond Wolff Convention . . . To retire without the right of re-entry is quite out of the question. Armenia has shown us what could happen if no civilised Power has the duty of policeman. Whatever might be the degree of local anarchy, international jealousy and the fear of European complications would effectively prevent any action . . . The French would not agree to our right of re-entry except on the unacceptable condition that they are to be the judges of whether the necessity for re-entry had arisen. Unless they agreed unconditionally the danger of complication with France would be greater after evacuation than they are now.'

Cromer went on to give examples of French obstruction in Egypt in answer to de Courcel's assertion that they were actuated by no unfriendly motives and to his suggestion for more French officials in the Egyptian service. He told Salisbury that the delay in building the Aswan reservoir, which had been the subject of surveys and discussions over the last four years, had been due to French opposition. 'Had the economies resulting from conversion been at the disposal of the Egyptian Government, the work would have been begun some years ago. Knowing that it was useless to approach the French Government, we waited. The financial position is now so improved that we can go ahead without touching the economies. But we must ask the Caisse. But there has been no decision yet from the French Government. After keeping us dangling for some months, they will return an evasive answer which will be tantamount to refusal . . . What we want in Egypt is financial liberty; I mean that, after the interest on the debt has been paid and an adequate sum—say £2 million—has been set aside to provide for the very improbable case of insufficiency of revenue pledged to the bondholders, the remainder of the revenue should be absolutely at the disposal of the Egyptian Treasury. The Caisse should have no voice in the matter. If the French were willing to treat on these grounds we might perhaps come to terms with them. But, unless they are prepared unconditionally to accept the principle of financial liberty . . . (there should be) . . . no administrative concessions by us.'

He concluded: 'These constant scares about evacuation do a great deal of harm . . . It must surely now be apparent to everyone that evacuation . . . is open to the strongest objections. Would it not be possible to get out of the vagueness which surrounds Egyptian policy? Might not the French be told clearly that we recognise our pledge to evacuate, that we have no wish to remain, but that the problem of putting the Egyptian Government on its legs has proved so much more difficult than was sup- posed at first that we see no present prospect of being able to withdraw the garrison? . . . (But) . . . though we could on no account agree to the re-establishment of the Condominium (*i.e.* the Anglo-French Control), we should be happy to discuss a *modus vivendi* and that the basis of any such arrangement should be (a) financial liberty for the Egyptian Government acting with British advisers, and (b) the bestowal on some French officials of positions which, although subordinate, would be of considerable importance.'

This proposal of Cromer's—indefinite postponement of evacuation and financial freedom for the Egyptian Government—was the basis of the Anglo-French Agreement arrived at eight years later. But, for the moment, nothing very much happened. In the Summer of 1896, when Cromer was in England, he had some inconclusive discussions with de Courcel, whom he found ill-informed on the subject of Egypt and unwilling to descend from generalities to details. By that time the Sudan campaign had started. Worsening relations with the French, culminating in the Fashoda incident in the Autumn of 1898, inhibited any further discussions between the two Governments about Egypt for the time being. By the time of the Sudan Condominium Agreement in 1899, the idea of a possible evacuation of Egypt had been tacitly abandoned by the British Government, and Salisbury, in an interview with the Turkish Ambassador, pointedly 'refused to reiterate the promises of evacuation at some unknown date which, on previous occasions, we had freely given.' (See p. 221 above.)

On the French side, the Fashoda débâcle can, in retrospect, be seen as marking the end of the traditional anti-British colonial policy, represented by the Comité de l'Afrique Française, and obsessed by the idea of ejecting the British from Egypt; and the beginning of a new policy, represented by l'Union Coloniale Française, and determined to build up a French hegemony in North and West Africa. 'Fashoda demonstrated *a fortiori* that Britain would fight rather than allow herself to be worried out of Egypt, and thereby destroyed an illusion which was widespread, not only among the French public, but in the bureaux and in the Diplomatic Corps . . . No responsible French statesman had ever contemplated a war for the sake of Egypt, except perhaps as a member of a Continental League, whose very existence would probably have made such a war unnecessary. To such a League, Germany was indispensable, and experience had shown that Germany would cooperate only at the impossible price of a final renunciation of the Lost Provinces. Except perhaps during 1884–85, when the temporary entente with Germany had brought some useful gains, the policy of opposing Britain because of her occupation of Egypt had been dictated by wounded pride rather than by any rational assessment either of French interests or of French diplomatic and military resources . . . A humiliation on the scale of Fashoda might well have been expected to freeze French opinion in this attitude of impotent but embittered protest. Instead, it convinced French opinion, other than the anti-Dreyfusard fanatics and traditionally anglophobe groups such as the nobility and the officer corps, that opposition to England in the Nile Valley was pointless because success was demonstrably impossible.'³

From 1898 onwards, French colonial ambitions began to concentrate on the possession of Morocco as the 'indispensable rounding-off of the French North African Empire,'⁴ which already included Tunisia and Algeria. In the context of French hostility, the British Government could be expected strenuously to oppose a French occupation of Morocco, since such an occupation would, in the event of war, facilitate a French denial of access to the Mediterranean by the British Navy. In the context of a general understanding with France, which would rule out the likelihood of war between the two countries, there would be no such objection. The desirability of such an understanding, both from the British and the French points of view, tended to increase as a result of the enlarged German naval building programme, and of the generally aggressive sabre-rattling encouraged by the megalomaniac German Kaiser and supported by German industrialists and by most of the officer class.

Discussions about Morocco and other colonial questions (but not Egypt) took place, on French initiative, between Sir Edward Monson, the British Ambassador in Paris, and Delcassé, the French Foreign Minister, in the Summer of 1902. These had no decisive result. During the following year, on 7 July 1903, an important conversation took place in London between Delcassé, and Lord Lansdowne, the British Foreign Secretary, during a State visit by the French President, in which various colonial matters—Siam, Newfoundland, Sokoto and New Hebrides—were discussed, and in which Lansdowne, for the first time, indicated that Egypt must be included in any general settlement of colonial matters outstanding between England and France. Delcassé, who in March had denied to a suspicious French Chamber that the question of Egypt had been linked with any Anglo-French discussions about Morocco, replied equivocally that the Egyptian question formed part of the larger African question which could be settled if the two countries came to an agreement over Morocco.

At that time Morocco, still nominally independent, was in a state of rebellion against the ruling Sultan, and the French Government were determined to add it to the French North African Empire by restoring the nominal authority of the Sultan and bringing the country under French protection.

After returning to Paris, Delcassé, in his instructions to Cambon, the French Ambassador in London, tended to 'drag his feet' over Egypt and, at the end of July, Lansdowne had to insist to Cambon that it would be impossible to exclude Egypt from consideration if a general colonial settlement were to be attempted. Advised of this by Cambon, Delcassé replied that he 'would not refuse' to discuss Egypt, provided France got what she wanted over Morocco.[5] On 5 August Lansdowne made it clear to Cambon that the Cabinet was 'unanimous as to the necessity of including Egypt in any arrangement which might be made' and that 'they would not entertain any proposals which did not include one for the regularisation of our position in that country.' Cambon replied that any French Government which recognised the British position in Egypt would require an immense amount of 'estomac' in face of French public opinion, which was very sensitive about Egypt, but indicated that Delcassé was prepared for this provided that he could obtain 'une grosse compensation' in Morocco and elsewhere. He then asked Lansdowne to formulate more precisely what the British wanted from France over Egypt.[6]

The cards were now on the table.

Cromer, who had been advised by Lansdowne of his conversation with Delcassé, was inclined to be sceptical of the possibility that French public opinion would permit any French Government to make real concessions over Egypt. But he had a keen eye for a bargain and quickly saw the possibility of using Morocco as a lever. He told Lansdowne: 'I most earnestly hope that advantage will be taken of the opportunity now offered . . . My own opinion is distinctly in favour of making concessions in Morocco in return for counter-concessions in Egypt . . . I have very little doubt that, when once the French are assured that they can make good their rights to the succession without any risk of serious interference on our part, Morocco will to all intents and purposes become before long a French Province. The question therefore . . . is this: have we any objection to Morocco becoming a French Province? Personally I see none provided we get an adequate quid pro quo in Egypt.'[7]

On 1 October Lansdowne, after consultations with Cromer (who was in England during the latter part of the Summer), submitted to Cambon a statement of what the British Government wanted in Egypt and what they were prepared to concede over Morocco. With regard to Egypt, Lansdowne declared that the British Government had no desire to alter its political status or to raise questions affecting England's international status there. What they did want was that the French Government should recognise the permanency of the British occupation and permit the British and Egyptian Governments to convert the whole of the Egyptian debt and abolish the international Railway Board. For the moment nothing was proposed about the Capitulations except that the French Government should declare themselves ready to examine subsequent British proposals for their abolition. With regard to Morocco the British Government were ready to recognise the preponderance of French influence there provided that British commercial rights remained intact, that the sea board was neutralised and an agreement reached about Spanish rights there.[8] Predictably, and in the normal course of diplomatic bargaining, the French Government objected that they were being asked for too much over Egypt and being offered too little over Morocco.

There were difficulties with public opinion both in France and England, and considerable popular opposition to any concessions made to the other side. But Lansdowne and Delcassé were both determined to see the thing through, provided they could drive a hard enough bargain. The French were 'playing it long.' Cambon told Delcassé in November: 'We should give in on nothing, should take our time, should not show haste. We are in a position to be difficult; the English have more interest in making an arrangement with us in Egypt than we have in concluding one with them for Morocco. They will become intractable if we seem too desirous of bringing things to an end.'[9] Lansdowne, on the other hand, egged on by Cromer, was trying to hurry things up. In his letter to Lansdowne on 17 July Cromer had expressed the opinion that 'in the present case, the danger lies rather on the side of moving too slow.' And, on 1 November, he told Lansdowne: 'I most earnestly hope . . . that you will continue the negotiations vigorously. Such an oppor⁄ tunity as the present is not likely to recur. We must manage to come to terms, though any display of excessive eagerness to do so would of course be inadvisable. Personally I regard this as by far the most important diplomatic affair that we have had in hand for a long time past . . . We must not fail . . . If we accept the French will have got all they want out of us and we shall have got little or nothing out of them. We should not have secured one of our main objects, which is to get a free hand for dealing with the finances of Egypt and the Sudan.'[10]

For Cromer, the two essentials for an agreement were (a) 'financial freedom,' i.e. the removal of the international restrictions over the disposal of Egypt's budgetary surpluses, for which he had fought for so long; and (b) French recognition of the British occupation. By this time, Cromer was even more anxious for an agreement over this than he was for 'financial freedom.' Nationalist agitation in Egypt was already beginning to assume serious proportions and this, combined with the hostility of the Khedive and the increasing unfriendliness of Turkey, made it particularly desirable to secure acceptance of the occupation by the Powers and so deprive the nationalists, the Khedive and the Sultan of the use of a potential weapon against the occupation. The acceptance of France was the key to the agreement of the other Powers, who would be deprived by a formal French acquiescence of their existing opportunities for *chantage*. But Cromer was adamant about the necessity for nothing less than an explicit, unequivocal, formal and public French acceptance of the British position in Egypt, which would be understood as such by the Powers, by the Egyptian nationalists, by the Sultan, and by all the other interests concerned. When Gorst, the Financial Adviser, who went to London in December, and later to Paris, to assist in the financial side of the negotiations, suggested to Cromer that something less formal might be acceptable, Cromer told him roundly that, keen as he was on an agreement, he would sooner see the negotiations broken off than accept anything less than a formal French acknowledgement of the British occupation.[11]

On points such as the Capitulations and conversion Cromer was prepared to be flexible. At the beginning of the negotiations Cromer and Gorst were busy on a plan to convert the whole of the Egyptian debt and Lansdowne, in his communication to Cambon on 1 October, had, at Cromer's instance, indicated that freedom to convert was one of the essential conditions for a settlement. When Delcassé showed signs of resisting this, owing to the opposition of the French bondholders, Lansdowne told Cromer: 'If you will allow us to postpone the conversion our difficulties will certainly be diminished and the retention of the Caisse, although with its wings clipped, will no doubt make the French easier to deal with.'[12] After obtaining Cromer's agreement, Lansdowne told Cambon that he would agree to compromise over conversion and to agree to the maintenance of the Caisse, provided that its function should be 'strictly limited to receiving the sums necessary for the service of the debt,' that the French Government agreed to join the British in addressing the other Powers for the purpose of securing their consent to whatever agreement was arrived at, and it was understood that, should the consent of the other Powers be refused, France would not oppose 'any steps which HMG may hereafter find it expedient to take for the purpose of giving effect to the agreement.'[13]

Apart from the questions of Egypt and Morocco, and apart from various more or less minor matters in dispute over Newfoundland and elsewhere, which it was desirable to have settled, both the British and French Governments were anxious for an agreement on wider grounds of international policy. The French, conscious of the darkening German menace, were anxious to bring England over to an association with the Dual Alliance of France and Russia, and regarded these negotiations as a first step towards this end. The British, conscious since the Boer War both of their isolation in Europe and of their military deficiencies, and alarmed by Germany's naval building and her aggressively unfriendly general attitude, were, for the first time, beginning to regard the Germans, rather than the French or Russians, as their principal potential enemies in Europe. But particular interests and traditional antipathies continued to stand in the way of agreement.

The great influence which Cromer had achieved with the British Government by this time is illustrated by the extent to which his opinion was consulted and deferred to during the negotiations, in connection not only with Egypt, but also with other matters. The British line over Egypt, in its stipulations and in its concessions, was taken entirely from Cromer. The French negotiators, knowing of Cromer's influence with the British Government, and knowing, or guessing, the extent of his anxiety for an agreement over Egypt, took advantage of this. In the middle of January, when there were difficulties over French demands in West Africa and Newfoundland, the French Consul-General in Cairo was told by his Government to 'see Lord Cromer and tell him, as though it came from you, that the sort of arrangement projected concerning Egypt is being subordinated to the compensation which is in question.'[14] As a result Cromer, who had already been told by Gorst that 'the spirit in which our Government and the FO are negotiating is much too stiff,'[15] sent an urgent telegram to Lansdowne: 'I am inclined to think that the risk of a breakdown is serious . . . It is worth some sacrifice to avoid this . . . I recommend settling the matter quickly. The negotiations are being allowed to drag on rather too long.'[16] This is more the language of a Foreign Secretary to an Ambassador than vice versa.

There were other difficulties. There was the threat of war between Russia, France's ally in Europe, and Japan, England's new ally in the Far East. There was the possibility that Germany might refuse to recognise any concessions made by France over Egypt and by England over Morocco. Cromer, who was very conscious of this, had been responsible for Lansdowne's original insistence on France's agreement to assist the British Government in securing the agreement of the other Powers to whatever might be agreed on between them over Egypt. In the event—and this was the only point on which Cromer's advice was overriden—Lansdowne, in face of French objections, withdrew his insistence on this.[17]

The negotiations dragged on until April. There were more difficulties over Newfoundland. Delcassé tried to retreat from any formal acknowledgement of the British occupation. Over this, in the light of Cromer's insistence, Lansdowne was adamant. He told Cambon: 'We cannot go to Parliament without at least an admission . . . that the French Government recognises the permanency of our occupation of Egypt.'[18] It must have been some satisfaction to Cromer that, for once, Parliamentary opinion was being invoked in favour of, instead of in opposition to, something for which he was pressing.

Eventually, on 8 April 1904, an Agreement, in the form of two Declarations and a Convention, was signed in Paris by the Representatives of the two Governments. The part concerning Egypt consisted of nine published and five secret Articles embodied in a 'Declaration between the United Kingdom and France respecting Egypt and Morocco.' The arrangements concerning 'financial freedom' for Egypt were contained in a draft Khedivial Decree annexed to the Declaration to which the French Government signified their assent in the first Article of the Declaration.

The principal terms of the Declaration[19] were as follows:

'HBMG declare that they have no intention of altering the political status of Egypt. The Government of the French Republic declare that they will not obstruct the action of HBMG in that country by asking that a limit of time be fixed for the British occupation or in any other manner, and that they give their assent to the draft Khedivial Decree annexed to the present Agreement containing the guarantees considered necessary for the protection of the interests of the Egyptian bondholders, on the condition that, after its promulgation, it cannot be modified in any way without the consent of the Powers signatory to the Convention of London of 1885.' (Article I.)

'The Government of the French Republic declare that they have no intention of altering the political status of Morocco. HBMG recognise that it appertains to France . . . to preserve order in that country, and to provide assistance for the purpose of all administrative, economic, financial and military reforms which it may require. They declare that they will not obstruct the action taken by France for this purpose, provided that such action shall leave intact the rights which Great Britain . . . enjoys in Morocco.' (Article II.)

'In order to ensure the free passage of the Suez Canal HBMG declare that they adhere to the stipulations of the Treaty of 20 October 1888 and that they agree to their being brought into force.' (Article IV.)

'In order to secure the free passage of the Straits of Gibraltar the two Governments agree not to permit the erection of any fortifications or strategic works on that portion of the coast of Morocco comprised within but not including Melilla and the heights which command the right bank of the river Sebou.' (Article VII.)

'The two Governments agree to afford to one another their diplomatic support in order to obtain the execution of the clauses of the present Declaration regarding Egypt and Morocco.' (Article IX.)

In one of the secret Articles, which were mainly concerned with the position of Spain in Morocco, it was provided: 'HBMG have no present intention of proposing to the Powers any changes in the system of Capitulations, or in the judicial organisation of Egypt,' but that 'in the event of their considering it desirable to introduce into Egypt reforms tending to assimilate the Egyptian Legislative system to that in force in other civilised countries, the Government of the French Republic will not refuse to entertain such proposals, on the understanding that HBMG will agree to entertain the suggestions which the Government of the French Republic may have to make to them with a view to introducing similar reforms in Morocco.'

The draft Khedivial Decree repealed forty-six of the existing fifty-two Decrees governing the international control of Egyptian finances and partly repealed the remaining six. This had the effect (a) of allowing the Egyptian Government free use of all their revenues other than those required for meeting the coupons on the debt; (b) of placing at the disposal of the Egyptian Government the two Reserve Funds in the hands of the Caisse—the General Reserve consisting of the Caisse 50 per cent share of all 'surplus' revenue as defined in the 1885 Convention, and the Special Reserve consisting of accumulated savings made on the conversion of the Preference Debt (apart from a sum of £E1,800,000 retained by the Caisse to make up for any future short-fall in the revenues set aside for the service of the debt); (c) of securing the payment of the debt coupons on the proceeds of the land-tax, thus making possible the abolition of the international Railways Board which had previously managed the railways and the port of Alexandria, whose revenues had been allocated to the service of the debt.

All this meant that the Caisse was relegated to the position of receiving and distributing agency for the bondholders and no longer had the power of dictating Egyptian financial policy, and that the Egyptian Treasury, in addition to being able freely to dispose of its own revenues, came in for a windfall of some £E7,800,000, being the accumulated sum standing to the credit of the two Reserve Funds, less the £E1,800,000 retained by the Caisse as a guarantee.

The Decree also provided that the Privileged Debt could be converted after 1910 and the Unified Debt after 1912. Austria and Italy gave their assent to the draft Decree, and to the Declaration generally, without difficulty. Both the Russian and German Governments took the opportunity to obtain various minor concessions in return.

On the day of the signature of the Agreement, Lansdowne, in a despatch to Monson, which was published, wrote: 'From a British point of view there is no more remarkable episode in recent history than that which concerns the establishment and gradual development of British influence in Egypt. Our occupation of that country, at first regarded as temporary, has, by force of circumstances, become firmly established.'[20]

The Agreement was, to a very large extent, Cromer's own achieve-ment. Lord Sanderson, the Permanent Under Secretary at the Foreign Office, wrote: 'The actual determining cause of the Entente was Lord Cromer's anxiety for an arrangement with France which would let him place Egyptian finances on a more satisfactory footing, and pave the way for abolishing the Capitulations. The proposals relating to Egyptian finance formed a sort of nucleus from which the further agreements developed themselves.'[21]

On the whole, the Agreement was well received both in England and France. In England it was approved by Parliament without a division in August. In the French Chamber it was approved by 436 votes to 94. In England most satisfaction was expressed at the regularisation of the British position in Egypt. In France most importance was attached to the wider implications of the Agreement, which was seen as the prelude to an understanding between England and Russia, and the beginning of a new alignment in European politics by which the power of the British Navy would be added to the military strength of the Dual Alliance. The difficulties which the German Government made over acceptance of the Agreement, and their contemporaneous and unsuccessful attempt to inaugurate a general negotiation with the British Government over various matters in dispute, were largely due to their realisation of this possibility.

The purely Egyptian effects of the Agreement, in which Cromer was mainly interested, and for which he had successfully worked, were two-fold. (1) Egypt had obtained virtually complete autonomy in, or rather had incurred unrestricted British control over, her finances, including disposal of her surpluses, control of her railways and ports, and manage-ment of her debts. (2) The British Government had secured formal French recognition of the British occupation of Egypt, and had put an end to the continual French 'sniping' which had persisted since the abolition of the Dual Control at the beginning of 1883. Henceforward, objections to the occupation and protests against it, were to come, not from the Powers, but from the Egyptians themselves.

The international regime of the Mixed Courts and the Capitula-tions remained unchanged, although these instruments were to be less assiduously exploited for the embarrassment of the British. And the Anglo-French Agreement paved the way for an arrangement arrived at in 1911 by which the General Assembly of the Mixed Courts was invested with the power of approving legislation affecting foreigners, thus obviating the necessity for referring all such legislation to the Governments of all the Capitulatory Powers before it could be promulgated. (In 1889

253

an agreement had been reached by which the Mixed Courts had been given a very limited criminal jurisdiction over foreigners in cases of minor 'contraventions,' with powers of imposing derisory fines in respect of legislation certified by the General Assembly of the Mixed Courts as not being contrary to the texts of existing Treaties and Conventions. This was the only relaxation of the Capitulations which took place during Cromer's term of office.)

Meanwhile Cromer, having secured financial autonomy and international acceptance of the occupation, and mindful of the secret Article in the Agreement regarding Egyptian legislation, devoted much of his attention, during his three remaining years of office, to trying to secure the legislative autonomy which still eluded Egypt. In his Annual Report for 1904[22] he noted that 'the only solution . . . would be that the Powers should transfer to Great Britain the legislative functions which they collectively possess . . . One of the necessary consequences would be the creation of some local machinery which would take a part in the enactment of laws applicable to Europeans.' In his Report for 1905[23] he developed his ideas about this 'local machinery.' He advocated the creation of a second Legislative Council composed 'wholly of subjects or protected subjects of the Powers who were parties to the Treaty under which the judicial reforms of 1876 (*i.e.* the Decree setting up the Mixed Courts) were accomplished.' Elsewhere[24] he suggested that legislation should be submitted to this Council by the Egyptian Government and, if approved by the Council, promulgated by the Egyptian Government with the consent of the British Government. He envisaged that such a Council—having powers of approving legislation which the indigenous Legislative Council did not at that time possess—should eventually be merged into an Assembly which would 'enable all the dwellers in cosmopolitan Egypt, be they Moslem or Christian, European, Asiatic or African, to be fused into one self-governing body.' But he added that 'it may take years, possibly generations, to achieve this object.' His more limited plan, as adumbrated in his 1905 Report, came to nothing. This was due, not so much to foreign objections, as to the increasingly exigent temper of Egyptian nationalism.

12

THE RISE
OF EGYPTIAN
NATIONALISM

THE MANIFESTATIONS OF Egyptian nationalism which had resulted
in the British occupation stemmed from three sources—the professional
resentment of the Egyptian officers of the Army against the alleged
preference shown to Circassian officers, the religious resentment of a
revivalist Islamic movement against Western influence and Western
domination, and the political resentment of a constitutional movement
against a domestic despotism sustained by foreign influence. The circumstances of the time made these three disparate forces coalesce into something like a coherent Egyptian nationalist movement. The Army officers,
by reason of the force at their command, became the leaders of this movement. Because the officers were uneducated men, because their original
grievance was inspired by ambition rather than principle, and because
the effectiveness of the movement depended on getting as much popular
support as possible, the religious and political principles contributed by
the Islamic Modernists and the Constitutionalists became coarsened and
popularised into manifestations of fanaticism and xenophobia on the one
hand, and advocacy of the overthrow of all existing authority and the
repudiation of existing obligations on the other. The movement was
discredited outside Egypt mainly by the content of its domestic propaganda; it was discredited inside Egypt by the humiliating circumstances
of its defeat. In the eyes of the British occupiers, this discredit extended
from the Army revolt which had been the spearhead of the movement,
and which had been largely responsible for its cruder manifestations, to
its constitutional and religious aspects. For the next twenty years, Cromer,
and British officialdom generally, were apt to dismiss manifestations of
political discontent as 'Arabism' or 'Moslem fanaticism' and thus, by
implication, to equate them with irresponsibility, ignorance and violence.

Among the generality of Egyptians, Arabi's conduct at Tel el-Kebir (where he fled from the field almost before the battle had started), and his abject behaviour afterwards (when he made a bargain with his accusers by which he pleaded guilty to treason on condition that he would not be punished for it by anything worse than exile), prevented any sort of mystique from growing up round his name or his movement. When, in 1901, he was allowed to return to Egypt from Ceylon, his place of exile (where he had spent his time petitioning for additional allowances and indulgences), he was regarded, by friends and foes alike, with good-natured contempt. Neither Mohamed Abdu, his old associate, by that time Grand Mufti, nor the new generation of nationalists, had any use for him.

The Islamic Modernists, after the confusion and discredit into which they had been cast as a result of their association with the débâcle of the Army movement, never re-emerged as a powerful political, nor indeed as a powerful religious or social, force in Egypt. Shaikh Mohamed Abdu, the principal Egyptian disciple of Jamal-ad-Din el-Afghani, who had been one of Arabi's closest associates, was forgiven by Taufiq for his part in the Arabi rebellion, and remained in Egypt, becoming Grand Mufti in 1899.[1] In this capacity he did his best to bring the practices and precepts of Islam, at el-Azhar and elsewhere, into line with modern thought, but he had little success during his six years of office. He died in 1905. Long before then, the Islamic Modernist movement had become almost completely detached from the mainstream of Egyptian nationalism and, during his period of office as Mufti, Mohammed Abdu was on good terms, politically and personally, with Cromer and had little friendly contact either with the Khedive or with the nationalists. The Islamic Modernist movement, failing, by and large, to equate the principles of Islam with the discoveries of modern science, gradually abandoned its incipient rôle of a bridge between the fanaticism of the masses and the agnosticism of the classes and, in much the same way as has happened in Christianity, became a somewhat self-conscious sect whose agnosticism repelled fanatics and whose faith repelled agnostics.

With the elimination of the Army and the virtual disappearance of Islamic Modernism from the political scene, the future development of Egyptian nationalism lay with the Constitutionalists—the third element in the Arabist movement. But it was not until the turn of the century— nearly twenty years after the British occupation—that constitutionalism—a demand for the subordination of government to a body of elected representatives—began to emerge as a recognisable, coherent expression of an Egyptian national movement directed, not only against the British occupation but also, and perhaps equally, against the despotic powers of the Khedive.

In 1882 there had been an almost complete identification, both in nationalist eyes and in fact, between foreign domination and the Khedive, since Taufiq had been placed and was being maintained on his throne by the British and French Governments who were, to all intents and purposes, ruling the country through the despotic powers vested in the Khedive. Ten years later, when Taufiq died and was succeeded by his son Abbas, the position changed. Although, in form, British rule continued to be exercised in the name of the Khedive, in fact, Abbas placed himself personally in opposition to British rule. He was compelled to continue to allow the Khedivate to be used as the formal channel for the exercise of British authority. But his known personal attitude made him a rallying-point for various disparate movements of discontent which had been gathering momentum during the ten years of the occupation.

During these ten years, the process of assimilation, by which the Turco-Egyptian aristocracy was gradually becoming absorbed into and identified with the native Egyptian upper class, had gone steadily on, and the social, linguistic and political gap between Turk and Egyptian had all but disappeared. Or rather, their affinities, in religion, in language, in habits, and in their common resentments, had become more important than their differences. Their common resentments included, generally, the political frustrations implicit in the British occupation and, more particularly, the jealousy with which they regarded the increasing influence of various Eastern Christian communities—Copts, Lebanese and Armenians—who, with their quick wits, their local knowledge, their wide connections, and their good relations with the British occupiers, were carving out for themselves an important place in the political and economic life of the country, and who had the more or less open ambition of succeeding the British as the real rulers of the country. Of this class Cromer wrote: 'They are much more intelligent than the Turks or Arabs . . . They want us to go . . . but they are all regarded as foreigners; most of them are Christians; they are inexperienced doctrinaires wholly out of touch with the population.'[2]

In the early days of Abbas' reign, Riaz was the principal spokesman of the Old Turco-Egyptian Pasha class, and Tigrane, Nubar's son-in-law, of the rising class of Levantine Christians. Abbas used both of them, Riaz as Prime Minister and Tigrane as Foreign Minister, and they both used Abbas, in an attempt to embarrass the British. At the same time the Egyptian Moslem Pashas tried to use the fanaticism of the Moslem masses to discredit their Christian rivals. And the British tried to use the increasing security and prosperity of the medium landed proprietor, which had been brought about by the British occupation, as a prophylactic against the political intrigues of the Khedive, the disgruntled Moslem Pashas, and the rising Levantine magnates.

The disgruntled factions who gathered round the new Khedive were neither reformers nor constitutionalists. They wanted to preserve the despotic powers of the Khedive intact because, like the British, they wanted to use these despotic powers as an instrument for ruling the country themselves once they had got rid of the British. When it became clear that they would be unable to get rid of the British, they either collaborated with them or, leaving politics alone, devoted themselves to self-enrichment under the favourable economic circumstances which the British occupation had created.

Meanwhile other, and more subversive, forces were beginning to make themselves felt. The rising generation of nationalists, unlike the old Constitutionalists, were mostly middle-class professional men. Many of them were lawyers and journalists; most of them had been educated in France and had there imbibed the anglophobia current at the time, particularly in all matters connected with Egypt. They were influenced, not only by French democratic institutions, but by constitutional aspirations and agitations in Turkey, which was still regarded by educated Egyptians as the 'Mother country' in much the same sense as educated Australians still think of England. Sympathising, as they did, with the ambitions of Turkish 'progressives' for a constitutional Sultanate, they were not prepared to accept for themselves a despotic Khedivate as the price for getting rid of the British. On the contrary, some of them would have been prepared to cooperate with the British, as a temporary but necessary evil, if the British had been prepared to make some progress in the direction of constitutional government. But the British were not so prepared.

In the absence of any effective representative institutions, the Press played an essential propagandist and educative rôle in the development of Egyptian nationalism and of Egyptian political life generally. Political journalism in Egypt had started in the 1870s, when a number of Lebanese writers found the political atmosphere of Cairo more favourable to the practice of their craft than that of Constantinople, Damascus or Beirut. By 1881 the freedom of the Press in Egypt had become so embarrassing to the Dual Control that a Press Law was promulgated giving the Government wide powers of licensing, suspension, seizure and suppression. But, after the occupation, owing to the operation of the Capitulations, and the attitude of France, as exemplified by the *Bosphore* incident, this Law became inoperative, since it was impracticable to apply to Egyptian journals restrictions from which foreign journals were exempt and which, in any case, Egyptian journals could easily evade by assuming a façade of foreign ownership. Consequently, newspaper comment and criticism became quite uninhibited. Contemporary British writers and officials frequently referred to the 'irresponsibility' and 'scurrility' of the Egyptian Press. But an uninhibited Press was a fortunate and necessary corrective to a politically irresponsible Administration and the only means by which criticism of the Administration could be voiced. And the Press was by no means unanimously anti-British or anti-Government. Cromer saw to it that the point of view of the Administration received appropriate publicity and several newspapers received regular subventions from the British Agency.

The use of the Press as an organ of propaganda, and the necessity for making a popular impact, inevitably led to all the familiar extravagancies inseparable from political campaigns conducted among relatively un-sophisticated peoples. There were simplifications amounting to ex-aggerations, suppressions of the truth amounting to falsehoods, mendacious allegations amounting, very often, to incitements to violence. In the particular circumstances of a potentially fanatical Moslem country ruled by the despotic agents of a Christian Power, with a large and privileged Christian population protected by that Power, there was also the endemic temptation, which was only occasionally resisted, of setting Moslem against Christian and of appealing to fanaticism against privilege. And there was an opposite temptation, equally not always resisted by the British occupiers, to equate the substance of nationalist demands with the emotions roused by nationalist propaganda, to denounce lawful aspirations as criminal subversion, and to dignify arbitrary tyranny with references to the preservation of law and order.

The leader of the new 'constitutional' Egyptian nationalist movement, which began to make itself felt at about the end of the century, was Mustafa Kamil. He had been born in 1874 and was thus still a very young man. He had been educated, first, at the Law School in Cairo and had then gone to study Law at the University of Toulouse. While in France he had become acquainted with M. Deloncle, an anglophobe French Deputy, with Mme Juliette Adam, editor of *Nouvelle Revue,* and with the writer, Pierre Loti. His Egyptian patriotism was nourished by the views of these French anglophobes and, while still at University, he became an ardent Egyptian nationalist. He began contributing articles to the Egyptian journal *el-Muayyad* which had been set up by Riaz Pasha under the editorship of Shaikh Ali Yusef. During the 1890s *el-Muayyad,* under Ali Yusef's editorship, had been the principal organ of nationalist opinion in Egypt. It was subsidised by the Khedive and adopted a generally pan-Islamic line. Its influence during these years was probably important in determining Cromer's later identification of Egyptian nationalism with pan-Islam. In 1899, after his return to Egypt, Mustafa Kamil started an Arabic-language newspaper of his own—*el-Liwa*—which soon replaced *el-Muayyad* as the principal organ of Egyptian nationalism.

Perhaps inevitably, given the necessity for seeking as much support as possible from wherever it was to be found, Egyptian nationalist objectives were never very precisely defined, but basically they consisted in the achievement of constitutional government, meaning a government which would be responsible to a popularly-elected parliament with supreme legislative authority. There were obvious difficulties about such a pro-gramme, from the point of view both of practicability and of popular interest and support. It was desirable not to antagonise those Powers who might support the nationalists against the British occupation, and, therefore, not to say too much about the necessity for removing the legislative and other restrictions imposed by the Capitulations; it was politic to champion the Khedive, who had become a sort of rallying-point for anti-British sentiment in Egypt, avoiding open advocacy of the elimination of his authority as Head of State; it was prudent to show respect to the Sultan, to whom the idea of a Constitution was anathema and whose influence, in his capacity as Caliph, was considerable among the Moslem masses, particularly since Abdul Hamid had put himself at the head of the pan-Islamic movement. This movement was intended by the Sultan to be a counterblast to constitutional tendencies and nationalist ambitions in his dominions, to European interference over his treatment of Christian minorities in Armenia, Lebanon and Macedonia, and to European domination in Egypt and North Africa. Until Abdul Hamid's fall in 1908 it was a force to be reckoned with, both by European occupiers and by aspiring nationalists.

For all these reasons, the Egyptian nationalist movement was equivocal both in its policies and in its relationships with other elements opposed to the British occupation. It is just possible that wise statesmanship might have reconciled nationalism to the occupation by constitutional con-cessions, by a more active policy of promoting Egyptian nationalists to responsible positions in the Administration, and by a more liberal attitude generally. But Cromer, with advancing age, was becoming more auto-cratic, more convinced of his own infallibility, more impatient of opposition, more complacent about British achievements in Egypt, and more convinced of Egyptian incapacity. And he was becoming less and less personally in touch with the Egyptian situation. On the one hand he was influenced by an increasing number of British officials who, proud of the efficiency of the administrative machine which they had built up, nourished by the robust Imperial sentiments fashionable at the time, and interested in the progress of the careers which they had adopted, were, for the most part, even more contemptuous than Cromer of the capacity of Egyptians to govern themselves. On the other, he was influenced by the Egyptian Ministers, such as Mustafa Fahmy, and by a handful of Lebanese journalists and bankers, such as Faris Nimr, the owner and editor of the newspaper *el-Muqattam*, who all had a vested interest in the occupation, and who were opposed to anything in the nature of constitutional government, which they feared would reflect the popular and nationalist prejudices against them.

And so Cromer treated the nationalist movement with contempt, attributing it to the intrigues of the Khedive or the Sultan, equating it with pan-Islam, and accusing its members of predatory or dishonest motives. In return, the nationalists gave some substance to Cromer's suspicions by flirting with the Khedive, with the Sultan, and with pan-Islam. These flirtations naturally blurred the constitutional outlines of their propaganda, which resolved itself into a series of uncoordinated attacks on various aspects and actions of the Administration. These attacks were made in the Press, in public speeches, and by such influence as the nationalists were able to bring to bear on the proceedings of the Legislative Council and the General Assembly, whose debates, from about 1900 onwards, became more and more critical of the Administration.

Partly because of the difficulties imposed by the Capitulations, and partly because Cromer seems genuinely to have believed in the virtues of a free Press and free speech as safety-valves for discontent, a very considerable measure of freedom of criticism continued to be permitted in Egypt. There was none of the tyranny which has come to be associated with the police State. When the atmosphere of debate became momentarily overheated, another battalion or so was added to the British garrison. It was hardly ever necessary to call this garrison out. Their mere presence, and the almost hypnotic authority which Cromer came to exert over Egypt, were sufficient to prevent serious political violence.

There were various factors in Cromer's favour. First, there was the undoubted fact that the agricultural population, and the Egyptian and foreign merchant and commercial communities, had benefited from British rule and were reasonably contented with it. Secondly, the various individuals and movements arrayed against the British were hopelessly divided by personal antipathies and in their political aims. The Khedive quarrelled alternately with the Sultan and with Mustafa Kamil. As an intelligent and Western-educated agnostic, he had no enthusiasm for pan-Islam, and no desire to emphasise his vassalage to the Sultan. As an autocrat *manqué*, he had no enthusiasm for Mustafa Kamil's con-stitutionalism. But, in view of his permanent quarrel with Cromer, he could not afford to isolate himself either from the traditional influence of the Sultan-Caliph on his right, or from the rising power of con-stitutional nationalism on his left. Meanwhile, having abandoned any hope of an accommodation with Cromer, he devoted himself to self-

enrichment by a number of devious and discreditable means which provided Cromer with ammunition for harassing and humiliating him, and
which confirmed Mustafa Kamil in the personal dislike he had taken to
him. Mustafa Kamil, whose personal and political affinities were with
the Turkish constitutionalists—the Committee of Union and Progress—
and who was scornful both of the Sultan and of the Khedive in private,
tried publicly to keep his lines open with both, and so far succeeded with
the Sultan that, in 1904, he was created a Pasha of the Ottoman Empire.

There was another, minor, Egyptian force with which Mustafa Kamil
and the Hizb el-Watani—the Nationalist Party founded under Mustafa
Kamil's leadership in 1906—had to reckon. Mohamed Abdu and the
Islamic Modernists, together with a number of Egyptian landlords and
professional men, were almost equally repelled by pan-Islam and by the
prospect of Khedivial absolutism, and were distrustful of Mustafa Kamil
because of his equivocal attitudes towards the Sultan and the Khedive.
In this group Cromer, or rather his Oriental Secretary Harry Boyle,
discerned the germ of a moderate and cooperative nationalism which
might be discreetly encouraged as an offset to what they regarded as
fanatical and extreme nationalism. It was with British encouragement
therefore that the Hizb el-Umma (People's Party) was formed. Cromer,
who overestimated its pro-British sympathies, lamented its lack of
influence. He referred in his last Annual Report[3] to 'a small but increasing
number of Egyptians of whom comparatively little is heard, but who
deserve that title (*i.e.* nationalist) quite as much as their competitors of a
different school of thought and action. I allude to the Party which . . . I
may call the followers of the late Mufti, Shaikh Mohamed Abdu . . .
Their fundamental idea is to reform the various Moslem institutions
without shaking the main pillars on which the faith of Islam rests. They
are truly nationalist in the sense of wishing to advance the interests of
their countrymen and co-religionists, but they are not tainted with pan-
Islamism. Their programme . . . involves not opposition to but cooperation with Europeans in the introduction of Western civilisation into the
country.'

Another factor in Cromer's favour, after the signature of the Anglo-
French Agreement in 1904, was the fact that the nationalists could no
longer rely on French support in opposing the British occupation. One
result of this was to convert the previous friendly sentiments which the
nationalist leaders had had towards France into feelings of bitter resentment at what they felt to have been a cynical betrayal.

With all these factors in favour of the British occupation, the activities
of Mustafa Kamil and his associates presented no very serious problem
until 1906, when three events combined to strengthen the nationalists on

the one hand and to weaken the validity of Cromer's policy on the other. The first, in point of time, was the defeat of Balfour's Conservative Government in the General Election held at the end of January, and the coming into office of a Liberal Administration, with Campbell-Bannerman as Prime Minister and Sir Edward Grey as Foreign Secretary. The second, in April, was a dispute with Turkey over the Sinai frontier. The third, in July, was the famous incident at Denshawai.

The first of these events brought into office a Government which seemed likely to be less sympathetic towards Cromer's autocracy and more amenable to nationalist pressure than its predecessor. The second brought the British Administration in Egypt into direct collision with the sentiments of pan-Islam. The third provided the nationalists with a long-awaited opportunity of discrediting Cromer's policy in the eyes both of English Liberals and of the Egyptian masses.

The Conservative Administration which had been in office for the previous ten years, first with Salisbury as both Prime Minister and Foreign Secretary, and then with Balfour as Prime Minister and Lansdowne as Foreign Secretary, had placed their unrestricted confidence in Cromer's policies in Egypt, which policies had, in fact, been initiated by Cromer rather than by the home Government. The signature of the Anglo-French Agreement had seemed to set the seal on these policies, which were fairly well-known to a wide circle as the result of the publication of the Annual Reports. Cromer's views, as expressed in these Reports, were generally shared in England, both by the Government and by the man-in-the-street, but there was a certain amount of criticism about lack of constitutional progress, and a little unease about Cromer's notoriously bad relations with the Khedive. In informed circles there was a feeling that something ought to be done about one or other of these matters, if not about both. But, so long as there appeared to be no trouble in Egypt, the criticism was muted and the unease no more than a penumbra of doubt about Cromer's masterful ways.

The advent of the Liberal Government was not marked by any sudden or open change in British policy towards Egypt, and full support was given to Cromer in a crisis over Egypto-Turkish relations which arose within a few weeks of their coming into office. This became known as the Aqaba incident and arose out of the old uncertainty about the precise location of the frontier between Egypt and Turkey in the Sinai Peninsula. This frontier had not been defined in the 1841 Firman conferring on Mohamed Ali the hereditary possession of Egypt and, in the Firman of appointment issued to Abbas Hilmi in 1892, the Sultan had made an attempt to define it as running from el-Arish to Suez. Cromer had successfully protested against this and, on his insistence, the Firman had been amended, in the form of a letter from the Grand Vizier to the Khedive, to provide that the frontier should be drawn in a direct line between el-Arish and Aqaba, with el-Arish in Egyptian and Aqaba in Turkish, territory (see p. 157). The matter did not appear to be of much practical importance, since the disputed region was uninhabited, except for a few Beduin, and was not regularly administered.

In March 1906 it was brought to Cromer's notice that a small detach-ment of Turkish troops had set up camp at a small village called Tabah, a few miles west of Aqaba and so within Egyptian territory according to the line laid down in the Grand Vizier's letter in 1892. There were already rumours that the Sultan intended to extend the Damascus–Medina rail-way, which he was then having built, by the construction of a branch line between Ma'an and Aqaba. Cromer, who had taken a firm line about this frontier in 1892, and who regarded any Turkish encroachment in the direction of the Suez Canal as a potential threat to the British occupation of Egypt, complained to London and asked that the Sultan should be told to withdraw his troops from Egyptian territory. The Sultan at first refused to do so and only gave way after what amounted to an ultimatum had been sent to Constantinople by the British Govern-ment. The frontier was subsequently defined by a mixed Commission which settled it in the sense of the Grand Vizier's letter in 1892.[4]

The importance of this apparently trivial incident lay in the extent of popular support for the Sultan manifested in Egypt. This support was of two kinds, both disquieting for the British Government. There was the 'tactical' support given, secretly, by the Khedive, and, more openly, by the nationalists. Neither the Khedive nor the nationalists could be suspected of any real enthusiasm for Abdul Hamid's alleged designs on Egypt, any more than for the British occupation. But evidence that, as between the Turks and the British, they apparently preferred the Turk as the lesser evil came as something of a shock to those who had prided themselves on the beneficence of the British occupation, who remembered something of the hatred with which the Turks had previously been regarded in Egypt, who knew of Abdul Hamid's bloodstained and reactionary record, and who realised that part of the price that had been paid for the continuance of the British occupation had been the severance of the traditional British alliance with Turkey. The other kind of support, which was even more disquieting, was the 'fanatical' backing given to the Sultan in his capacity as Caliph in a dispute, which was seen as a dispute between the Moslem Suzerain and the Christian occupier of Egypt over a matter which had explosive implications in that the disputed territory was on the pilgrim route between Cairo and Mecca. Cromer stated later[5] that 'we were within measurable distance of an outburst in

Egypt last Spring' and expressed the view that such an outburst was only averted by a timely increase in the British garrison, which he had requested and received.

As a result of the Aqaba incident it began to be appreciated in British political circles, perhaps for the first time, that the occupation, on which the British position in the Near East was now seen to depend, was endangered, not by the attitude of the European Powers, who had been 'squared' by the 1904 Anglo-French Agreement, but by the unpopularity of that occupation among the Egyptians themselves.

It is against this background that the effect of the Denshawai incident on British Government and Parliamentary opinion must be viewed, bearing in mind that the new House of Commons contained a large majority of Liberal backbenchers who were, many of them, sympathetically inclined towards emergent nationalism and traditionally suspicious of benevolent despotism.

In June 1906 a detachment of British mounted infantry marching from Cairo to Alexandria encamped outside the village of Denshawai in the Delta. A party of British officers went pigeon-shooting and became embroiled with the villagers. A fracas ensued in which some villagers were wounded when a shotgun accidentally went off while the officers were being forcibly disarmed. The officers were badly knocked about before making their escape and one of them, Captain Bull, collapsed and died from the combined effects of sunstroke and the wounds he had received.

Under the terms of a Decree promulgated in 1895, provision had been made for the convening of Special Tribunals, consisting partly of British and partly of Egyptian judges, with unlimited powers of sentence and from whose judgements there was no appeal, to try offences alleged to have been committed against members of the Army of Occupation. Such a Tribunal was set up within a few days of Captain Bull's death to try a number of Denshawai villagers accused of murdering him and assaulting the other British officers. The President of this Tribunal was Butros Pasha Ghali, a Copt, who, as Foreign Minister, had signed the 1899 Sudan Convention on behalf of the Egyptian Government, and who was later to be Prime Minister. But the dominant figure on the Tribunal was the English Vice-President, Sir Walter Bond, Vice-President of the National Court of Appeal. As a result of the trial, four of the villagers were condemned to death, four to life imprisonment, three to fifteen years, six to seven years, three to one year with fifty lashes, and five to fifty lashes. Thirty-one were acquitted. The sentences of death by hanging, and the floggings, were carried out in public outside the village of Denshawai the day after they were pronounced in the presence of a strong British military guard.[6]

It is unlikely that the execution of these sentences, excessive and indeed barbarous as they were, would have provoked very much organised protest in Egypt had it not been for the explosion of feeling which took place in England. Left to themselves, it would probably not have occurred to the nationalist leaders to make very much of an issue about the hanging and flogging of a few peasants. But, from the British reactions to the incident, Mustafa Kamil and his associates soon realised that the British Administration in Egypt had incurred the violent disapproval of a large body of opinion in England and that Cromer's whole policy of benevolent despotism was being seriously called in question as being less benevolent and more despotic than had generally been assumed. As a result of Denshawai, Egyptian nationalism could count on a favourable hearing in England for the first time since 1882.

Cromer, who had caused the Special Tribunal to be convened, was on his way to England at the time of the trial. Immediately after the trial, Findlay, the First Secretary who was acting for Cromer, telegraphed Grey advising him of the sentences, informing him that they were to be carried out immediately, and stating that 'any interference on the part of HMG is earnestly to be deprecated.' The telegram went on: 'I am convinced that Lord Cromer would concur in my opinion that the Court was not inspired by panic or vindictiveness; the evidence proved premeditation and concerted action.'⁷ Grey, in spite of the fact that he regarded the sentences as 'startlingly severe,' and in spite of the obviously defensive note in Findlay's telegram, decided, after consultation with CampbellBannerman, the Prime Minister, and Asquith, the Home Secretary, that the Cabinet should not interfere. He recorded, however, that 'when the full facts were before me, I felt that what had been done was open to question.'⁸ Cromer came to see Grey immediately after he had arrived in England and heard about the sentences and their execution. 'He was greatly disturbed; he realised to the full the bad effect on public opinion. He said that if he had had any notion that such things might happen he would never have left Egypt before the trial was over.' But 'he was very emphatic that it would have been a capital error to overrule the Tribunal when once the sentences had been pronounced, taking very strongly the view that to throw over the authority on the spot would be disastrous, especially in the state of feeling then in Egypt.'⁹

There was a great deal of agitation in England. The *Manchester Guardian,* primed by Wilfrid Blunt, took the matter up. There were questions in Parliament. Mustafa Kamil, who had been in Paris at the time of the incident, came over to London and was introduced by Blunt, with whom he had been in touch for some time, to J. M. Robertson, the Radical MP for NewcastleuponTyne, and other backbench MPs, who formed an unofficial Egyptian Committee with the object of pressing upon the Government the necessity for reforms in Egypt. Robertson paid a visit to Egypt the following Winter to see things for himself. Although he annoyed Cromer by his criticisms, he seems to have taken a fairly objective view of things.

The agitation caused in England by the Denshawai incident, the criticisms of the Cromer régime voiced in the British Press and in the House of Commons, the sympathetic reception accorded to Mustafa Kamil and other Egyptian nationalists who visited England (Mustafa Kamil had an interview with Campbell-Bannerman), led to a tremendous increase in the volume and fervour of nationalist activity. Something of the euphoria which they were feeling was expressed by Blunt in his diary at the end of 1906. 'My half-dead hopes connected with Egypt have come into political blossom. We have smitten Cromer hip and thigh from Tabah to Denshawai . . . Never since Tel el-Kebir have the fortunes of Egyptian nationalism seemed so smiling.'[10]

The result of this euphoria, paradoxically, was not to strengthen and consolidate the position of Hizb el-Watani under the leadership of Mustafa Kamil, but to encourage a proliferation of 'splinter' nationalist parties and groups, each with its own newspaper, each competing with the other to secure the attention and support both of Egyptian audiences and of European sympathisers and, before long, each denouncing the others for venality, lack of patriotism and double-dealing. During the Winter of 1906–07, Hafiz Awad, the Editor of el-Mimbar, the organ of the Islamic Modernists, paid a visit to London, talked with British sympathisers and, later, acted as Robertson's guide during that MP's tour of Egypt. At about the same time, Shaikh Ali Yusef, the Editor of el-Muayyad, with whom Mustafa Kamil had started his journalistic career, and who had formed a political club called the Constitutional Reform League, also visited London. This sort of competition was not at all to Mustafa Kamil's taste and there was a brisk exchange of polemics in the various organs of the nationalist Press.

The published programmes of the various nationalist groups were relatively moderate and not dissimilar. The programme of Mustafa Kamil's Hizb el-Watani included: (1) The autonomy of Egypt under Ottoman suzerainty as established in 1841 by the Treaty of London; (2) The institution of representative government 'so that the governing authority may be responsible to a parliament possessing authority like that of European parliaments'; (3) Respect for treaties and financial conventions; (4) The transference of criminal jurisdiction over foreigners from the Consular to the Mixed Courts; (5) The inculcation of harmony between Moslems and Copts.[11]

In this there was no specific demand for evacuation, although the first item of the programme could be taken to imply it; there was (in items 3 and 4) an implicit acceptance of existing international restrictions on Egypt's sovereignty; item 5 provides evidence of the sensitivity always shown by Mustafa Kamil (who was not himself by any means a fanatical, or even a devout, Moslem) and Hizb el-Watani generally about the accusations of fanaticism with which their opponents tried to discredit them.

Hafiz Awad's programme, as communicated in a petition to Grey during his visit to London in 1906, included demands for: (1) Free and compulsory education in kuttabs (kindergartens) and primary schools; (2) Arabic as the medium of instruction in all schools; (3) Increased powers for the Legislative Council; (4) The gradual replacement of European Government officials by Egyptians; (5) The transfer of criminal jurisdiction over foreigners from the Consular to the Mixed Courts.[12] The programme of Shaikh Ali Yusef and the Constitutional Reform League comprised the first, second and fourth items of the Hizb el-Watani programme and the first, second, fourth and fifth items of Hafiz Awad's programme. It was, in one respect, more extreme than the Hizb el-Watani programme in that it claimed the fulfillment of 'the pledges given and the declarations made by Great Britain at the time of the occupation.'[13]

There was nothing very alarming or unreasonable about any of these programmes, although there was some reason for disquiet, and a considerable element of unreason, in the polemics of the nationalist Press, whose threats, exaggeration and vituperation, and whose internecine quarrels, gave an impression of immaturity, irresponsibility and disunity which discouraged British sympathisers with, and encouraged British denigrators of, the aims of Egyptian nationalism. In the eyes of nearly all Anglo-Egyptian officials, of most of the Conservative Party and Press in England, and perhaps of those of the not very liberal Foreign Secretary, the real offence of the nationalists was not the content of their programmes, nor even the sometimes childish behaviour of their supporters. What they really objected to was that people whom they considered, almost as an article of faith, to be incapable of ruling themselves, and to have been redeemed from barbarism by the wise and altruistic efforts of the British Administration, should have the presumption and ingratitude to criticise and to call in question the beneficent dispositions of that Administration. The incidental violence, immaturity and disunity displayed by the nationalists were really welcomed by Cromer and by the other British opponents of nationalism as providing a plausible reason for discrediting and dismissing demands which, presented in a less emotional way, would have been difficult to ignore.

During the fifteen months which elapsed between the accession of the Liberal Government to office in the Spring of 1906 and Cromer's resignation in the early Summer of 1907, relations between the Foreign Office and the British Agency in Cairo became progressively more strained. While Grey was firm in declaring that it was 'the settled intention of HMG to maintain the continuance of the British occupation,'[14] he complained that the effect of the Denshawai sentences had been mischievous, suggested the advisability of revising some of the prison sentences imposed,[15] criticised the 'want of public spirit' on the part of some of the British officials in Egypt[16] and hinted generally at the desirability of moving a little faster in the direction of giving more responsibility to Egyptians. (By this he meant conceding more power and independence to Egyptian Ministers and officials; at no time did he urge or even suggest the desirability of the 'democratic' reforms being urged by the nationalists.)

In reply to these criticisms and suggestions, Cromer drew attention to the recent appointment of Saad Zaghlul as Minister of Education, and went on: 'Of course it is anticipated that we shall go further in the direction of pushing on the natives. I am quite prepared to do so, but I shall not be in too great a hurry. I want to see how the present experiment succeeds. What I want from natives in the higher positions is by no means absolute submission to British advice, but intelligent cooperation . . . I fear that the Khedive remains as hostile as ever. I am convinced that he personally is the heart and fount of all the opposition here.' About Denshawai he wrote: 'I will not go so far as to say that no portion of the sentences should ever be remitted but it would be altogether premature to raise the question now.'[17]

Later, in March 1907, Cromer wrote a long private letter to Grey plainly indicating his view that he was not getting sufficient support from him. 'There is a growing tendency to believe that the Government at home do not understand the hollowness of the Robertsonian policy.[18] The main reasons why I stay on here are (i) because I want to carry through the reform of the Capitulations which I doubt whether anyone else can get, even if I can do it; and (2) because I feel very strongly the hopelessness of the situation in general if I have any appearance of being driven out by the Mustafa Kamils, Khedives, Robertsons, Diceys,[19] and all the rest of the pack who are now barking and snarling at my heels. Also, I do not like to see the work of a lifetime wrecked by simple folly . . . The difficulties of the situation are, in reality, not in the least local . . . They arise entirely from the supposed sympathy in England with the ultra-opposition here . . . I know the difficulty of reconciling an Imperial policy with democratic tendencies at home . . . Unless great care is taken . . . the Government will have to face this difficulty in

Egyptian affairs before long. You will be driven into one of two courses—
(1) evacuation or (ii) annexation . . . The Robertson policy is to maintain
the occupation and rapidly to advance in the direction of Egyptian
autonomy. Gradual development in this direction is possible but . . . to
suppose that, while the occupation lasts, we can leave the extremely
incompetent Egyptians to do what they like about local affairs is madness.
I should really prefer evacuation . . . The only method of avoiding a crisis
is that you, in the name of HMG, should take an early opportunity of dis-
sociating yourself in the strongest and most emphatic terms from Robertson
and his crew; if you do not do so . . . they will land you in difficulties
greater than you realise.'[20]

Over the next three weeks Cromer wrote several further letters to Grey
complaining about Parliamentary criticism,[21] commenting adversely on
the unaccustomed control which the Government sought to exercise from
London,[22] and protesting against a Cabinet decision that in future
alleged offences against British troops in Egypt should be tried by the
National Courts.[23] Eventually, on 28 March, he cabled his resignation.
In a letter written to Grey the same day he gave his health as a reason,
telling him that 'in spite of all my efforts at decentralisation, the tendency
is to throw the work and responsibility more and more on my shoulders.
Gorst's departure[24] has made a great difference to me. Except for Garstin
I have absolutely no one who is not departmental in the narrow sense.'
He asked that the announcement of his resignation should be accom-
panied by a public statement emphasising that no change of policy was
intended in Egypt, and recommended that Gorst should succeed him.[25]
He left Egypt less than a month later.

When Wilfrid Blunt heard the news of Cromer's resignation, he
recorded in his diary that he 'was feeling like a huntsman at the end of
his day's sport, with Cromer's brush in my pocket and the mask of that
ancient red fox dangling from my saddle.'[26] Mustafa Kamil, in a letter
to his mentor Juliette Adam, expressed much the same feelings in more
sober language: '*Le mouvement national se developpe beaucoup et la chute de
Lord Cromer est une excellent chose pour nous. Si Dieu me donne les forces pour
continuer la lutte cinq ans seulement, nous arriverons à des grands resultats.*'[27]

In a public comment on Cromer's resignation, published in his newspaper *el-Liwa* on 12 April, Kamil wrote that Egypt would remember
that Cromer had usurped Khedivial authority, that he had conquered
the Sudan with Egyptian men and money and then denuded Egyptians
of every influence there, that he had deprived Egyptians of any influence
in the government of their own country, that he had attacked the Moslem
religion, that he had deprived Egyptians of their right to education, that
he had insisted that Egyptians be ruled by Englishmen, that he had

denigrated Egyptian nationalism, and that he had made of Egypt a British colony. The verdict of the more moderate nationalists was given next day by Lutfi-as-Sayyid in an article in *el-Jarida*, the organ of Hizb el-Umma. He paid tribute to Cromer as an economist and financier but accused him of depriving Egypt of the kind of political life to which every nation aspired. Though he had given personal freedom to Egyptians, he had deprived Egyptian Government servants of all initiative. Through his educational policy he had tried to keep Egyptians subservient to British interests, for the low level at which he had kept Egyptian education had given him the excuse to import Englishmen to do jobs which other-wise Egyptians would have been capable of doing.

In his last Annual Report before his departure[28] Cromer summed up his impressions of Egyptian nationalism. He described it as an 'entirely novel idea,' 'a plant of exotic rather than of indigenous growth,' and 'deeply tinged with Panislamism.' After giving a warning about the implications of pan-Islam which 'certainly requires to be carefully watched by all European nations which have political interests in the East,' which 'means, in Egypt, more or less complete subservience to the Sultan' and which 'almost necessarily connotes a recrudescence of racial and religious animosity,' he recognised that constitutionalism existed side by side with pan-Islam in the nationalist movement, but expressed his conviction that 'Panislamism is the predominant partner.' Referring to the constitutional element, he stated that 'what is demanded is a wide and immediate extension of Parliamentary institutions,' meaning 'first the creation of a Ministry responsible to the Chamber and dependent for its existence on the maintenance of a majority; and secondly complete control over the finances of the country such as that exercised by the elected Chambers in the United Kingdom and in other European countries.' He expressed the opinion that 'the adoption of the first of these proposals would produce a state of things which may without exaggeration be termed chaotic,' and that 'the adoption of the second proposal . . . would almost inevitably lead to national bankruptcy.' He concluded that there was 'no hope for Egyptian nationalism in the form in which that idea is conceived by the Egyptian National Party' (*i.e.* Hizb el-Watani) and went on to commend the 'moderate' Hizb el-Umma in the terms which have already been quoted.

He had already, soon after his return to Egypt in the Autumn of 1906, signified his approval of this Party, and recognised the validity of some of the criticisms which had been made of the Administration's educational policy, by arranging for the elevation of the Department of Public Instruction into a Ministry, and for the appointment of Saad Zaghlul, a member of Hizb el-Umma, as Minister. This involved the promotion of Mr Dunlop, the Adviser, from Departmental to Ministerial Adviser, an appointment which nullified any educational advantages which might otherwise have been gained. (See Chapter 13.)

In his farewell speech at the Opera House, delivered to a mainly European audience, Cromer deprecated 'any brisk change and any violent, new departure' and stated: 'The British occupation is to continue for an indefinite period. So long as that occupation continues the British Government must of necessity be responsible, not indeed for the details, but for the main lines on which the Administration is conducted. I shall urge that the wholly spurious and manufactured development of parliamentary institutions should be treated for what it is worth, and gentlemen, let me add that it is worth very little.' He appealed, as one who 'claims always to have been their true friend' to the 'blue-shirted fellahin on whose labours the prosperity of the country really depends,' not to allow themselves 'to be duped and misled by their pseudo-representatives who, without a shadow of real authority, credit them with ideas which they neither entertain nor fully comprehend, and who advocate a political programme, the immediate adoption of which, while detrimental to all other interests, would . . . be specially hurtful to those of the poorest classes of the community.'

Sir Eldon Gorst who, on Cromer's recommendation, succeeded him as British Agent and Consul-General, was forty-six years of age at the time of his appointment. He had first come to Egypt in 1886 as an Attaché at the British Agency. In 1890 he had transferred to Egyptian Govern-ment service and entered the Ministry of Finance as Controller of Direct Taxes. In 1892 he had succeeded Milner as Under Secretary at the Ministry of Finance. In 1894 Cromer arranged for his appointment as Adviser to the Interior in pursuance of his policy of introducing more British control into that Ministry. In 1898 he was promoted to Financial Adviser, the senior British official post in the Egyptian Government, on the retirement of Sir Elwin Palmer. By this time, the measure of sub-ordination of the Egyptian Ministers was such that the Financial Adviser was, to all intents and purposes, a Prime Minister ruling the country under Cromer's dictatorship. Gorst established good relations with the Khedive and seems to have been instrumental in keeping the peace between the Khedive and Cromer during his term as Financial Adviser, which lasted until 1904. His last important work before leaving this position was to go to London and Paris in the Winter of 1903-04 to negotiate the financial clauses of the Anglo-French Agreement. In the Spring of 1904, just after the signature of the Agreement, he went to the Foreign Office as Assistant Under Secretary. He had already been given to understand that he was earmarked as Cromer's successor and regarded his long career in Egypt as an ideal apprenticeship for what was in store for him. He looked forward keenly to the appointment, noting that 'throughout the British Empire there is no place of which the occupant enjoys greater freedom of action than that of British Agent and Consul General in Egypt. The Consul-General is the *de facto* ruler of the country, without being hampered by a Parliament or by a network of Councils like the Viceroy of India, and the interference of the home Government has hitherto been limited to such matters as are likely to arouse interest or criticism in the British House of Commons. Otherwise, HM's Representative can practically run the government on whatever lines he thinks right.'[29]

Gorst appears to have received no detailed instructions from Grey when he took over as British Agent on 7 May 1907. 'My first care was to take stock of the existing situation . . . Things had for some time being going from bad to worse and it was time that they were taken in hand. The whole machinery of government absolutely depended on one man . . . Lord Cromer . . . was no longer able to keep his team in hand. The team itself was far from satisfactory . . . Lord Cromer's local policy had in my opinion got on to the wrong lines. The growth of the national spirit had pushed him into an attitude of antagonism to the Egyptian Moslems generally, and he was trying to counterbalance (them) by leaning towards the European colonies and the various sections of native Christians . . . The chief result of encouraging them was to strengthen the Moslem opposition to the occupation. The anti-Egyptian attitude into which Lord Cromer had gradually drifted . . . was rendered more acute by the hostility . . . between himself and the Khedive (and) had greatly strengthened the influence of the extreme nationalists over respectable Egyptian Moslems.' He went on to list two factors which had further embittered the situation. The first was the Denshawai affair which he described as 'our worst mismanaged piece of work since the beginning of the occupation.' The second was 'the increasing number of the Anglo-Egyptian officials and their increasingly anti-Egyptian and anti-Khedive attitude.'[30]

After taking stock of the situation, Gorst noted the general lines of the policy which he intended to pursue:

'(1) While outwardly proclaiming that Cromer's policy was unchanged, to apply the prescriptions laid down in his Annual Reports rather than to follow the actual practice of recent years; in a word, to carry into execution the many excellent and statesmanlike maxims which abounded in Cromer's writings, but which had remained in the stage of pious opinions.

'(2) To avoid setting up contentious questions or providing new points of attack for the nationalist party in Egypt or for hostile critics in the House of Commons.

'(3) To render our rule more sympathetic to the Egyptians in general and to the Moslems in particular by restoring good feeling between the Anglo-Egyptian officials and the natives of the country, and preventing the British element from riding roughshod over the Egyptians, by putting a check on the annual British invasion of new recruits, by giving greater encouragement to the Egyptian official class, and . . . by giving a more national character to the educational system.

'(4) To resume Cromer's original attitude of hostility to European privilege and to try and unite English and Egyptian interests by the policy of one and the same law for all the inhabitants of the country.

'(5) To cultivate good relations with the Khedive, so that his influence and prestige—whatever they may be worth—may be an asset on our side of the account. My trump card . . . was to hold out to HH the prospect of reconciliation with the King and Royal Family provided he behaved well in local matters.

'(6) To settle various matters regarding pay and pensions of officers and officials which had been allowed to remain open.

'(7) To supervise the administration of the Sudan on sound lines, to provide for material development, to keep a tight rein on expenditure, but to interfere with the man on the spot as little as possible.'[31]

The salient point about Gorst's policy was that it was a serious attempt to implement, and to accelerate, what was, in theory, a declared object of British policy under Cromer—the giving of increased responsibility to Egyptians in the machinery of administration. In practice, over the previous twelve years, things had been moving in the opposite direction. In the capital, the Ministers had become puppets. Each had a British Adviser attached to him who really ran the Ministry, assisted by a band of senior British officials. There was hardly any Egyptian official in any position of real responsibility, and it was becoming almost impossible even for a capable Egyptian to attain any such position. In the Provinces the authority of the Mudirs and Mamurs (Governors and District Commissioners) was circumscribed and almost nullified by numbers of British Mufattishin (Inspectors) from the various Ministries, reporting direct to the British Adviser at his particular Ministry. Many of these British officials, particularly the younger ones, were neither very well qualified, nor very tactful, nor very experienced in the ways of the country. More importantly, they impaired the authority and prestige of senior Egyptian officials, blocked the advance of junior ones, and prevented the employment of others.

The British occupation, at the time of Gorst's arrival, was simultaneously faced with two forms of indigenous discontent. There was the vociferous discontent of the nationalists who, encouraged by the European *Zeitgeist,* wanted representative government, parliamentary institutions, and all the rest of the fashionable nostrums. And there was the quiescent, but none-theless deep-seated, discontent of the official and ruling class, from the Khedive downwards, who saw themselves and their descendants being pushed further and further away from the prospect of exercising real authority, however well-educated, or however well-qualified, they might become. In retrospect, it seems obvious that a continuation of the policy of anglicising the Administration, which had been drifted into rather than adopted deliberately, would, by depriving educated Egyptians of the chance of responsible careers, compel them to be nationalist agitators as a means of getting rid of the British. However hostile they might have been to the concept of representative institutions, they could hardly be expected to incur the odium of resistance to the nationalists in order to preserve a despotism wielded not by themselves but by the British.

Gorst's deliberate policy was to give real and increasing authority to Egyptian Ministers and senior officials and, by so doing, to give the Egyptian ruling and official class a vested interest in opposing that demand for representative institutions which both they and the British considered premature and unwise. Cromer's policy of encouraging 'moderate' nationalism was not viable since, apart from the solitary example of appointing Saad Zaghlul Minister of Education, it was not accompanied by a policy which made it worth any responsible Egyptian's while to support. Gorst equated 'moderation' with the old tradition of indigenous autocracy and sought to ally himself with it against the newer democratic ambitions of the nationalists. It has generally been assumed that he failed. But, in fact, in spite of an apparent reversion under Kitchener, and in spite of conditions of martial law and intensified British control during the First World War, Egyptian Ministers, under the impetus given by Gorst, never returned to the state of puppetry to which Mustafa Fahmy and his Cabinet had descended. The vested interest in indigenous autocracy which Gorst revived was, in course of time, to create a balance in Egyptian domestic affairs which had the effect, both of prolonging British influence in Egypt and of moderating inevitable Anglo-Egyptian dissensions.

Because Cromer was merely a Consul-General and not an Ambassador, and in spite of the fact that he had been receiving Ambassadorial emolu-ments of over £6,500 a year during his last years in Egypt, he was only entitled to a pension of £900 a year on retirement instead of an Ambas-sador's pension of £1,700 a year. In order to make up for this, and as a mark of appreciation for his outstanding services, the Government asked the Commons to vote 'that a sum not exceeding £50,000 be granted to

HM to be issued to the Earl of Cromer OM, GCB, GCMG, KCSI, CIE, in recognition of his eminent services as Agent and Consul-General in Egypt.' Sir Henry Campbell-Bannerman, the Prime Minister, proposing the vote in the Commons on 24 May 1907,[32] and referring to 'the great Province whose reconstruction he made the business of his life,' delivered the following eulogy:

'The external trade of Egypt has doubled since he became Agent and Consul-General in 1883. The irrigation works carried out during his Consulate have been the means of creating out of the desert fair and fertile tracts of vast extent. In the same period the population of Egypt has increased from $6\frac{3}{4}$ to $9\frac{3}{4}$ million. Egypt has suffered, and still suffers, from heavy taxation but, notwithstanding the great outlay which all the improvements effected in the public services entailed, Lord Cromer succeeded in reducing the burden of taxation by 25 per cent and the charge for interest on the debt was reduced by £890,000 p.a. . . . He never lost sight of the paramount duty of economical administration or forgot that the taxes were paid by the peasants out of their poverty . . . But his countrymen are even prouder of the security and liberty which his labours have secured for Egypt, and of the revival of justice and the work he did for education, than of the material results which he obtained . . . Lord Cromer belongs to a school of administrators who hold it wise to hasten slowly in superimposing the civilisation of one race upon another, and we must bear that in mind if we are to appreciate the methods he employed and the spirit he brought to his work . . . He profoundly disbelieved in any attempt to force the Egyptian people into a Western mould. He sought to preserve what was vital and characteristic in their habits, laws and customs . . . and made it his business to understand their character and to study their grievances and their needs . . . By working through mediums familiar to them and employing as far as possible native agents, he hoped in time to enable them to develop along their own lines . . . When I see him criticised for his want of sympathy with the national spirit I am disposed to ask whether his wise and patient and understanding administration and the respect shown by him to the Egyptian race do not entitle him to be called a great national administrator . . . He saw that the regeneration of Egypt could only be effected by the Egyptians themselves, and in devising means of emancipating the peasantry from debt and preserving them on their own holdings, he laid the foundations of an agrarian policy which is equally the foundation of modern Egypt.'

Balfour, Leader of the Conservative Opposition, supporting the motion, was even more eulogistic. 'Lord Cromer's services have raised Egypt from the lowest pitch of social and economic degradation until it now stands among Oriental nations absolutely alone in its prosperity, financial and moral. There is no triumph of civilisation to which he has not contributed—material, moral and intellectual. Everything he has touched has succeeded, every cause he has taken in hand he has furthered, and he left Egypt to look back on an administration longer, more beneficent, more fruitful, the results of which are more obviously apparent to all who have eyes to see and ears to hear than can be boasted of by any of his great predecessors . . . who have carried on a great civilising work among natives who . . . cannot rise to the level of those whose lot it is to govern.'

This was the official and, to some extent, the real opinion of the Establishment. But, when the debate on the vote was resumed on 30 May,[33] other points of view were expressed. John Redmond, the Irish nationalist leader, opposing the vote, asked whether Cromer 'was to receive £50,000 because, instead of carrying out the policy of evacuation which he was ordered to do, he had made Egypt into a British Province occupied by an Army which could not for the moment be withdrawn.' He went on: 'Apart from Public Works and finance, Lord Cromer's work in Egypt has been singularly unsuccessful and unfortunate . . . His policy over the Egyptian Army has been a total failure. With very few exceptions every command is held by an Englishman and the greatest possible irritation and indignation is felt by Egyptians in consequence . . . The position in Egypt is much the same as in Ireland, where every position of trust and emolument is in the hands of Englishmen, and the Egyptian people are made to feel that they are hewers of wood and drawers of water in their own country.' He pointed out that Cromer himself had admitted that crime in Egypt was increasing and that, in education, 'the almost unanimous opinion of the people of Egypt is that the educational policy has been that of checking education so as to keep the mass of the Egyptian people in such ignorance that there should be no political advancement.' He said that the Ministry of Justice was almost entirely under British direction and that 'justice was administered by people ignorant of the language.' He cited the Denshawai trial and sentences as evidence that Cromer had not placed the administration of justice on a satisfactory basis and, again referring to Denshawai, charged that 'things have been done in Egypt under Lord Cromer's administration at which civilisation stands shocked.' He concluded: 'I do not grudge Lord Cromer the honours and titles he has received, but I do draw the line at asking for the money of Irish as well as English taxpayers for a gentleman whose name would ever be associated with what was a blot and a disgrace on the name of the British Empire.'

There were other critical speeches in the same sense. Grey, the Foreign Secretary, defending Cromer over Denshawai, said that it was unfair to 'make him responsible for every detailed act of the Egyptian Administration,' and pointed out that Cromer was not in Egypt when the Denshawai sentences were carried out. Robertson, the member for Newcastle-upon-Tyne, who had been one of Cromer's foremost critics, made a fair and moderate speech in which he supported the vote but regretted that Cromer had been referred to by supporters of the grant in such terms of panegyric, 'which could not possibly be the verdict of history.' He went on: 'Egypt is clearly not getting the standard of good government which we exact in this country . . . There has been a failure to maintain higher education at the level at which Lord Cromer found it.' Lord Cromer had instituted 'an absolutely autocratic system of government of which the natural result was such an abuse of justice as Denshawai. No matter what a man's abilities are—and those of Lord Cromer have on some grounds been overstated—no man can act as an autocrat without suffering deterioration.' 'But,' he concluded, 'the nation, having created an autocracy in Egypt, having sent Lord Cromer to Egypt to occupy the post so created, and having backed up the system of which Lord Cromer was the representative, is not entitled to haggle over the grant.'

In the division which took place the grant was approved by 254 votes to 107.

13

THE EGYPTIAN
ACHIEVEMENT

AS ROBERTSON, THE Radical Member for Newcastle-upon-Tyne, stated in the Commons debate on Cromer's grant, the panegyrical accounts of Cromer's achievement in Egypt given by Campbell-Bannerman and Balfour 'could not possibly be the ultimate verdict of history,' any more than the attacks made on his administration by his more extreme critics, whether British or Egyptian, could be.

The extent and nature of that achievement were conditioned in part by the circumstances of the occupation, and by the policy of the British Government, which imposed a pattern of indirect rule, maintained the existing international restrictions on administrative freedom of action, and thereby inhibited any drastic changes in the administrative and social order. Within these general limitations, the extent and nature of Cromer's achievements in Egypt were very largely dictated by Cromer's own very definite views and prejudices, as they developed and hardened during his twenty-three years of office.

These views and prejudices were set down in didactic form in several writings by Lord Cromer after his retirement. It is useful to quote from some of these, as they provide a clue to the policy he pursued while in Egypt, and help to explain the political and administrative achievements and limitations of his régime.

'It is essential that each separate issue should be decided mainly with reference to what, by the light of Western knowledge and experience, tempered by local considerations, we conscientiously think is best for the subject race, without reference to any real or supposed advantage which may accrue to England as a nation or . . . to the special interests represented by some one or more influential classes of Englishmen . . . We need not always enquire too closely what those people who are, nationally speaking, more or less *in statu pupillari,* themselves think is best in their own interests.'

'Though we can never create a patriotism akin to that based on affinity

279

of race or community of language, we may perhaps foster some sort of cosmopolitan allegiance grounded on the respect always accorded to superior talents and unselfish conduct and on the gratitude derived both from favours conferred and from those to come.'

'Whether Imperialism will continue to rest on a sound basis depends in the degree to which the moralising elements in the nation can, without injury to all that is sound and healthy in individualist action, control the defects which may not improbably spring out of the egotism of the commercial spirit.'

'Free institutions, in the full sense of the term, must, for generations to come, be wholly unsuitable to countries such as India and Egypt . . . Do not let us for one moment imagine that the fatally simple idea of despotic rule will readily give way to the far more complex conception of ordered liberty. This transformation, if it takes place at all, will probably be the work, not of generations but, of centuries.'

'The method of Parliamentary institutions is thoroughly uncongenial to Oriental habits of thought. It may be doubted whether, by the adoption of that exotic system, we gain any real insight into native aspirations and opinions . . . Our primary duty is, not to introduce a system which, under the specious cloak of free institutions, will enable a small minority of natives to misgovern their countrymen, but to establish one which will enable the mass of the population to be governed according to the code of Christian morality. A freely elected Parliament, supposing such a thing to be possible, would not improbably legislate for the protection of the slave-owners, if not the slave-dealers . . . Before Orientals can attain anything approaching the British ideal of self-government they will have to undergo numerous transmigrations of political thought.'

'It may be laid down as a principle of universal application that high taxation is incompatible with assured stability of Imperial rule.'

'We cannot . . . effectively prevent the manufacture of demagogues without adopting measures which would render us false to our acknow-ledged principles of government and to our civilising mission. But we may govern in such a manner as to give the demagogue no fulcrum with which to move his credulous and ill-informed countrymen and co-religionists. The leading principles of a Government of this nature should be that low taxation is the most potent instrument with which to conquer discontent . . . If it is to be adopted, two elements of British society will have to be kept in check at the hands of the statesmen acting in concert with the moralist. They are military and commercial egotism. The Empire depends in a great degree on the strength and efficiency of its Army. It thrives on its commerce. But, if the soldiers and the traders are not kept under some degree of control, they are capable of becoming the most formidable, though unconscious, enemies of the British Empire.'[1]

'The main feat accomplished by the rulers of Egypt during the last quarter of a century is not so much that they learnt to do well as that they ceased to do evil. They abstained from misgovernment. For the first time during the long course of Egyptian history Nature was not only given a chance but received some intelligent aid from Man.'

'The rulers and people in this country must be very careful lest, in their well-intentioned . . . efforts to give self-governing powers to the Egyptians, the interests of the masses are not sacrificed to those of the classes.'[2]

'It should never be forgotten that . . . there are certain broad features which always exist when the European . . . is brought into contact with the Oriental—be he Algerian, Indian or Egyptian. When the former once steps outside the influence acquired by the power of the sword and seeks for any common ground of understanding with the subject race, he feels that he is . . . debarred from using all the moral influence which, in more homogeneous countries, binds a society together. These are—a common religion, a common language, common traditions, inter-marriage, and really intimate social relations. What remains? Practically nothing except the bond of material interest . . . But experience shows that a wise statesmanship can build a political edifice . . . of a character which will give some solid qualities of stability . . . No one who was well acquainted with the facts could at any time have thought that it would be possible to create in the minds of the Egyptians a feeling of devotion towards England which might in some degree take the place of patriotism . . . But it was thought that, by careful attention to the material interests of the people, it might be possible to bring into existence a conservative class who, albeit actuated by no great love for their foreign rulers, would be sufficiently content to prevent their becoming easily the prey either of the nationalist demagogues who were sure sooner or later to spring into existence, or that of some barbarous religious fanatic, such as the Mahdi, or that of some wily politician such as Sultan Abdul Hamid, who would, for his own purposes, fan the flame of religious and racial hatred . . . The methods adopted, which were in the main carried out before any large sums were spent on education, were the relief of taxation, the abolition of fiscal inequality and of the *corvée*, the improvement of irrigation and . . . a variety of measures having for their object the main-tenance of a peasant propertied class . . . The best, and indeed the only, way to combat successfully the proceedings of the demagogue and the agitator is to limit his field of action by the removal of any real grievances which, if still existent, he would be able to use as a lever to awaken the blind wrath of Demos.'[3]

'The principle which lies at the root of all sound administration . . . is that administrative and commercial exploitation should not be entrusted to the same hand.'

'The British, though they succeed less well when once the full tide of education has set in, possess in a very high degree the power of acquiring the sympathy and confidence of primitive races.'

'There has been no thorough fusion, no real assimilation between the British and their alien subjects and, so far as we can now predict, the future will be a repetition of the past . . . The foundations of which the barrier wall of separation are built may be . . . the result of prejudice rather than of reason but . . . for generations to come, they will probably defy whatever puny efforts may be made to undermine them.'

(The Englishman) 'is in truth always striving to attain two ideals which are apt to be mutually destructive—the ideal of good government, which connotes the continuance of his own supremacy, and the ideal of self-government, which connotes the whole or partial abdication of his supreme position. The country over which the breath of the West, heavily charged with scientific thought, has passed, and has in passing left an enduring mark, can never be made the same as it was before. The new foundation must be of the western and not the eastern type . . .'

'The idea (*i.e.* of self-government for India) is not only absurd, it is not only impracticable . . . (but) . . . to entertain it would be a crime against civilisation and especially against the voiceless millions in India whose interests are committed to our charge.'[4]

To these sentiments may be added a firm, almost fanatical, belief in *laissez-faire*—free trade, self-help, and a system of social services initiated and financed either by feelings of family solidarity or by the charitable enterprise of well-to-do people, rather than by Government action. (In his political activity after his retirement, Cromer finally broke with the Liberal Party as a result of his opposition to Old Age Pensions and Sick Benefit introduced by the Liberal Government.)

The application of Cromer's views to Egypt is well summed up by a writer on the subject: 'Baring . . . despaired of assimilating the Orient to European religion and culture. The one hope he could see for progress in the East lay in gradually reforming its government and in improving its material condition. Only when all this had been done could the Orient adopt that liberal and humanitarian code of ethics which the Victorians still held must triumph throughout the world. There was something of Bentham and much of the younger Mill in Baring's certainty that scientific administration was the key to progress. His ideas of government were inspired by Indian experience interpreted in the light of the laws of Utilitarian political economy. To him political order was obviously the first requirement for the improvement of character. He was fond of comparing the role of the *Pax Britannica* to that of the *Pax Romana*. Political stability to his mind depended above all upon the contentment and prosperity of the productive classes, especially the mass of the peasantry. For him, as for Mill, the backwardness and "inhumanity" of Oriental society were to be blamed on its quasi-feudal parasitic rulers who throttled freedom and killed enterprise. The task of administration, in Baring's eyes, was to break this vicious circle, to release the peasantry from injustice and extortion, to cleanse the government of corruption, and to achieve a surplus of revenue. The surplus in turn would permit him to lighten taxes, to develop agriculture and public works, and so to improve the lot of the peasant and the prospect of order . . . In the eyes of this financier and administrator, mere politics seemed ineffectual and dishonest . . . He looked upon Egypt with a high sense of duty towards the fellah, contempt for the Pasha, and detestation for the politician . . . His outlook indeed had many virtues, but it was hardly congenial to the business of nursing the country quickly back to independence.'[5]

For his first four years in Egypt, when his primary task was to create conditions which would make evacuation practicable, Cromer concentrated on the achievement of solvency and, apart from the building up of the Egyptian Army under British supervision, avoided any interference in Egyptian administration which was not devoted to this end. He told the British Government that it was necessary to restore the effective authority of the native Government and that any reforms tending to undermine that authority were to be deprecated. But he gradually became convinced that a mere restoration of the authority of the native Government was impracticable. The process of Westernisation was too far advanced, the hopes and aspirations of the masses too much awakened, the *facultas regendi* of the ruling class too much impaired, to make a reversion to a crude Ismailian despotism possible without the near-certainty of serious disturbance. And so, as the near prospect of evacuation receded, and as the financial position improved, Cromer's philosophy of Imperial administration, derived largely from his Indian experience, began to be applied to Egypt. This philosophy implied a steadily increasing measure of British control in order to provide, on the one hand for increased agricultural productivity leading to reduced taxation and greater prosperity, and on the other hand for the improved conduct of the day-to-day administration, with the object of creating a climate of opinion which, for material reasons, would be favourable to the occupation and provide an antidote to the inevitable discontents arising from the political inhibitions and frustrations implicit in prolonged, intensified, and auto-cratic British control of the administration.

Because Cromer believed that Egypt had passed the point of no return in respect of Westernisation, and that consequently any reforms must proceed on Western lines, and because he believed that the Oriental mind was fundamentally different from and essentially inferior to the Western mind, he regarded it as axiomatic that reforms must be introduced and maintained by Western agency and that there was no foreseeable prospect of entrusting these reforms to an indigenous agency without nullifying them in the process. In spite of several official asseverations to the contrary in his Annual Reports, he set his face against any effective Egyptian participation in the higher direction of an increasingly anglicized administration. Still more did he set his face against any development of 'parliamentary institutions' in the form of increased powers for the Legislative Council. He was scornful of the effects of 'parliamentary institutions' even in England and expressed his vehement disapproval of Disraeli's 'leap in the dark' in 1868 which, as he saw it, had set England on the dangerous and slippery slope towards universal franchise. He was utterly contemptuous at the prospect of any kind of parliamentary democracy among 'subject races' and considered that it would make orderly and benevolent government impossible and subordinate the interests of the masses to the wiles of voluble and half-educated demagogues who would manipulate the machinery of democracy in their own interests.

Cromer realised that his prescription for Egypt would lead to political discontent, but he was confident that the material benefits accruing from the occupation—which, as he saw it, could only be obtained by an indefinite prolongation of the occupation and by the maintenance and intensification of effective British control—would create a contented, non-political and conservative body of opinion which would more than outweigh the political discontent. As time went on, he tended more and more to underrate the discontent and to exaggerate the material benefits.

He came to attribute this discontent primarily to the machinations of the Khedive and, in a lesser degree, to the intrigues of Sultan Abdul Hamid. His quarrel with Abbas certainly encouraged this discontent, in that it deprived British rule of that façade of consent which it had enjoyed under Taufiq. Abdul Hamid's pan-Islamic policy, and his successful defiance of the European Powers over Armenia and other matters, certainly encouraged that Moslem fanaticism which was an ingredient, although not so large a one as Cromer professed to believe, in Egyptian nationalism. But, even without these special factors, a foreign autocracy, however benevolent, however efficient, and however tactful, given the spirit of the time, and given the Western influences to which Egypt was exposed, was bound to lead to nationalist protest and opposition, particularly when, as Cromer made quite plain in his Annual Reports and elsewhere, there was no intention in the foreseeable future either of 'egyptianizing' the administration or of subjecting it to any sort of parliamentary check or control.

Even had the British-controlled administration been as benevolent, as efficient, and as tactful as Cromer and the Anglo-Egyptian officials were in the habit of assuming, it is doubtful whether the material prosperity and the relief from oppression thus created would have been sufficient to outweigh the discontents of a politically-conscious minority, many of whom had been educated in Europe, all of whom were in touch with Western ideas, who were contemptuously treated as a subject race, and who were not only deprived of any voice in the government of their country, but who also found themselves, to any increasing extent, debarred from any responsible positions in Government service.

But the beneficent effects of British administration were neither as great nor as widespread as Cromer came to believe. British officials, particularly as they became more numerous, were not invariably efficient and even less invariably tactful. In the Police and in the Ministry of Justice particularly, as Cromer himself admitted,[6] the standard left very much to be desired. English judges in the National Courts were, for the most part, neither very good lawyers nor very good linguists. The general standard of Arabic among British officials was poor. Their habit of segregating themselves among their own countrymen outside office hours (any British official who was 'too friendly with the natives' was regarded as suspect by his fellow-countrymen) prevented them from obtaining any deep understanding of the Egyptian character. The Anglo-Indian tradition, imported into Egypt, of regarding 'Orientals' as inferior beings, deficient in moral sense, unamenable to kindness, and only responsive to a 'firm hand,' inhibited any mutual feelings of sympathy between British officials and their Egyptian colleagues. The indirect nature of British rule blunted much of the impact of genuinely reformist measures introduced by the British Advisers. The beneficent effects of less arbitrary and more humane methods of justice and punishment introduced by the British were to a large extent outweighed, as far as the general well-being was concerned, by a massive increase in crime.

The great positive achievements of Cromer's administration, and the ones of which he was most proud, were the development of irrigation, the abolition of the *corvée* and the reduction of the incidence of taxation.

The development of irrigation included the rehabilitation and re-activation of the Delta barrage, the construction of the Aswan dam and reservoir, the cutting of the Sudd in the Sudan, the digging of new and the realignment of old irrigation canals, the start of a proper agricultural drainage system, and improvements in the maintenance of the canals and in the efficient and equitable distribution of water. The reactivation of the Delta barrage and the construction of the Aswan dam and reservoir enabled the cultivated area to be increased from 4,742,610 feddans to 5,339,638 feddans and the crop area from 4,762,178 feddans to 7,480,546 feddans between 1877 and 1906.[7] This large increase in the crop area, due to the possibility of growing Summer crops on perennially-irrigated land, was the greatest single cause of increased Egyptian prosperity during the first twenty-five years of the British occupation. Evidence of this increased prosperity is provided by the following figures:

Cotton Cultivation

Year	Area under cotton feddans	Av. yield per feddan kantars	Crop 1,000 kantars	Exports 1,000 kantars	Av. price per kantar talaris	Value of cotton exports £E000
1883–84	969,000	2·77	2,686	2,565	13·52	8,385
1905–06	1,567,000	3·80	5,960	6,033	15·11	18,872

(A feddan is about an acre; a kantar is just under one hundredweight, a talari is equivalent to twenty Egyptian piastres or about four shillings.)[8]

Foreign Trade[9]

Year	Imports	Exports
1883	£E8,021,000	£E12,310,000
1906	£E23,980,000	£E25,301,000

During the same period, revenue increased from £E10,587,436 in 1883 to £E16,337,667 in 1906, although as the result of an increase in population from 6¾ to 9¾ million, the incidence of taxation per head decreased by about 25 per cent. More important perhaps, as regards the mass of the rural population, was the abolition of forced labour (*corvée*) except for emergency flood protection. Moreover, some progress had been made towards a more equitable distribution of the land-tax and, in particular, the previous large tax differential between Kharaj and Ushuri lands in favour of the latter, which weighed heavily on small landowners, had been abolished.

These were considerable achievements. As a result of this access of relative prosperity, the problem of peasant indebtedness, which Dufferin had considered the most serious problem facing Egypt in 1883, had been greatly alleviated, though by no means solved. (Another attempt made by Cromer to alleviate it was the creation of an Agricultural Bank in 1902 with the object of enabling small landowners to contract loans on the security of their land at reasonable rates of interest. This was not very successful since the majority of Egypt's peasants, with holdings of five feddans or less, had financial requirements which were on too small a scale to make conventional banking operations practicable.)

But this increased prosperity had certain limitations and disadvantages. Cromer's avowed object of maintaining in existence the peasant proprietor and encouraging his growth was not altogether successful. The combination of the Moslem Law of Inheritance—which divides a man's property equally between his children with the sons getting two shares and the daughters one share each without right of primogeniture—and the pressure of peasant indebtedness tended to squeeze out the peasant proprietor with a small viable holding, who was the object of Cromer's solicitude, and to increase, on the one hand the size and number of large landholdings, and on the other hand the number of holdings too small to provide an adequate living for a peasant family. This is illustrated by the following figures:[10]

	1896		1906	
	No.	Feddans	No.	Feddans
Small holdings (under 5 feddans)	608,000	988,000	1,002,000	1,259,000
Medium holdings (5–50 feddans)	141,000	1,769,000	132,000	1,642,000
Large holdings (over 50 feddans)	10,300	1,666,000	10,900	1,763,000

The increased crop yields and reduced taxes benefited landowners, both large and small, but were of little use or benefit either to tenant farmers, whose rent tended to increase *pari passu* with the increased yield of the land they cultivated, or to the landless labourer in the towns and villages, who was too poor to pay taxes and who had no produce to sell. And the spread of perennial irrigation had some effects which were not beneficial. The increased productivity was achieved at the expense of a great increase in the amount of work to be done. Under perennial irrigation fields had to be prepared, sown, irrigated and harvested two and sometimes three times a year instead of once; continual care and vigilance had to be employed in the obtaining and distribution of water during eleven out of the twelve months of the year. After a time the soil tended to become impoverished through overcropping, necessitating the application of imported artificial manures, which had to be purchased, in addition to the home-produced pigeon and cattle manure which the peasant normally used. And, later, the soil tended to become waterlogged owing to overwatering and yields began to decrease until adequate drainage was, somewhat belatedly, put in hand. Various plant diseases, which had before been unknown, began to become endemic. Human diseases, such as bilharzia, malaria and ankylosis began to flourish in the humidity generated by the perennial water, and soon became a very grave problem, afflicting a large proportion of the fellahin with their debilitating effects. Soon after the beginning of the twentieth century the fatal epidemic diseases, such as cholera and bubonic plague, which had periodically swept Egypt during the nineteenth century and which had been largely eradicated (not so much by improved sanitation, of which there was very little outside the main towns, as by efficient and ruthless quarantine and isolation measures), were being replaced by non-fatal endemic diseases. It was not long before Egypt, instead of having a small and relatively healthy population, had an increasingly large and very unhealthy one.

None of this, or very little of it, could reasonably have been foreseen. But Cromer's *laissez faire* philosophy, which aimed at low taxation, and concentrated government expenditure on revenue-producing projects like irrigation, and left 'social services' such as hospitals and poor relief to private enterprise, charitable organisations and family solidarity, rendered Egypt ill-equipped to deal with the social problems created by a rapidly increasing population, by a growing urban proletariat, by the onset of new and unfamiliar diseases, and by the beginning of industrial activity.

In his Report for 1902[11] Cromer gave details of Egyptian Government expenditure under various headings for the first twenty years of the British occupation. £E12,368,000 had been spent on the Army, £E10,419,000 on Public Works, £E79,448,786 in interest on the foreign debt, £E13,393,910 on the Ottoman Tribute, £E3,678,889 on the Sudan, £E7,054,000 on the administration of Justice, £E5,919,000 on the Civil List, £E1,852,000 on medical and sanitary services, and £E1,822,000 on education. An average of something less than £E100,000 p.a. had been spent on each of the last two items. These amounts were not sub-stantially increased after the Reserve funds in the hands of the Caisse were released as a result of the Anglo-French Agreement in 1904. This parsimony was not entirely, or even mainly, the result of financial stringency. It was the result of Cromer's *laissez faire*, low taxation, self-help philosophy. By the end of his term of office, outside Cairo and Alexandria and the Canal Zone, there was no main drainage and very few towns or villages had supplies of piped water. In 1906 the death rate in Alexandria was 34·9 per 1,000 and in Cairo 37·7 per 1,000. Of this, approximately ⅓ consisted of children under one year old and ⅓ of children between one and five years old.[12]

Apart from a tightening-up of quarantine measures against the spread of epidemic diseases, the principal public health measures undertaken by the Anglo-Egyptian Administration during Cromer's term of office con-sisted of a programme of elementary training and certification for the village barbers, who performed the duties of medical and dental prac-titioners in the villages, and the establishment, in 1900 of some travelling 'tent' hospitals to treat eye-diseases. These 'tent' hospitals were so successful that the experiment was later extended for the treatment of bilharzia.

There was no system of poor relief at all, except what was provided by private charity. 'If an Egyptian be hungry, roofless and wanting in raiment to keep out the cold . . . the Government will do nothing for him, no, not even if he be a confirmed invalid, a helpless cripple, or too young or too old to gain his livelihood . . . so long as he is not guilty of an offence punishable by law. He must first commit a crime and then, and then only, will the State interest itself on his behalf . . . Hence we see, even in our opulent capital of Cairo, children, half clad and desperately hungry, roaming the streets at all hours of the day and night and fighting with the pariah dogs for the garbage thrown out of the houses for removal by the dust carts. Our streets are so infested also with beggars and cripples that ladies hardly dare venture out alone for fear of their importunate molestation.'[13]

Cromer's answer to all this, given by the Under Secretary for Foreign Affairs in reply to a question asked in the House of Commons on 5 August 1904, was that 'foundations in Egypt dispose of considerable revenues for the maintenance of the poor and aged, and large sums are granted yearly by the Mussulman Benevolent Society. There is also a foundling home which receives children irrespective of creed, and various religious communities have funds devoted to the relief of the poor. There is at present no need of any further institutions of this character.'[14] There was, in Cromer's view, still less need for any Government-financed system of poor relief. This was not due to any belief that destitution in an Oriental country was less deplorable than in a Western one. A few years later, he adopted precisely the same attitude towards proposals for old age pensions and sick and unemployment benefit in England. He had a doctrinaire and unreasoning belief in the virtues of self-help, and genuinely believed that any system of Government 'dole,' either in England or in

Egypt, would 'pauperise' the recipient, erode the bases of individual and family responsibility, and dry up the sources of voluntary charitable relief. He also genuinely believed that the relations between ruler and ruled, whether in England or in Egypt, should be 'founded on the granite rock of the Christian moral code,' and was quite unconscious of, and would indignantly have repudiated, any suggestion of incompatibility between the one belief and the other.

Contemporary criticism of Cromer's régime was largely concentrated on his educational policy. Cromer himself defined this policy[15] as having four principal objects. 'The first object is to raise the general level of the mass of the population through the village schools,' at which only the three R's were taught. The illiteracy rate in Egypt was 91·2 per cent male and 99·3 per cent female. The village schools, or kuttabs, of which there were about 10,000, had been entirely in the hands of the religious auth‑ orities. Cromer's policy was to establish a few State kuttabs under the direct control of the Department of Public Instruction and to encourage the rest to improve their standards by inspection and the offer of grants‑in‑ aid to those coming up to a certain level of efficiency. 'The second object is to create an efficient civil service. The ultimate aim is to compose the civil service entirely of young men who have got their secondary certificate.' Entry to State higher primary and secondary schools was limited by the payment of fees, a practice on which Cromer was insistent. In 1905 there were 7,175 pupils at the State higher primary and 1,345 at the State secondary schools. The principal object of these schools was to train their pupils for Government service and an endeavour was made to limit the entry to the requirements of Government service. Entry to the secondary schools was made conditional on having obtained a primary certificate and entry to the senior ranks of Government service was con‑ ditional on having obtained a secondary certificate. A very limited amount of State higher education was provided by the Schools of Law, Medicine, Agriculture and Engineering, at which 743 pupils were being educated in 1905.

Cromer's third object was to see that entry to the State higher primary schools was restricted as far as possible to those who would eventually go on to secondary schools and secure secondary certificates, in order to avoid creating a class whose 'partial education unfits them for manual labour and which looks almost exclusively to Government for the means of providing them with a livelihood.' In fact, many more pupils were educated at the higher primary than ever went on to the State secondary schools, of which there were only three in existence at the end of Cromer's term of office. Thus, the creation of that quarter‑educated, more or less unemployable, element, which Cromer dreaded, was not altogether avoided. His fourth object was to encourage the growth of technical education, particularly in the Provinces, in order to provide training for artisans and mechanics.

Cromer's ideas about Egyptian education were extremely limited in scope, even by the standards of the day. As in other 'social services,' financial stringency was only part of the reason for the parsimony displayed. The principal reason was Cromer's *laissez faire*, self-help philosophy, which dictated the payment of fees for higher primary and secondary education, and which believed in the encouragement of private education.

But, even within the limits of this philosophy, there was much lack of foresight and imagination. This seems to have been largely due to the British Education Adviser, Douglas Dunlop, who was selected by Cromer for the post during the 1890s and who remained in it until after the First World War. Dunlop was an ex-missionary who seems to have been a living illustration of Joseph Conrad's dictum that 'truth is stranger than caricature.' He was reported to have said that he would not have any Englishmen under him who came to Egypt knowing a word of Arabic. 'It would only give them romantic ideas about the natives and they would waste their time explaining what they taught to the natives in Arabic instead of making them learn English.'[16] Another observer, who was himself a teacher under Dunlop for a time, wrote: 'Efficiency of a sort there undoubtedly was, but there was a complete lack of elasticity . . . Originality and initiative on the part of the British staff were not encouraged; if an Egyptian dared to show them he was regarded with positive disfavour.'[17]

The same writer gives the following account of the English teachers. '"Dunlop's young men," as the newcomers were called, arrived in annual batches, callow and inexperienced. They were called upon to teach the Egyptian boys for some twenty-four hours a week, but the rest of their time, except the few hours devoted to preparation and correction, was their own to spend as they liked. It can hardly be said that they were ideal schoolmasters. They had been educated at good public schools and universities; they soon learnt to maintain discipline; they carried out their duties adequately, if not always very conscientiously; they did something to teach the young Egyptians gentlemanly behaviour. But there was little or no friendly intercourse between them and their pupils . . . There was in fact almost a feeling of discredit at being in the P.I. (Public Instruction) at all; "Dunlop's young men" came out to Cairo full of enthusiasm, not for their work, but for early escape from it. Their one ambition was to transfer to another Department as soon as this could conveniently be arranged. They referred slightingly to their pupils as the "walads" and hardly less so to their Egyptian colleagues as the "effendis." Their teaching work was regarded as drudgery, to be put out of their minds as soon as the hours of duty were over. Once they left the school precincts, they took little or no interest in their pupils' welfare . . . All this was thoroughly bad policy, quite apart from bad manners; and it is reasonable to suppose that many of the difficulties which ensued in Egypt in the early years of the twentieth century would have been avoided, or at least minimised, had it been otherwise. Certainly, in the schools, the effect was disastrous. Up to 1903, and even for some years after, there was a constant influx of British recruits who, by the time they were beginning to be of some value as teachers, were transferred to other and more promising spheres. As the years went on, the gulf separating British and Egyptians widened rather than lessened. It was during this period that the nationalist move-ment began to show its strength, led by Mustafa Kamil and Shaikh Abdul Aziz Shawish, the latter an ex-inspector of the Ministry of Education. It was in the schools that the movement was chiefly fostered, and it was the students who led the demonstrations.'[18]

Hardly any attempt was made to train Egyptian teachers for the secondary schools, with the result that most secondary subjects were taught in English by English schoolmasters who had no knowledge of Arabic to pupils who had an imperfect knowledge of English, which they had had 'crammed' into them, to the exclusion of most other sub-jects, at the higher primary schools. The Department of Public Instruction, as it was called before it became the Ministry of Education in 1906, was, as regards British staff, regarded largely as a training ground for other Departments, and promising British schoolmasters were usually soon transferred to other Ministries where pay and prospects were better. There was no attempt to use the educational system to commend Western ideals, Western techniques, or Western modes of thought, to Egyptian youth. Hardly anything was done about female education, in spite of some high-minded sentiments on the subject emitted by Cromer (an ardent anti-feminist) from time to time in his Annual Reports. Education was regarded neither as an instrument of policy to try to reconcile Egyptian youth to the British occupation, nor as an instrument of regeneration to enable the end of that occupation to be hastened. It was simply used as an instrument, and an inefficient instrument at that, for providing the necessary *main d'oeuvre* for Government clerkships. Its most popular and successful branch was the School of Law, which was conducted by French staff and in the French language, and which helped to train a number of the coming generation of nationalist politicians. Apart from the School of Law, ambitious Egyptians who could afford to do so sent their sons to one of the numerous, and mostly non-British, foreign private schools in Egypt for primary and secondary education, and to France, Germany, Austria or Italy (and very occasionally to England) for higher education.

Cromer's elevation of the Department of Public Instruction into the Ministry of Education, and his securing the appointment of Saad Zaghlul, a rising nationalist politician, and son-in-law of Mustafa Fahmy, the Prime Minister, as Minister of Education, was due more to political reasons than to any enthusiasm for education. At the same time Dunlop was elevated from departmental to Ministerial Adviser, which was more or less of a guarantee against the influx of any liberal or imaginative ideas into the Ministry.

Lord Lloyd, who cannot be regarded as a severe critic of British achievements in Egypt, wrote: 'Egypt . . . got a system of education whose only goal was to turn out more and more young men fitted for nothing else but to be government officials. The existing model of education was adhered to, and what is sometimes described as a "liberal" education was imposed upon a country to which it could bring no profit.'[19]

In his reflections on Imperial rule, Cromer frequently referred to the necessity of controlling 'commercial egotism.' And Campbell-Bannerman, in his speech to the Commons proposing a grant of £50,000 to Cromer after his retirement, said: 'If he (Cromer) had cared to dazzle the world with swift and sensational results, there were plenty of capitalists ready to develop Egypt on the lines of European finance, and he would have saved himself infinite trouble if he had yielded to pressure to let them in.' The mountain of foreign debt with which Egypt had become encumbered before the occupation was an object lesson in the harm which un-restricted 'commercial egotism' could do to a country. Even if Cromer's strict financial orthodoxy and administrative principles had not forbidden it, restrictions on the Egyptian Government's borrowing powers imposed by the 1885 London Convention would have prevented any large piling-up of Government indebtedness under the occupation. Outside the very strict limits imposed by international obligations, capital develop-ment in Egypt had to take place through private enterprise. This was so even with the Government-sponsored Aswan dam and reservoir, where most of the money was advanced, nominally to the contractors, by the financier Sir Ernest Cassell. Apart from this, there was a large amount of foreign investment in Egypt during Cromer's term of office, after the rehabilitation of the finances and the prospect of a continued British occupation had restored the confidence of investors.

'From the time of the repair of the Delta barrage in 1890, foreign capital began to manifest increasing interest in Egyptian affairs. In 1892 the various units of the sugar industry in Egypt united into a single company, Societé Générale des Sucreries, under the control of French capital; between 1895 and 1898 a number of concessions were given to transport companies, and Egypt was endowed by foreign capital with light railways in the Delta and trams in Cairo and Alexandria . . . At about the same time several industrial companies were formed to con‑dition or prepare for marketing the products of the country, such as cotton ginners, salt and soda manufacturers, and two cotton spinning mills. In the same period a number of land companies were formed, notably the Daira Sanieh Land Company which took over the estates of the Daira Sanieh in order to liquidate the Daira Sanieh Loan of 1877. The mortgage companies increased their loans and had to obtain more capital from abroad. The burst of prosperity at the beginning of the twentieth century was followed by a rush of capital to Egypt, chiefly in the form of investment in companies. The paid‑up capital of companies operating only in Egypt (*i.e.* excluding branches of foreign banks and other foreign companies) increased from £E7,326,000 in 1892 to £E26,280,000 in 1902 and to £E87,176,000 in 1907 . . . The greater part of the new capital was loan capital, in the form of mortgage com‑panies lending money on land, land companies selling land on credit, or financial companies lending money on shares, land, or other security. The presence of this large sum of capital, the rapidly rising value of land owing to the rising prices of agricultural products and mortgage loans and the effect of the irrigation works, led to a burst of speculation that culminated in the disastrous slump of 1907.'[20]

This large increase in foreign investment was not nearly covered by the difference between imports and exports. In consequence, Egypt accumulated a large load of private foreign indebtedness which was probably not less, and may have been more, than the public indebtedness incurred under Ismail.

This was not necessarily a bad thing. The difficulty was that most of the imported capital was controlled by foreign companies who, because of the Capitulations, were largely exempt from Egyptian laws, and indeed from any sort of control at all. Restraints on 'commercial egotism' were thus necessarily of a very feeble kind. Standards of conduct could not adequately be supervised; profits of exploitation could not adequately be taxed. One writer, referring to the 'modernizing' activities of private enterprise in Cairo, complained of 'the myriad converging interests, the hedge of new monopolies—this builder on one side, that purveyor of traction on another, and all the rest, with their self‑constituted and irregular policies, will have made of the city a pile of insanitary incongruity. Houses raised to five, six, and even seven stories high, the wholesale destruction of trees, and a still tolerated system of refuse collection which will find its parallel in some forgotten corner of medieval times . . . So

indifferently do the Inspectors of Buildings discharge the duty of supervision that hardly a week passes but one hears of houses in the poorer
districts tumbling down and oftimes burying the inhabitants in their
ruins ... Cairo is probably the worst lighted city in the civilised world ...
Street illumination is a monopoly owned by a company paying handsome
dividends and the Government has a very tender regard for monopolists
... The Cairo Water Company too owns a monopoly. It is probably
the richest company in all Egypt. Yet it not infrequently happens that
during a spell of hot weather ... there is a water famine. People are
constantly complaining that the pressure at the mains is not sufficient to
provide a constant supply on the second and third stories.'[21]

Most of this foreign investment was concentrated either in urban
building and public utilities or, in the form of ginning factories, cotton
seed oil factories, spinning factories and light railways (for transporting
the cotton crop), closely tied to the cotton industry. The supply of capital
depended upon conditions and was devoted to developments largely
beyond Egyptian control. There was an absence of capital for many
forms of local industry, the development of which would have diversified
the reliance of the Egyptian economy on cotton, which made it particularly
vulnerable to fluctuations in world prices. 'In spite of vast amounts of
capital attracted to Egypt, little was allocated for industrial development.
European financiers did not want to develop Egypt as a competitor with
Europe in manufactured products. Rather, they wanted to extract the
raw materials from Egypt, making it a consumer of European finished
products. The few efforts to promote industrialisation ... were generally
unsuccessful. In the 1890s, for example, a group of enterprising Englishmen tried to establish local textile factories in Egypt. These of course
would have competed with the Lancashire factories aimed at the Egyptian
consumer market. The British administrators in Egypt, realising full well
that they would be under attack from this powerful English lobby,
impeded the venture, although Cromer was not able to prevent the establishment of the cotton mills. In fact, Cromer was aware of a similar
controversy in India which had led to very strong attacks against the
British administration by the Lancashire industrialists for allowing local
textile factories to be established. To forestall this kind of criticism Cromer
had an excise of 8 per cent levied on locally manufactured goods, the tax
being equivalent to the tariff on imported goods. Cromer's official reason
for this excise was that he was opposed in theory to the practice of supporting industry behind protective tariff barriers. There is no reason to
discount this, for Cromer was a dedicated apostle of free trade. But there
can be no question that he also felt the pressure from the cotton manufac-
turing community in England ... In like fashion, excise taxes roughly

equivalent to the tariffs on imported products were placed on other locally manufactured goods.'[22]

Cromer frequently referred to the necessity for controlling 'military egotism.' In this he was more successful than he was with 'commercial egotism.' He kept a tight hold of military expenditure over the reconquest of the Sudan, and even induced the British Treasury to bear some of it. He successfully resisted the attempts of successive Sirdars to expand the strength of the Egyptian Army beyond what he considered necessary. He prevented the War Office from using Egypt as a training-ground for the British Army at the expense of the Egyptian Government and insisted on keeping the British garrison down to the minimum level he considered appropriate to ensure the security of the occupation. But he was unsuccessful in his continual efforts to induce the British Government to pay part of the costs of the occupation troops on the ground that the occupation was primarily a British rather than an Egyptian interest.

Judged by comparison with any likely alternative, Cromer's regime was a favourable one for Egypt. What were the alternatives? If a possible one had been an independent indigenous government, which Europe would have allowed to repudiate the foreign debt and sweep away all the various international restrictions with which Egypt was encumbered, such a regime, whether a traditional one under a despotic Khedive, or a revolutionary one of the Arabist type, might have satisfied more of the Egyptian people more of the time than the Cromer regime did. It would not have been reformist in the Western sense. It would, by Western standards, have been corrupt and inefficient. Its repudiation of the debt, and its abolition of international privileges and restrictions, would have cut off most of its contacts with the West. Under such a regime, Egypt might eventually have attained the same sort of social, political and economic stability and viability as Turkey did under Ataturk and Persia under Reza Shah. But this was not a remotely possible alternative. In the circumstances of the time, the countries of western Europe would never have allowed, and would have been able to prevent, any Egyptian Government from repudiating the debt and from abolishing international privileges. The only alternative to a British occupation was a reversion to the kind of international financial control as had existed before the Arabi rebellion and the British occupation—enough control for collecting debts and maintaining foreign privileges, but not enough for effecting any worth-while reforms. Subject to this, the Egyptian Government would have been run by Egyptians, but it is doubtful whether there would have been any more development in the direction of representative government than there was under Cromer's regime.

Cromer introduced a limited but very real measure of reform at the price of virtually handing over the whole machinery of administration to British officials. The productivity of the country was greatly increased as a result of irrigation improvements. Alleviations of the burden of the foreign debt were negotiated in a sense far more favourable to Egypt than the Egyptians would have been able to negotiate for themselves. These two achievements enabled the *corvée* to be abolished and taxation to be reduced. In addition, the Administration, in Cromer's words, 'ceased to do evil' and 'abstained from misgovernment,' in that gross acts of oppression were no longer regularly perpetrated, and in that, generally speaking, taxation and punishment were imposed according to law and not according to the whims or exigencies of some local potentate. Apart from the alleviation in the burden of the foreign debt, virtually nothing was achieved in relieving Egypt from the weight of foreign privileges and immunities inherent in the Capitulations.

Two questions arise. One, did these limited, but real, reforms necessitate the extent of autocratic British control and the denial of representative institutions which accompanied them? Two, was the beneficent effect of these reforms on the Egyptian people as a whole sufficient to compensate them for being degraded to the status of a subject race, and being deprived of any responsible share in, or control over, the administration, always bearing in mind that the only practicable alternative was a reversion to the kind of internationally-controlled regime which had existed prior to the British occupation?

The answer to the first question almost certainly is that the reforms effected could have been accomplished under conditions of much more responsible Egyptian participation in and control over the administration, and the principal reason why this did not happen was that Cromer himself had very definite views about the essential inferiority of 'Orientals' and the essentially disruptive nature of representative institutions in Oriental countries. The answer to the second question is that the political impotence and personal frustration and humiliation to which educated Egyptians were reduced under the Cromer regime would have out-weighed any material benefits gained had it not been that the only practicable alternative would have involved most of the political impotence and much of the personal frustration and humiliation without any com-pensating material benefits at all.

In the long run, it is doubtful whether the impact of the Cromer regime on Egypt, whether for good or ill, was very important, except in one respect. Balfour's panegyric about Cromer having 'raised Egypt from the lowest pitch of social and economic degradation until it now stands among Oriental nations absolutely alone in its prosperity,' was, like many of that statesman's utterances, nonsense. Egypt's development as a modern State was started under Mohamed Ali and continued under Ismail. This development was accompanied by many mistakes and false starts, by corruption, extravagance, improvidence, oppression and absurdity. But a start was made. Railways, telegraphs, Banks, capital investments, news-papers, an educational system, steam engines, and all the basic apparatus of modernisation were introduced into the country. In the process a fearful mess of debt, social upheaval, and administrative confusion was generated. Cromer's real contribution to Egypt was to clear up this mess and give Egypt a breathing-space of ordered administration, so that she could adapt herself to and absorb the modernisation which had so incontinently been thrust upon her. As part, and an important part, of the process he restored Egypt's official finances to solvency and, by so doing, enabled the process of modernisation, which depended on a continued process of capital investment, to go on. And, as a result of restoring Egypt to solvency, he was able to relieve the people of Egypt from some of the burdens which a powerful and ruthless creditor is able to inflict on a defenceless and defaulting debtor.

The one important and enduring mark which the Cromer regime left on Egypt was its contribution to the Egyptian irrigation system. Perennial irrigation was not introduced into Egypt by the British. It had been introduced by Mohamed Ali in the 1820s as a means of providing Summer water for the cotton crop which he, on the advice of European experts, had started to develop for the export market. At first, this involved the laborious business of digging deep canals and raising the low Nile water on to the Summer crops by means of primitive lifting devices such as the *saqia* and the *shadoof*, worked by animal or man-power. In the mid-1830s, advised by French engineers, Mohamed Ali conceived the idea of building a barrage at the apex of the Delta to raise the level of the Summer water behind it, which would then be led off into the Delta fields by canals. The barrage was not completed until 1861 and it was then found that, through defects in its construction, it could not retain enough water to raise appreciably the level of the low Nile. It was therefore not used, and the old method of deep canals and lifting apparatus was continued.

The great contribution of the British irrigation engineers was, by the application of correct engineering methods, first to bring the Delta barrage into use to raise the level of the low Nile, and then to supplement the total amount of water available at low Nile by retaining and storing part of the flood water behind the Aswan dam. They thus embarked on a scientifically calculated process of gradually making all the water of the Nile flowing through Egypt available for the benefit of Egypt, instead of letting most of the flood water escape into the sea, and of so regulating its flow to rescue Egypt from the perennial threats of drought due to an exceptionally low Nile and flood from an exceptionally high one.

But for the incidence of autocratic British rule, which happened to have at its command the technical experience of Anglo-Indian irrigation engineers, and which was actuated by an urgent desire to commend the British occupation of Egypt both to the Egyptians themselves and to European opinion, the development of the Egyptian irrigation system which, in its cumulative effects, has had an impact on Egypt akin to that of the Industrial Revolution on England, would probably have had to await the advent of some other enlightened despot, native or foreign. For this development, unlike the Industrial Revolution in England, which took place as a result of the initiative and enterprise of thousands of separate individuals, was dependent for its realisation on the act of a solvent, autocratic and civilised Government, both willing and able to embark on a long-term, large-scale, and well-thought-out enterprise.

14

THE IMPERIAL
ACHIEVEMENT

In 1886 both Government and Opposition in England were agreed in regarding the occupation of Egypt as an 'incubus' and were anxious to get out of the country as soon as possible. In 1907, when Cromer left Egypt, both Government and Opposition were agreed in regarding the continued occupation of Egypt as an Imperial necessity. To some extent, this fundamental change was due to a change in European alliances and alignments. But it was also due, to a large extent, to Cromer's earlier successful insistence on the importance of Egypt in the Imperial scheme of things.

It was largely as a result of Cromer's influence that Salisbury gradually adopted the theses (a) that the consolidation of British influence in Cairo was a necessary compensation for its decline in Constantinople; and (b) that British control of the whole Nile Valley was a necessary condition of safeguarding the continuance of British influence in Cairo. These theses were adopted by Rosebery in face of the opposition of most of the Liberal Cabinet and, later, accepted almost as articles of faith, not only by the Conservative Administrations in office between 1895 and 1906, but also by the Liberal Administration which came into office early in 1906. They had become so much accepted that it occurred to no one that the Anglo-French Entente of 1904 might possibly have modified the position, by contributing to the removal of that threat to Imperial communications which had been the reason for occupying Egypt in the first place.

In the light, particularly, of the Entente with France and the decline of British influence at Constantinople, there was no good reason why the Mediterranean strategy of the past 100 years should not have been abandoned and communications with British possessions around the Indian Ocean and in the Far East and Australasia secured by concentration on the blue water route round the Cape of Good Hope, where Britannia ruled the waves and the Royal Navy was supreme. To some extent, the building up of the British position in Egypt, as a means of maintaining the by-now-traditional Mediterranean strategy, was a case of the tail wagging the dog. It is arguable that the resultant concentration on building up massive, British-controlled bastions on both sides of the Suez Canal—leading, *inter alia*, to the declaration of a British Protectorate over Egypt in 1914, to the Balfour Declaration of 1917, and to the assumption of British Mandates over Palestine, Transjordan and Iraq in 1920, was an important factor in the process of British Imperial decline.

Up to about 1890, Cromer was wont to advance Imperial necessity as a principal reason for staying in Egypt. Thereafter, he came increasingly to regard continued British control in Egypt as an end in itself, as a necessary means of accomplishing the rehabilitation and civilisation of Egypt, without very much reference to Imperial strategy, except in so far as he continually pointed out to successive Chancellors of the Exchequer that, since British Imperial interests were being served by the British occupation, the British taxpayer should in fairness be asked to contribute part of the cost. In reply the various Chancellors tacitly accepted the premise but explicitly rejected the conclusion.

During the campaign for the reconquest of the Sudan, Cromer, who had originally suggested to Salisbury the necessity for British control of the whole Nile Valley, showed very little interest in a doctrine which, so far as he was concerned, had already served its purpose, and concentrated most of his attention on trying to ensure that Egyptian financial stability would not be endangered by the acquisition of 'large tracts of useless territory.' His plans for the administration of the Sudan, as expressed in the Condominium Agreement, were motivated, not by a desire for British strategic control of that territory, but by a determination that its administration should not be subject to the same international controls and restrictions which encumbered Egypt.

Similarly, the Anglo-French Agreement was welcomed by Cromer in its local aspect as a means of facilitating his administration of Egypt, and not in its international aspect as a major realignment in British policy. He would certainly have baulked, and indeed did baulk, at any suggestion that his requirements for French concessions in Egypt might be waived in deference to other, and possibly wider, considerations.

During the twenty-three years of Cromer's Proconsulship, there was a curious reversal in the rôles of the British Government and the British Agent in Egypt. During 1883–85 Gladstone's Liberal Government, anxious to justify their intervention in Egypt to their supporters, were principally concerned with the progress of domestic reforms in Egypt, while Baring tried to impress on them that a strong indigenous government, rather than a reformist one, was necessary in order to make evacuation possible. In 1906, when a Liberal Government was again in office, it was Cromer who was intent on reforms and the British Government who were interested in the restoration of a stronger indigenous government as a means of safeguarding the continuance of the occupation.

By that time, British Imperial policy was, largely as a result of Cromer's influence, firmly committed to a maintenance of British control in Egypt. This was not disputed even by Cromer's Radical critics like Robertson who argued, in effect, that Cromer's policy was jeopardising the maintenance of that control. Just as, in 1883, the desirability of a rapid evacuation was common ground, so, in 1906, the maintenance of British control was common ground among almost all shades of political opinion.

This was Cromer's most enduring, if not his most beneficent, achievement. He achieved it as a by-product of what came to be his principal interest—the rehabilitation, as he saw it, of Egypt. He had become an Anglo-Egyptian rather than a British statesman. As Salisbury put it: 'If the world were falling to pieces round his ears, but Egypt was left intact, Lord Cromer would not ask for more.'[1] He had become genuinely attached to Egypt, in a somewhat patronising way, and regarded its rehabilitation, according to the tenets of Victorian Imperialism, as his life-work. At various times during the Nineties he had declined offers of the Constantinople and Vienna Embassies in order to remain in Egypt. By staying there, he became a much more powerful influence on British policy than he ever would have been in Constantinople or Vienna.

Cromer's influence on British Imperial strategy—his arguments about the shifting of the centre of gravity of British interests from Constantinople to Cairo, and the necessity for keeping other European Powers out of the Nile Valley—had been means to the end of ensuring continued, effective British control of Egypt for the purpose of achieving the rehabilitation of Egypt. The profound effect of these arguments on the course of British Imperial policy was, as far as he was concerned, incidental and accidental. He may not even have realised the extent and far-reaching consequences of his influence. When, in 1916, as the last public duty of his life, he became Chairman of the Dardanelles Commission, one wonders whether he realised that, but for his influence on British Imperial strategy during his time in Egypt, there would probably not have been a Dardanelles expedition.

It is not suggested that Cromer deliberately propagated an Imperial strategy centred on Egypt with the conscious intention of forwarding his own ambitions in Egypt. Like many Viceroys of India who viewed Imperial strategy almost exclusively from an Indian point of view, and became obsessed with Russian designs on the Indian Empire, Cromer, quite naturally, came to take an Egypt-oriented view of Imperial strategy. And because he remained in Egypt much longer than any Viceroy had remained in India, and because he became identified with Egypt in the

British official and public mind much more than any Viceroy became identified with India, his views had more authority in England than those of any Viceroy ever had. Largely because of that increasing and continuing authority, British Imperial policy, almost imperceptibly, became Egypt-oriented.

There were several factors, in addition to Cromer's personal prestige, which contributed to this result. There was the tradition of 100 years of Mediterranean strategy, which had been inaugurated by the battle of the Nile, which was not easily relinquished, but which was seen to be becoming impracticable in its traditional form as a result of declining British influence at Constantinople. There was the fatal fascination of the prospect of sharing in the eventual division of the Ottoman heritage. There was the growing commercial and missionary interest in the opening-up of Central Africa. There was, in the Imperialist atmosphere of the Nineties, a growing pride in the much-publicised, and greatly exaggerated, British administrative achievement in Egypt, which came to be regarded as a jewel in the British Imperial crown second only in splendour to India. There was the prevalent Jingo sentiment, well expressed by Queen Victoria, who once told her Ministers that it was a mistake to give up what one has got. There was a growing feeling, almost a superstition, about the Suez Canal as an 'Imperial life-line,' the severing of which would imperil England's national existence.

All these things, through the 1890s and during the early years of the twentieth century, developed a momentum of their own, quite independent of Lord Cromer, who was no Jingo, who mistrusted commercial, and was suspicious of missionary, enterprise. But most of it sprung from the seeds he had sown in Salisbury's mind during the late 1880s, and from the careful publicity which he started giving to British achievements in Egypt during the early 1890s. Possibly without realising it, probably without intending it, he was the major influence, not in effecting a fundamental change in British Imperial strategy, but in ensuring a continuance of traditional strategy under changing conditions. At the beginning of the nineteenth century British influence at Constantinople had been fostered, and Malta and the Ionian Islands occupied, as a means of devising a Mediterranean strategy in face of potential French and Russian threats to British Indian possessions. At the beginning of the twentieth century the possession of Egypt, and a desire to continue possessing it, were used as reasons for continuing this strategy when the threats originally inspiring it had almost ceased to be operative, and when political developments, such as nationalism among 'subject peoples,' and technical developments, such as the aeroplane and the submarine, were already beginning to make it obsolete.

303

NOTES

see page 321 *et seq.* for explanation of abbreviations

CHAPTER I Egypt In 1876
1 Malet-Granville 19.12.81 FO 141/144
2 Bruce-Clarendon 23.3.57 FO 78/1313
3 Beauval-Thouvenel 15.5.61 Correspondence Politique Egypte 29
4 Colquhoun-Russell 24.1.62 FO 78/1675
5 Stanton-Derby 6.11.75 and 27.11.75 FO 78/2404
6 Derby-Stanton 6.12.75 FO 78/2403
7 Derby-Stanton 6.12.75 FO 78/2403
8 Cave-Derby 25.12.75 FO 78/2538
9 Parliamentary Papers Commons 1876 LXXXIII 99 in FO 2539A
10 Derby-Stanton 26.5.76 FO 78/2498
11 Vivian-Derby 21.11.76 FO 78/2720
12 See text of opinion in FO 78/2750
13 Derby-Cookson 7.8.76 FO 78/2499
14 For what purports to be a detailed account of his murder, see McCoan, *Egypt Under Ismail,* pp. 191–204
15 Derby-Vivian 12.12.76 FO 78/2499
16 Cromer, *Modern Egypt,* Vol. I, p. 15

CHAPTER 2 Commissioner of the Debt
1 Baring-Goschen 18.12.77 FO 633/2
2 Derby-Vivian 25.4.77 FO 78/2630
3 Vivian-Derby 2.3.77 FO 78/2361
4 Vivian-Derby 11.8.77 FO 78/2503
5 Vivian-Derby 7.7.77 FO 78/2633
6 Vivian-Derby 5.9.77 FO 78/2634
7 Baring-Goschen 19.12.77 FO 633/2
8 Baring-Goschen 21.12.77 FO 633/2
9 Baring-Goschen 28.12.77 FO 633/2
10 Baring-Goschen 8.2.78 FO 633/2
11 Derby-Vivian 27.12.77 FO 78/2630
12 Baring-Goschen 2.2.78 FO 633/2
13 Baring-Goschen 10.2.78 FO 633/2
14 Baring-Goschen 15.2.78 FO 633/2
15 Baring-Goschen 1.3.78 FO 633/2
16 Derby-Vivian 26.2.78 FO 78/2851
17 Baring-Goschen 8.3.78 FO 633/2
18 Baring-Goschen 22.3.78 FO 633/2
19 Baring-Goschen 25.3.78 FO 633/2
20 Baring-Goschen 22.3.78 FO 633/2
21 Baring-Goschen 22.3.78 FO 633/2
22 HMG were interested in this as the Egyptian tribute was part of the security for a Franco-British loan to the Ottoman Government
23 Vivian-Derby 15.4.78 FO 78/2854

24 Salisbury-Vivian 16.4.78 FO 78/2851
25 Baring-Goschen 19.4.78 FO 633/2
26 Baring-Goschen 19.4.78 FO 633/2
27 Baring-Goschen 29.4.78 FO 633/2
28 Cromer, *Modern Egypt*, Vol. I, pp. 36–37
29 Salisbury-Northcote 19.4.78 Iddesleigh Papers Vol. VII BM Add. MS. 50019
30 Cromer, *Modern Egypt*, Vol. I, p. 38
31 For text see FO 78|2856
32 Salisbury-Northcote 25.8.78 Iddesleigh Papers Vol. VII BM Add. MS. 50019
33 Vivian-Salisbury 13.7.78 FO 78/2854
34 Salisbury-Vivian 17.7.78 FO 2851
35 R. Wilson, *Chapters from My Official Life*, p. 123
36 R. Wilson, *Chapters from My Official Life*, p. 123
37 Salisbury-Vivian 29.7.78 FO 78/2851
38 Vivian-Salisbury 25.8.79 FO 78/2856 and Salisbury-Vivian 27.8.78 FO 78/2851
39 Wilson-Salisbury undated FO 78/2852
40 Cromer, *Modern Egypt*, Vol. I, pp. 70–71
41 R. Wilson, *Chapters from My Official Life*, p. 187
42 Salisbury-Vivian 21.2.79 FO 141/123
43 Cromer, *Modern Egypt*, Vol. I, p. 97
44 R. Wilson, *Chapters from My Official Life*, p. 186
45 Cromer, *Modern Egypt*, Vol. I, pp. 126–27

CHAPTER 3 Controller-General

 1 Public Record Office. Cabinet 41/12/7 quoted by Lowe, *The Reluctant Imperialists*, Vol. II, p. 13
 2 Salisbury-Lascelles 25.4.79 FO 141/123
 3 Iddesleigh Papers Vol. VII BM Add. MS. 50019
 4 Cromer, *Modern Egypt*, Vol. I, pp. 108–109
 5 Blunt, *Secret History*, pp. 65–66
 6 Salisbury-British Ambassador in Berlin 15.5.79. Copy in FO 141/123
 7 Salisbury-Vivian 30.5.79 FO 141/123. Vivian, after recriminations in London between him and Wilson and the Foreign Office, had been sent temporarily back to Cairo as a 'face saver.' He formally handed over to Lascelles and left Egypt in June
 8 Iddesleigh Papers Vol. VII BM Add. MS. 50019
 9 Lowe, *The Reluctant Imperialists*, Vol. I, p. 41
10 Lady Gwendoline Cecil, *Salisbury*, Vol. II, pp. 331–32
11 Iddesleigh Papers Vol. VII BM Add. MS. 50019
12 Salisbury-Lyons 15.7.79. Quoted in Cecil, *Salisbury*, Vol. II, p. 355
13 Lascelles-Salisbury 8.8.79 FO 141/125
14 Zetland, *Cromer*, p. 57
15 Cromer, *Modern Egypt*, Vol. I, p. 159
16 Baring-Salisbury 20.9.79 FO 633/2
17 Lascelles-Salisbury 8.8.79 FO 141/125
18 These Powers were those which enjoyed the privileges of the Capitulations and numbered fourteen—France, Italy, Great Britain, Holland, Greece, Sweden, Portugal, Austria-Hungary, Belgium, Spain, Germany, Russia, Denmark and the United States
19 Baring-Salisbury 15.9.79 FO 633/2
20 Salisbury-Malet 19.9.79 State Papers, Vol. 73, pp. 1127–28
21 State Papers, Vol. 70, p. 622

22 Baring-Salisbury 19.9.79 FO 633/2
23 Salisbury-Baring 25.9.79 FO 633/2
24 Salisbury-Baring 3.10.79 FO 633/2
25 Memo by Baring dated 1.11.79 in FO 633/2
26 Salisbury-Baring 29.10.79 FO 633/2
27 Lascelles-Salisbury 17.7.79 FO 141/125
28 Lascelles-Salisbury 19.8.79 FO 141/125
29 Cromer, *Modern Egypt*, Vol. I, p. 165
30 Cromer, *Modern Egypt*, Vol. I, p. 165
31 Cromer, *Modern Egypt*, Vol. I, p. 166
32 Baring-Goschen 19.3.80 FO 633/2
33 Cromer, *Modern Egypt*, Vol. I, p. 168
34 Cromer, *Modern Egypt*, Vol. I, p. 168
35 Baring-Salisbury 21.1.80 FO 633/2
36 Salisbury-Baring 6.2.80 FO 633/2
37 Malet-Salisbury 26.4.80 FO 141/134
38 Baring-Salisbury 16.2.80 FO 633/2
39 Malet-Salisbury 31.3.80 FO 141/134
40 Butros Ghali, a future prime minister
41 For the text of Law of Liquidation see, *inter alia*, Borelli, *Choses Politiques d'Egypte 1883–1895*, p. 448 *et seq.*
42 Baring-Goschen 17.1.80 FO 633/2. Baring is referring to the Cyprus Convention, a secret agreement arrived at between England and Turkey just before the Berlin Congress by which Turkey agreed to lease Cyprus to England. The news of the Convention was 'leaked' to the Press during the course of the Congress and Baring believed that Salisbury had had to make some concessions to Waddington, the French Foreign Minister, in order to appease him. On the whole, now that all the relevant diplomatic correspondence is available, it would seem that Baring's suspicions were unfounded, and that British policy in Egypt was unaffected by the Cyprus Convention
43 Blunt, *Secret History of the British Occupation*, p. 97
44 Cromer, *Modern Egypt*, Vol. I, pp. 173–74

CHAPTER 4 The British Occupation

1 In 1882 there were 1,263 European officials in Egyptian Government service. Although this only represented about five per cent of the total strength of the civil service, the European officials drew fifteen per cent of its total emoluments. See Egypt No. 4 and Egypt No. 6 (1882)
2 Granville-Malet 6.1.82 FO 141/152
3 Cromer, *Modern Egypt*, Vol. I, p. 235
4 Cromer, *Modern Egypt*, Vol. I, p. 235
5 Granville-Malet 19.5.82 No. 22 Egypt No. 8 1882
6 FO circular 31.5.82 No. 147 Egypt No. 8 1882
7 Memo to Cabinet quoted in J. L. Garvin, *Life of Joseph Chamberlain*, Vol. I, p. 446
8 Hartington-Granville 20.6.82 Public Record Office 30/29/132
9 See Cabinet minute by Bright 7.7.82 PRO 30/29/143
10 Gladstone-Granville 9.7.82 PRO 30/29/126
11 Granville-Queen 12.7.82 QVL 2nd series 3, p. 309
12 Gladstone-Granville 22.7.82 PRO 30/29/126
13 Childers, *Life of Childers*, Vol. II, pp. 96–97
14 Hansard 3rd series CCLXXII 1586–90 24.7.82

15 Hansard 3rd series CCLXXII 1720 25.7.82
16 Hansard 3rd series CCLXXII 1590 24.7.82
17 Granville–Dufferin 3.11.82 FO 141/167
18 Egypt No. 6 1883
19 Dufferin–Granville 7.12.82 FO 141/168
20 Suleiman Sami, who was convicted and executed for organising the burning of Alex-
    andria after the bombardment, was undoubtedly guilty but, equally undoubtedly, had
    been acting on orders from Arabi. Even Arabi's defending counsel considered that it
    would have been difficult for Arabi to have been acquitted on this charge, on which he
    was never tried. See, *inter alia*, Broadley, *How We Defended Arabi*
21 Egypt No. 6 1883
22 State Papers, Vol. 74, p. 1104
23 Dufferin–Granville 18.11.82 FO 141/168
24 State Papers, Vol. 74, p. 1095
25 Granville–Circular to Ambassadors 3.1.83 FO 141/167
26 Dufferin–Granville 14.1.83 Egypt No. 4 1883
27 Malet–Granville 29.8.83 FO 141/174

CHAPTER 5 The House of Bondage
1   See correspondence with Granville in PRO 30/29/199 and with Northbrook in FO 633/4
2   Afterwards Lord d'Abernon
3   PRO 30/29/161
4   It was HMG's policy at the time to publish, in the form of Blue Books, edited versions of
    official correspondence about British policy in Egypt and elsewhere
5   PRO 30/29/161
6   PRO 30/29/199
7   FO 633/5
8   Baring–Childers 4.3.84 FO 633/5
9   PRO 30/29/161
10 Baring–Granville 22.12.83 FO 78/3561
11 PRO 30/29/161
12 Granville–Baring 3.1.84 FO 78/3695
13 Cromer, *Modern Egypt*, Vol. I, pp. 424–25
14 Note by Granville 29.12.83 PRO 30/29/146
15 Baring–Granville 10.12.83 PRO 30/29/161
16 PRO 30/29/162
17 Baring–Granville 16.1.84 FO 78/3696
18 Cromer, *Modern Egypt*, Vol. I, pp. 437–38
19 For an elucidation of the times of the various telegrams see B. M. Allen, *Gordon in the
    Sudan*, pp. 225–26
20 For this see, *inter alia*, the author's *Mission to Khartum*
21 Cromer, *Modern Egypt*, Vol. I, p. 563
22 Cromer, *Modern Egypt*, Vol. I, p. 567
23 Baring–Granville 3.4.85 PRO 30/29/165
24 PRO 30/29/161
25 Baring–Granville 21.10.83 PRO 30/29/161
26 18.4.84 PRO 30/29/200
27 PRO 30/29/162
28 Baring–Granville 3.3.84 PRO 30/29/162
29 Baring–Granville 3.3.84 PRO 30/29/162

30 Baring-Granville 3.3.84 PRO 30/29/162
31 Baring-Granville 24.3.84 PRO 30/29/162
32 Baring-Granville 14.4.84 PRO 30/29/162
33 14.9.84 PRO 30/29/163
34 Scott Moncrieff relates that Nubar, when forming his administration, asked him whether he would like as Minister of Public Works *un homme capable ou un nullité.* '*Un nullité, s'il vous plait Excellence.*' '*Ah, mon cher, vous avez raison.*' And a nullity was duly appointed who, Moncrieff recorded, 'always backed me up and agreed with what I wanted'. (N. Hollings, *Life of Sir C. Scott Moncrieff*, p. 176)
35 3.6.85 PRO 30/29/165
36 PRO 30/29/162
37 For a full account of the Conference and of the conversations preceding it, see Cocheris, *Situation Internationale de l'Egypte et du Soudan*, pp. 178–87
38 Egypt No. 1 1885
39 Cromer, *Modern Egypt*, Vol. II, p. 367
40 For a text of Northbrook's Reports see, *inter alia*, PRO 30/29/289
41 PRO 30/29/163
42 Baring-Childers 3.4.84 FO 633/5
43 26.12.84 PRO 30/29/200
44 16.12.84 PRO 30/29/163
45 Egypt No. 6 1885
46 Baring-Goschen 7.2.87 FO 633/5
47 3.3.85 PRO 30/29/164
48 24.2.85 PRO 30/29/164
49 1.5.85 PRO 30/29/201
50 30.4.85 PRO 30/29/165
51 12.5.85 PRO 30/29/165
52 24.2.85 PRO 30/29/164
53 20.5.85 PRO 30/29/165
54 3.6.85 PRO 30/29/165
55 20.5.85 PRO 30/29/165
56 12.6.85 PRO 30/29/201
57 Baring-Granville 25.1.85 PRO 30/29/164
58 Baring-Granville 29.2.84 FO 78/4194
59 Hollings, *Life of Sir C. Scott Moncrieff*, p. 172
60 Hollings, *Life of Sir C. Scott Moncrieff*, p. 182

CHAPTER 6 The Drummond Wolff Negotiations

 1 Cecil, *Salisbury*, Vol. III, p. 218
 2 Cecil, *Salisbury*, Vol. III, p. 232
 3 Egypt No. 1 1886
 4 Cecil, *Salisbury*, Vol. III, p. 235
 5 Cecil, *Salisbury*, Vol. III, p. 236
 6 Baring-Salisbury 19.9.85 SP Unbound letters
 7 For text of Convention and details of negotiations leading up to it see Egypt No. 1 1886
 8 SP Unbound letters
 9 For text of Mukhtar's Report see Egypt No. 3 1886
10 9.2.86 FO 633/6
11 15.2.86 FO 633/6
12 5.7.86 FO 633/7

13 31.10.86 FO 633/6
14 Baring-Dufferin 15.12.86 FO 633/5
15 Salisbury-Baring 21.1.87 SP A/55
16 Egypt No. 7 1887
17 Cecil, *Salisbury*, Vol. IV, p. 41
18 Cecil, *Salisbury*, Vol. IV, p. 39
19 21.1.87 AP A/55
20 21.1.87 SP A/52
21 31.1.87 SP Unbound letters
22 4.3.87 SP A/52
23 1.4.87 SP A/52
24 6.4.87 SP A/52
25 23.4.87 SP A/52
26 6.5.87 SP A/55
27 15.5.87 SP A/52
28 For text of Convention and correspondence connected with it see Egypt No. 7 1887
29 1.6.87 FO 633/4
30 Cecil, *Salisbury*, Vol. IV, p. 48
31 Cecil, *Salisbury*, Vol. IV, p. 47
32 Cecil, *Salisbury*, Vol. IV, p. 49
33 Cecil, *Salisbury*, Vol. IV, p. 50
34 See *Egypt in 1887*, an unpublished work in the d'Abernon Papers BM Add. MS. 48960/61
35 Under the terms of the debt settlement a certain fixed percentage of gross railways receipts had to be devoted to the service of the debt, leaving any resultant deficit on railway working to be met out of 'unaffected' revenue
36 Vincent quotes figures to show that the price of unginned cotton had fallen from PT 300 to PT 220 per kantar between 1881 and 1886. The average cotton yield was 3 kantars per feddan. This involved a fall in gross income from PT 900 to PT 660 per feddan on cotton growing land as against fixed charges of about PT 400 per feddan. The incidence of land-tax varied from a minimum of PT 50 per feddan on the privileged 'ushuri' land, which made up about a quarter of the whole, to a maximum of PT 160 per feddan on the ordinary 'kharaj' lands
37 14.2.67 SP A/52
38 5.3.87 FO 633/5
39 7.3.87 FO 633/5
40 28.3.87 FO 633/5
41 9.7.87 FO 633/5
42 4.2.87 SP A/55
43 11.2.87 SP A/55
44 1.4.87 SP A/55
45 H. E. Hurst, *The Nile*, pp. 38–40
46 Cromer, *Modern Egypt*, Vol. 2, p. 458
47 M. A. Hollings, *Life of Sir C. Scott Moncrieff*, p. 194, *et seq.*
48 Hollings, *Life of Sir C. Scott Moncrieff*, p. 194 *et seq.*
49 Hollings, *Life of Sir C. Scott Moncrieff*, p. 194 *et seq.*
50 Cromer, *Modern Egypt*, Vol. 2, p. 412
51 No. 59 Salisbury-Baring 15.2.87 Egypt No. 11 1887
52 No. 86 Salisbury-Baring 30.3.87 Egypt No. 11 1887
53 21.1.87 SP A/55

54 7.2.87 SP A/52
55 18.2.87 SP A/52
56 7.3.87 FO 633/5
57 The Conservatives and Liberal Unionists
58 18.2.87 SP A/55
59 Hollings, *Life of Sir C. Scott Moncrieff*
60 27.2.87 FO 633/5
61 7.2.87 SP A/52
62 Hollings, *Life of Sir C. Scott Moncrieff*
63 18.11.87 FO 633/5
64 22.10.87 SP A/52
65 8.5.87 SP A/52
66 W. S. Blunt, an influential English sympathiser with and propagandist for Egyptian nationalism, who had taken a prominent part in arranging for Arabi's legal defence and who had thereafter, for a time, been debarred from visiting Egypt, where he owned property. Later he was allowed to return, and was on visiting terms with Baring, although he continued to be politically opposed to the British occupation
67 1.5.87 SP A/52 in reply to a letter from Wilfrid Blunt making various suggestions for the government of Egypt which Salisbury had forwarded to him for comment

CHAPTER 7 The Velvet Glove
1 Cecil, *Salisbury*, Vol. IV, p. 187
2 Robinson and others, *Africa and the Victorians*, p. 268
3 2.11.87 Cecil, *Salisbury*, Vol. IV, p. 65
4 14.12.87 Cecil, *Salisbury*, Vol. IV, p. 65
5 Salisbury-White 2.11.87 Cecil, *Salisbury*, Vol. IV, p. 65
6 17.2.88 SP A/55
7 For text of Convention see Egypt No. 2 1889
8 6.4.88 SP A/53
9 25.8.88 Cecil, *Salisbury*, Vol. IV, p. 106
10 29.4.88 FO 633/4
11 28.12.88 FO 633/4
12 15.12.89 SP A/54
13 I am indebted for many of the above details to W. L. Langer, *The Diplomacy of Imperialism 1880–1902*, Vol. I, p. 103 *et seq.*
14 No. 35 Riaz-Baring 9.12.88 Egypt No. 1 1889
15 Proceedings of the Royal Institute of Great Britain 1895, pp. 405–18
16 Cecil, *Salisbury*, Vol. IV, p. 392
17 17.2.88 SP A/55
18 Cecil, *Salisbury*, Vol. IV, p. 137
19 18.10.89 SP A/53
20 Who had replaced Nubar as Prime Minister in 1888
21 15.6.89 SP A/53
22 27.9.91 SP A/55
23 Cecil, *Salisbury*, Vol. IV, p. 393
24 Cecil, *Salisbury*, Vol. IV, p. 392
25 29.10.91 SP A/53
26 25.10.91 SP A/53
27 4.12.91 SP A/55
28 29.11.87 SP A/52

29   2.2.88 SP A/53
30   15.2.88 SP A/53
31   18.2.88 SP A/53
32   17.2.88 SP A/55
33   10.3.88 SP A/53
34   10.3.88 SP A/53
35   10.3.88 SP A/53
36   11.6.87 SP A/53
37   15.6.88 SP A/53
38   Lord d'Abernon, *Portraits and Appreciations*, pp. 13–24
39   2.11.88 SP A/55
40   10.11.88 SP A/53
41   Baring-Salisbury 30.12.88 SP A/53
42   18.4.89 SP A/53
43   Baring-Barrington 27.6.90 SP A/53
44   9.7.90 SP A/53
45   See Chapter 9
46   9.11.90 SP A/53
47   29.12.90 SP A/53
48   17.1.91 SP A/53
49   Sir Elwin Palmer who had replaced Vincent as Financial Adviser towards the end
     of 1889
50   19.1.91 SP A/53
51   26.1.91 SP A/53
52   23.1.91 SP A/55
53   27.2.91 SP A/55
54   See *inter alia* Blunt, *Secret History*, pp. 40–41
55   Baring-Pauncefote 27.8.85 SP Unbound letters
56   18.10.89 SP A/53
57   Portal-Salisbury 9.7.90 SP A/53
58   27.2.91 SP A/55
59   9.3.91 SP A/53
60   Egypt No. 3 1891
61   Egypt No. 2 1891. A Kantar is just under 1 cwt.
62   Baring-Salisbury 20.2.90 FO 78/4308
63   Egypt No. 3. 1891
64   MP 231
65   Baring-Salisbury 11.12.91 SP A/53
66   19.1.91 SP A/53
67   Baring-Salisbury 10.1.92 SP A/53
68   16.1.92 SP A/53
69   21.2.92 SP A/53
70   Cocheris, *Situation Internationale de l'Egypte et du Soudan*, p. 61
71   Salisbury-Baring 18.3.92 SP A/55
72   9.2.92 SP A/53
73   13.2.92 SP A/53
74   Sirdar of the Egyptian Army
75   21.2.92 SP A/53
76   17.4.92 SP A/53

CHAPTER 8 The Iron Hand

1 Abbas II, p. 17
2 No. 180 Cromer-Rosebery 13.1.93 FO 633/6
3 Rosebery-Cromer 1.1.93 FO 141/299
4 No. 19 Cromer-Rosebery 15.1.93 FO 141/299
5 Nos 20 and 21 Cromer-Rosebery 15.1.93 FO 141/299
6 No. 12 Rosebery-Cromer 16.1.93 FO 141/299
7 No. 13 Rosebery-Cromer 16.1.93 FO 141/299
8 No. 22 Cromer-Rosebery 16.1.93 FO 141/299
9 No. 24 Cromer-Rosebery 17.1.93 FO 141/299
10 No. 25 Cromer-Rosebery 17.1.93 FO 141/299
11 No. 15 Rosebery-Cromer 17.1.93 FO 141/299
12 No. 16 Rosebery-Cromer 17.1.93 FO 141/299
13 No. 23 Cromer-Rosebery 18.1.93 FO 141/299
14 The Khedive afterwards denied that he had said this and said that he had merely promised Cromer that he would consult him over all important decisions. See Blunt, *My Diaries*, Vol. I, p. 113
15 No. 17 Rosebery-Cromer 18.1.93 FO 141/299
16 No. 22 Cromer-Rosebery 17.1.93 FO 141/299
17 R. R. James, *Rosebery*, p. 276
18 Crewe, *Rosebery*, p. 419
19 No. 31 Cromer-Rosebery 19.1.93 FO 141/299
20 No. 32 Cromer-Rosebery 19.1.93 FO 141/299
21 James, *Rosebery*, p. 276
22 James, *Rosebery*, p. 276
23 James, *Rosebery*, p. 276
24 James, *Rosebery*, p. 276
25 No. 18 Rosebery-Cromer 20.1.93 FO 141/299
26 No. 282 21.1.93 FO 633/6
27 No. 283 21.1.83 FO 633/6
28 No. 284 22.1.93 FO 633/6
29 No. 20 Rosebery-Cromer 23.1.93 FO 141/299
30 No. 21 Rosebery-Cromer 23.1.93 FO 141/299
31 No. 181 Cromer-Rosebery 22.1.93 FO 633/6
32 No. 122 Rosebery-Cromer 27.1.93 FO 633/7
33 No. 125 14.2.93 FO 633/7
34 No. 184 Cromer-Rosebery 11.2.93 FO 633/6
35 No. 185 Cromer-Rosebery 17.3.93 FO 633/6
36 No. 185 Cromer-Rosebery 17.3.93 FO 633/6
37 No. 187 Cromer-Rosebery 17.3.93 FO 633/6
38 Rosebery-Cromer 16.2.93 Egypt No. 2 1893
39 No. 192 Cromer-Rosebery 28.4.93 FO 633/6
40 No. 197 Cromer-Rosebery 25.12.93 FO 633/6
41 Abbas II, p. 50
42 FO 141/304
43 Abbas II, p. 56
44 Abbas II, pp. 56–57. Cromer's telegram to Rosebery is missing from the archives
45 Rosebery-Cromer 21.1.94 FO 141/304
46 Cromer-Rosebery 23.1.94 FO 141/304

47 Cromer-Rosebery 23.1.94 FO 141/304
48 Milner had spent about three years, from 1889 to 1892, as an official in the Egyptian Ministry of Finance, first as Director-General of Accounts and then as Under Secretary. During his period of service in Egypt, he had, with Cromer's permission, published several articles in the British Press extolling the benefits brought to the Egyptian people by the British occupation.
49 Cromer-Rosebery 24.1.94 FO 141/304
50 Magnus, *Kitchener*, p. 89
51 Cromer-Rosebery 24.1.94 FO 141/304
52 Cromer-Kimberley 10.4.94 FO 141/304
53 Abbas II, p. 60
54 No. 38 Cromer-Kimberley 14.4.94 FO 141/304
55 No. 59 Cromer-Kimberley 14.4.94 FO 141/304
56 Blunt, *My Diaries*, Vol. I, p. 135
57 6.2.97 FO 633/6
58 Cromer-Kimberley 17.1.95 FO 633/6
59 5.6.98 SP A/III
60 Rosebery-Cromer 21.2.95 FO 141/308
61 A Lutfi as-Sayyid, *Egypt and Cromer*, p. 128

CHAPTER 9 The Reconquest of the Sudan

1 For accounts of the 'rescue' expedition, see *inter alia* V. Casati, *Dix Années en Equatoria: Retour avec Emin Pasha, 1891;* H. M. Stanley, *In Darkest Africa,* 1890; Vita Hasan, *La Verité sur Emin Pasha,* 1893; K. Schynse, *Mit Stanley und Emin Pasha dürch Deutsch Ostafrika,* 1890
2 Baring-Salisbury 15.12.89 SP A/53
3 4.4.90 SP A/54
4 23.2.90 SP A/54
5 This was soon after the battle of Toski
6 4.4.90 SP A/54
7 15.12.89 SP A/55
8 31.8.90 SP A/55
9 28.3.90 SP A/55
10 3.8.90 SP A/55. As well as the Agreement with Germany, an Agreement with France had been reached over Madagascar and some disputed areas in West Africa
11 For text of Agreement see Cocheris, *Situation Internationale de l'Egypte et du Soudan*, p. 381
12 21.11.90 SP A/55
13 28.11.90 SP A/54
14 28.11.90 SP A/54
15 9.3.91 SP A/54
16 13.2.91 SP A/5517
17 For full details of this Convention see, *inter alia*, Robinson, *Africa and the Victorians*, pp. 290–94 and Cocheris, *Situation Internationale de l'Egypte et du Soudan*, pp. 363–67
18 See Cocheris, *Situation Internationale de l'Egypte et du Soudan*, p. 391
19 Robinson, *Africa and the Victorians*, p. 328
20 Rosebery had become Prime Minister in March 1894 on Gladstone's final retirement
21 See Cocheris, *Situation Internationale de l'Egypte et du Soudan*, pp. 425–26
22 Bulletin de l'Institut d'Egypte Serie 3 No. 4 1893, pp. 180 *et seq.*
23 For text of Convention see Africa No. 4 1894
24 Cocheris, *Situation Internationale de l'Egypte et du Soudan*, p. 414

25 Hansard 4th series Vol. XXXII cols. 405–06
26 No. 235 8.3.95 FO 633/6
27 No. 236 29.3.95 FO 633/6
28 No. 166 21.6.95 FO 633/7
29 Cromer had probably had his attention drawn to Scott Moncrieff's recent lecture on the subject in London—see Chapter 7, p. 139 back—and he almost certainly knew about Prompt's speculations in Cairo two years before
30 Nos. 205 and 206 11.4.95 and 14.4.95 FO 633/6
31 No. 137 22.4.95 FO 633/7
32 No. 19 Salisbury-Cromer 8.11.95 FO 633/7 and No. 245 Cromer-Salisbury 15.11.95 FO 633/6
33 G. N. Sanderson, *England, Europe and the Upper Nile*, p. 69
34 Cromer-Salisbury 26.2.96 SP A/109
35 Sanderson, *England, Europe and the Upper Nile*, p. 243
36 Sanderson, *England, Europe and the Upper Nile*, p. 244
37 See, *inter alia*, Blunt, *My Diaries*, Vol. I, p. 272
38 Rodd, *Social and Diplomatic Memories*, Vol 2, 1894–1901, p. 86
39 J. L. Garvin, *Life of Joseph Chamberlain*, Vol. 3, pp. 169–70
40 Rodd, *Social and Diplomatic Memories*, Vol. 2, 1894–1901, pp. 85–89
41 No. 17 12.3.94 FO 78/4893
42 13.3.96 SP A/113
43 14.3.96 SP A/109
44 Sanderson, *England, Europe and the Upper Nile*, p. 247
45 Cromer-Salisbury 15.3.94 SP A/109
46 No. 69 Cromer-Salisbury 28.3.96 FO 78/4893
47 Cromer-Salisbury 20.3.96 SP A/109
48 Blunt, *My Diaries*, Vol. I, p. 272
49 21.3.96 SP A/109
50 15.3.96 SP A/109
51 27.3.96 SP A/109
52 1.4.96 SP A/113
53 19.4.96 SP A/109
54 No. 259 13.6.96 FO 633/6
55 Cromer-Salisbury 14.10.96 SP A/109
56 30.6.96 SP A/109
57 14.10.96 SP A/109
58 27.11.96 SP A/113
59 The Treasury originally asked for $3\frac{1}{2}$ per cent and reduced it as the result of an angry protest from Cromer
60 27.11.96 SP A/113
61 Magnus, *Kitchener*, p. 103
62 For these details of the origins of the Marchand expedition see Sanderson, *England, Europe and the Upper Nile*, pp. 271–78
63 Rodd, *Social and Diplomatic Memories*, Vol. 2, 1894–1901, p. 187
64 16.4.97 SP A/110
65 22.10.97 SP A/110
66 5.11.97 SP A/110
67 12.11.97 SP A/110
68 Magnus, *Kitchener*, pp. 115–16
69 Magnus, *Kitchener*, p. 116

70 He was at that time negotiating for a sale of the right to construct a railway between Suakin and Berber by the Egyptian Government to a British syndicate; it never came to anything
71 25.12.97 SP A/110
72 15.1.98 SP A/111
73 27.1.98 SP A/111
74 8.1.98 SP A/113
75 Lowe, *The Reluctant Imperialists*, Vol. 2, p. 107
76 Telegram No. 47 Salisbury-Cromer 3.6.98 FO 78/5050
77 SP A/111
78 Salisbury-Rodd 2.8.98 FO 78/5050
79 Magnus, *Kitchener*, p. 140
80 Cromer-Salisbury 15.11.98 SP A/111
81 Salisbury-Cromer 9.12.98 SP A/113
82 For text see British and Foreign State Papers, Vol. 91, p. 19
83 Suakin, as forming part of Egypt, was at first excluded from the provisions of the 1899 Convention, but a year later this exception was dropped and Suakin was formally incorporated into the Sudan
84 Treaty Series No. 16 1902
85 3.2.99 SP A/113

CHAPTER 10 The Power and the Glory
1 Cromer-Rosebery 2.3.93 FO 141/297
2 Cromer, *Modern Egypt*, Vol. 2, p. 481
3 Cromer-Grey 3.3.07 Egypt No. 1 1907
4 Cromer-Salisbury 30.10.95 SP A/108 and 29.2.96 SP A/108
5 5.6.97 SP A/110
6 19.6.97 SP A/113
7 16.12.97 SP A/110
8 Cromer-Salisbury 27.2.98 Egypt No. 1 1898
9 Cromer-Lansdowne 26.2.04 Egypt No. 1 1904
10 Cromer-Grey 8.3.06 Egypt No. 1 1906
11 Milner, *England in Egypt*, 4th ed., 1907, pp. 386–87
12 Blunt, *My Diaries*, Vol. 2, p. 81
13 Blunt, *My Diaries*, Vol. 2, p. 83
14 Blunt, *My Diaries*, Vol. 2, p. 89
15 Blunt, *My Diaries*, Vol. 2, p. 114
16 Blunt, *My Diaries*, Vol. 2, p. 87
17 Clara Boyle, *Boyle of Cairo*, p. 114
18 Cromer-Pauncefote 6.11.87 FO 633/5 Cromer stated that he had paid £100 down to the *Egyptian Gazette* and had arranged to pay it £25 a month
19 Boyle, *Boyle of Cairo*, p. 121
20 Rodd, *Social and Diplomatic Memories*, Vol. 2, 1894–1901, p. 18 *et seq.*
21 Rodd, *Social and Diplomatic Memories*, Vol. 2, 1894–1901, p. 309
22 d'Abernon, *Portraits and Appreciations*, p. 14
23 9.12.94 FO 633/6
24 28.3.07 FO 633/13
25 Magnus, *Kitchener*, p. 89
26 Dawkins-Milner 6.12.96 MP
27 Willcocks, *Sixty Years in Egypt*, p. 269

28   Dawkins-Milner 18.9.96 MP
29   Dawkins-Milner 16.8.96 MP
30   4.11.93 FO 633/6
31   Clara Boyle, *A Servant of the Empire*, p. 107
32   Clara Boyle, *Boyle of Cairo*, pp. 48–55
33   R. Wingate, *Wingate of the Sudan*, p. 45
34   Boyle Papers
35   Cromer-Salisbury 27.2.98 Egypt No. 1 1898
36   Cromer-Salisbury 26.2.99 Egypt No. 3 1899
37   Cromer-Salisbury 20.2.00 Egypt No. 1 1900
38   Cromer-Lansdowne 1.3.01 Egypt No. 1 1901 and Cromer-Lansdowne 21.2.02
     Egypt No. 1 1902
39   The reduction in the incidence of taxation per head was entirely due to the increase in
     population which had taken place over these twenty years
40   Cromer-Lansdowne 26.2.03 Egypt No. 1 1903
41   Cromer-Lansdowne 26.2.04 Egypt No. 1 1904
42   Cromer-Lansdowne 15.3.05 Egypt No. 1 1905
43   Cromer-Grey 8.3.06 Egypt No. 1 1906

CHAPTER 11 The Anglo-French Agreement
 1   20.2.96 SP A/113
 2   29.2.96 SP A/109
 3   Sanderson, *England, Europe and the Upper Nile*, p. 374
 4   Sanderson, *England, Europe and the Upper Nile*, p. 376
 5   Delcassé-Cambon 2.8.03 DDF Serie 2 III, p. 511
 6   Lansdowne-Monson 5.8.03 BD II, p. 306
 7   Cromer-Lansdowne 17.7.03 BD II, p. 299
 8   Lansdowne-Monson 7.10.03 BD II, pp. 317–18
 9   Cambon-Delcassé 18.11.03 DDF Serie 2 IV, p. 116
10   1.11.03 FO 633/6
11   Zetland, *Cromer*, p. 271
12   Lansdowne-Cromer 17.11.03. Newton, *Life of Lansdowne*, p. 285
13   Lansdowne-Cambon 19.11.03 BD II, pp. 325–26
14   Cogordan-Boulinière 19.1.04 DDF Serie 2 IV, p. 274
15   Gorst-Cromer 6.1.04. Zetland, *Cromer*, p. 280
16   Cromer-Lansdowne 21.1.04. Newton, *Life of Lansdowne*, p. 289
17   Lansdowne-Cromer 15.3.04 BD II, p. 356
18   Lansdowne-Cambon 1.4.04 BD II, pp. 361–62
19   Treaty Series No. 6 1905
20   Lansdowne-Monson 8.4.04 BD II, p. 365
21   *The Cambridge History of British Foreign Policy*, 1783–1919, editors Ward and Gooch,
     Vol. III, p. 309 note 1
22   Cromer-Lansdowne 15.3.05 Egypt No. 1 1905
23   Cromer-Grey 8.3.06 Egypt No. 1 1906
24   Cromer, *Modern Egypt*, Vol. 2, pp. 568–69

CHAPTER 12 The Rise of Egyptian Nationalism
 1   The three principal Ulema in Egypt were (1) the Grand Mufti, or chief Islamic legal
     authority, (2) the Rector of el-Azhar University, the principal centre of Islamic studies,
     and (3) the Grand Qadi, Head of the Shari'a—Islamic religious—Courts

2   See Chapter 6 Note 65

3   Egypt No. 1 1907

4   For official correspondence over this matter see Egypt No. 2 1906

5   Annual Report for 1906 Egypt No. 1 1907

6   For official correspondence on the incident see Egypt Nos. 3 and 4 1906

7   Findlay-Grey 28.6.06, Grey, *Twenty Five Years*, Vol. I, p. 135

8   Grey, *Twenty Five Years*, Vol. I, p. 137

9   Grey, *Twenty Five Years*, Vol. I, p. 138

10 Blunt, *My Diaries*, Vol. 2, p. 164

11 See text of programme in Alexander, *The Truth about Egypt*, pp. 121-22

12 Alexander, *The Truth about Egypt*, p. 126

13 Alexander, *The Truth about Egypt*, p. 130

14 Grey-Cromer 18.1.07 FO 633/13

15 Grey-Cromer 1.3.07 FO 633/13

16 Grey-Cromer 3.3.07 FO 633/13

17 Cromer-Grey 15.11.06 FO 633/13. Some of the prison sentences were remitted in January 1908, after Cromer's departure, on the occasion of the anniversary of the Khedive's accession

18 A reference to the reforms being advocated by J. M. Robertson MP who had just visited Egypt

19 Edward Dicey, a well-known English publicist who, just before the occupation, had been extremely critical of HMG's softness towards Egypt in the matter of debt collection, was now a foremost critic of Cromer's dictatorial policies

20 Cromer-Grey 3.3.07 FO 633/13

21 8.3.07 FO 633/13

22 15.3.07 FO 633/13

23 22.3.07 FO 633/13

24 After his part in negotiating the Anglo-French Agreement in 1904, Sir Eldon Gorst, at that time Financial Adviser, had left Egyptian Government service to become an Under Secretary at the Foreign Office

25 28.3.07 FO 633/13

26 Blunt, *My Diaries*, Vol. 2, p. 173

27 Kamil, *Lettres Egyptiennes-Françaises*, p. 204

28 Egypt No. 1 1907

29 Gorst, *Autobiographical Notes*

30 Gorst, *Autobiographical Notes*

31 Gorst, *Autobiographical Notes*

32 Parliamentary Debates Commons 4th series CLXXIX, paragraph 835 *et seq.*

33 Parliamentary Debates Commons 4th series, CLXXIX, column 858 *et seq.*

CHAPTER 13 The Egyptian Achievement

1   From article on 'The Government of Subject Races,' *Edinburgh Review* January 1908 No. CCCCXXIII

2   From 'The Situation on Egypt', Address delivered by Lord Cromer to the Eighty Club on 15 December 1908 (Macmillan 1908)

3   From an article on 'The French in Algeria,' *Spectator* 31 May 1913, reprinted in *Political and Literary Essays 1908-13* (Macmillan 1913)

4   From 'Ancient and Modern Imperialism,' Address given by Lord Cromer to the Classical Association (Murray 1909)

5   Robinson and others, *Africa and the Victorians*, p. 275

6   See, *inter alia*, Cromer-Grey 29.10.09 FO 633/14

7   A. E. Crouchley, *The Economic Development of Modern Egypt*, p. 259. A feddan is about an acre

8   Crouchley, *The Economic Development of Modern Egypt*, pp. 263–64

9   Crouchley, *The Economic Development of Modern Egypt*, pp. 167–68

10 Egypt No. 1 1907

11 Egypt No. 1 1903

12 *Letters Upon the Affairs of Egypt*, pp. 72 and 77. Comparable figures for the Provinces were almost certainly much worse

13 *Letters Upon the Affairs of Egypt*, pp. 107–08

14 *Letters Upon the Affairs of Egypt*, p. 110

15 Egypt No. 1 1903

16 Blunt, *My Diaries*, II, p. 39

17 H. E. Bowman, *Middle East Window*, p. 42

18 H. E. Bowman, *Middle East Window*, pp. 39–41

19 Lloyd, *Egypt Since Cromer*, Vol. I, p. 162

20 Crouchley, *The Economic Development of Modern Egypt*, pp. 178–80

21 *Letters Upon the Affairs of Egypt*, pp. 96–103

22 R. Tignor, *Modernisation and British Colonial Rule in Egypt 1882–1914*, pp. 364–65. The writer's view is confirmed by a FO minute on Findlay-Lansdowne No. 53A FO 78/5233 which states, 'In order to avoid the trouble which arose between Manchester manufacturers and the Government of India owing to the alleged protectionist tendencies of India cotton duties, and also in the interests of free trade, Lord Cromer obtained the imposition of the excise duty on cotton made in Egypt equivalent to the import duty on such goods manufactured abroad'

CHAPTER 14 The Imperial Achievement

1   de Chancel-Hanotaux 3.10.96 DDF XIII No. 468

LIST OF SOURCES

1 Unpublished Private Papers

BOYLE PAPERS. Letters from Harry Boyle CMG to his mother from Cairo 1885–1907. St Antony's College, Oxford

CROMER PAPERS. Official and demi-official correspondence between Lord Cromer and Lords Granville, Iddesleigh, Rosebery, Salisbury, Kimberley, Goschen, Lansdowne, Grey and others. 1876–1908. FO/633. Public Record Office

D'ABERNON PAPERS. MS. of unpublished book on Egypt written in 1889 by Sir Edgar Vincent (afterwards Viscount D'Abernon). Department of Manuscripts, British Museum. Add. MSS. 48960–61

GLADSTONE PAPERS. Department of Manuscripts, British Museum. Add. MSS. 44466 f. 231. Letter Cromer–Gladstone 1880. Add. MSS. 44467 f. 6. Letter Cromer–Gladstone 1880. Add. MSS, 44776 f. 40. Letter Gladstone–Rosebery re Cromer 1894

GORST PAPERS. Autobiographical Notes by Sir Eldon Gorst. St Antony's College, Oxford

GRANVILLE PAPERS. Private and official papers of the Earl of Granville, including official and demi-official correspondence with Sir Evelyn Baring 1883–85. Public Record Office PRO 30/29

HAMILTON PAPERS. Department of Manuscripts, British Museum. Add. MSS. 48620 Vol. XXII. Correspondence between Edward Hamilton and W. S. Blunt

IDDESLEIGH PAPERS. Correspondence between Sir Stafford Northcote and Lord Salisbury 1878–79. Department of Manuscripts, British Museum. Add. MSS. 50019

MILNER PAPERS. Diary kept by Alfred (later Viscount) Milner dated 1889 to 1892 and sundry correspondence to and from Lord Milner in connection with Egypt 1889–1906. New College, Oxford, deposited in Bodleian Library. (Referred to in Notes as MP)

SALISBURY PAPERS. Official and demi-official correspondence between Lord Salisbury and Lord Cromer 1885–1892 and 1895–1900. Christ Church Library, Oxford. (Referred to in Notes as SP)

WINGATE PAPERS. Private and official papers of Sir Reginald Wingate. School of Oriental Studies, University of Durham

2 Unpublished State Papers

PUBLIC RECORD OFFICE
> F.O. 78 Series (Turkey). Diplomatic correspondence between Foreign Office and British Agency Cairo 1877–1905
> F.O. 371 Series (Egypt). Diplomatic correspondence between Foreign Office and British Agency Cairo 1906–1907
> F.O. 141 Series (Egypt). Telegrams and other correspondence between Foreign Office and British Agency Cairo 1877–1907
> (For detailed catalogue, refer to Enquiries Room, Public Record Office, Chancery Lane, London WC 2)

3 Published State Papers

> (Available at Foreign Office Library, Cornwall House, Stamford Street, London SE 1)

PARLIAMENTARY PAPERS (BLUE BOOKS)
> Egypt Series 1876–1907
> Sundry papers in 'Africa,' 'Abyssinia,' and 'Treaties' Series
> (For detailed catalogue see *A Century of Diplomatic Blue Books 1814–1914* (ed. Harold Temperley and Lilian Penson. Cass 1966)

BRITISH AND FOREIGN STATE PAPERS
> Vols. 74–99 (ed. Sir E. Herslet. Published by Ridgway)

LETTERS OF QUEEN VICTORIA (ed. G. E. Buckle)
> Series 2 1862–85. 3 Vols.
> Series 3 1886–1901. 3 Vols.
> (Referred to in Notes as QVL)

BRITISH DOCUMENTS ON THE ORIGINS OF THE WAR (ed. G. P. Gooch and Harold Temperley. HMSO 1926–32)
> Vols. I–V. (Referred to in Notes as BD)

DOCUMENTS DIPLOMATIQUES FRANÇAISES
> Accords Conclus de 8 Avril Entre la France et l'Angleterre au Sujet du Maroc, de l'Egypte, de Terre Neuve. Ministere des Affaires Etrangeres, Quai d'Orsay, Paris. 1904. (Referred to in Notes as DDF)

4 Published Books

AHMAD RISHAD. *Mustafa Kamil.* 1958
ARTHUR, G. C. A. *Life of Earl Kitchener.* 3 Vols. 1920
ALEXANDER, J. *The Truth About Egypt.* 1911
BARETIER, A. E. A. *Souvenirs de la Mission Marchand.* 3 Vols. 1941
BELL, E. H. C. M. *The Life and Letters of Moberly Bell.* 1927
BLUNT, W. S. *The Secret History of the British Occupation of Egypt.* 1906
> *Gordon at Khartum.* 1911
> *My Diaries.* Part I 1888–1900. 1919
> *My Diaries.* Part II 1900–1914. 1920

BORELLI, O. *Choses Politiques; Egypte.* 1883–1895. 1896

BOWMAN, H. E. *Middle East Window.* 1942

BOYLE, CLARA. *A Servant of the Empire.* 1938
   Boyle of Cairo. 1965

CECIL, LADY GWENDOLEN. *Life of Robert, Marquess of Salisbury.* 4 Vols. 1921–32

CHESNIL, E. *Plaies d'Egypte: Les Anglais dans la Vallée du Nil.* 1888

CHILDERS, E. S. C. *Life of Rt Hon. Hugh C. E. Childers.* 1901

COCHERIS, J. *Situation Internationale de l'Egypte et du Soudan.* 1903

COLLINS, R.O. *The Southern Sudan 1883–1898. A Struggle for Control.* 1962
   King Leopold, England and the Upper Nile. 1968.

COLVIN, SIR A. *The Making of Modern Egypt.* 1906

COUPLAND, R. *The Exploration of East Africa 1856–90; The Slave Trade and the Scramble
   for Africa.* 1939

CREWE, MARQUIS OF. *Lord Rosebery.* 1932

CROMER, EARL OF. *Modern Egypt.* 2 Vols. 1908
   Abbas II. 1915

CROUCHLEY, A. E. *The Economic Development of Modern Egypt.* 1938

D'ABERNON, VISCOUNT. *Portraits and Appreciations.* 1931

DE CAIX, R. *Fashoda, la France et l'Angleterre.* 1899

DE HERREROS, E. G. *Les Tribunaux Mixtes d'Egypte.* 1914

ELGOOD, P. G. *Egypt and the Army.* 1924
   The Transit of Egypt. 1928

FITZMAURICE, E. G. P. *Life of Earl Granville.* 2 Vols. 1905

GARDINER, A. G. *Sir William Harcourt.* 2 Vols. 1923

GARVIN, J. L. *Life of Rt Hon. Joseph Chamberlain.* 3 Vols. 1932–34

GIFFEN, M. B. *Fashoda: The Incident and Its Diplomatic Setting.* 1930

GORDON, C. G. *The Journals of Major-General Gordon at Khartoum* (ed. A. E. Hake).
   1885

GOSSE, E. *Lord Cromer as a Man of Letters.* 1917

GRENVILLE, J. A. S. *Lord Salisbury and Foreign Policy.* 1964

GREY OF FALLODEN, LORD. *Twenty-Five Years: 1892–1916.* 2 Vols. 1925

GWYN, S. L. and TUCKWELL, G. M. *Sir Charles Dilke.* 2 Vols. 1917

HASSAN, VITA. *La Verité sur Emin Pasha.* 1893

HOLLAND, B. H. *Life of Spencer Compton, 8th Duke of Devonshire.* 2 Vols. 1915

HOLLINGS, M. A. *The Life of Sir C. Scott Moncrieff.* 1917

HOLT, P. M. *The Mahdist State in the Sudan, 1881–1898.* 1958

ISSAWI, C. *Egypt: An Economic and Social Analysis.* 1947

JACKSON, H. C. *Osman Digna.* 1926

JAMES, R. R. *Rosebery.* 1963

LANGER, W. L. *European Alliances and Alignments, 1871–1890.* 1931
   The Diplomacy of Imperialism. 2 Vols. 1935

LLOYD, LORD. *Egypt Since Cromer.* Vol. I. 1933

LOWE, C. J. *Salisbury and the Mediterranean, 1886–96.* 1965
   The Reluctant Imperialists. 2 Vols. 1967

LUTFI-AS-SAYYID, A. *Egypt and Cromer: A Study in Anglo-Egyptian Relations.* 1968

LYALL, A. C. *Marquess of Dufferin and Ava.* 1909

MAGNUS, PHILIP. *Kitchener: Portrait of an Imperialist.* 1958

MALLET, SIR B. *Thomas George, Earl of Northbrook.* 1908

MATTHEWS, J. J. *Egypt and the Formulation of the Anglo-French Entente of 1904.* 1939

MILNER, ALFRED. *England in Egypt* (4th ed.). 1907

MORLEY, JOHN. *Rt Hon. W. E. Gladstone.* Vol. 3. 1903

MUSTAFA KAMIL. *Lettres Egyptiennes-Françaises, 1895-1908.* (Undated)

NETON, A. *Delcassé.* 1952

NEWTON, LORD. *Lord Lyons.* 2 Vols. 1913
 Life of the Marquess of Lansdowne. 1929

PENSON, L. M. *Foreign Affairs Under the 3rd Marquess of Salisbury.* 1962

POLITIS, N. *La Condition d'Egypte d'Après l'Accord Franco-Anglais de 1904.* 1905

PORTAL, G. M. *My Mission to Abyssinia.* 1892
 The British Mission to Uganda in 1893. 1894

PORTER, C. W. *The Career of Theophile Delcassé.* 1936

RAGATZ, C. J. *The Question of Egypt in Anglo-French Relations.* 1922

RAMM, A. *Political Correspondence of Mr Gladstone and Lord Granville, 1876-1886.* 1962

ROBERTSON, J. M. (ed.) *Letters From Egypt to an English Politician on the Affairs of Egypt.* 1908

ROBINSON, R. E. and Others. *Africa and the Victorians: The Official Mind of Imperialism.* 1961

RODD, SIR J. RENNELL. *Social and Diplomatic Memories.* Vol. 2. 1923

SAFRANI, N. *Egypt in Search of a Political Community.* 1961

SANDERSON, G. N. *England, Europe and the Upper Nile, 1882-1899.* 1965

SHIBEIKA, MEKKI. *British Policy in the Sudan, 1882-1902.* 1952

SLATIN, R. *Fire and Sword in the Sudan.* 1896

STANLEY, H. M. *In Darkest Africa.* 1890

STEEVENS, G. W. *Egypt in 1898.* 1898

TIGNOR, R. L. *Modernisation and British Colonial Rule in Egypt.* 1966

TRAILL, H. D. *Lord Cromer.* 1897

TREVELYAN, G. M. *Lord Grey of Falloden.* 1937

WILLCOCKS, W. *Sixty Years in the East.* 1935

WILSON, C. RIVERS. *Chapters from My Official Life.* 1926

WINGATE, F. R. *Mahdism in the Egyptian Sudan.* 1891

WINGATE, RONALD. *Wingate of the Sudan.* 1955

ZETLAND, LORD. *Lord Cromer.* 1932

5 Published Papers, Articles etc.

CHURCHILL, W. S. 'The Fashoda Incident.' *North American Review.* CCXVII (1898), pp. 736-43

CROMER, LORD. 'Army Reform.' *Nineteenth Century and After.* Feb. 1904
 'The Government of Subject Races.' *Edinburgh Review.* Jan. 1908
 'The Situation in Egypt.' Address Delivered to the Eighty Club 15.12.08. Macmillan. 1908

'Ancient and Modern Imperialism.' Address Given to the Classical Association. Murray. 1909

'The French in Algeria.' *The Spectator.* 31.5.13

'An Indian Idealist.' *The Spectator.* 12.7.13

DEHERAIN, H. 'L'Occupation Egyptienne du Haut Nil.' *Revue des Deux Mondes.* Nov. 1898, pp. 187–200.

'Le Successeur de l'Egypte Dans la Province Equatoriale.' *Revue des Deux Mondes.* May 1899, pp. 312–47

'DIPLOMATIST.' 'Fashoda: Lord Salisbury's Vindication.' *Fortnightly Review.* Dec. 1898, pp. 1002–14

GILLARD, D. R. 'Salisbury's African Policy in the Heligoland Offer of 1890.' *English Historical Review.* LXXV 297 (1960), pp. 53–63

GIRADEAU, C. 'Après Adowa Avant Dongola.' *Revue Politique et Litteraire.* Nov. 1896, pp. 362–64

JACKSON, H. W. 'Fashoda 1898.' *Sudan Notes and Records.* III 1 1920, pp. 1–9

MANGIN, C. M. E. 'Lettres de la Mission Marchand, 1895–1899.' *Revue des Deux Mondes.* Sep. 1931, pp. 241–83

MILLER, T. B. 'The Egyptian Question and British Foreign Policy, 1892–94.' *Journal of Modern History.* XXXII 1960, pp. 1–15

PENSON, L. M. 'Salisbury's Foreign Policy.' *Cambridge Historical Journal.* VI (1935), pp. 87–106

PROMPT, V. 'Soudan Nilotique.' *Bulletin de l'Institut d'Egypte,* Serie 3. No. 4 (1893), pp. 71–116

RENOUVIN, P. 'Les Origines de l'Expedition de Fashoda.' *Revue Historique.* CC 408 (1948), pp. 180–87

RICHES, T. W. 'A Survey of British Policy in the Fashoda Crisis.' *Political Science Quarterly.* XLIV 1 (1929), pp. 54–78

TAYLOR, A. J. P. 'Prelude to Fashoda: the Question of the Upper Nile, 1894–95.' *English Historical Review.* LXV 254 (1950), pp. 52–80

THORNTON, A. P. 'Rivalries in the Mediterranean, the Middle East, and Egypt, 1870–1898.' *New Cambridge Modern History.* Vol. XI, Chapter XXI, pp. 567–92

INDEX